OXFORD PHILOSOPHICAL TEXTS

Spinoza

Ethics

OXFORD PHILOSOPHICAL TEXTS

Series Editor: John Cottingham

The Oxford Philosophical Texts series consists of authoritative teaching editions of canonical texts in the history of philosophy from the ancient world down to modern times. Each volume provides a clear, well laid out text together with a comprehensive introduction by a leading specialist, giving the student detailed critical guidance on the intellectual context of the work and the structure and philosophical importance of the main arguments. Endnotes are supplied which provide further commentary on the arguments and explain unfamiliar references and terminology, and a full bibliography and index are also included.

The series aims to build up a definitive corpus of key texts in the Western philosophical tradition, which will form a reliable and enduring resource for students and teachers alike.

PUBLISHED IN THIS SERIES:

FORTHCOMING TITLES INCLUDE:

SPINOZA

Ethics

EDITED AND TRANSLATED BY

G. H. R. PARKINSON

OXFORD

UNIVERSITY PRESS

OXFORD
UNIVERSITY PRESS

Great Clarendon Street, Oxford OX2 6DP

Oxford University Press is a department of the University of Oxford.
It furthers the University's objective of excellence in research, scholarship,
and education by publishing worldwide in

Oxford New York

Athens Auckland Bangkok Bogotá Buenos Aires Calcutta
Cape Town Chennai Dar es Salaam Delhi Florence Hong Kong Istanbul
Karachi Kuala Lumpur Madrid Melbourne Mexico City Mumbai
Nairobi Paris São Paulo Singapore Taipei Tokyo Toronto Warsaw

with associated companies in Berlin Ibadan

Oxford is a trade mark of Oxford University Press
in the UK and in certain other countries

Published in the United States
by Oxford University Press Inc., New York

© G. H. R. Parkinson 2000

The Moral Rights of the Author have been asserted.

British Library Cataloguing in Publication Data

Data available

British Library Cataloging in Publication Data

(Data applied for)

ISBN 0-19-875214-8

5 7 9 10 8 6

Typeset in Dante
by RefineCatch Limited, Bungay, Suffolk
Printed in Great Britain by
Biddles Ltd., Guildford, Surrey

Contents

Contents

PART 3: SUPPLEMENTARY MATERIAL

PART 1
Introductory Material

How to Use this Book

This book is intended primarily for readers who are new to Spinoza. Accordingly it contains a long Editor's Introduction, which tries to elucidate Spinoza's often difficult concepts, and which also tries to show how his philosophy is important by relating it to present-day concerns. It is not necessary to begin by reading the entire Editor's Introduction; however, Sections 2 and 3 should be read at an early stage, since they not only explain why the *Ethics* has the unusual form that it has—namely, that of a geometrical treatise—but also introduce some of Spinoza's fundamental ideas. Sections 4 to 8 cover roughly the first two Parts of the *Ethics*, and the remaining three Parts are covered by Sections 9 to 11.

To help the reader further, I have provided a Summary of the *Ethics*. This may be used either as a guide to what is to come, or as a help to the assimilation of what has just been read. I have also provided a Select Bibliography, in which emphasis is placed on recent work, together with full explanatory Notes. There is a comprehensive Index of References, as well as an Index of Names and Subjects. Finally, although each technical term used in the *Ethics* is explained either in the Editor's Introduction or in the Notes, I have added a Glossary, so that the reader who is puzzled by some of Spinoza's technicalities can easily obtain help.

Abbreviations

Spinoza's Works: Texts and Translations

DIE   *Tractatus de Intellectus Emendatione*

E   *Ethics*

      A   Axiom

      C   Corollary

      D   Definition

      DE Definition of the Emotions (Part 3)

      L   Lemma

      P   Proposition

      S   Scholium

      (So, for example, 'E2 P40 S2' refers to *Ethics*, Part 2, Proposition 40, Scholium 2)

      References followed by page number are to the pagination of this translation

Ep.   Letter(s)

G   *Spinoza, Opera* ed. C. Gebhardt, 4 vols. (Heidelberg: Winter 1925)

KV   *Short Treatise on God, Man and his Well-Being*

PPC   Geometrical version of Descartes's *Principles of Philosophy*

SL   *Spinoza: The Letters*, trans. S. Shirley (Indianapolis: Hackett, 1995)

TTP   *Tractatus Theologico-Politicus*

Other Works

PWD   *The Philosophical Works of Descartes*, trans. J. Cottingham, R. Stoothoff, D. Murdoch, and A. Kenny, 3 vols. (Cambridge: Cambridge University Press, 1985, 1991)

Editor's Introduction

1. Life and Works

Spinoza's *Ethics* is, beyond doubt, one of the classics of philosophy; but it is also beyond doubt that it that it is one of the most difficult. This difficulty has two main sources. Most, if not all, major philosophers introduce new technical terms, or give old ones a new sense; but few philosophers have taken this practice further than Spinoza. This would not be so great a difficulty if Spinoza's new usages had entered the main stream of philosophy. However, few if any have done so, with the result that readers of the *Ethics* have to wrestle with terms that are often strange to them. A second source of difficulty is provided by the form in which the book is written. As the title-page proclaims, it is 'demonstrated in geometrical order'; that is, Spinoza presents his work in the form of a deductive system, taking as his model the most perfect deductive system known in his epoch, the geometry of Euclid. This makes his argument appear needlessly long-winded, and may seem to obscure the nature of his thought.

These difficulties have led to a wide variety in the interpretations of the *Ethics*. Some scholars think that Spinoza is best understood in the context of the philosophy of Descartes; others see him as deeply influenced by the largely Aristotelian thought of the Middle Ages, and so as having his roots in a philosophy which was very different from that of Descartes.[1] There are other disagreements between Spinoza scholars. Some, for example, see his philosophy as culminating in a kind of mystical insight,[2] whereas others dispute this. There is no easy way to settle these disputes; to a large extent the problems are best solved as one goes along, trying to produce an interpretation which is coherent and which fits the texts. However, one can make a useful start by placing his life and works within their historical context.

---

[1] See e.g. H. A. Wolfson, *The Philosophy of Spinoza* (Cambridge, Mass.: Harvard University Press, 1934), vol. I, p. vii.

[2] See e.g. P. Wienpahl, 'Spinoza and Mysticism', in Jon Wetlesen (ed.), *Spinoza's Philosophy of Man* (Oslo: Universitetsforlaget, 1978), 211–24.

Spinoza was born in Amsterdam on 24 November 1632.[3] His father, Michael de Spinoza, was one of many Portugese Jews who had settled in the Netherlands, fleeing from persecution by the Inquisition. Michael was a well-off merchant, carrying on a general import business, and he was a respected member of the Jewish community. Archival evidence has shown that the young Spinoza was intended by his father to carry on the family business, and in fact he and his brother did so after Michael's death in 1654. However, Spinoza's career as a merchant did not last long; on 27 July 1656 he was expelled from the Jewish community for what were called his 'wrong opinions' and 'horrible heresies'. What these opinions were is not certain, but the evidence suggests that Spinoza interpreted the Bible in a critical way, and that he defended a kind of deism, arguing that God does not interfere in the natural world, but is manifested in the laws of Nature.[4] After his expulsion from the Jewish community, Spinoza ceased to use the Portugese form of his first name, Bento, together with its Hebrew form, Baruch, and referred to himself henceforth by their Latin equivalent, Benedictus. Cut off from his former associates—the formula of excommunication forbade Jews to have any association with him—Spinoza had to find a new way of earning a living, and new friends. He found a new way of earning a living by grinding and polishing lenses, at which he became very skilled, and he found new friends among the members of two Christian sects, the Collegiants and the Mennonites. The Collegiants were so called because they dispensed with priests, and met for worship in small groups, *collegia*; the Mennonites, named after their founder Menno Simons, were noted for holding aloof from politics and for preaching a doctrine of non-resistance.

What drew Spinoza towards these people was not so much a concern with the nature and truth of Christianity as a shared concern with the philosophy of Descartes.[5] It is not known just when Spinoza first studied

[3] For scholarly accounts of Spinoza's life, see W. N. A. Klever, 'Spinoza's Life and Works', in D. Garrett (ed.), *The Cambridge Companion to Spinoza* (Cambridge: Cambridge University Press, 1996), 13–60, and S. Nadler, *Spinoza: A Life* (Cambridge: Cambridge University Press, 1999). A valuable survey of Dutch politics and culture during Spinoza's epoch may be found in J. I. Israel, *The Dutch Republic: Its Rise, Greatness and Fall, 1477–1806* (Oxford: Clarendon Press, 1995), 595–807, 889–933.

[4] It has been suggested that the young Spinoza was influenced by the French *libertins* (free-thinkers). On these, see R. H. Popkin, *The History of Scepticism from Erasmus to Spinoza* (Berkeley: University of California Press, 1979), 87–109.

[5] It appears that Spinoza's friends were attracted by Descartes's refusal to base his views on mere tradition, and his view that what we know is known by the 'natural light of reason'. This seemed to them to harmonize with the importance of the 'inner light'. This was

Descartes, but that he owed much to Descartes is not in doubt.[6] However, he was by no means a slavish follower of Descartes; by 1661, the
year in which published correspondence begins, he emerges (Ep. 2, G iv.
8–9: *SL* 62–3) as a man who has his own views, and who is critical of
Descartes in many respects. At this stage Spinoza was living in Rijnsburg,
a village near Leiden, and it was at Rijnsburg that he wrote his first
philosophical works. These were the *Tractatus de Intellectus Emendatione*
('A Treatise on the Correction of the Intellect') and the *Korte Verhandeling
van God, de Mensch en deszelfs Welstand* ('A Short Treatise on God, Man
and his Well-Being'). The first of these is a treatise on methodology.
Spinoza did not complete it, but his editors said that he always intended
to do so, and they decided to include it among his posthumous works
when these were published in 1677. Spinoza's intention was to comple-
ment it by another work, which would deal with metaphysics and ethics,
and at about the same time as the *Tractatus* he wrote what is evidently a
draft of such a work, the *Korte Verhandeling*. This book (which was not
published until the nineteenth century) raises many problems; there are
disagreements as to whether it was written before or after the *Tractatus*,
and whether what has come down to us is an original text or a Dutch
translation of a Latin original.[7] What one can say of both these works is
that, in them, Spinoza's distinctive philosophy is clearly present, though
the philosophy is often immature and obscurely expressed. Of the two,
the *Treatise on the Correction of the Intellect* is of much greater value to the
student of the *Ethics*, and I shall refer to it on several occasions. The *Short
Treatise*, on the other hand, seems to me to raise more problems than it
solves. It is, however, interesting for the light that it throws on Spinoza's
sources. The influence of Descartes is plain;[8] however, the book also

---

described by one of them, Pieter Balling, in terms that are reminiscent of Descartes, namely
as 'a clear and distinct knowledge of the truth, in the understanding of every man, and
through which we are so convinced that we cannot have any doubt'. (Balling, *The Light on the
Candlestick* (1662); see *Chronicon Spinozanum*, 4 (1924–6), 189.)

[6] This was accepted by Spinoza's friends, one of whom, Jarig Jelles, said in his preface to
Spinoza's posthumous works that 'the philosophical writings of the great and famous René
Descartes were of great service to him'. Spinoza's interest in Descartes may have been
kindled by Franciscus van den Enden (d. 1674), who founded a school in Amsterdam in 1652,
and under whom Spinoza studied Latin. Van den Enden is regarded as an important influence on the young Spinoza, but when the two first met is not certain. On Van den Enden see,
e.g. Klever, 'Spinoza's Life and Works', 17–19.

[7] The textual problems that arise are well summarized by E. Curley, *The Collected Works
of Spinoza* (Princeton: Princeton University Press, 1985), 46–53.

[8] See e.g. the a posteriori argument for the existence of God in *KV* I. 1 (G i. 15–16), which
is based on an argument contained in Descartes, *Meditations*, III: *PWD* ii. 31–6.

displays the influence of Dutch sources—more precisely, of two Leiden professors, Franco Burgersdijk (d. 1636) and his successor, Adrian Heereboord (d. 1651).[9] Heereboord is especially interesting, because he sympathized both with Descartes and with the Scholastics, and in particular with the late Scholastic Suárez (1548–1617). Spinoza, like Descartes, often used Scholastic terms in his philosophy, but this does not imply a close study, at first hand, of Scholastic texts; he could have derived the terms from Heereboord.[10]

Whilst still at Rijnsburg Spinoza began work on his first published book. This appeared in Amsterdam in 1663, and was a geometrical version of the first two parts of Descartes's *Principles of Philosophy*, together with an appendix, *Cogitata Metaphysica* ('Metaphysical Thoughts'), which deals with metaphysical problems in a Cartesian way. Spinoza's declared aim in publishing the book was to attract the attention of powerful people who might make it possible for him to publish his more controversial work (Ep. 13, G iv. 63–4: *SL* 110–11). In a preface one of his friends explained that Spinoza regarded as false much that was contained in it (G i. 131). However, he did not say that Spinoza regarded the contents of the book as entirely false, and indeed Spinoza sometimes quotes from it in his later work (*E*I P19 S; *TTP*, note 4, G iii. 253; Eps. 19, 21, 35, 50, 58).

We come now to the circumstances surrounding the writing and publication of the *Ethics*. Spinoza appears to have begun work on the book before he left Rijnsburg in April 1663.[11] From Rijnsburg he moved to Voorburg, near The Hague, and stayed there until 1670. By June 1665 a draft of the *Ethics* (apparently in a three-part form) was near completion (Ep. 28, G iv. 163: *SL* 180). However, Spinoza laid the book aside at this stage, in order to begin work on his *Tractatus Theologico-Politicus* ('A Treatise on Theology and Politics'). In this work he claimed to show (as the subtitle of the work indicates) that 'the freedom of philosophizing

---

[9] In *KV* I. 3 Spinoza uses a classification of causes introduced by Burgersdijk in his *Institutionum Logicarum Duo* (Leiden, 1626). On this classification, see *Spinoza's Short Treatise on God, Man and his Well-Being*, trans. A. Wolf (London: Black, 1910), 190–5. Whether he got this directly from Burgersdijk is not certain; he could have derived it from Heereboord, who expounded it in his *Hermeneia Logica* (Leiden, 1650) and in his *Meletemata Philosophica* (Leiden, 1st edn. 1654, 2nd edn. 1659, 3rd edn. 1665). Spinoza is known to have studied Heereboord, whom he mentions in his *Cogitata Metaphysica* (1663), II. 12: G i. 279.

[10] For Spinoza's use of the works of Heereboord, see H. de Dijn, 'Historical Remarks on Spinoza's Theory of Definition', in J. G. van der Bend (ed.), *Spinoza on Knowing, Being and Freedom* (Assen: Van Gorcum, 1974), 41–50.

[11] He sent (see Ep. 8) what seems to be a draft of the first definitions of the work to friends in Amsterdam in Feb. 1663.

not only can be granted without damaging piety and public peace, but cannot be destroyed without destroying them as well'.

Freedom of speech, Spinoza said in a letter of 1665 (Ep. 30, G iv. 166: *SL* 185–6), was being suppressed in the Netherlands by 'the excessive authority and impudence of demagogues'. Here, Spinoza had in mind the Dutch Calvinists, or more precisely a certain sect, the 'strict' or 'precise' Calvinists. However, the republican statesman Jan de Witt, the political leader of the Netherlands between 1653 and 1672, succeeded in upholding the ideals of tolerance. Despite the fury of the Calvinists,[12] who objected above all to the critical attitude that Spinoza took to the Bible, the book was published in 1670, and several editions appeared during Spinoza's lifetime. In 1670 Spinoza moved from Voorburg to The Hague. There he resumed work on the *Ethics*, and the book was ready for publication by September 1675 (Ep. 68). However, his position had become more precarious. In 1672 de Witt had been murdered by a mob on the occasion of a French invasion of the Netherlands, and it was doubtless the lack of de Witt's protection, and the fact that the new leader, Prince William III of Orange, looked to the Calvinists for support, that led Spinoza to decide to delay publication. In fact the book did not appear until after Spinoza's death on 21 February 1677, when it appeared as part of his *Opera Posthuma* ('Posthumous Works'), which were published, together with a Dutch translation, in December 1677.[13] During the last months of his life Spinoza had been working on a *Tractatus Politicus* ('A Treatise on Politics'), though he did not live to complete it. This, too, appeared as part of his posthumous works, along with the *Tractatus de Intellectus Emendatione*, an unfinished Hebrew grammar, and Spinoza's philosophical correspondence.

This correspondence is of great value to the student of Spinoza. Not only does it throw direct light on the views contained in his philosophical books, but it also sheds some indirect light on them, since it displays some of his interests, and in particular his interest in the sciences. Of the eighty-nine letters to or from Spinoza that have been preserved, nineteen touch on mathematical or scientific topics. In view of Spinoza's work as a lens-grinder, it is not surprising that some of the letters (Eps. 36, 39, 40, 46) should deal with problems of optics. But

---

[12] On this, see J. I. Israel, 'The Banning of Spinoza's Works in the Dutch Republic, 1670–1678', in W. van Bunge and W. Klever (eds.), *Disguised and Overt Spinozism around 1670* (Leiden: Brill, 1996), 3–14.

[13] On the use of the Dutch translation made by Spinoza scholars, see Notes on the Translation.

several letters display wider interests, such as the nature of fluidity and firmness (Eps. 6, 11), the movement of the planets and of comets (Eps. 26, 29–32), the calculation of chances (Ep. 38), and the physics of pressure (Ep. 41). Evidence of Spinoza's interest in the sciences is also provided by a catalogue of the books from his library that were put up for sale after his death.[14] Of the 161 books that are listed, roughly a quarter are mathematical or scientific works. This interest in the sciences is not merely peripheral; on the contrary it takes us, as will be seen later, to the heart of Spinoza's thought.

2. 'Demonstrated in Geometrical Order'

In this Introduction I shall attempt to explain the main themes of the *Ethics*, and the arguments by which Spinoza supported them. In doing so, I shall concentrate on those topics that are of most interest to a modern audience. I begin with a question which must strike every reader. The *Ethics*, as stated on its title-page, is 'demonstrated in geometrical order'. Spinoza sets out a number of definitions, axioms, and postulates, and from these he claims to derive, by rigorous logical deduction, a number of what would now be called 'theorems', but which he calls 'propositions'. Spinoza is the only philosopher to have written an important philosophical treatise in the form of a geometrical work, and it is natural to ask what led him to do this. An important clue to the answer is to be found in Descartes. Descartes had said that the long chains of reasoning employed by geometers in their proofs had given him the idea that everything that we can know can be interconnected in the same way (*Discourse on Method*, part 3: PWD i. 120). One of his correspondents, Father Mersenne, suggested that Descartes was well qualified to present his philosophy in such a way (*Second Objections*: PWD ii. 92). In his reply Descartes made use of a familiar mathematical distinction[15] between 'analysis' and 'synthesis'. In the former, one starts with what has to be proved and works back to primitive concepts. In synthesis, on the other hand, one proceeds by means of 'a long series of definitions, axioms, theorems and problems' (PWD ii. 111); in other

[14] The catalogue was originally published by J. Freudenthal, *Die Lebensgeschichte Spinozas* (Leipzig: Veit, 1899), 160–4.

[15] It goes back to Pappus, a Greek mathematician of the 4th century AD. One can be sure that Spinoza was aware of this distinction, which was mentioned (G i. 129) by his friend Lodewijk Meyer in his Preface to Spinoza's geometrical version of Descartes's *Principles* .

words, one proceeds as Euclid did. In this way, Descartes says, one can compel the reader's assent. There is an echo of this in the *Ethics*, when Spinoza remarks that mathematics convinces, even when it does not attract (*E*I, Appendix, p. III).

Descartes declared (*PWD* ii. III) that he preferred the method of analysis for philosophical purposes, and that it was this method that he employed in his *Meditations*. However, he conceded that the method of synthesis could be applied to philosophy, and he illustrated this remark by putting into geometrical form some arguments for the existence of God and for the distinction between mind and body (*Reply to Second Objections*: *PWD* ii. II3–20). One may say, then, that what Descartes did in only a summary fashion, Spinoza carried through to completion. His motives seem clear enough; he used the geometrical method because he wanted to convince the reader by producing cast-iron proofs.

But by no means the whole of the *Ethics* is set out in geometrical form; much of its argument is informal in character. In particular, Spinoza often inserts into his geometrical framework what he calls (using a word from classical scholarship) 'scholia'. In the *Ethics* these are passages of philosophical argument—often quite long—in which Spinoza adds to what he has stated in his propositions, and in which the argument is not presented in geometrical form. There is no suggestion that the arguments contained in the scholia are inferior to those contained in the formal propositions; Spinoza seems to have used the scholia either because he thought that they would be more accessible to the reader, or because a presentation of the arguments in a strict geometrical form might have proved unduly cumbrous. Certainly the scholia (along with a number of prefaces and appendices) are among the most attractive passages of the *Ethics*.

I said just now that Spinoza wants to present cast-iron proofs by means of his use of the geometrical method. However, his version of Descartes's *Principles* may seem to present a problem; for this is a work which is cast in geometrical form, but which presents views not all of which Spinoza believed to be true. This has led to the suggestion[16] that the geometrical method of the *Ethics* was intended to be, not a method of proof, but a method of presentation, inspired by the impersonality of such works as Euclid's *Elements*. But this suggestion rests on a confusion between the truth of a conclusion and the validity of a proof. The fact that Spinoza deduces theorems from a number of definitions, axioms,

---

[16] L. Roth, *Spinoza* (London: Benn, 1929), 24.

and postulates does not oblige him to say that all these theorems are true. Certainly, if he starts from true statements, and if the deductions made from them are valid, then the theorems must be true. But Spinoza does not have to say that, in the case of his geometrical version of Descartes's philosophy, the statements from which he starts are uniformly true. In the case of the *Ethics*, of course, he would say that the situation is different. Here, he would say, the starting-points are true, as are the statements derived from them.

3. The Starting-Points of the *Ethics*: Axioms, Postulates, and Definitions

I have said that, by casting his philosophy in geometrical form, Spinoza wants to prove that his is a true philosophy. But the geometrical method is more than a method of proof. To see what other function the method has, it is necessary to look more closely at the starting-points of the *Ethics*—namely, its definitions, axioms, and postulates. In the *Ethics* Spinoza is on the whole content to use these rather than to talk about them; however, the few remarks that he does make can be supplemented from the *Tractatus de Intellectus Emendatione* and from his correspondence.

Like Euclid, Spinoza begins his work with definitions, but it will be convenient for expository purposes to comment first on the axioms. Spinoza would not claim that his views on these were in any way new or controversial. For him, an axiom is a truth; further, it is a truth that does not have to be proved, but is 'self-evident', in the sense that it will be accepted as true by any rational being.[17] However, an axiom is not just a self-evident truth; it is also a starting-point. From axioms, propositions are deduced; but axioms themselves are not deduced from other propositions.[18]

---

[17] Compare the remark made by Meyer in his Preface to Spinoza's geometrical version of Descartes's *Principles*: 'Axioms . . . are statements so clear and evident that all who simply understand correctly the words they contain can in no way refuse their assent to them' (G i. 127).

[18] In one case (E5 A2) Spinoza suggests that an axiom could have been derived from an earlier proposition, namely E3 P7. Perhaps his reason for introducing an axiom at this point is to simplify exposition. The desire to simplify exposition may explain another feature of the *Ethics*. Spinoza often says in the course of the work that a proposition is 'self-evident' (E1 P11, P20 C2, P31; E2 P5, L1, L3 C, L6, P28, P43; E3 P4; E4 P10, P25, P39, P72; E5 P28, P37), but does not grant such a proposition the status of an axiom.

Euclid's geometry contains a number of 'postulates'—one indeed, the 'postulate of parallels', is famous. Spinoza, too, makes use of postulates; six come immediately before E2 P14, and two are stated at the beginning of Part Three. For Spinoza, as for Euclid, a postulate is a statement for which no proof is offered; however, unlike an axiom, it is not known to be true, but is only assumed to be true. Obviously, one cannot assume whatever one pleases, and it emerges from the *Ethics* that Spinoza means by a postulate a proposition for whose truth we have considerable, but not conclusive, evidence. This is made clear by a passage in E2 P17 S, in which Spinoza defends the postulates of Part Two by saying that they contain scarcely anything that is not supported by experience.

I said earlier in this section that Spinoza's geometrical method of procedure is more than a method of proof. That this is so can be seen by considering his use of definitions in the *Ethics*. The question what Spinoza is doing when he offers definitions in the course of the work has an obvious answer: namely, that he is informing his readers how he proposes to use certain words. This is made clear by the structure of the definitions themselves, which are usually of the form 'By . . . I understand . . .'. That is, Spinoza is offering what are now called 'stipulative' definitions; he tells his readers how he proposes to use certain terms, regardless of the way in which others may use them. This may seem to imply that we cannot say whether Spinoza's definitions are true or false, since they merely indicate his intention to use certain words in certain ways. But if that is so, then one may ask why one should accept Spinoza's definitions; why one should indulge in what may seem to be an idiosyncratic game with words. However, this would involve a misunderstanding. Spinoza states clearly (Ep. 4, G iv. 13: *SL* 67; Ep. 9, G iv. 43: *SL* 91; *DIE*, sect. 95) that, in his view, there are both true and false definitions, and that his definitions are true. What he has in mind here is indicated by a passage from the *Ethics* (E3 DE20), where he says, in connection with what may appear to be an unusual definition, that his purpose is to explain, not the meaning of words, but the nature of things. A true definition, then, will be one that gives a satisfactory account of 'the nature of things'. One may illustrate this by considering the definition of the term 'velocity'. In popular usage, this may be defined simply as speed; but in its scientific usage it is defined as speed in a certain direction. Spinoza would doubtless say that the latter is the true definition of the word 'velocity'. To connect this with the fact that Spinoza's definitions are stipulative, consider a scientist introducing a definition that has since become standard. Such a scientist might say, for example, 'Although the word "velocity" is commonly used simply to mean speed, I propose to use it in another way, namely . . . etc.' This would correspond to the way in which Spinoza defines terms in the *Ethics*.

Spinoza's concept of definition is closely related to his concept of essence, a term that is often used in the *Ethics*. In the *Tractatus de Intellectus Emendatione* (sect. 95) Spinoza says that if a definition is to be perfect, it must explain the 'inmost essence' of a thing, rather than refer to any of the thing's 'properties'. Suppose, for example, that a circle is defined as a figure such that the lines drawn from the centre to the circumference are equal; 'everyone sees', Spinoza says, that this definition does not explain the essence of a circle, but explains only a property of it. This can also be illustrated from the *Ethics*, where Spinoza says, of a definition of love which states that love is the will of the lover to unite himself with the beloved, that it states only a property, not the essence of love (*E3* DE6).[19] Spinoza does not define the word 'property', and it may be assumed that he was taking it in what he regarded as a standard sense. In late Scholasticism a property of X is not a part of the essence of X, though (like the essence) it does belong necessarily to X,[20] and this seems to be what is in mind here. Spinoza adds that not only must a definition state the essence, as opposed to the properties, of a thing; it must also be such that from it all the properties of the thing defined can be derived (*DIE*, sect. 96; see also Eps. 82 and 83). The interesting question here is the relation between essence and property. Spinoza is saying in effect that although a property of (say) Socrates is a feature of Socrates that belongs necessarily to him, yet that feature is less fundamental than some other necessary feature of Socrates, because the former feature can be derived from the latter. It is this latter feature that one must know if one is really to understand what Socrates is.

Let us now take stock of Spinoza's use of the geometrical method. It has been seen to have two main functions. The first is to prove the truth of certain propositions, by showing that they follow logically from certain definitions, axioms, and postulates. The second is to explain the nature of things, i.e. to enable us to understand. It performs this second task, above all, by producing true definitions, from which necessary consequences are logically derived. These two tasks are interlinked in so far as, roughly speaking, to explain something is to deduce it from

---

[19] In fact, one that is offered by Descartes, in *The Passions of the Soul*, ɪɪ. 79: *PWD* i. 356.

[20] See e.g. Suárez, *Disputationes Metaphysicae*, 3. 1. 1. The definition of a property given by Aristotle (*Topics*, 1. 5. 102ᵃ 18–19) is more complex. According to this, a property of X is peculiar to and convertible with X, though not essential to X.

definitions and self-evident truths. (I say 'roughly speaking', as this will require some qualification later, in Section 8; but it is true on the whole.)

In taking the view that to explain something is to produce deductive arguments, Spinoza was saying nothing new; such a view goes back as far as Aristotle. Consider, for example, Aristotle's explanation of the fact that the planets shine steadily (*Posterior Analytics*, 1. 13. 78^{a}38–^{b}3). Aristotle argues that this can be done by constructing a deductive argument—more specifically, a syllogism—of which 'All planets shine steadily' is the conclusion. The argument runs as follows:

> All bodies near the earth are bodies that shine steadily
> All planets are bodies near the earth
> Therefore all planets are bodies that shine steadily.

This leads to the question why Spinoza should cast his system in a Euclidean form, and not in the form of syllogisms. The answer is to be found in Spinoza's interest in the science of his time, mentioned earlier (Section 1). For the new science, mathematics was the key to the understanding of Nature. The book of Nature, as Galileo said in a remark that has become famous, is written in the language of mathematics.[21] Spinoza took the same view. Truth, he says in the Appendix to Part One of the *Ethics* (p. 108), might have lain hidden from the human race throughout all eternity had it not been for mathematics. It was, then, for this reason that he took as the pattern for the *Ethics* what was in his epoch the paradigm of a mathematical system—the geometry of Euclid.

4. Substance and Attributes

Like many works of moral philosophy, Spinoza's *Ethics* presupposes a view about the nature of human beings. Spinoza insists that we are not to be regarded as beings which are fundamentally different from all others, a kind of empire within an empire (*E*3, Preface). Rather, we are part of a wider order of things, and cannot be understood without a knowledge of that order. Such knowledge, Spinoza believes, must involve a knowledge of foundations; in other words, a moral philosophy demands a metaphysics. It also involves some knowledge of the sciences, but Spinoza thinks it sufficient, for his purposes, to give only a sketchy account of these. The *Ethics*, then, begins with a metaphysics. The first part of the

---

[21] See e.g. J. Losee, *A Historical Introduction to the Philosophy of Science*, 1st edn. (London: Oxford University Press, 1972), 17.

book concerns the general nature of reality; only in the second part does Spinoza begin to discuss the topic of the human being in particular.

Part One of the *Ethics* is entitled 'On God'. There is a sense in which the whole work is about God, and the first part could have been entitled 'On Substance and Cause', which are its main topics. In discussing substance, Spinoza is discussing a subject which has deep roots in the history of thought. In his time there were two main concepts of substance, each derived from Aristotle. In the first sense of the term, substance is that which depends on nothing else for its existence; in the second, a substance is that which remains the same through change. Although Spinoza is by no means a commentator on Aristotle, it will be useful to look at the account of these senses in chapter 5 of the *Categories*, for this account determined the standard use of the term 'substance' in Spinoza's time. With regard to the first sense, Aristotle says of a substance (*Categories*, 5. 2^a12–13) that it is 'that which is neither said of a subject nor is in a subject'.[22] By the first part of the definition he means that a substance is an ultimate subject of predication. For example, one may predicate several things of Socrates—that he is Greek, is a philosopher, is snub-nosed, and so on—but one cannot predicate Socrates of anything. In saying that substance is 'not in' a subject, Aristotle is giving the term 'in' a special sense. To say, in this sense, that something is 'in' a subject is not to say that it is a part of it, as, say, the heart is in the body; rather, it is to say (*Categories*, 2. 1^a24–5) that it cannot exist separately—as, for example, the colour of a white horse cannot exist by itself, apart from the horse. A substance, then, is what Aristotle calls elsewhere (e.g. *Metaphysics*, Δ 8. 1017^b25) 'separable'; in other words, it is that which has an independent existence, as distinct from (say) colour, whose existence is only dependent. The second sense of the term, i.e. substance as that which remains the same through change, is introduced by Aristotle when he says (*Categories* 5. 4^a10 ff.) that 'it seems most distinctive of substance that what is numerically one and the same is able to receive contraries'—as, for example, a man who becomes hot at one time and cold at another.

Though Spinoza is interested in the problem of how a thing can remain the same through change, he does not discuss it in the context of the concept of substance.[23] Substance, he says, is to be defined as 'that

---

[22] Trans. J. L. Ackrill, *Aristotle's 'Categories' and 'De Interpretatione'* (Oxford: Clarendon Press, 1963). More exactly, this is a definition of substance in Aristotle's primary sense of the term. Aristotle also recognizes a secondary sense of the term, in which a substance is a universal rather than a particular.

[23] He discusses it when he considers the nature of 'individuals'; see Sect. 5

which is in itself (*in se*)[24] and is conceived through itself' (*E*I D3). In saying that substance is 'in itself', Spinoza is close to the Aristotelian view that substance is that which has an independent existence. He differs from Aristotle, however, over the question of what satisfies this criterion of substance. In the *Categories* Aristotle recognizes as substances such things as an individual man or an individual horse. For him, then, there are very many substances. Spinoza, on the other hand, argues (*E*I P14) that there can only be one substance, and that this substance is God.[25] We turn now to Spinoza's assertion that substance is 'conceived through itself'. He explains (*E*I D3; cf. *E*I P8 S2, p. 79) that this means that a substance is such that, in thinking of it, we do not have to think of anything else. The point of including this within the definition of substance becomes clear later, when it emerges (see *E*I P10 and S) that the notion of being 'conceived through itself' has a vital part to play in Spinoza's theory of the relations between mind and matter.

There is much more to be said about the substance that is God. In *E*I D6, after saying that God is a substance, Spinoza goes on to say that God is a substance 'consisting of infinite attributes, each of which expresses eternal and infinite essence'. This makes use of the concept of attribute, defined by Spinoza (*E*I D4) as 'that which intellect perceives of substance, as constituting its essence'. The concept of an attribute is one of Spinoza's most important, and difficult, concepts. A problem arises from the reference in the definition to the intellect; an attribute is that which intellect perceives of substance *as constituting* (*tanquam constituens*) its essence. Some scholars take this to mean 'as if', and say that Spinoza means that intellect ascribes attributes to a reality which is in reality without attributes. However, the textual evidence is strongly against this, the so-called 'subjective interpretation' of the attributes;[26] all indications are that, for Spinoza, the attributes are as real as substance. In fact,

---

[24] This is not to be rendered as 'which exists in itself', since Spinoza later claims to *prove* that existence belongs to the nature of substance (*E*I P7).

[25] The argument, contained in *E*I P14, rests on the thesis that there cannot exist two substances of the same nature or attribute (*E*I P5, P8 S2). For these arguments, which are notoriously difficult, see e.g. J. Bennett, *A Study of Spinoza's Ethics* (Cambridge: Cambridge University Press, 1984), 66–70, and R. J. Delahunty, *Spinoza* (London: Routledge & Kegan Paul, 1985), 108–16.

[26] For a defence of the subjective interpretation of the attributes, see e.g. Wolfson, *The Philosophy of Spinoza*, i. 146–7. This interpretation is strongly attacked by, for example, F. S. Haserot, 'Spinoza's Definition of Attribute', repr. in S. P. Kashap (ed.), *Studies in Spinoza* (Berkeley: University of California Press, 1972), 28–42, and by Delahunty, *Spinoza*, 116–17.

attributes *are* substance; any attribute is substance as conceived (and truly conceived) by intellect, and for this reason Spinoza speaks in *E1* P19 as 'God, i.e. all the attributes of God'. This leaves unanswered the question why Spinoza introduces intellect into his definition of substance. Perhaps his point is that the relation between substance *S* and attribute *A* is not one between separate entities. In a sense, nothing exists but *S*; but it is *S* as being (and really being) *A*, and this is something that can be grasped by an intellectual operation.

Spinoza declares that the one substance, God, has an infinity of attributes (*E1* D6), but the only two attributes that he discusses are extension and thought. Indeed, in a late letter (Ep. 64 (1675), G iv. 278: *SL* 299) he goes so far as to say that these are the only two attributes that human beings can know. His view, then, is that we know that there are attributes other than these, but that we do not know what they are. This view has puzzled scholars,[27] but for our purposes we may leave this problem aside and concentrate on the two attributes that we do know. We can say at once that Spinoza's view that thought and extension are attributes of God (*E2* P1, P2) has important consequences. It means that Spinoza would reject the view that everything is really matter (mind being in some sense material) and also the view that everything is really mind (matter being in some sense mind). But it also means that the one substance, God, is matter, even though not exclusively matter.

The view that there is one, and only one, substance is commonly termed 'monism', and there is no doubt that Spinoza is a monist in this sense of the term. However, the term 'monism' has another sense; it can be used to refer to a theory which states that there is a plurality of substances, each of which is of one and the same kind. An example of this would be the 'neutral monism' of William James. For James, minds and bodies consist of entities of the same basic kind (hence the term 'monism'), each of which is neutral in that it is neither mental nor physical. For Spinoza there can be no plurality of substances, nor is his substance of just one basic kind; the attributes which express the essence of God are infinite in number.

There is more to be said about Spinoza's attributes. Spinoza says that

---

[27] It has been argued that in speaking of an infinity of attributes of God, Spinoza means 'all the attributes there are', which could refer to just the two attributes of thought and extension. (See A. Wolf, 'Spinoza's Concept of the Attributes of Substance', repr. in Kashap, (ed.), *Studies in Spinoza*, 24–7.) This would rule out the idea of unknown attributes of substance; however, the evidence seems to be against this view. (See *E2* P7 S (especially the phrase 'or under any other attribute') and Ep. 64.)

each attribute must be 'conceived through itself' (*E*I PIO and S). By this he means that if we are considering anything that is physical, we must think of it in terms of matter alone, and if we are considering anything that is mental, we must think of it in terms of mind alone. Here Spinoza is incorporating into his own system a distinction that had been made by Descartes. Descartes had said that although in the strict sense God is the only substance—for God alone is truly independent—yet it is proper to speak of physical and mental substances, in that they are almost independent, dependent only on the God who creates them and keeps them in existence (*Principles of Philosophy*, I. 51–2: *PWD* i. 210). Descartes also held that such substances, i.e. minds and bodies, are 'really distinct' (*Meditations*, VI: *PWD* ii. 54): that is, that mental substances must be understood in terms of thought alone, and physical substances in terms of matter alone. Spinoza would say that this constitutes an important part of the truth. There is only one substance; but what Descartes puts in terms of extended and mental substances can be put in terms of the attributes of the one substance, by saying that each attribute must be 'conceived through itself'. Descartes's sharp distinction between mind and body created problems both for himself and for subsequent philosophers: namely, the problems of how mind and body can interact, and how they can form a unity. These problems concern particular beings—this human body, this human mind—and before examining Spinoza's answers (into which, incidentally, the concept of an attribute will enter) it is necessary to look at his views about particular things.

5. The Modes of Extension

We have seen that Spinoza claims that there is just one substance; he also claims (*E*I PI2) that this substance is indivisible. This raises the question how he can find room within his system for the existence of particular things; that is, whether he is committed to the view that such things are no more than illusory appearances of the one seamless being. His answer to the problem is to be found in his doctrine of modes. He defines a mode as (*E*I D5) an 'affection' of substance; in other words, a mode is, in complete contrast to substance, 'that which is in something else, through which it is also conceived'. Here he is drawing on Descartes, who asserts (*Principles of Philosophy*, I. 56: *PWD* i. 211) that we use the term 'mode' 'when we are thinking of a substance as being affected or modified'. Descartes gives shape as an example of a mode of an extended thing, saying that 'shape is unintelligible except in an extended thing'; similarly, imagination, sensation, and will are modes of the mind, in that they are 'intelligible only in a thinking thing' (ibid. 1. 53; see also 1. 61). This is clearly close to Spinoza's definition in that it says that modes are 'in' something else.

In these passages Descartes speaks of the modes of particular things, whether corporeal or mental. For Spinoza, particular things are themselves modes (*E1* P25 C). I begin with his account of particular extended things. One might suppose that, when he speaks of such things, Spinoza has in mind the particular things of everyday experience—this man, this horse—that Aristotle would have regarded as substances. Certainly, Spinoza's theory of modes includes such things; but it is important to note that the particular extended things of which Spinoza speaks are, in the main, grasped by the intellect and not by the senses. That is to say, they have to be understood within the context of a physical theory, of which Spinoza offers a sketch in Part Two of the *Ethics*, between *E2* P13 S and *E2* P14. The basic units of Spinoza's physical theory are what he calls 'most simple bodies' (A2 after L3, following *E2* P13 S); that is, bodies which are not composed of other bodies. There is no suggestion that these most simple bodies are observable entities; they are simply, according to Spinoza, the units with which a rational physical theory has to operate. We may take it that these are what Spinoza would call 'particular things'; the question now arises how such things are to be distinguished from one another. For an atomist, the answer is straightforward; the 'most simple bodies' would be corporeal substances. For Spinoza, however, there can be no more than one substance, and the 'most simple bodies' have to be regarded as modes of the one substance, or more precisely of the one substance conceived under the attribute of extension. How, then, can these modes be differentiated from one another? Spinoza's answer is that extension is not an inert mass; on the contrary, it is axiomatic that all bodies either move or are at rest, and move now more slowly and now more quickly (A1 and A2 after *E2* P13 S). It is by virtue of these differences (L1 after A2) that the most simple bodies are differentiated from one another.

Spinoza has more to say about motion and rest. I have made the point that, for him, particular things are modes; but it must also be realized that not all modes are particular things, whether extended or thinking. According to Spinoza (Ep. 64 (1675), G iv. 278: *SL* 299) motion and rest are modes;[28] not finite modes, however, but what scholars call 'immediate infinite modes'.[29] These are described in very abstract and obscure terms in *E*1 P21. Put informally, Spinoza's position is that motion and rest are of great importance to the physicist. They are not absolutely basic, since to talk of motion and rest is to talk of something extended that moves or is at rest. They are therefore modes of the attribute of extension; but they are *infinite* modes, as it is the infinite attribute of extension that either moves or is at rest. They are also 'immediate', as they require nothing but the attribute of extension in order to exist.

To revert to the 'most simple bodies': Spinoza says that these combine in groups, each of which has a certain structure. Such a group Spinoza proposes to call one (composite) body, or, and this is his preferred term, an 'individual' (D after A2, following L3). What makes an individual one is its structure. So long as this remains the same, the individual remains the same; this is how we can say, for example, that the same individual becomes larger or smaller, or can change the direction of its motion (L4–L7). Individuals are of various degrees of complexity. At the lowest level of complexity are those whose constituents are most simple bodies; such individuals can combine to form a class (*genus*) of individuals, whose members may combine to form a third class, and so on (L7 S). The human body, Spinoza says, is composed of many such individuals, each of which is highly composite (Postulate 1 after L7 S). At this stage we have reached what Aristotle would call 'substances', such as this particular man, and we see how we can ascribe change to one and the same thing without regarding such a thing as a substance.

Spinoza adds (*E*2 L7 S) that the containment of individuals within individuals is something that can be thought of as continuing to infinity, with the result that we can conceive 'the whole of Nature to be one individual, whose parts—that is, all bodies—vary in infinite ways without any change of the whole individual'. He calls such an individual (Ep. 64) the 'aspect of the whole universe' (*facies totius universi*). What he has in mind here is the fact that the physical universe, taken as a whole, manifests a certain law: namely, that the same ratio of motion and rest is preserved in the entire universe (cf. Ep. 32 (1665), G iv. 172: *SL* 194).

---

[28] Some scholars regard motion and rest as constituting *one* mode, and to emphasize this they speak of 'motion-and-rest'. The position is not clear, but the evidence seems to be against this view; see e.g. A. Gabbey, 'Spinoza's Natural Science and Methodology', in Garrett (ed.), *The Cambridge Companion to Spinoza*, 189 n. 60.

[29] To be exact, they are infinite and *eternal* modes. For Spinoza's concept of eternity, see below, Sect. 8.

Scholars call the 'aspect of the whole universe' a 'mediate' infinite mode of extension; it is mediate, in that it presupposes motion and rest.

All this provides an answer to the question raised at the beginning of this section, namely, whether Spinoza regards the modes as merely illusory. It is now clear that he does not. In saying that 'individuals', such as compound bodies, are diversified by structure, and that the 'most simple' (i.e. non-compound) bodies are diversified by motion and rest, Spinoza is not saying that material things are illusory. Of course, it would be illusory to suppose that material things are substances; but that would be a different matter.

A mode, by definition, is something that exists in and is conceived through something else, and this 'something else' is God (*E1 P15*). From what has just been said about the modal nature of particular things, it is clear why Spinoza's philosophy should often be said to be a form of 'pantheism'. Some scholars[30] think that this is misleading; it suggests that Spinoza's God is identical with the universe, whereas in fact his God is more than the universe. Such scholars prefer the term 'panentheism', which suggests that although the world is in God, yet it is not God. Certainly, if it were supposed that Spinoza's God is just the material universe, this would be a serious error, for it would neglect the attribute of thought, of which much remains to be said. However, one need not take the word 'pantheism' in this restricted way. One of its standard senses is that God is everything and everything is God, which is what Spinoza asserts.

6. The Modes of Thought

We now turn to the attribute of thought. Spinoza declares (*E2 P5*) that the modes of this attribute are 'ideas'. His use of this term is distinctive. In effect, he offers a critical commentary on what Descartes has to say about ideas, so his own views are best approached by way of those of Descartes. Descartes had taken the word 'idea' to mean whatever is immediately perceived by the mind (*Reply to Second Objections*, sect. 5: *PWD* ii. 127). Ideas are also *of* something; they are 'thoughts which are as it were the images of things', as when one thinks of 'a man, of a chimaera, or the sky, or an angel, or God' (*Meditations*, iii: *PWD* ii. 25). For Descartes, then, an idea is a representative entity, perceived immediately

---

[30] See e.g. G. Lloyd, *Spinoza and the 'Ethics'* (London: Routledge, 1996), 38–41.

by the mind. Spinoza, on the other hand, takes an idea to be an action of the mind (*E2 D3*). Descartes himself had noted that the term 'idea' could be taken to mean an activity (Preface to the *Meditations*: PWD ii. 7), but added that he preferred to use the term to mean, not an operation of the intellect, but the thing represented by that operation. The use of the term that Descartes rejected, Spinoza adopts.

The answer to the question why he did so, and what he meant by calling an idea an action of the mind, is to be found at the end of Part Two of the *Ethics* (*E2 P49* and S). In *E2 P49* Spinoza states that 'There is in the mind no volition, or, no affirmation and negation, apart from that which an idea involves in so far as it is an idea.' This shows that Spinoza is thinking of an idea as involving judgement, in the philosophical sense of the term; that is, he is saying that to have an idea of X is not to have in the mind some picture-like entity, but is to affirm or deny something of X. His use of the term 'volition' in this context shows that he is thinking of, and also distancing himself from, Descartes's theory of judgement. Descartes had argued that when a person judges something, two faculties are involved, namely the intellect and the will (*Meditations*, IV: PWD ii. 39). Suppose, for example, that I judge that the sun is shining. It is by virtue of the intellect that I have the idea of the sun's shining, and by virtue of the will that I affirm that it is shining. Here Descartes is trying to account for the fact that to judge something is in a way to commit oneself. In judging that the sun is shining I do not just consider the proposition that the sun is shining. Rather, I commit myself, I give others my word for saying that the sun is shining, and this commitment comes from something that is other than the intellect. This 'something other' is the will. Spinoza argues that this theory of the judgement is false, for intellect and will are one and the same (*E2 P49 C*). To have an idea of something, he argues, is to make a judgement about it; so, for example, to think of a winged horse is to affirm wings of a horse (*E2 P49 S*, p. 160). Spinoza has a further objection against Descartes (*E2 P43 S*). Suppose that we take an idea to be an image-like entity, which we compare with reality; how can we know that an idea is true? How know that it agrees with that of which it is the idea?[31]

Spinoza's disagreement with Descartes goes even deeper. In his definition of the term 'idea', Spinoza makes use of the term 'mind'; an idea,

---

[31] For a discussion of the question whether Spinoza's criticisms of Descartes's theory of the judgement are fair, see J. G. Cottingham, 'The Intellect, the Will and the Passions: Spinoza's Critique of Descartes', *Journal of the History of Philosophy*, 26 (1988), 239–57.

he says, is a 'conception' of the mind (*E*2 D3), by which he means (as we have seen) that it is an action of the mind. But what is a mind? More specifically, what is a human mind, which is Spinoza's chief concern in the *Ethics*? For Descartes, the answer was clear. Minds are thinking substances—not substances in the sense that they are absolutely independent, for only God is a substance in that sense, but substances in the sense that they need only God in order to exist (*Principles of Philosophy*, I. 51: *PWD* i. 210). Ideas, for Descartes, are what are perceived by such thinking substances. For Spinoza, on the other hand, to talk of a mind is to talk of an idea; or, more precisely, the human mind is an idea which is composed of very many ideas (*E*2 P15). Here the line of thought parallels what Spinoza has said earlier about the human body. Just as the human body is a highly complex 'individual', composed of other individuals, so the human mind is composed of very many ideas; and just as the human body, despite its complexity, may be regarded as one body, so the human mind may be regarded as one idea. There is a further parallel. Just as Spinoza does not offer an atomistic account of human bodies (cf. Section 5), so he does not offer an atomistic account of the mind. Ideas are not atomic entities; they are modes, and that of which they are modes is the attribute of thought.

In Ep. 64 Spinoza gave motion and rest as an example of an immediate infinite mode of extension. (Cf. Section 5 above.) In the same letter he gives as an example of an immediate infinite mode of thought what he calls the 'absolutely infinite intellect'. The notion of an infinite intellect has a part to play in the *Ethics* (*E*1 P16 C1, P30; *E*5 P40 S). What Spinoza means by the term is not obvious, though some remarks about the eternal and infinite intellect of God made towards the end of the *Ethics* (*E*5 P40 S) may suggest that he has in mind the way in which true ideas fit together into an explanatory system.[32] But this implies his theory of truth, which will be discussed in Section 8. As to a mediate infinite mode of thought, Spinoza gives no hint of what this might be, and scholars have not been able to produce an agreed answer.[33]

We have spoken of the human body and of the human mind; there remains the important question of how Spinoza conceives the relations

---

[32] Cf. G. H. R. Parkinson, *Spinoza's Theory of Knowledge* (Oxford: Clarendon Press, 1954), 107, 115–18, 178–80.

[33] See e.g. H. H. Joachim, *A Study of the Ethics of Spinoza* (Oxford: Clarendon Press, 1901), 94; M. Gueroult, *Spinoza: Dieu* (Paris: Aubier, 1968), 316–19; Y. Yovel, 'The Infinite Mode and Natural Laws in Spinoza', in Y. Yovel (ed.), *God and Nature: Spinoza's Metaphysics* (Leiden: Brill, 1991), 89.

between them. His discussion of this topic is one of the best-known parts of his philosophy. It was mentioned earlier (Section 4) that Descartes's sharp separation between mind and body caused him serious problems; more specifically, it made it hard to explain how mind can act on body, and how the two form one human being. It is generally agreed that Descartes's answers to these problems are unsatisfactory. Spinoza was one of Descartes's severest critics;[34] but it must also be realized that Spinoza did not think that Descartes's views about mind and body were wholly wrong. Descartes was right, Spinoza would say, in insisting that mental events must be explained in mental terms alone, and physical events in physical terms alone. At the same time there is a connection between mental and physical events; 'the order and connection of ideas', Spinoza says in E2 P7, 'is the same as the order and connection of [material] things'. Spinoza explains how this is possible in an important Scholium (E2 P7 S). He says that it follows from his theory of attributes that 'a mode of extension and the idea of that mode [sc. the idea that corresponds to that mode[35]] is one and the same thing, but expressed in two ways . . . For example, a circle existing in Nature and the idea of the existing circle, which is also in God, is one and the same thing, which is explained through different attributes.'

For Spinoza, then, the problems that faced Descartes about the relations between mind and body do not arise. This is because mind and body are not separate substances, as Descartes supposed; rather, to talk of X's mind and X's body is to talk of one and the same mode of substance, which is expressed through different attributes. Nor, since each attribute is conceived through itself, can it be said that X's mind acts on X's body, or conversely. Spinoza recognizes that this last assertion may seem paradoxical. Suppose (E3 P2 S) that a craftsman is performing some delicate operation; surely, one may say, the mind must guide the hand in this case? Spinoza replies that this is not, and indeed cannot be, so; to suppose that the mind must guide the body rests on our ignorance of what the body can do by its own powers.

The theory of mind–matter relations that Spinoza offers is not a mere historical curiosity; on the contrary, it is the recognized ancestor of what

---

[34] See, in particular, his scathing critique of Descartes's views about the functions of the pineal gland in the Preface to Part Five of the *Ethics*.

[35] This must be what he means here and in similar contexts. He also uses the term 'idea of X' in what is perhaps its usual sense, where X is that of which one thinks. See, e.g. E2 P17 S, with its reference to the idea of Peter which Paul has; compare also Descartes's view about the representative character of ideas, discussed at the beginning of Sect. 6

is termed the 'double-aspect' theory of mind–matter relations, which is still discussed.[36] According to this theory, physical and mental states or events are independent manifestations of one and the same reality, of which they are different aspects or expressions. Spinoza does not in fact assert that thought and extension are different aspects of the same substance, but he does say that attributes 'express' the essence of substance (E1 D6, P10 S, P11, P16, P19, P29 S). He does not define the term 'express', so it may be assumed that he believed that he was using the term in a standard way, and that he meant (roughly speaking) that *A* expresses *B* if, from a knowledge of *A* alone, we can derive some knowledge of the nature of *B*. This, however, is not enough to explain mind–matter relations, for there are various kinds of expression. It may be said, for example, that one mathematical figure expresses another, as when it is said that an ellipse expresses a circle; or again, one may say that a certain action expresses a person's character, or that a person expresses his meaning now in one language, now in another. Of these sorts of expression, perhaps the last is the closest to what Spinoza means. Languages are, on the whole, mutually independent systems; to understand a sentence written in Latin we need a knowledge of the vocabulary and syntax of Latin, and of no other language. This would correspond to the fact that an attribute is 'conceived through itself'. Again, the same thought that is expressed in Latin can be expressed in other languages; this would correspond to Spinoza's point that the one substance is expressed through different attributes. Yet, when all this has been said, the differences are great. Spinoza's substance is not a thought, nor is an attribute a language. What we are offered is only a rough analogy, and we are left asking just what it is that is expressed both by extension and by thought.[37]

7. Causation and Necessity

Now that the concepts of substance, attribute, and mode have been discussed, we have in place much of the framework of Spinoza's account of the nature of the human being. But there is still more to be said about this account. First, it is necessary to explore what Spinoza has to say

[36] See e.g. G. N. A. Vesey, 'Agent and Spectator: The Double-Aspect Theory', in Vesey (ed.), *The Human Agent* (London: Macmillan, 1968), 139–59.

[37] This is a general objection to double-aspect theories: cf. J. Hospers, *An Introduction to Philosophical Analysis*, 2nd edn. (London: Routledge, 1967), 398.

about causation and necessity, in the context of both substance and the modes. Not only is God a substance consisting of an infinity of attributes, in each of which there is an infinity of modes; God is also a cause. The one substance, God, is declared to be a 'cause of itself' (*causa sui*; *Ei* P7); further, Spinoza declares that 'infinite things in infinite ways' (that is, an infinity of things in an infinity of attributes) follow from God's nature (*Ei* P16), from which he derives the corollary (*Ei* P16 C1) that God is the cause of absolutely all modes. In the course of his discussion of God's causality, Spinoza makes use of the concept of necessity. The one substance, God, exists necessarily (*Ei* P11), and the modes follow from the necessity of the divine nature (*Ei* P16).

Spinoza defines the term 'cause of itself' as (*Ei* D1) 'that whose essence involves existence, or, that whose nature cannot be conceived except as existing'. This definition plays an important part in the first of the arguments for God's existence contained in *Ei* P11. Here, Spinoza puts forward a version of the so-called 'ontological argument' for the existence of God,[38] in which the existence of God is argued to follow from the definition of God. This argument has been severely criticized, and is now widely regarded as fallacious; it is unlikely, too, that modern philosophers would accept any of the other three arguments for the existence of God put forward by Spinoza in *Ei* P11 and S. This may seem to have disastrous consequences for Spinoza's philosophy. The function of Spinoza's proofs of the existence of God, it may appear, is to anchor his concepts in reality, i.e. to show that there really is a substance of the sort that he describes. If these proofs fail, then Spinoza's philosophy becomes (as many critics have supposed it to be) a mere game with words. However, the situation is not so desperate for Spinoza as may at first sight appear. The claim to absolute certainty, based on self-evident truths, must indeed be abandoned; but it may well be that the concepts that Spinoza elaborates in the *Ethics* may throw some light on the enduring problems of philosophy, of which the nature of substance and cause are just two.

---

[38] What is called the 'ontological argument' covers at least two arguments, which have in common the fact that they proceed from a definition of God to the existence of what is defined. The first version is the one contained in the fifth of Descartes's *Meditations*: PWD ii. 44–9. Here, Descartes operates with the concept of God as a most perfect being, together with the assertion that existence is a perfection. (A similar argument had been put forward in the 11th century by St Anselm, who started from the concept of God as 'that, than which nothing greater can be thought'.) Spinoza, on the other hand, starts from the concept of a being which has to be thought of as existing—sometimes called a 'necessary being'. Cf. G. H. R. Parkinson, *Logic and Reality in Leibniz's Metaphysics* (Oxford: Clarendon Press, 1965), 77–85.

The term 'cause of itself' (however useless it may be as a means of proving the existence of Spinoza's God) is valuable for the light that it throws on Spinoza's concept of cause. It might be objected to Spinoza that the notion of a cause of itself is an evident absurdity; for if a thing is to bring about its own existence, it must first of all exist, i.e. it would have to exist before it exists. Spinoza would reply that this objection presupposes that a cause must precede its effect in time; but this, he would say, is not so. Rather, a cause has to be viewed as a reason—hence his famous phrase 'cause or reason' (*causa seu ratio*; E1 P11, first Alternative Proof).[39] What Spinoza has in mind here can be illustrated from elementary geometry. Suppose that one says that the reason why the base angles of a triangle are equal to one another is that the triangle is isosceles. In this case, one is not saying that first there is an isosceles triangle, and then there is a triangle whose base angles are equal; rather, the reason involved here is the timeless one of logical relationship. To say, then, that God is 'cause of himself' is not to say that God first exists and then brings about his own existence; it is to say that God's existence follows logically from the concept of God.[40] This concept of causality, according to which the relation between cause and effect is a logical one, is commonly called 'the rationalist theory of causality', and Spinoza is perhaps its most famous exponent. The attraction of the theory for Spinoza was doubtless the fact that it offered an explanation of the necessary character of causality; that is, the fact that given that *A* is the cause and *B* the effect, then given *A*, there *must be B*.[41]

Not only is God a self-caused being; God is also the cause of absolutely all things, inasmuch as all things follow necessarily from the divine nature (E1 P16 C1).[42] This means, then, that God is the cause of particular things. This is not to say that God as it were stands outside such things; particular things, as has been seen, are modes of the one infinite sub-

---

[39] Descartes, too, said that the concept of cause does not require that a cause should precede its effect in time, and that for this reason it is appropriate to speak of God as a 'cause of himself' (*Reply to First Objections*: PWD ii. 78–9).

[40] For Spinoza's view that causality is a timeless relation, see E1 P16 and its three corollaries. Here Spinoza begins by talking about what follows logically from the divine nature, and then proceeds to describe God in terms of causality.

[41] Compare E1 A3: 'From a given determinate cause an effect follows *of necessity*' (my emphasis).

[42] More exactly, God is the 'efficient cause' of absolutely all things. Spinoza does not define an 'efficient cause', which was a standard Aristotelian term (Aristotle, *Physics*, 2. 3. 194[b] 29–32); he seems to mean by it something that produces or generates its effect. He has no use for the other three types of Aristotelian cause—final, formal, and material—and is indeed very hostile to the notion of final causality (cf. Sect. 9).

stance. In Spinoza's language, God is (E1 P18) an 'immanent' and not a 'transitive' cause.[43] Besides recognizing a relation between God and particular things, Spinoza also recognizes a causal relation between particular things themselves, saying that (E1 P28) 'Every particular thing, or, any thing which is finite and has a determinate existence, cannot exist or be determined to operate unless it is determined to existence and operation by another cause, which is also finite and has a determinate existence.' The same can be said of that determining cause, and in turn of its cause, and so on to infinity. It is important to note here that Spinoza does not regard such a chain of causes as terminating in a God who is outside the chain; rather, all this causal activity takes place in God.[44]

In sum, God exists of necessity, and the modes of God follow from him of necessity. From this it follows, Spinoza says (E1 P29), that 'In Nature there exists nothing contingent, but all things have been determined by the necessity of the divine nature to exist and operate in a certain way.' This is a clear and concise statement of Spinoza's determinism, a determinism which is noteworthy in two respects. First, it is a universal determinism. *All* things—and, consequently, human minds and human bodies—are determined to exist and operate in a certain way. Secondly, Spinoza's determinism may be called a logical determinism, in that everything that exists (God included) exists with logical necessity; no other state of affairs than that which exists is really thinkable.

This second point may seem to indicate a grave weakness in Spinoza's determinism. Spinoza is here presupposing the rationalist theory of causality of which we have just spoken; but it has to be added that Hume[45] produced a criticism of this theory which many consider decisive. For the rationalist theory, to say that *A* causes *B* is to say that *B* is a logical consequence of *A*. But if this were so, it would be logically contradictory

---

[43] *Causa immanens* and *causa transiens* were standard terms in Spinoza's time. Heereboord (on whom, see Sect. 1, p. 8) explains them as follows: 'An immanent cause is one which produces an effect within itself; thus the intellect is called the cause of its concepts. A transitive cause is that which produces an effect outside itself' (Heereboord, *Hermeneia* (1650); cf. M. Gueroult, *Spinoza: Dieu* (Paris: Aubier, 1968), 246). On immanent or internal causality, see also Spinoza, Ep. 60, *SL* 290.

[44] Spinoza does call God the 'first cause' (E1 P16 C3), but this must be taken to mean something like 'the ultimate explanation'. It follows from this that the existence of an infinity of causes does not rule out the existence of a first cause in Spinoza's sense of the term, for these finite causes are different ways in which God's causality is manifested. Cf. Ep. 12, G iv. 61–2: *SL*, 106–7.

[45] Hume, *Abstract of a Treatise of Human Nature*; to be found, for example, in Hume, *An Enquiry concerning Human Understanding*, ed. A. G. N. Flew (La Salle, Ill.: Open Court, 1988), 34.

to assert *A* and deny *B*—but it is not. Hume put this by saying that in the case of a demonstration, 'the contrary is impossible, and implies a contradiction'. But, he continued, 'the mind can always *conceive* any effect to follow from any cause, and indeed any event to follow upon another', and 'whatever we conceive is possible'. It seems, then, that a logical determinism such as Spinoza's cannot be true. However, this does not mean that what Spinoza has to say about the necessity of what happens is wholly without value. There is a version of determinism which, like Spinoza's, involves the thesis that the causal relation is a necessary one, but which (unlike Spinoza's version) is not committed to the view that the causal relation is a logical relation . This version may be called 'causal determinism'. Briefly, it asserts that every human act has a cause or causes, which has the consequence that every such act is necessitated; there can, therefore, be no place for free will. This theory is not stated on a priori grounds, but rests on a view about the development of the sciences. The argument is that, over a period of many years, the sciences have made great progress in the discovery of the causes of human actions, and there is no reason to suppose that such progress must stop short of the ability to give a complete explanation of everything that any human being does. This theory is probably the version of determinism that is now most often thought to have damaging consequences for the possibility of human freedom. What makes Spinoza's views interesting is that they offer a way of reconciling human freedom with causal determinism. How they do so will be discussed later (see Section 11). First, however, there are other topics to be considered.

8. Truth and the Kinds of Knowledge

Immediately after the digression on physics that follows *E2 P13 S* Spinoza turns to questions about the nature of truth and knowledge, in a discussion that is concluded at the end of Part Two. It may seem strange that Spinoza should defer his discussion of knowledge until the second half of the second part of the *Ethics*; it might seem to be more logical to follow the order of Descartes's *Meditations*—that is, to begin with an account of the nature of knowing, and then to consider what may properly be said to be known. However, that would be to follow the 'analytic' method of procedure, whereas the *Ethics* is written by the 'synthetic' method (cf. Section 2). That is, Spinoza begins with axioms and definitions which he believes to be such that they cannot rationally

be doubted, and then proceeds to demonstrate their logical consequences.[46] This is not to deny that there are important things to be said
about knowledge and truth, and Spinoza thinks that he is in a position to
discuss these issues once he has given a general account of the modal
structure of the universe.

Spinoza does not offer a formal definition of truth in the *Ethics*, but he
shows what he means by the term 'true' in an axiom of Part One (*E1* A6),
which states that 'A true idea must agree with that of which it is the
idea.' Closely related to a true idea is what Spinoza calls an 'adequate'
idea (*E2* D4: cf. Ep. 60 (1695), *SL* 290). An adequate idea and a true idea
are the same, except that in the case of an adequate idea we do not
consider the idea to be related to something, but consider the idea
simply as it is in itself. This may seem clear enough; what Spinoza says
about adequate ideas, it seems, has as its basis a form of the correspondence theory of truth. But this is not so. It emerges that when Spinoza is
talking about 'truth', he is really talking about what we would call
'knowledge'. That there is something unusual about Spinoza's use of the
term 'true' is indicated by a striking remark in *E2* P43: 'Someone who has
a true idea knows at the same time that he has a true idea.' I call this
remark striking because, in a standard sense of the word 'true', it is a
gross error. Suppose, for example, that I predict successfully the outcome of a football match. My prediction may be said to be a true
statement; nevertheless (given that there has been no skulduggery of
which I happen to know), I do not, at the time of my prediction, know
that it is true. However, in the case of *E2* P43 the appearance of error
only indicates that a term is being used in an uncommon sense. What
this sense is Spinoza explains in *E2* P43 S, when he says that 'to have a true
idea simply means knowing a thing perfectly, or, in the best way'. This is
why Spinoza says (*E2* P35) that falsity consists in a privation of knowledge. As he remarks in the *Tractatus de Intellectus Emendatione*,[47] if someone says that Peter exists, but does not know that Peter exists, then his
utterance is false even if Peter does exist.

There is a complication here. Spinoza does not assert that a man who

---

[46] For Spinoza's view that the axioms and propositions of the *Ethics* cannot meaning-
fully be doubted, see *E1* P8 S2, P11 S; *E2* P17 S, P43; and *E5* P36 S.

[47] *DIE*, sect. 69: 'If anyone says that Peter, for example, exists, but does not *know*
that Peter exists, his thought is, as far as he is concerned, false—or, if you prefer, is not true—
even though Peter really does exist. The assertion "Peter exists" is true only with respect to a
person who knows for certain that Peter exists.' Here Spinoza suggests that one might
distinguish between a thought that is false and one that is not true, but there is no hint of
such a distinction in the *Ethics*.

has a false or inadequate idea of *X* has no knowledge of *X*; he may have knowledge of *X*, but it is knowledge of an inferior sort. (Hence the remark in *E2 P43 S* that to have a true idea of something is to know it in the best way.) Spinoza has in mind here a distinction drawn in the *Ethics* between three kinds of knowledge,[48] of which the first kind, which he commonly calls 'imagination',[49] is constituted by 'all those ideas which are inadequate and confused' (*E2 P41*). What Spinoza says about imagination is important, not just for the light that it throws on the nature of false or inadequate ideas, but also for the light that it throws on his theory of knowledge in general. At first sight, what Spinoza calls 'imagination' may seem to be a mixed bag. In the *Ethics* he divides it (*E2 P40 S2*) into 'knowledge from inconstant experience' and 'knowledge from signs'. The latter is involved in our use of language; but although what Spinoza has to say about this is of interest in its own right,[50] it is of less importance for an understanding of his philosophy than is 'knowledge from inconstant experience' (*ab experientia vaga*). This concerns the knowledge of particular things that we get from the senses, together with inductive knowledge, such as (*DIE*, sect. 20) my knowledge that I shall die, or that oil is suitable for feeding a flame.[51]

Spinoza says of knowledge from inconstant experience that it is mutilated and confused (*E2 P40 S2*). In describing sense-experience in this way, Spinoza does not mean that it provides us with nothing but illusions. Suppose, for example, that I look at a piece of paper which is lying on my desk; by virtue of this, I know that there is a piece of paper on my desk. But, Spinoza would say, this is knowledge of a low grade. His point is that my seeing the paper is the mental correlate of a complex physical process, which involves both the paper and my sense-organs and brain. But in so far as I merely see the paper, I have no knowledge of these processes, nor of the relation between these processes and my idea of the paper. In other words, my knowledge is fragmentary (hence 'mutilated') or it is like a consequence without its premises (hence 'confused';

---

[48] In *DIE*, sects. 19–24, Spinoza recognizes four kinds of knowledge, the first two of which constitute what is called in the *Ethics* the first kind of knowledge.

[49] Spinoza also says (*E2 P40 S2*) that he will call it 'opinion'; perhaps the point is that knowledge of this kind is such that, even though true in the standard sense of the term, it could have been false—as opposed to knowledge of the second and third kinds.

[50] See D. Savan, 'Spinoza and Language', in M. Grene (ed.), *Spinoza: A Collection of Critical Essays* (New York: Doubleday, 1973), 60–72; G. H. R. Parkinson, 'Language and Knowledge in Spinoza', ibid . 73–100.

[51] Cf. *E2 P40 S2*, in which Spinoza refers to a merchant's knowledge of a rule for finding a fourth proportional, based on the fact that he has often found the rule to work with small numbers.

E2 P28). In sum, when Spinoza says that sense-experience involves inadequate ideas, he means that the possession of such knowledge is not sufficient for us to understand or to explain. The same can be said of inductive knowledge. If I say that oil serves to feed a flame, and base this on my past experience of cases in which oil did just this, then though I know *that* this is the case, I do not know *why* it is the case.

This leaves open the question why induction and sense-experience, despite their deficiencies, should be called *knowledge*. The answer is not clear as far as induction is concerned, but a passing remark in *E2* P17 S gives some indication of why Spinoza should say that sense-experience gives us knowledge of a kind. When discussing Spinoza's use of postulates (Section 3), I mentioned his remark in this Scholium that the postulates used in Part Two of the *Ethics* are acceptable in that they contain hardly anything that is not supported by experience. He then says that we may not doubt experience 'now that we have shown that the human body exists as we sense it'. In other words: sense-experience may be accepted as giving us knowledge, provided that it is underpinned by the deductive system of the *Ethics*.

This remark about sense-experience has wide implications for Spinoza's philosophy as a whole. Spinoza is often called a 'rationalist' philosopher, and in so far as rationalism is taken to be the thesis that some truths of fact—such as, for example, the existence and nature of God—can be known by reason alone, then Spinoza is a rationalist. But it is important to realize that Spinoza does not take up the position that it is in principle possible for human beings to know absolutely everything by means of pure reason. He states this clearly in an early letter (Ep. 10, 1663, *SL* 95), saying that we need experience in the case of those things which 'cannot be inferred from the definition of a thing, as, for example, the existence of modes'. In other words, it does not follow from the definition of a sheet of paper, lying on my desk, that such a piece of paper exists. It is true, Spinoza would say, that from a definition of God we can infer that God exists. But to know that the piece of paper exists I need more than definitions and axioms; I need sense-experience.

Not only do inadequate ideas belong to the first kind of knowledge; all such ideas belong to it (*E2* P41). When we know things by the second and third kinds of knowledge, therefore, we have adequate ideas (ibid.). The question now arises what Spinoza means by these kinds of knowledge. Of the second kind of knowledge, 'reason', Spinoza says that it consists of 'common notions and adequate ideas of the properties of things' (*E2* P40 S2). In Spinoza's time the term 'common notions' (*communes notiones*) was generally used[52] to refer to axioms; so, for example, Descartes speaks of 'axioms or common notions' (*Replies to Second Objections: PWD* ii. 116). As to 'adequate ideas of the properties of things', it is probable that Spinoza means by a property of X something that belongs necessarily to X, but does not constitute X's essence (cf. Section 3). To have an adequate idea of a property—for example, that the lines from the centre of a circle to the circumference are equal—is to be able to show that this follows from the axioms and definitions of a system.

Spinoza has to show how such knowledge is possible for us. For we are finite beings, and so it may seem that every idea that we have must be 'mutilated and confused'. Spinoza's answer is based on the thesis that there are certain things which are 'common to all things', and equally in the part and in the whole (*E2 P37*). In *E2 P38* he begins by considering those things that are common to all bodies. By virtue of the theory of attributes, such things must also have their parallels in the attribute of thought, which means that there are ideas which are equally in the part and in the whole. These ideas will equally be part of the divine and of the human mind; consequently, we must possess adequate ideas, for in such cases we are operating with ideas which are not fragmentary and confused, but are in a sense God's ideas (*E2 P38*). Spinoza puts this by saying (*E2 P34*) that when we have an adequate idea, there is an adequate idea in God, in so far as he constitutes the human mind. In sum: the person who knows things by means of reason has adequate ideas inasmuch as God is manifested through the mind of that person.

One of Spinoza's most famous phrases is *sub specie aeternitatis*. The phrase makes its first appearance in the *Ethics* in *E2 P44 C2*, in which Spinoza says that 'It is of the nature of reason to perceive things under a certain species of eternity (*sub quadam aeternitatis specie*)'.[53] In Part One of the *Ethics* Spinoza explains that to talk about eternity is to talk about existence of a certain kind: namely, the existence that follows from the nature or definition of God (*E1 D8* and *P19*). He is emphatic that 'eternity' does not mean 'everlasting existence'. Rather (*E1 D8*), eternity

---

[52] Hence Spinoza speaks of 'notions which are called common' (*E2 P40 S1*). The Latin term is a literal translation of the Greek *koinai ennoiai*, by which Euclid refers to his axioms.

[53] Cf. *DIE*, sect. 108; *TTP*, ch. 6: G iii. 86. The shorter expression 'under a species of eternity' is more common in the *Ethics* (*E5 P22, P23 S, P29* and *S, P30, P31* and *S, P36*). The distinction does not seem to be of any significance; e.g. in *E5 P23 S* the expression 'under a species of eternity' comes soon after 'by a certain eternal necessity' in *P23*.

'cannot be explained by duration or time, even though the duration is conceived as without beginning and end'; or, as he says elsewhere (*E1 P33 S2*, p. 104), 'there is no "when", "before", or "after" in eternity'. So when reason grasps things 'under a certain species of eternity',[54] this means that it conceives them as timelessly related to a timeless God—just as when, in mathematics, we consider the relations between figures, we conceive these as timeless relations.

Spinoza has two arguments for his view that reason perceives things under a certain species of eternity (*E2 P44 C2*). First, reason regards things as necessary, and necessary relations are timeless relations. Secondly, the foundations of reason are the common notions, which explain what is common to all and do not explain the essence of any particular thing. Spinoza means that when (say) scientists investigate the nature of silver, they are not concerned with just this piece of silver, in all its particularity; they are concerned with silver in general. This is why Spinoza says (*E4 P62 S*, *E5 P36 S*) that reason is 'abstract' or 'universal'. This does not mean, however, that whenever we know things under an aspect of eternity, our knowledge is abstract; this, as will be seen shortly, is not true of the third kind of knowledge.

Knowledge of the third kind, or 'intuitive knowledge', has been regarded as exceptionally obscure. Some writers regard it as a kind of mystic vision; others regard it as simply unintelligible. I would suggest that Spinoza is here making an important point about knowledge, which can be placed within the context of Descartes's philosophy. To begin with, it may be noted that at any rate some features of intuitive knowledge are clear and uncontroversial. It resembles reason in two respects. First, it is necessarily true (*E2 P41*), i.e. it consists of adequate ideas. Secondly, it conceives or understands things under a species of eternity (*E5 P31* and S). It also differs from reason in two respects. First, it is not 'universal', but is a knowledge of particular things (*E5 P36 S*). Secondly, it is (as its name suggests) intuitive. All this, however, is very abstract, leaving us to ask just what intuitive knowledge is. In *E2 P40 S2*, in which Spinoza explains his view about the three kinds of knowledge, he offers a mathematical example, namely, the problem of finding a fourth proportional. (That is, given three numbers, to find a fourth number which is to the third as the second is to the first.) Spinoza points out that there

---

[54] Why a *certain* species of eternity? Spinoza does not explain, but by it he probably means that, in using reason, one does not grasp God in the totality of his necessary existence. So if, for example, one is to understand a law of physics, one does not have to grasp the connections between absolutely everything.

is a well-known rule for solving this problem: multiply the second number by the third, and divide the product by the first. The first two kinds of knowledge offer different methods of justifying this rule. Someone who uses the first kind of knowledge has found the rule to work with small numbers, and argues from these particular cases that the rule will hold in the case of all numbers. Someone who uses reason will justify the rule by relating it to a mathematical proof, such as that to be found in Euclid, 7. 19. But in the case of intuitive knowledge, there is no need of the rule just described. When the numbers are small—e.g. 1, 2, and 3—we *see* that the fourth proportional is 6, because 'we infer the fourth number from the very ratio that we see with one intuition that the first has to the second'. It is useful to compare this with what Spinoza says about intuitive knowledge in the *Tractatus de Intellectus Emendatione*, section 23: one sees the proportionality of the numbers, not by the force of Euclid's demonstration, but 'intuitively, without performing any operation'.

The difficulty is that there seems to be a self-contradiction in what Spinoza says about intuitive knowledge. On the one hand we do not (as in the case of the second and third kinds of knowledge) carry out the operation of applying a rule to a specific case. It seems, then, that no process of inference is involved. But on the other hand we find Spinoza saying that, in intuitive knowledge, a fourth number is *inferred* (*E*2 P40 S2). However, this apparent contradiction can be reconciled. In doing so, it is helpful to consider what Descartes said in connection with his famous utterance *Cogito, ergo sum*—'I think, therefore I exist'. Descartes insisted (*Reply to Second Objections: PWD* ii. 100) that this is not a syllogistic argument, proceeding from premises to a conclusion. That is, it is not of the form 'Everything that thinks exists; I am a thing that thinks; therefore I am a thing that exists'. Rather, it is recognized as self-evident 'by a simple operation of the mind'. In a conversation with Frans Burman, held in 1648 (*PWD* iii. 333), Descartes put his point by saying that the general proposition 'Everything that thinks exists' is logically prior to 'I think, therefore I exist', but that I do not know the general proposition before I recognize the truth of 'I think, therefore I exist'. 'We do not', said Descartes, 'separate these general propositions from the particular instances; rather, it is in the particular instances that we think of them.' This is close to what Spinoza says about the third kind of knowledge. When, in his example of this kind of knowledge, he says that we infer the fourth number intuitively, this could be put in Descartes's terms by saying that we think of the general rule in the particular instance. This is not to suggest that Spinoza knew of Descartes's conversation with Burman,[55] or indeed that he would have counted 'I think, therefore I exist' as an example of the third kind of knowledge; all that is claimed is that there is an illuminating parallel here.

This leads to the question whether the *Ethics* offers any interesting examples of what is known by the third kind of knowledge. The example of the fourth proportional is merely illustrative, and does not form a part of Spinoza's philosophical system. However, an important example is to be found in *E5 P36 S*. Here Spinoza asserts that, from what he has said, 'it becomes evident to us how, and in what way, our mind follows from the divine nature, and continually depends on God in respect of essence and existence'. This, he says, shows how the second kind of knowledge differs from the third; for although he has shown in general terms in Part One of the *Ethics* (the reference is probably to *E1 P25 S*) that 'all things (and consequently the human mind as well) depend on God in respect of essence and existence, yet that demonstration—although legitimate and beyond doubt—does not so affect our mind as when it is inferred from the very essence of any particular thing which we declare to depend on God'. This Scholium is also interesting in that it shows that the second kind of knowledge is not inferior to the third kind *as knowledge*; the demonstration of *E1 P25 S*, he says, is 'legitimate and beyond doubt'. The difference is (ibid.) that the third kind of knowledge is *more powerful* than the second. What this means will be discussed later, in Section 11.

9. *Conatus*

By the end of Part Two of the *Ethics* Spinoza has explained what the human mind is and how it is related to the human body; he has also said something about what human minds do—namely, that they make judgements, and so understand (or fail to understand) the nature of things. So far, however, Spinoza has said nothing about the fact that we endeavour to do certain things, nor has he mentioned the fact that we have emotions. In traditional terms, he has discussed only one of the three main features of the mind. He has considered intellection, but he

---

[55] This was not published until 1896. Of course, Spinoza could in principle have had access to the manuscript, but there is no evidence that he did.

has said nothing about conation and emotion. These deficiencies are made good in Parts Two and Three of the *Ethics*.

Spinoza's account of the conative aspect of human beings rests on two important propositions of Part Three. In *E3* P6 he asserts that 'Each thing, in so far as it is in itself, endeavours (*conatur*) to persevere in its being.' It should be noted first that this—commonly known as Spinoza's theory of *conatus*—is of universal application; all things, and not just human beings, manifest this endeavour.[56] In the next proposition, *E3* P7, Spinoza explains what *conatus* is, when he states that the endeavour by which each thing endeavours to persist in its own being simply is the essence of the thing. At first sight this may seem puzzling, as may the further statement made in *E3* P7 that the *conatus* of a thing may also be called its power. However, it emerges that Spinoza means that we should consider the essence of a thing as having certain necessary consequences. Suppose that such a consequence is *X*; to say that the thing endeavours to do *X* is to say that it will necessarily do *X* unless it is hindered by something that is external to it (cf. *E3* P4 and P5). Similarly, to say that something has the power to do *X* is to say that it will do *X* unless impeded by external things. I mentioned earlier that Spinoza's concept of *conatus* is of universal application. Spinoza's view about the nature of *conatus* can be illustrated from the sketch of physics contained in Part Two. In the Corollary to Lemma 3 after *E2* P13 S Spinoza says that a body in motion will continue to move unless determined to rest by another body. Spinoza would say of such a body that it endeavours to continue to move.

Spinoza has said of each thing that it endeavours to persevere in its being 'in so far as it is in itself'. The need for this qualifying phrase is obvious. It was pointed out earlier that the phrase 'in itself' means 'independent' (Section 4). By saying that each thing endeavours to persevere in its being in so far as it is independent, Spinoza is providing an answer to a possible objection: namely, that many human beings kill themselves out of sheer misery, or suffer torture and death for the sake of some cause, or sacrifice themselves for the sake of their children. Such acts, Spinoza would say, are not the acts of people who are independent. The phrase 'in itself' also has metaphysical implications, in so far as it is reminiscent of the definition of substance in *E1* D3 (cf. Section 4). This is no mere coincidence. In arguing in *E3* P6 for the

---

[56] Cf. *E3*, Preface, for Spinoza's view that human beings do not form a distinctive realm within Nature.

existence of *conatus*, Spinoza refers to the fact that each particular thing is a mode which expresses in a certain way the power of God, i.e. of substance.[57] This means that a particular thing's endeavour to persevere in its being does not spring from itself alone; rather, its endeavour is derived from God, the only being which is 'in itself'.

Spinoza claims to offer, in E3 P6, a deductive proof of his doctrine of *conatus*. It cannot be said that the proof is successful;[58] however, Spinoza's doctrine is of great interest as an attempt to give a philosophical account of the nature of purposive behaviour. Spinoza rejects the standard Aristotelian account, and puts forward an alternative view. In Aristotelian theory purposive behaviour is to be explained in terms of 'final causation', a final cause being the end or purpose of an activity. So, for example, health is the final cause of taking a walk, in that one takes a walk *for the sake of* one's health (Aristotle, *Physics*, 2. 3. 194^{b}32–195^{a}3). In the Appendix to Part One of the *Ethics*, which contains a sustained attack on the idea of God as a purposive being, Spinoza criticizes the notion of final causality in general. He says of it that 'that which is really a cause it considers as an effect, and conversely' (ibid., p. 108). What he means can be explained by a passage from the Preface to Part Four of the *Ethics*, in which Spinoza returns to the topic of final causes. There he says that a so-called final cause is simply a human appetite, considered as a cause. So, if someone says that habitation was the final cause of the building of a certain house, this means that 'a man, from the fact that he imagined the advantages of domestic life, had an appetite for building a house'. This appetite, says Spinoza, is an efficient cause,[59] by which he means that the building of a house follows from the appetite. It will be seen shortly that 'appetite' is a form of *conatus*, which means that Spinoza is proposing to explain purposive activity in terms of *conatus*. He is saying that each man, in so far as he is 'in himself', endeavours to persist in his own being. So if a man thinks that building a house will help him to persist in his own being, then he will (unless something impedes him) build a house.[60]

It was said just now that appetite is a form of *conatus*. It is in fact one

---

[57] Cf. E2 P45 S, where Spinoza says that the force (*vis*) by which each particular thing persists in existing follows from the eternal necessity of the nature (sc. the essence) of God. We shall return to this point later (Sect. 11).

[58] Cf. G. H. R. Parkinson, 'Spinoza on the Power and Freedom of Man', in E. Freeman and M. Mandelbaum (eds.), *Spinoza: Essays in Interpretation* (La Salle, Ill.: Open Court, 1975), 11, 32 n.11.

[59] On efficient causality, see n. 42, above.

[60] It is instructive to compare Spinoza's account of purposive behaviour with that given by Jonathan Bennett, *Linguistic Behaviour* (Cambridge: Cambridge University Press, 1976), 38–42.

of several types that Spinoza distinguishes when he discusses in detail the *conatus* that is displayed by human beings. He says (*E*3 P9 S) that in so far as *conatus* is related to the human mind alone, it is called 'will' (*voluntas*).[61] In so far as it is related to the mind and body simultaneously, it is called 'appetite' (*appetitus*). Appetite, Spinoza adds, is the essence of man.[62] Spinoza also takes account of the fact that human beings are sometimes unaware of their *conatus*, and to do so he makes use of the term 'desire' (*cupiditas*). Desire, he says (ibid.), is the same as appetite, except that desire is ascribed to human beings in so far as they are conscious of their appetite. When Spinoza considers the *conatus* of human beings, 'desire' is the term that he uses most often.

10. The Emotions

There remains for discussion the third member of the trio of intellection, conation, and emotion mentioned at the beginning of Section 9. By the emotions I understand here what would commonly be regarded as feelings; feelings such as love, hatred, fear, and compassion. Spinoza's account of these is confused. He says of the feelings just mentioned that they are *affectus*.[63] All the *affectus*—and there are many of them—can be reduced to a small number of primary ones, two of which are pleasure (*laetitia*) and pain (*tristitia*) (*E*3 P11 S, P59 S, and DE 48).[64] So far, all seems clear; the *affectus* in general are what we would call emotions, and pleasure and pain are two of the primary or basic emotions. Spinoza now tries to fit pleasure, pain, and the *affectus* in general into his system by offering definitions of them; in doing so, he claims to be explaining their nature. He does so by relating the *affectus* to *conatus*. He defines the *affectus* (*E*3 D3) as 'the affections of the body, by which the body's power of acting is increased or diminished, helped or hindered, and at the same time the ideas of these affections'.[65] In other words, the *affectus* are defined in terms of our power of acting, whether mental or physical, which is

---

[61] As he notes later (*E*3 DE6), this sense of the term differs from that which it has in the context of his theory of knowledge, where it stands for judgement, in the sense of affirming or denying something. Cf. sect. 6, above.

[62] Cf. *E*3 P7, discussed earlier in this section; *conatus* is the essence of each thing.

[63] A note for the non-Latinist: *affectus* here is a plural form. (The nominative singular is spelt in the same way.) For love, hatred, fear, and compassion as *affectus*, see *E*3 DE6, DE7, DE13, DE18.

[64] On the translation of these terms, see n. 20, on *E*3 P11 S.

[65] Note that the *affectus* are defined in terms of both body and mind.

another way of referring to *conatus*. The point that he is making here is perhaps most easily grasped through his account of pleasure and pain (*E3* DE2, DE3; cf. *E3* P11 S). He explains the nature of these *affectus* by arguing that in so far as our endeavour to persevere in our being is increased or assisted, we experience pleasure, and in so far as it is diminished or hindered, we experience pain. *Conatus*, then, is fundamental—as indeed one would expect from what Spinoza has said about *conatus* and essence, discussed early in the last section. This is confirmed by *E3* P57, in which Spinoza says that 'Pleasure and pain are desire, i.e. appetite, in so far as it is increased or diminished, helped or hindered, by external causes.'

So far it seems that when Spinoza discusses the *affectus*, he is discussing what are commonly regarded as emotions, and relating them to his basic concept of *conatus*. However, the issue is confused by what Spinoza says about the primary *affectus*. We have mentioned two of these, pleasure and pain; but there is also a third, and this third member is desire (*E3* P11 S, P59 S, DE48). This seems to suggest that desire (which, it will be recalled from Section 9, is a form of *conatus*) is not to be regarded as more fundamental than pleasure and pain; rather, it seems to be treated on equal terms with them. How this could have come about is not clear, but it may be that Spinoza discovered that not all the *affectus* can be defined in terms of pleasure and pain, but that some involve a reference to desire (*E3* DE32–DE48). He may have argued that desire cannot be inferred from pleasure or pain alone, which means that desire has to be recognized as a primary *affectus*.

It is not clear how this confusion can be reduced to something like order. What can be said is that the view that *conatus*, or desire, is fundamental, in that all the *affectus* can be derived from it, fits most easily into Spinoza's system as a whole. This leaves us with a problem of translation. Since Spinoza regards desire and its forms as *affectus*, and since desires are commonly distinguished from emotions, how is one to translate the word *affectus*? Some translators use the word 'affect', but this has the disadvantage that it is a technical term that itself stands in need of explanation. I follow those translators who have rendered *affectus* as 'emotion'; for there is no reasonable doubt that when Spinoza uses the word *affectus* he is trying to fit into his system what are commonly regarded as emotions.

Spinoza draws an important distinction (*E3* D3, Explanation) between those emotions which are actions and those which are passions. He explains (*E3* D2) that X is said to act when something occurs, either in X or outside *X*, which can be understood through *X*'s nature alone. On the other hand, *X* is said to be passive when something occurs of which *X* is only a partial cause. In other words, to say that *X* is passive is not to say that *X* does absolutely nothing. *X* does something, but what *X* does has to be explained by (which, for Spinoza, means that it is caused by) something else. Action and passion are linked by Spinoza to his theory of knowledge when he remarks (*E*3 P1) that in so far as the mind has adequate ideas it acts, and in so far as it has inadequate ideas it is passive. Spinoza's meaning can be illustrated by considering an idea which one has in so far as one perceives something by the senses (cf. Section 8). This, for Spinoza, is an inadequate idea, since it is the thought-correlate of a physical system, involving both the human body and something outside it. In Spinoza's terminology, our body is only the 'partial cause' of our physical state (*E*3 D2), and we are said to be passive both in respect of our physical state and in respect of the idea which is its correlate. However, if we have an adequate idea—say, a 'common notion'[66]—then we are not determined by what is outside us, and our mind is active. Spinoza draws a similar distinction between the emotions. Suppose that we have a certain emotion, and that the idea that is involved in that emotion is inadequate, then the emotion is a 'passion'. But just as not all ideas are inadequate ideas, so not all emotions are passions. Spinoza says expressly (*E*3 P58), 'Besides the pleasure and the desire which are passions, there exist other emotions of pleasure and desire which are related to us in so far as we act.'

The concept of the passions is of great importance in Spinoza's moral philosophy. Put in general terms, his view is this. To have a passion is to lack power, and this implies that in so far as we have a passion, we are the less able to succeed in our endeavour to persevere in our being. It is therefore important to replace the passions by actions of the mind. Accordingly, Spinoza devotes much of the *Ethics*—Part Three, and the first eighteen propositions of Part Four—to an analysis of the passions, showing how all the passions, and indeed all the emotions, can be derived from pleasure, pain, and desire.[67] There is no need to provide a

[66] Cf. Sect. 8, above.

[67] Something must be said here about the relation between Spinoza's account of the passions and that given by Descartes in *The Passions of the Soul* (*PWD* i. 325–404). It has been pointed out by H. A. Wolfson, in *The Philosophy of Spinoza*, ii. 209–10, that of the forty-eight emotions defined in the *Ethics*, no fewer than forty-three are to be found in Descartes's book. But this is not to say that Spinoza's definitions correspond to those given by Descartes; further, whereas Spinoza recognizes only three primary emotions, Descartes recognizes six primitive passions. See Descartes, *The Passions of the Soul*, II. 69: *PWD* i. 353.

detailed account of this analysis here; enough has now been said to explain the foundations of Spinoza's moral philosophy. To this philosophy we now proceed.

11. The Moral Philosophy of the *Ethics*

It is clear from what has already been said that the moral philosophy expounded in the *Ethics* is of the kind known as 'naturalistic', in that it is based on the view (strongly emphasized by Spinoza) that man is a part of Nature. Such theories have been severely criticized on the ground that they fail to give due weight to a fundamental distinction that exists between the words 'is' and 'ought'.[68] A critic of such theories would say that Spinoza's account of Nature is an account of what there *is*; a moral judgement, on the other hand, is about what *ought* to be, and such judgements cannot be reduced to judgements about what there is. Certainly, the concept of obligation is to be found in Spinoza's moral philosophy. It is true that the common Latin word for 'ought', *debet*, which occurs often in the *Ethics*, tends to have the sense there, not of 'ought', but of 'must'.[69] However, there is certainly one place in the *Ethics* in which Spinoza talks about what there ought to be. In the Preface to Part Four, in which he discusses the strength of the passions, he talks about what he calls 'exemplars', that is, models or ideal patterns. In the course of this discussion, he speaks of 'an idea of man, as an exemplar of human nature towards which we may look', which is in effect to say that there is a pattern of human nature at which we ought to aim.

Can Spinoza, then, explain the concept of 'ought' as it figures in moral judgements? He does not pose the problem explicitly, but he would doubtless point out that in his view the finite modes (which include human beings) are not static, but dynamic, because they endeavour to persevere in their own being. But (and this is the important point) they do not always succeed in their endeavour. However, success can be achieved; further, there are rational precepts which, if followed, will bring success. To say that we ought to follow these precepts is to say that these precepts are those which a rational agent who is trying

---

[68] The issue has been much debated in 20th century philosophy; see e.g. W. D. Hudson (ed.), *The Is/Ought Question* (London: Macmillan, 1969).

[69] Another commonly used word for 'ought', *oportet*, is not to be found in the *Ethics*.

to persevere in his being *must* follow if his endeavour is to be successful.[70]

A moral philosophy may be expected to give some account of the words 'good' and 'bad', and Spinoza does not fail to provide such an account.[71] At first sight, his account may seem to be a relational one. He argues that we form the concepts of good and bad from the fact that we compare things with one another, and this means that one and the same thing can at the same time be good, bad, and indifferent. So, for example (*E*4, Preface, final paragraph), music is good to the melancholy man, bad to the man who mourns, and neither good nor bad to the deaf. This, he notes, has given rise to scepticism (*E*1, Appendix, p. 111); however, relativism is not his final view. It is, he says (*E*4, Preface, final paragraph), useful to retain the words 'good' and 'bad' in a sense that he defines. He has spoken of an 'exemplar' of human nature—an ideal pattern of human nature and conduct—and he proposes to call 'good' that which we *know* to be a means towards the attainment of that exemplar, and 'bad' that which we know to impede us from attaining it (ibid.). In short, he proposes to call 'good' that which we know to be useful to us, and 'bad' that which we know will hinder us from attaining something good (*E*4 D1–D2).

The question now arises how we know that something is advantageous or disadvantageous to us. Spinoza does not suggest that 'the good' or 'the bad' is something that we know by some kind of intellectual vision; instead, he introduces into his account of such knowledge the concepts of pleasure and pain. To have a knowledge of good or bad, he says, is simply to be aware of (*conscius*) one's pleasure or pain (*E*4 P8), for pleasure (*E*3 P11 S) just is the emotion by which the mind passes to a greater, and pain the emotion by which it passes to a lesser, state of perfection. So to be aware of an emotion of pleasure is to be aware of the fact that we are being successful in our endeavour to preserve our being, and conversely in the case of our awareness of pain. However, Spinoza draws an important distinction here. Some pleasures, he says,

---

[70] Kant might object that Spinoza, in so far as he says in effect, 'Act in such a way as to preserve your own being', is offering a hypothetical rather than a categorical imperative; that is, he is saying, 'If you want such-and-such, then do such-and-such'. Such an imperative, Kant argues, does not capture the essence of a moral judgement, which must involve a categorical imperative, having no 'if' about it. (For Kant's distinction, see e.g. R. C. S. Walker, *Kant* (London: Routledge & Kegan Paul, 1978), 151–9.) Spinoza would doubtless reply that no 'if' is involved here. We *must* endeavour to preserve our being, and if we are to succeed in our endeavour we *must* act in the ways that reason prescribes.

[71] On the translation of the words *bonus* and *malus*, see n. 51 to Part 3.

can be bad and, conversely, some pains can be good. This is because the pleasures that relate to one particular part of that highly complex individual that we call the human body can harm the body as a whole. Conversely, localized pains can prevent such pleasures from harming the body as a whole (*E4 P43*).

To the extent that we succeed in our endeavour to preserve our being—that is, to the extent that we master our passions—we are in what Spinoza calls a state of 'happiness' (*felicitas*) (*E4 P18 S*). Spinoza has other terms for this condition, including 'blessedness' (*beatitudo*; *E2 P49 S*; *E4*, Appendix, sect. 4; *E5 P36 S*) and 'salvation' (*salus*; *E5 P36 S*, P42 S*). Another term that he uses in the same sense is 'freedom' (*libertas*; *E5 P36 S*). The concept of freedom is very important in the *Ethics*; indeed, it figures in the subtitle of Part Five. In calling someone 'free' Spinoza is drawing attention to the fact that to be successful in one's *conatus* is to act, in his sense of the term. That is, it is to be the true source of what one does; it is not to be determined by what is outside oneself, i.e. it is not to be controlled by one's passions. This means that for one to be free is not for one's deeds to have no cause (this has been ruled out: cf. Section 7); it is for these deeds to be caused by oneself alone.

This may seem to present Spinoza with an insoluble problem. He has said (*E1 P17 C2*) that God alone is a free cause, as God alone acts solely by the necessity of his nature. How, then, can finite beings such as ourselves possibly be free? Spinoza would agree that there is a sense in which human beings are not free. There is, he says, no free will, but the mind 'is determined to will this or that by a cause, which is again determined by another, and that again by another, and so on to infinity' (*E2 P48*). However, he would deny that this is inconsistent with freedom in his sense of the term. We have already seen (cf. Section 9) that no particular thing is the independent source of its endeavour to persevere in its being; rather, its *conatus* or power comes from God. As Spinoza puts it in *E2 P45 S*, although each particular thing is determined by another in a certain way, yet 'the force by which each one perseveres in existing follows from the eternal necessity of the nature of God'. In short: the power by which a free man perseveres in being is really the power of God, as manifested in that person.

This throws further light on Spinoza's moral philosophy. Spinoza has said that each person endeavours, in so far as he is in himself, to preserve *his own* being, and this is emphasized when he says (*E4 P25*) that no one endeavours to preserve his being for the sake of another thing. This might give the impression that Spinoza's moral philosophy is a type of what is known as psychological egoism, according to which human beings always, as a matter of fact, look to their own interests. However, it has become clear that Spinoza does not think of a free man as one among many independent entities, each of which is trying to preserve its own separate being. For Spinoza, there are no independent beings, with the exception of God, and the free man knows this. His endeavour to preserve his being is in effect a cancellation of his own particularity. This is brought out in a striking fashion when Spinoza says (E4 P72 and S) that a free man may act in a way that involves his own death. A free man, he says, never acts deceitfully, even if this were a way of freeing himself from the danger of death; for it is reason that tells us not to act deceitfully, and the propositions of reason have no exceptions.

I have just argued that Spinoza's monism is an important part of his theory of human freedom. So, too, is his determinism. The free man is not subject to the passions, and Spinoza has much to say about the power over the passions that is possessed by the mind. I will not discuss all the remedies for the passions that are discussed in the first twenty propositions of Part Five and summarized in E5 P20 S; it will be sufficient here to consider just one, which Spinoza regards as the best (E5 P4 S). This remedy consists in the formation of true ideas of the passions (E5 P3–P4). What Spinoza means here can perhaps be grasped most easily from a hypothetical example. Suppose that someone, B, has caused pain to another person, A, and that A thinks of this pain as caused by B. This means that A will hate B (E3 P13 S, DE7). Now, hatred is a passion, and as such it involves inadequate ideas; that is, in so far as A hates B he does not understand what B did. Suppose, next, that A comes to understand what B did, i.e. that he has an adequate idea of it. He will now see the act as necessary, and he can no more hate A than he can hate a frightened cat which scratches him.

Here, Spinoza has to take account of the difficulties posed by what is commonly called *akrasia*, or weakness of will, which has exercised both ancient and modern philosophers.[72] For it may be said that it is possible, for example, both to understand what a man did and yet to hate him for it. In more general terms, it is possible to recognize that something (in the example, ceasing to hate someone) is the rational course of action,

[72] On this problem, see e.g. W. Charlton, *Weakness of Will: A Philosophical Introduction* (Oxford: Blackwell, 1988).

and yet not to do it. Spinoza was well aware of this; three times in the *Ethics* (*E*3 P2 S; *E*4 Preface; *E*4 P17 S) he refers to Ovid's lines, 'I see and approve the better; I follow the worse.'[73] Spinoza does not give explicit answers to the problems that *akrasia* poses, but it is not difficult to see what his answers would be. He is concerned with two problems. First, how is *akrasia* possible? That is, how can we see the better and yet do the worse? Secondly, how can *akrasia* be overcome? His answers to both problems involve his theory of knowledge. Someone who 'sees', i.e. knows the better and yet follows the worse, must, Spinoza would say, have the second kind of knowledge. Consider again the case just cited. *A* (who understands what *B* did, and yet still hates him for it) may have followed the arguments of the *Ethics*, and as a result of this knows that hatred can never be good (*E*4 P45), i.e. can never be truly useful to him. But this is knowledge of the second kind, which means that it is universal or abstract (*E*4 P62 S), and it is because of this abstractness that it cannot master the hatred that *A* has for *B*. Spinoza's answer to the second question—how *akrasia* can be overcome—involves the third kind of knowledge. Such knowledge (cf. Section 8) is not universal, but is of particular things, in the sense that we grasp the rule in the particular instance. If we had such knowledge, it would 'affect our mind' (*E*5 P36 S) with such power that our passions would be overcome. All this throws light on what Spinoza means when he says that the third kind of knowledge has greater power than the second. But whether Spinoza succeeds in showing that the third kind of knowledge can be guaranteed to overcome *akrasia*—whether, for example, it can overcome hatred of an exceptionally virulent and deep-seated kind—may be doubted.[74]

---

[73] The reference is to Ovid, *Metamorphoses*, 7. 20–1.

[74] Spinoza's concept of intuitive knowledge also plays an important part in his doctrine of the eternity of the human mind, expounded in *E*5 P21–P40. This doctrine is notoriously obscure, and has been severely criticized. Since Spinoza himself makes clear (*E*5 P41) that his moral philosophy does not depend on this doctrine, I do not discuss it here, though a few comments will be found in the notes. Critical accounts of the doctrine may be found in, for example, Bennett, *A Study of Spinoza's Ethics*, 357–63, 369–75; Delahunty, *Spinoza*, 279–305; Martha Kneale, 'Eternity and Sempiternity', in Grene (ed.), *Spinoza: A Collection of Critical Essays*, 227–40. More sympathetic accounts can be found in, for example, G. Lloyd, *Part of Nature* (Ithaca: Cornell University Press, 1994), 118–41; D. Savan, 'Spinoza on Duration, Time and Eternity', in G. Hunter (ed.), *Spinoza: The Enduring Questions* (Toronto: University of Toronto Press, 1994), 3–30.

12. The Influence of the *Ethics*

I conclude this Introduction by saying something about the influence of the *Ethics* on later philosophy. Immediate reaction to the work was predictably hostile. The Leiden Reformed Consistory spoke for many when it declared, at its meeting of 4 February 1678, that the *Ethics* was a work which, 'perhaps since the beginning of the world until the present day, surpasses all others in godlessness and which endeavours to do away with all religion and set godlessness on the throne'.[75] However, the Dutch authorities seem not to have prosecuted Spinoza's publisher; they simply made it difficult to buy the book by applying pressure on booksellers. Despite this, copies of the *Ethics* did circulate. But it is not surprising that, in view of the dominant position still occupied by the Christian Church in the intellectual life of Europe, the book remained on the fringe of European philosophy for the whole of the century that followed Spinoza's death, or that the relatively few people who did owe something to Spinoza tended to disguise their debt under a mask of opposition to Spinozism.[76] Many of these individuals—whether overt or disguised Spinozists—are known only to specialists. But there is good reason to believe that Spinoza's influence was felt by members of an important movement in British philosophy and theology. This was the 'deistic' movement which began late in the seventeenth century and lasted well into the eighteenth. The deists were not anti-Christian, but they sought a Christianity which, in the words of one of their members,

---

[75] Israel, 'The Banning of Spinoza's Works in the Dutch Republic', 11–12.

[76] See esp. Van Bunge and Klever, *Disguised and Overt Spinozism*. This is perhaps a suitable place to discuss the relations between Spinoza and his younger contemporary Leibniz. It has been argued by Bertrand Russell that Leibniz owed much to Spinoza, though he did not acknowledge his debt (Russell, *The Philosophy of Leibniz*, 2nd edn. (London: Allen & Unwin, 1937), 5). Later, Russell went even further, arguing that Leibniz was a crypto-Spinozist who had two philosophies—a public philosophy which was theistic and superficial, and a private philosophy which was profound and largely Spinozistic (Russell, *History of Western Philosophy* (London: Allen & Unwin, 1946), 604). Recent research has not favoured Russell's view; see esp. Georges Friedmann, *Leibniz et Spinoza*, 3rd edn. (Paris: Gallimard, 1962). The fact seems to be that Leibniz, throughout his philosophical career, believed in the truth of theism and in the existence of a plurality of substances. It is true that at one stage in his career Leibniz seems to have explored the possibility that particular things might be modes and not substances (Leibniz, *De Summa Rerum: Metaphysical Papers, 1675–6* (New Haven: Yale University Press, 1992), 93). But the relevant paper breaks off without a conclusion, and it may be conjectured that Leibniz was trying to decide whether Spinoza's monistic philosophy could be made to fit his own, and broke off when he decided that it could not.

John Toland, was 'not mysterious'.[77] Christianity, the deists argued, had no need of a divine revelation, but could be established by reason alone, and for this reason they were attracted to Spinoza.[78]

A major revival of interest in Spinoza, and in the *Ethics* in particular, occurred in Germany late in the eighteenth century. In conversations with the philosopher Jacobi, held in July 1780, the great dramatist and critic Lessing proclaimed himself a disciple of Spinoza, and more specifically of Spinoza's monism.[79] Lessing said that he took as his motto the Greek phrase 'hen kai pan' ('the one and the all'), which he regarded as expressing the essence of Spinoza's doctrine. The explanation of Lessing's enthusiasm seems to lie in one of the aspects of that long and complex intellectual movement known as the Enlightenment, which dominated Europe in the second half of the eighteenth century. The aspect in question was a critical attitude to Christian doctrine, and it is significant that Lessing had already made available to the public, in 1774–7, excerpts from an attack on Christian revelation by Hermann Samuel Reimarus (1694–1768). After the death of Lessing in 1781 Jacobi drew the attention of another German philosopher, Moses Mendelssohn, to Lessing's pantheism; a correspondence developed between the two which culminated in the publication, in 1785, of Jacobi's book *On the Doctrine of Spinoza, in Letters to Moses Mendelssohn*. Spinoza, and especially his pantheism, became an object of keen interest in Germany; in the 1790s many German writers—notably Lichtenberg, Novalis, Herder, and Schleiermacher—expressed an enthusiasm for Spinoza. In Jena in 1802–3 there appeared the first collected edition of Spinoza's works, edited by a professor of theology, H. E. G. Paulus.

A small part in this edition was played by Hegel, and it was through Hegel above all others that Spinoza entered the main stream of European philosophy.[80] Spinozism, Hegel said, is 'in essence, the beginning of all philosophizing'.[81] The phrase 'the beginning' is significant here. Hegel is far from asserting that Spinozism is to be accepted as a whole; but he does hold that Spinoza's monism is a necessary stage on the way to an

---

[77] John Toland, *Christianity not Mysterious* (1696).

[78] On Spinoza and the deists, see Rosalie L. Colie, 'Spinoza and the Early English Deists', *Journal of the History of Ideas*, 20 (1959), 23–46.

[79] Cf. T. McFarland, *Coleridge and the Pantheist Tradition* (Oxford: Clarendon Press, 1969), 77–9.

[80] On Hegel and Spinoza, see G. H. R. Parkinson, 'Hegel, Pantheism and Spinoza', *Journal of the History of Ideas*, 38 (1977), 449–59.

[81] Hegel, *Geschichte der Philosophie*, iii: *Werke*, Jubilee Edition, ed. Glockner (Stuttgart, 1927–37), xix. 376.

idealistic monism of the kind that he himself proclaimed. In this sense, Spinoza's doctrine of substance may be called the truth, though it is not the whole truth.[82]

Spinoza's reputation was probably never higher than it was between the publication of Jacobi's book in 1785 and the death of Hegel in 1831. After 1831 the main currents of Western philosophical thought—and, in particular, that current which is known as modern analytical philosophy—moved away from Hegel, and indeed from metaphysics in general. But an interest in Spinoza still remains, even among philosophers who would regard themselves as belonging to the analytical tradition. Such philosophers may study Spinoza for a variety of reasons. Some value Spinoza for his aims rather than for his achievements; as such they value him for his attempt to bring human beings within the framework of the natural sciences, or more specifically for his programme of a naturalistic psychology, or for his attempt to marry psychology to ethics.[83] But there is another reason for studying the *Ethics*. One can regard it as what Spinoza would have called an 'exemplar'; namely, as a paradigm of the endeavour to push rational inquiry as far as it can go, without any regard for current opinions.

[82] Ibid. 337.
[83] See respectively A. Gabbey, M. de la Rocca, and D. Garrett in Garrett (ed.), *The Cambridge Companion to Spinoza*, 181, 193, 307.

Select Bibliography

COMPLETE WORKS OF SPINOZA: ORIGINAL-LANGUAGE EDITIONS

Benedicti de Spinoza Opera, ed. J. van Vloten and J. P. N. Land, 3rd edn. (The Hague: Nijhoff, 1914).
Spinoza: Opera (Heidelberg: Winter, 1924–8).

WORKS OF SPINOZA: ENGLISH TRANSLATIONS

The Collected Works of Spinoza, ed. and trans. E. Curley, i (Princeton: Princeton University Press, 1985).
The 'Ethics' and Selected Letters, trans. S. Shirley (Indianapolis: Hackett, 1982).
The 'Ethics' and 'Treatise on the Correction of the Intellect', trans. A. Boyle, rev. G. H. R. Parkinson (London: Dent, 1993).
Principles of Cartesian Philosophy, with Metaphysical Thoughts, trans. S. Shirley (Indianapolis: Hackett, 1998).
Spinoza: The Letters, trans. S. Shirley (Indianapolis: Hackett, 1995).
Spinoza: The Political Works. The 'Tractatus Theologico-Politicus' in part and the 'Tractatus Politicus' in full, ed. and trans. A. G. Wernham (Oxford: Clarendon Press, 1958).
Tractatus Theologico-Politicus, trans. S. Shirley (Leiden: Brill, 1989).

BIBLIOGRAPHIES AND INDEXES

GUERET, M., ROBINET, A., and TOMBEUR, P., *Spinoza, 'Ethica': Concordances, Index, Listes de fréquences, Tables comparatives* (Louvain-la-Neuve: CETEDOC, 1977).
OKO, A. S., *The Spinoza Bibliography* (Boston: Hall, 1964).
VAN DER WERF, T., *A Spinoza Bibliography, 1971–1983* (Leiden: Brill, 1984).
WETLESEN, J. A., *A Spinoza Bibliography, 1940–1970* (Oslo: Universitetsforlaget, 1971).

Select Bibliography

THE PHILOSOPHY OF SPINOZA: GENERAL SURVEYS

BENNETT, J. F., *A Study of Spinoza's Ethics* (Cambridge: Cambridge University Press, 1984).

DELAHUNTY, R. J., *Spinoza* (London: Routledge & Kegan Paul, 1985).

DONAGAN, A., *Spinoza* (London: Harvester, 1988).

FREEMAN, E., and MANDELBAUM, M. (eds.), *Spinoza: Essays in Interpretation* (La Salle, Ill.: Open Court, 1975).

GARRETT, D. (ed.), *The Cambridge Companion to Spinoza* (Cambridge: Cambridge University Press, 1996).

GRENE, M. (ed.), *Spinoza: A Collection of Critical Essays* (New York: Doubleday, 1973).

HAMPSHIRE, S. N., *Spinoza*, 1st edn. (Harmondsworth: Penguin, 1951).

HUNTER, G. (ed.), *Spinoza: The Enduring Questions* (Toronto: University of Toronto Press, 1994).

JOACHIM, H. H., *A Study of the Ethics of Spinoza* (Oxford: Clarendon Press, 1901).

KASHAP, S. P. (ed.), *Studies in Spinoza: Critical and Interpretive Essays* (Berkeley: University of California Press, 1972).

KENNINGTON, R. (ed.), *The Philosophy of Baruch Spinoza* (Washington: Catholic University of America, 1980).

LLOYD, G., *Spinoza and the 'Ethics'* (London: Routledge, 1996).

SHAHAN, R. W., and BIRO, J. I. (eds.), *Spinoza: New Perspectives* (Norman: University of Oklahoma Press, 1978).

VAN DER BEND, J. G. (ed.), *Spinoza on Knowing, Being and Freedom* (Assen: Van Gorcum, 1974).

WOLFSON, H. A., *The Philosophy of Spinoza* (Cambridge, Mass.: Harvard University Press, 1934; reissue: New York, Meridian, 1958).

METHODOLOGY AND THEORY OF KNOWLEDGE

DE DIJN, H., *Spinoza: The Way to Wisdom* (West Lafayette: Purdue University Press, 1996).

JOACHIM, H. H., *Spinoza's 'Tractatus de Intellectus Emendatione'* (Oxford: Clarendon Press, 1940).

PARKINSON, G. H. R., 'Definition, Essence and Understanding in Spinoza', in J. A. Cover and M. Kulstad (eds.), *Central Themes in Early Modern Philosophy* (Indianapolis: Hackett, 1990), 49–68.

——'Language and Knowledge in Spinoza', *Inquiry*, 12 (1969), 15–40; repr. in Grene (ed.), *Spinoza: A Collection of Critical Essays*, 73–100.

——*Spinoza's Theory of Knowledge* (Oxford: Clarendon Press, 1954; reissue: Aldershot, Gregg Revivals, 1993).

SAVAN, D., 'Spinoza and Language', *Philosophical Review*, 67 (1958), 212–25; repr.

in Grene (ed.), *Spinoza: A Collection of Critical Essays*, 60–72, and in Kashap (ed.), *Studies in Spinoza*, 236–48.

WALKER, R. C. S., 'Spinoza and the Coherence Theory of Truth', *Mind*, 94 (1985), 1–18.

YOVEL, Y. (ed.), *Spinoza on Knowledge and the Human Mind* (Leiden: Brill, 1994).

METAPHYSICS AND PHILOSOPHY OF MIND

BARKER, H., 'Notes on the Second Part of Spinoza's Ethics', *Mind*, 47 (1938), 159–79, 281–302, 417–39; repr. in Kashap (ed.), *Studies in Spinoza*, 101–67.

CURLEY, E., *Spinoza's Metaphysics* (Cambridge, Mass.: Harvard University Press, 1969).

DELLA ROCCA, M., *Representation and the Mind–Body Problem in Spinoza* (New York: Oxford University Press, 1997).

DONAGAN, A., 'Essence and the Distinction of Attributes in Spinoza's Metaphysics', in Grene (ed.), *Spinoza: A Collection of Critical Essays*, 164–81.

GUEROULT, M., *Spinoza: Dieu ('Éthique', 1)* (Paris: Aubier, 1968).

—— *Spinoza: L'Âme ('Éthique', 2)* (Paris: Aubier, 1974).

HASEROT, F. S., 'Spinoza's Definition of Attribute', *Philosophical Review*, 62 (1953), 499–513; repr. in Kashap (ed.), *Studies in Spinoza*, 28–42.

KNEALE, M., 'Eternity and Sempiternity', *Proceedings of the Aristotelian Society*, 69 (1968–9), 223–38; repr. in Grene (ed.), *Spinoza: A Collection of Critical Essays*, 227–40.

LLOYD, G., *Part of Nature: Self-Knowledge in Spinoza's 'Ethics'* (Ithaca: Cornell University Press, 1994).

PARKINSON, G. H. R., 'Spinoza on Miracles and Natural Law', *Revue Internationale de Philosophie*, 31 (1977), 145–57.

SPRIGGE, T. L. S., 'Spinoza's Identity Theory', *Inquiry*, 20 (1977), 419–45.

WOLF, A., 'Spinoza's Conception of the Attributes of Substance', *Proceedings of the Aristotelian Society*, 27 (1927), 177–92; repr. in Kashap (ed.), *Studies in Spinoza*, 16–27.

WOOLHOUSE, R. S., *Descartes, Spinoza, Leibniz: The Concept of Substance in Seventeenth Century Metaphysics* (London: Routledge, 1993).

MORAL PHILOSOPHY

BROAD, C. D., *Five Types of Ethical Theory* (London: Kegan Paul, 1930), 15–52.

EISENBERG, P. D., 'Is Spinoza an Ethical Naturalist?', in S. Hessing (ed.), *Speculum Spinozanum, 1677–1977* (London: Routledge, 1977), 145–64.

GARRETT, D., 'Spinoza's Ethical Theory', in Garrett (ed.), *The Cambridge Companion to Spinoza*, 267–314.

HAMPSHIRE, S. N., 'Spinoza and the Idea of Freedom', *Proceedings of the British Academy*, 46 (1960), 195–215; repr. in Kashap (ed.), *Studies in Spinoza*, 310–31.

—— *Two Theories of Morality* (Oxford: Oxford University Press, 1977); amended version in S. N. Hampshire, *Morality and Conflict* (Oxford: Blackwell, 1983), 10–68.

JAMES, S., 'Spinoza the Stoic', in T. Sorell (ed.), *The Rise of Modern Philosophy* (Oxford: Clarendon Press, 1993), 289–316.

NEU, J., *Emotion, Thought and Therapy: A Study of Hume and Spinoza* (London: Routledge, 1977).

PARKINSON, G. H. R., 'Spinoza on the Power and Freedom of Man', *Monist*, 55 (1971), 527–53; repr. in Freeman and Mandelbaum (eds.), *Spinoza: Essays in Interpretation*, 7–33.

SPINOZA'S LIFE AND INFLUENCE

COLIE, R. L., 'Spinoza and the Early English Deists', *Journal of the History of Ideas*, 20 (1959), 23–46.

FRIEDMANN, G., *Leibniz et Spinoza*, 3rd edn. (Paris: Gallimard, 1962).

KLEVER, W. N. A., 'Spinoza's Life and Works', in Garrett (ed.), *The Cambridge Companion to Spinoza*, 13–60.

MCFARLAND, T., *Coleridge and the Pantheist Tradition* (Oxford: Clarendon Press, 1969), 53–106.

PARKINSON, G. H. R., 'Hegel, Pantheism and Spinoza', *Journal of the History of Ideas*, 38 (1977), 449–59.

POPKIN, R., *The History of Scepticism from Erasmus to Spinoza* (Berkeley: University of California Press, 1979), 214–48.

VAN BUNGE, W., and KLEVER, W. (eds.), *Disguised and Overt Spinozism around 1700* (Leiden: Brill, 1996).

YOVEL, Y., *Spinoza and Other Heretics: The Marrano of Reason* (Princeton: Princeton University Press, 1989).

Summary of Spinoza's *Ethics*

PART ONE: ON GOD

Spinoza's *Ethics* is about human beings, and about the best way in which such beings can live. However, the human being—*homo*—is not formally introduced into the *Ethics* until Proposition 10 of the second Part; before this, Spinoza sets out the framework within which human beings have to be understood. In setting out this framework, he goes back to what is basic, which for him means a being by reference to which absolutely everything has, in the last analysis, to be explained. This being he calls God. In Part One Spinoza considers God first as substance (P1–P15) and second as cause (P16–P25). This leads to a third topic, related to the second: the universality and necessity of causation, or what may be called the thesis of determinism (P26–P36).

1. Roughly, Spinoza means by 'substance' that which has an absolutely independent existence, or is 'in itself' (D3). This sense of the term 'substance', which can be traced back to Aristotle's *Categories*, would not have alarmed his contemporaries; what did alarm them were the consequences that he derived from this and from some related terms. One important such term was the term 'attribute'. An attribute of substance (D4) is that which constitutes the essence of substance, in the sense of a fundamental feature of substance, in terms of which substance must be understood. In the first ten propositions of Part One Spinoza uses the concept of an attribute in the process of explaining what X must be, if X is to be a substance. It emerges that one substance cannot be produced by another (P6); further, it belongs to the nature of substance to exist (P7), and each substance is infinite (P8). Here Spinoza is already moving towards two important conclusions: that the substance that is called God exists (P11), and that there is no substance besides God (P14). Spinoza also looks towards future arguments when he says (P10) that each attribute of a substance must be conceived through itself, i.e. without the help of another. He will argue in Part Two that thought and extension are not (as Descartes had supposed) different substances, but different attributes of one substance.

So far all this has been, strictly speaking, hypothetical; it tells us what substances must be, if there are any substances. This hypothetical character is removed in P11, in which Spinoza argues that there necessarily exists at least one substance, namely God, an entity that consists of infinite attributes. This absolutely infinite substance is indivisible (P12–13), and it is the only substance that there is (P14). There is, therefore, no substance other than God, and whatever exists exists in God (P15). What exist in God are termed by Spinoza 'modes' (D5); nothing, therefore, exists besides substance and its modes (P15). This means that it is wrong to suppose, as theists do, that corporeal substance was created by a God who is fundamentally different from it (P15S).

2. In P15 S Spinoza touched on the question of God's creativity; in P16–25 he considers in detail the nature of God's causal activity. He argues that the consequences of the divine nature are infinite; from God, infinite things follow in infinite ways (P16). From this, Spinoza infers that God can be called a cause (P16 C1–C3), since in his view to say that X causes Y is to say that Y follows from X with logical necessity. Because God acts solely from the laws of his own nature, he may be called a 'free' cause, in that there is nothing outside him that can compel him to act (D7, P17 and C2). But it is wrong to think of God's freedom in the way that theists do; God does not consider alternatives by his intellect and decide between them by his will (P 17 S). Nor, again, should God be thought of as something that is outside that which he creates; God is an 'immanent' cause (P18).

After discussing God as cause, Spinoza begins to consider the effects of God when he speaks of the so-called 'infinite modes', which follow from the attributes of God (P21–P23). The nature of these infinite modes, which are divided into the 'immediate' and the 'mediate', is obscure, but it seems that Spinoza is trying to fit into his system the basic concepts of physics and psychology, and of certain universal laws into which these concepts enter. Besides infinite modes, Spinoza recognizes finite modes (P25 C). These play an important part in his system, in that they are involved in his analysis of the nature of particular things. Such things, he argues, do not have an independent existence, but are the particular forms in which an attribute manifests itself.

3. Spinoza now moves to a statement of his determinism. Taking up P16, he says (P26) that whatever was determined to produce some effect was necessarily so determined by God. This means (P28) that each particular thing was determined by another, and that by another, and so on to infinity—it being understood that what are involved here are the modes of God, so that God is the ultimate cause of this chain of events.

Spinoza now draws the conclusion (P29) that there is nothing contingent in the universe, but that all things are determined by the necessity of the divine nature. This means (P32 C1) that God does not act from freedom of will; things could not have been produced by God in any other way than that in which they were produced (P33). It is therefore wrong to say, as some do, that God is free in that he could have created something other than that which he did produce (P33 S2). God is not free in this sense; God is free, not in that he is undetermined, but in that he is self-determined (cf. D7). Discussions of freedom tend to involve discussion of what an agent has the power to do; Spinoza explains his view of power by saying (P34) that God's power is his essence, and that to say that something is in God's power is to say (P35) that it follows from his essence. Whatever is in God's power necessarily exists (P35), which implies that the universe is completely full, in that whatever is possible exists. Not only is the universe completely full, but nothing in it is inert; nothing exists from whose nature some effect does not follow (P36).

Spinoza adds to Part One an appendix in which he tries to remove certain prejudices which stand in the way of an acceptance of his views. These prejudices involve the assumption that everything in the universe has been created by a purposive God, the end or aim of whose activity is the benefit of mankind. Spinoza discusses how this view has arisen, why it is false, and how it has given rise to popular but faulty notions of good and bad, order and confusion. Spinoza does not mean that such notions have no use in philosophy; quite the contrary. What he objects to is the use of such terms within the context of a belief that God made everything for man.

PART TWO: ON THE NATURE AND ORIGIN OF THE MIND

The concept that is fundamental to Spinoza's account of the mind is that of the idea. For Spinoza, an idea (E2 D3) is not an inactive entity, the object of some kind of contemplation; it is an act of thinking, which involves affirmation or denial. The discussion of ideas in Part Two may be divided into four sections. In the first (P1–P7 S), Spinoza considers the relation between minds and bodies. In the second (P8–P15), he examines the relation between ideas and minds, and in doing so gives a general account of the human mind. The next topic of discussion, the scope and limits of human knowledge, is dealt with in two sections, which concern respectively 'inadequate' and 'adequate' ideas. Of these, Section Three (P16–P31) concerns the mind as externally determined, and Section Four (P32–P49 S) considers it as internally determined.

1. After arguing that thought and extension are two of the attributes of God (P1–P2), Spinoza states that the modes of each attribute can be understood only in terms of that attribute (P5–P6); we cannot, for example, explain thinking if we try to do so by means of physical concepts. But thought and extension are not totally independent of one another; they are different expressions of one and the same substance, so that, for example, a physical thing and the idea of that thing are one and the same thing, expressed through different attributes (P7–P7 S).

2. Human beings are not substances, but are finite modes of the attributes of God (P10 and C). To talk of a human mind is to talk (P11 C) of a part of the infinite intellect of God, one of the 'infinite modes'. But we are not just minds; we are minds and bodies (P13 C). The human mind is what Spinoza calls the 'idea of' the human body' (P11, P13). This means that it exists and acts in parallel with its body; or rather, it is the expression in the attribute of thought of that of which its body is the expression in the attribute of extension. In order to understand the distinguishing features of the human mind, we must have at least an outline knowledge of the nature of the human body (P13 S). To achieve this end, Spinoza inserts (between P13 S and P14) a sketch of the nature of bodies in general, and of the human body in particular. The human body is an example of what Spinoza calls an 'individual', that is, a number of fundamental corpuscles or 'most simple bodies' which communicate their motions to one another in a certain specific way. Spinoza explains (L4–L7, after P13 S) how the human body, a highly complex individual, can retain its identity through a series of changes. The human mind, too, is complex; the idea that constitutes it is composed of many ideas (P15). Spinoza's point could also be made by saying that the human mind does not *have* ideas; it *is* an idea, an idea that is composed of ideas.

3. Spinoza now begins a discussion of human knowledge, a topic that occupies him until the end of Part Two. He begins by considering what he later calls (P29 C) knowledge 'through the common order of Nature'; that is, knowledge that we have when the mind is determined externally. Our bodies are acted on by external things; in terms of thought, this means that we perceive external things. We are also able to imagine things that are not present to us, and also to recollect them (P14,

P16–P18 S). Besides knowing external things, the mind also knows itself (P22–P23). Spinoza now undertakes to show (P24–P29) that knowledge through the common order of Nature is what he calls 'inadequate'. (An 'adequate' idea, he has explained in D4, is closely related to a true idea, the difference being that to call an idea 'true' is to consider it as agreeing with its object, whereas an 'adequate' idea is a true idea considered without relation to its object.) The basic pattern of his argument is this. When the human body is acted on by some external body, it constitutes only part of a complex physical system (P16), which involves not only the human body but also the bodies that affect it. Correspondingly, the idea that is the thought-parallel of the human body is a mere fragment of a whole. Such an idea cannot agree perfectly with its object, and must therefore be false, or, as Spinoza says here, inadequate. This is what Spinoza means when he says later in Part Two that falsity consists in the privation of knowledge (P35).

4. What was said about perception 'through the common order of Nature' might seem to imply that human beings cannot have any adequate ideas; for we are finite things, which may suggest that all our ideas are fragmentary. However, we do have adequate ideas, for we are determined internally as well as externally (P29 S). Spinoza explains how this is possible by arguing (P37–P40 S1) that certain things are common to all bodies, so the ideas that correspond to these in the attribute of thought are not fragmentary, but must be adequate. Such ideas are what were traditionally called 'common notions'; they are the axioms which are the bases of all our reasoning (P40 S1). In P40 S2 Spinoza sums up what he has said about knowledge, and looks ahead. What he has previously called perception from the common order of Nature he now calls knowledge of the first kind, or 'imagination'. Our use of common notions he now calls knowledge of the second kind, or 'reason'. Besides these kinds of knowledge there is also a third kind, which Spinoza calls 'intuitive knowledge', whose advantages will be discussed in Part Five. At the present stage Spinoza hints that to know things in this way is to grasp a universal rule in a particular instance. He continues (P44) by saying more about the nature of reason, the second kind of knowledge. He has already said (P31 C) that when we think of things by means of the imagination, we think of them as contingent; when we think of them by means of the reason, we think of them as necessary, and we perceive them (P44 C2) 'under a certain species of eternity'—that is, we regard them as timeless. He now relates what he has said to our knowledge of God. We have, he says (P44–P47), an adequate knowledge of the eternal

and infinite essence of God, though our knowledge of God is obscured by the fact (P47 S) that we tend to think of God in terms of what we can imagine. Spinoza concludes Part Two by taking up again (P49 and S) his theory of the idea. Criticizing Descartes, he argues that it is wrong to say that judgement involves two faculties, the will (which in effect says 'Yes' or 'No'), and the intellect, which provides that which we affirm or deny by means of the will. An idea, Spinoza insists, is not something other than the judgement; rather, it involves judgement.

PART THREE: ON THE ORIGIN AND NATURE OF THE EMOTIONS

In Part Two Spinoza has discussed the intellectual functions of the mind, in the sense of the making of judgements and the various ways in which human beings know. What he says in that Part has a bearing on Part Three, in which he expands his theory of the mind by taking into account our emotions and our endeavours.

1. After a short Preface, in which he defends his use of the geo-metrical method to give an account of the emotions, Spinoza introduces some important concepts in the course of a series of definitions. He draws a contrast (D2) between action and passion. To be active is to do things which can be understood solely through the agent's nature; to be passive is to do things of which the agent is only a partial cause. Linking this with a topic raised in Part Two, Spinoza adds (P1) that our mind acts in so far as it has adequate ideas, and is passive in so far as it has inadequate ideas. Another important concept contained in the defi-nitions of Part Three is that of an emotion (*affectus*). In speaking of the emotions, Spinoza is considering the human being—regarded in terms of both body and mind—as a dynamic being. An emotion (D3) is an increase or diminution of the power either of the body or of the mind.

2. The reference to power is picked up in an extremely important proposition, P6. This states what is commonly called Spinoza's theory of *conatus*, which concerns the basic endeavour (*conatus*) that each thing has. Spinoza claims that each thing, in so far as it is itself (i.e. in so far as it is not affected by other things), endeavours to persevere in its own being. Spinoza also calls this endeavour the 'power' by which each thing endeavours to persevere in its own being, and he says that it is the 'essence' of each thing (P7). He has various terms for this endeavour

(P9 S). When related to the mind alone, it is called 'will'; when related to mind and body simultaneously it is 'appetite'. Closely related to the term 'appetite' is the term 'desire'—a term which, in the *Ethics*, is the most used of this group. There is, Spinoza says, no difference between an appetite and a desire, except that to talk of a desire is to talk of an appetite of which we are conscious.

Two other important concepts of Part Three remain to be introduced: these are 'pleasure' and 'pain'. They are closely related to the concept of an emotion, which was defined in terms of the increase or diminution of power; pleasure (P11 S) is said to be the emotion by which the mind passes to a greater perfection, i.e. has more power, and pain the emotion by which it has less power. Spinoza declares desire, pleasure, and pain to be (ibid.) the three 'primitive' or 'primary' emotions—primitive in the sense that it is possible to derive from them all the other emotions.

3. In the remainder of Part Three Spinoza attempts to derive all other emotions—or to be exact, all those that are of any practical interest—from the three that are primary. In doing so, he refers to the way in which pleasure or pain can be accompanied by the idea of an external cause; this explains the nature of the important emotions of love and hatred (P13 S). He also makes use of what might be called psychological laws. So, for example, he explains by means of the association of ideas the emotions of sympathy and antipathy (P14, P15 S); again, he uses what might be called the law of the imitation of the emotions (i.e. the fact that, on seeing others to have a certain emotion, we feel a similar emotion) to explain the emotions of compassion and emulation (P27 and S1). But he is not concerned to explain just what a given emotion is; he is also concerned to show how the emotions act on each other—how, for example, hatred can be destroyed by love (P43).

Spinoza also derives from his views about the primary emotions some conclusions about popular morality. The term 'good', he says (P39 S), means every sort of pleasure, and especially that which satisfies a desire, whatever that may be; 'bad' is the opposite of 'good'. This has the consequence (ibid.) that each person judges what is good or bad in accordance with his own emotions. This view is repeated in the Preface to Part Four, but it does not by any means constitute the whole of Spinoza's view about the nature of good and bad. First, however, it is necessary for Spinoza to expand his views about the emotions of the human being. The first steps towards this are taken towards the end of Part Three.

4. In most of Part Three Spinoza has been concerned with those emotions which are passions. There has been frequent reference to the imagination (e.g. P16–P32, P34–P35, P40–P41), i.e. to inadequate ideas, but so far there has been no reference to adequate ideas. In P58, however, Spinoza says that besides the pleasure and the desire which are passions, there are also pleasure and desire which are related to us in so far as we act—i.e. in so far as we have adequate ideas. This will be of great importance in the rest of the *Ethics*, in which Spinoza describes the power over the emotions possessed by the rational human being.

5. Before proceeding with his account, Spinoza adds to Part Three what is in effect an Appendix, in which he states in a more easily accessible form what he has so far deduced about the emotions step by step. He does so in the form of a series of 'Definitions of the Emotions', which are set out as follows:

(a) The three primary emotions, namely desire, pleasure, and pain (DE1–DE3).
(b) An aside about wonder and contempt (DE4–DE5).
(c) The emotions which arise from pleasure or pain, involving either an external (DE6–DE24) or an internal (DE25–DE31) cause.
(d) The emotions which are related to desire (DE32–DE48).
(e) Finally, a 'General Definition of the Emotions', which is in fact a definition of the passions.

PART FOUR: ON HUMAN SERVITUDE, OR, ON THE STRENGTH OF THE EMOTIONS

Although the Fourth Part of the *Ethics* is subtitled 'On the Strength of the Emotions', this is misleading in two respects. First, Spinoza's concern here is with the passions rather than with the emotions in general; secondly, the power of the passions is the subject of the first eighteen propositions only. After this, Spinoza is concerned with the active rather than with the passive life, and his concern is to show what the active life would be; Part Five will establish how one can live such a life.

1. In Part Three Spinoza has mentioned the terms 'good' and 'bad', and has said (*E*3 P39 S) that each person judges what is good and bad in accordance with his own emotions. He returns to the topic in a Preface to Part Four. He first supplements his attack on the idea of a purposive God, made in the Appendix to Part One, with an attack on the whole

Aristotelian concept of final causes. There are, he argues, no final causes; there are only efficient causes. He then turns to the concepts of good and bad, saying that these are relative terms, in that what X may think to be good, Y may think to be bad. However, Spinoza has a use in his philosophy for the terms 'good' and 'bad', and explains that in his sense of the terms, that is good which we know to be useful to us, and that is bad which we know to hinder us from possessing something good. 'Good' and 'bad' are formally defined in $E4$ D1–D2; another important concept defined at the beginning of Part Four is that of 'virtue'. Virtue, Spinoza says, is power ($E4$ D8) and the virtue of man is the very nature of man, in so far as what Spinoza calls 'actions' (i.e. the opposite of passions) follow from that nature. 'Good', 'bad', and 'virtue' are key concepts of Part Four.

2. In P1–P17 Spinoza explains the causes of our lack of power, and of the fact that we do not always do what reason recommends. We are, he says, necessarily liable to passions (P4 C), and our knowledge of good and bad seems to have little control over them. To know that something is good or bad is simply to be conscious of the emotion of pleasure or pain (P8)—for to feel pleasure or pain ($E3$ P11 S) is simply for one's power to be increased or diminished. Such knowledge does not, of itself, restrain an emotion; it can do so only in so far as it is regarded as an emotion (P14). There is indeed a type of desire that arises from a knowledge of good and bad, but this can be destroyed or hindered in many ways (P15–P17).

3. After this account of human weakness Spinoza turns (P18–P28) to the strength, i.e. the 'virtue', of man. The doctrine of *conatus* re-enters when Spinoza observes (P20) that the more we are successful in our endeavour to preserve our own being, the more virtue we have. He then makes a connection between virtue and reason; to act from virtue is to be determined by the fact that we understand (P23), i.e. it is to act under the guidance of reason (P24).

4. Although Spinoza states (P25) that no one attempts to preserve his being for the sake of anything else, he does not think that a life guided by reason is a solitary life, and in P29–P40 he explains the nature and the usefulness of life in society. The more a thing agrees with our nature, the more useful, i.e. the better, it is for us (P30–P31); now, we do not agree in nature in so far as we are liable to the passions (P32–P34), but we do agree in so far as we live under the guidance of reason (P35), from which it follows (P35 C1) that those who live in this way are most useful to one another. However, Spinoza has already argued (P4 C, P14) that we are

necessarily liable to those emotions which are passions, and that an emotion can be restrained only by an emotion. If we are to live in harmony with one another, there must therefore be a form of association which uses a passion—fear—to restrain the passions, and this form of association is the commonwealth (P37 S2). From this it follows (P40) that whatever produces harmony in the commonwealth is good, and that whatever introduces discord is bad.

5. Spinoza now gives a detailed account (P41–P58) of various forms of the emotions of pleasure and pain, and asks whether they are good or bad, virtues or defects. Here he refines on his views about good and bad. Pleasure, for example, is always good in itself; however (P41), it can be bad in certain contexts—namely, if the pleasure felt by one part of an organism impedes the activity of the organism as a whole. In the same way pain, which is bad in itself, can be good in so far as it checks the power of a part which would, if unchecked, damage the whole (P 43). But some passions, such as hatred, can never be good (P45). In the course of his account of the emotions Spinoza may seem to say some harsh things about what would normally be regarded as one of the virtues—namely, pity. Pity, he says (P50), is bad in itself, since it is a form of pain; the rational man, therefore, will not be guided by this emotion. But this does not mean that the rational man will not help others; he will indeed help them, but he will do so because this is the rational thing to do, and not because he is led solely by emotion (P50 C).

6. Finally (P59–P73) Spinoza gives a sketch of a life that is governed by reason. It is not fear, he says, but a desire that arises from reason that leads the rational man to do good (P63 and C). Led, as he is, by reason, he follows no one's will but his own, and so he is properly called 'free' (P66 S). He is not governed by considerations about a life after death (P67), he is not rash (P69), and he always acts in good faith (P72). In the last Proposition of Part Four (P73) Spinoza emphasizes the importance of a political society; a man who is led by reason is more free in a commonwealth than in solitude. Part Four closes with an Appendix, in which Spinoza states in a more perspicuous form what he has said about the right way of life.

PART FIVE: ON THE POWER OF THE INTELLECT, OR, ON HUMAN FREEDOM

This part of the *Ethics* is the culmination of the work. In Part Four Spinoza has explained what human freedom would be, if we could achieve it; he now shows how it can be achieved, and what is the relation of free human beings to God. The Part falls into three main sections. In the first (P1–P13) Spinoza explains how we can be active rather than passive, and so live a free life. The second (P14–P20 S) discusses the emotions of the free man, when it considers the topic of God's love and of our love for God. In the third (P21–P40 S) Spinoza discusses the eternity of the human mind, and takes further the topics of God's love and of the love of the human mind for God. This is followed by what is in effect a short postscript about the motives for moral action (P41–P42 S).

1. Spinoza begins by considering the power that the intellect has over the passions. He first (*E*5, Preface) attacks Descartes's view that the human mind has an absolute power over the passions, based on his theory of the pineal gland and its functions. This theory, Spinoza argues, is demonstrably false, and therefore Descartes does not establish his desired conclusion. Spinoza's own view is that although we do not have total power over the passions, we do have some power over them; freedom, then, is something that we can attain. For this thesis he produces a number of arguments. We can (P2 and P4 S) detach the passions from the confused ideas that we have of their causes and attach them to clear and distinct ideas. More generally, a passion ceases to be such once we form a clear and distinct idea of it, i.e. once we understand it (P3 and P4 S). Again, the more we understand things as necessary, the less we suffer from them, i.e. the less we are subject to passions (P6). Next, Spinoza appeals to what he has said in Part Two about reason, the second kind of knowledge. An emotion which arises from reason (P7) always remains the same, since it is based on properties which are common to all things (cf. *E*2 P40 S2), which we always regard as present; it is therefore stronger than the impermanent emotions which are based on the imagination. Again, an emotion which is based on the common properties of things is fostered by a vast number of causes, and so is stronger than a passion (P9 and P11). Finally (P10 S and P12–P13), we can make use of the imagination to support the reason, supplementing the abstract rules with which reason supplies us by imagining concrete

situations which we may meet in everyday life, and considering what the rational response to these would be.

2. In the earlier Parts of the *Ethics* Spinoza has discussed the love that human beings have for finite things; he now discusses the love that we have for God, and also the love that God has. In so far as we understand ourselves and our emotions, we love God (P14–P15). God, on the other hand, does not feel pleasure or pain, and for this reason he cannot strictly be said to love or hate any finite thing, such as ourselves (P17 and C). For our part, although we love God, we cannot (as beings who understand, that is, are active) hate God, for hatred is a passion (P18). Again, we cannot rationally try to bring it about that God loves us, for to do so would involve a misunderstanding of God's nature (P19; cf. P17 C). Finally, our love for God cannot (unlike our love for finite things) be tainted by envy or jealousy; on the contrary, our desire is that all shall share in this love (P20).

3. Spinoza now goes on to what is clearly indicated (end of P20 S) as a separate section of the *Ethics*, in which he argues that the human mind, or at any rate a part of it, is capable of an existence which is eternal—that is (P23 S) which cannot be explained by duration. He notes first (P21) that the mind has imagination and memory only as long as the body endures, which in effect rules out personal survival after death. However, we can have ideas which express, not the temporal existence of our body, but its essence. This essence we conceive under a certain species of eternity, and to that extent the mind's existence is eternal (P23 and S; cf. P29). To conceive things under a certain species of eternity is the work of the second and third kinds of knowledge, 'reason' and 'intuitive knowledge' (E2 P44 C2; E5 P31 and S), and Spinoza next explains the importance of intuitive knowledge, which is an adequate knowledge of particular things. A mind that understands things by such knowledge has the greatest power, and also enjoys the greatest contentment (P25, P27). Further, in so far as the mind knows itself and its body under a species of eternity, it has knowledge of God and knows that it is in God (P30). So the more a person knows by intuitive knowledge, the more he is aware of God; that is, the more perfect or blessed he is (P31 S). Such knowledge also has an emotive aspect; that is, the person who has intuitive knowledge loves God with a kind of love that Spinoza calls 'intellectual' (P32 and C). This love is eternal (P33); God loves himself with such love (P35) and the mind's intellectual love of God is the love with which God loves himself (P36). It follows from this (P36 C) that God has an intellectual love for men. Spinoza has already argued (P17 and C) that

God cannot strictly be said to love human beings, and in speaking of God's intellectual love he hints (P36 S) that such love is of a special kind, which does not involve pleasure. The point is that pleasure is a transition to a higher state of perfection, whereas God's love is something that is ascribed to an absolutely perfect being. Spinoza adds (P36 S) that our eternal love for God, or, God's love for men, constitutes our blessedness or freedom. In the same Scholium he makes an important remark about intuitive knowledge, saying that its superiority over reason lies in the greater power that it has by virtue of its concreteness. Spinoza continues by arguing (P37) that nothing can destroy intellectual love, and that the more the mind understands—and Spinoza includes here both the second and the third kinds of knowledge—the less it is subject to the passions (P38). Spinoza now reminds his readers of his theory of the relations between mind and matter when he says (P39) that to have a mind which is to a large extent eternal is to have a body which is capable of very many activities. But the person who has a mind only a part of which is eternal need not despair; however small that part may be, it is still more perfect than the rest of the mind (P40 C).

4. Having argued for the eternity of the mind, Spinoza emphasizes that what he said about this is not essential to the ethical content of his work. For even if we did not know that the mind is eternal, we would still follow the precepts of reason (P41). He concludes with an attack on conventional views about an afterlife, criticizing those people who are led to behave morally only by a hope of rewards in the afterlife for the virtuous, or a fear of punishment for the wicked (P41 S). It is wrong, he says, to regard blessedness as a reward for good behaviour. Blessedness is not the reward of virtue; it is virtue itself (P42).

Notes on the Translation

The translator of Spinoza's *Ethics* is faced with a problem, inasmuch as there is at present no entirely satisfactory edition of the original text. For many years the edition published by Carl Gebhardt, in volume II of his edition of Spinoza's complete works (Heidelberg, 1925), was regarded as a paradigm. Certainly, Gebhardt was a fine scholar, and his edition of the *Ethics* is still useful. However, Gebhardt has been severely criticized for a thesis about the text that he propounded. The *Ethics* was published in Latin in December 1677 as part of Spinoza's *Opera Posthuma*. At about the same time there appeared a Dutch translation of the same works, *De Nagelate Schriften van B.d.S.* The importance of the Dutch version as a means of correcting a number of printer's errors in the *Opera Posthuma* has long been recognized. Gebhardt, however, went much further. He noted that there are many textual differences between the Latin and the Dutch versions, and also that most of these differences are to be found in the first two parts of the *Ethics*. This led him to conclude that the Dutch version of the first two parts was based on an earlier manuscript than that used by the editors of the Latin version. In his edition he indicated the differences between the two manuscripts by inserting into the text of the *Opera Posthuma* various passages from the Dutch translation, where this differed from the published Latin text. However, there is now general agreement among scholars that Gebhardt's thesis was mistaken. Passages that he regarded as stemming from an earlier version of Parts One and Two do not in fact do so, but spring from what one might call translator's licence. As to the fact that these passages are concentrated in the first two parts of the *Ethics*, this is explained by the plausible hypothesis that different people translated the first two and the last three parts respectively. My translation, accordingly, is not based on Gebhardt's text. (Readers interested in the differences between the Latin text and the Dutch translation will find helpful material in E. Curley's translation of the *Ethics*, in volume I of his *Collected Works of Spinoza*.) I have based my translation on the third edition, published in 1914, of an earlier version of the text made by two nineteenth-century scholars, van Vloten and Land. This is by no means perfect—it is, for example, marred by a large number of typographical errors—but at least it does not involve a false hypothesis, as Gebhardt's does. I have corrected the text where necessary in the light of later scholarship.

I have tried to produce a translation which is both readable and faithful to the original. In the interests of clarity I have often been led to break up long and complex Latin sentences into shorter English ones. I have, however, retained the paragraphs of the original Latin text. These may often seem long to the modern reader, but it seemed to me that to subdivide them would be to impose on the text my own concept of the structure of the arguments. I have also been faced by some problems that meet any translator of seventeenth-century Latin. First, Spinoza makes much use of the terms *seu* or *sive* on the one hand, and *aut* or *vel* on the other. Any member of this group of words can be translated by the English word 'or'; but there is an important difference between, say, the phrase 'Deus seu Natura' (*E*4 Preface), which indicates that the terms 'God' and 'Nature' may correctly be used of the same thing, and the assertion that it is of the nature of substance to exist 'vel finita, vel infinita', which states that it is false to say that a substance is both finite and infinite. To mark this difference, I render terms from the second group as 'or', and sometimes 'either . . . or'. *Seu* and *sive* I render, sometimes by placing commas round the word 'or', sometimes by 'or, in other words', and sometimes by 'i.e.'. The other problem concerns quotation marks. These were unknown to Spinoza's printers, who would normally use italics in their place. In such cases, I have followed modern practice; I also use quotation marks where the phrase is not in italics, but the sense demands it.

PART 2
The Text

ETHICS

Demonstrated in Geometrical Order

PART ONE

ON GOD

Definitions[1]

1. By cause of itself[2] I understand that whose essence involves existence, or, that whose nature cannot be conceived except as existing.

2. That thing is called finite in its own kind which can be limited by another of the same nature. For example, a body is called finite because we can always conceive another which is greater. In the same way, a thought is limited by another thought. But a body is not limited by a thought, nor a thought by a body.

3. By substance[3] I understand that which is in itself and is conceived through itself; that is, that which does not need the concept of another thing, from which concept it must be formed.

4. By attribute[4] I understand that which intellect perceives of substance, as constituting its essence.

5. By mode[5] I understand the affections of substance, or, that which is in something else, through which it is also conceived.

6. By God[6] I understand an absolutely infinite entity, that is, a substance consisting of infinite attributes, each of which expresses eternal and infinite essence.

Explanation. I say 'absolutely infinite', but not 'infinite in its own kind'. For of anything which is only infinite in its own kind we can deny infinite attributes. But in the case of that which is absolutely infinite, there belongs to its essence whatever expresses essence, and involves no negation.

7. That thing is called free[7] which exists solely by the necessity of its own nature, and is determined to action by itself alone. However, that thing is called necessary, or rather compelled, which is determined by another to exist and to operate in a certain and determinate way.

8. By eternity[8] I understand existence itself, in so far as it is conceived to follow necessarily solely from the definition of an eternal thing.

Explanation. For such existence is conceived as an eternal truth, just as is the essence of the thing, and consequently it cannot be explained by duration or time, even though the duration is conceived as without beginning and end.

Axioms[9]

1. Each thing that exists exists either in itself or in something else.
2. That which cannot be conceived through something else must be conceived through itself.
3. From a given determinate cause there necessarily follows an effect; conversely, if no determinate cause exists, it is impossible that an effect should follow.
4. Knowledge of an effect depends on the knowledge of the cause, and involves it.
5. Those things which have nothing in common with each other cannot be understood through each other, or, the conception of the one does not involve the conception of the other.
6. A true idea must agree with that of which it is the idea.[10]
7. The essence of whatever can be conceived as not existing does not involve existence.

Proposition 1

Substance is prior in nature to its affections.

Demonstration. This is evident from Defs. 3 and 5.

Proposition 2

Two substances[11] which have different attributes have nothing in common with one another.

Demonstration. This also is evident from Def. 3. For each one must be in itself and must be conceived through itself, or, the conception of the one does not involve the conception of the other.

Proposition 3

Of things which have nothing in common with one another, one cannot be the cause of another.

Demonstration. If they have nothing in common with each other, it follows (by Ax. 5) that they cannot be understood through each other, and so (by Ax. 4) one cannot be the cause of another. QED.

Proposition 4

Two or more distinct things are distinguished from one another either by a difference of the attributes of substances, or by a difference of their affections.

Demonstration. Each thing that exists exists either in itself or in something else (by Ax. 1). That is (by Defs. 3 and 5), nothing exists outside the intellect apart from substances and their affections. Outside the intellect, therefore, nothing exists by which several things can be distinguished from one another apart from substances, or, what is the same (by Def. 4), their attributes and their affections. QED.

Proposition 5

There cannot exist in the universe two or more substances of the same nature, i.e. of the same attribute.[12]

Demonstration. If several distinct substances were to exist, they would have to be distinguished from one another either by a difference of their attributes or by a difference of their affections (by the preceding Proposition). If they were distinguished only by a difference of attributes, it would be granted that only one substance of the same attribute exists. But if they were distinguished only by a difference of their affections, then since substance is prior in nature to its affections (by Prop. 1), if the affections are set aside and the substance is considered in itself (that is, by Def. 3 and Ax. 6, truly considered), it could not be conceived to be distinct from another. That is (by the preceding Proposition), there cannot exist several substances; there can exist only one.[13] QED.

Proposition 6

One substance cannot be produced by another substance.

Demonstration. There cannot (by the preceding Proposition) exist in the universe two substances of the same attribute), that is (by Prop. 2), which have something in common. So (by Prop. 3) one cannot be the cause of the other, or, cannot be produced by another. QED.

Corollary

It therefore follows that a substance cannot be produced by something else. For nothing exists in the universe apart from substances and their affections, as is evident from Ax. 1 and Defs. 3 and 5. But a substance cannot be produced by a substance (by the preceding proposition); therefore, absolutely, a substance cannot be produced by something else. QED.

ALTERNATIVE PROOF

This is demonstrated even more easily by the absurdity of the contradictory. For if a substance could be produced by something else, the knowledge of that substance must depend on the knowledge of its cause (by Ax. 4), and so (by Def. 3) it would not be a substance.

Proposition 7

It belongs to the nature of substance to exist.

Demonstration. A substance cannot be produced by something else (by the Corollary of the preceding Proposition); therefore, it will be the cause of itself. That is (by Def. 1), its essence necessarily involves existence, or, it belongs to its nature to exist. QED.

Proposition 8

Every substance is necessarily infinite.

Demonstration. A substance of one attribute[14] cannot exist except as unique (by Prop. 5), and it belongs to its nature to exist (by Prop. 7). By its own nature, therefore, it will exist either as finite or as infinite. But it will not exist as finite. For (by Def. 2) it would have to be limited by another substance of the same nature, which would also have to exist necessarily (by Prop. 7). So there would exist two substances of the same attribute, which is absurd (by Prop. 5). It therefore exists as infinite. QED.

Scholium 1

Since to be finite is in fact a partial negation, and to be infinite is the absolute affirmation of the existence of some nature, it therefore follows from Prop. 7 alone that every substance must be infinite.

Scholium 2

I do not doubt that all those who judge about things in a confused way, and have not become used to knowing things through their primary causes, will find it difficult to grasp the demonstration of Prop. 7. This is because they do not distinguish between the modifications of substances and the substances themselves, and do not know how things are produced. So it comes about that they ascribe to substances the beginning that they see that natural things have. For those who are ignorant of the true causes of things confuse everything, and without any mental aversion they suppose trees as well as human beings to speak, and imagine human beings to be formed from stones as well as from semen, and any forms to be changed into any others. So also those who confuse the divine nature with human nature readily ascribe human emotions[15] to God, especially as long as they are also ignorant of the way in which emotions are produced in the mind. But if people would pay attention to the nature of substance, they would by no means doubt of the truth of Prop. 7. On the contrary, everyone would regard this proposition as an axiom, and it would be counted as one of the common notions.[16] For they would understand by substance that which is in itself and is conceived through itself, that is, that the knowledge of which does not need the knowledge of another thing. But they would understand by modifications that which is in something else, and that the conception of which is formed from the conception of the thing in which they are. It is on account of this that we can have true ideas of the modifications of non-existent things. For although such things do not exist actually outside the intellect, yet their essence is included in something else in such a way that they can be grasped through it. But the true nature of substances is not outside the intellect except in the substances themselves, for they are conceived through themselves. If anyone were to say, therefore, that he has a clear and distinct, that is, a true idea of substance and yet doubts whether such a substance exists, then that would be the same as if he were to say, if you please, that he has a true idea and yet is inclined to think that it may be false (as is clear to anyone who pays attention to the matter). Or again, if anyone judges that a substance is created, he has at the same time judged that a false idea has been made true, and nothing more absurd than this can be conceived.[17] So it must necessarily be admitted that the existence of a substance is, like its essence, an eternal truth. From this we can infer in another way that there exists only a unique substance of the same nature, and I have thought it worth while to show this here. So that I can do this in a systematic way, it must be noted (1) that the true definition of each thing neither involves nor expresses anything apart from the nature of the defined thing. From this it follows (2) that no definition either involves or expresses a certain number of individuals, since it expresses nothing other than the nature of the defined thing. For example, the definition of a triangle expresses nothing other than the simple nature of the triangle, and not a certain number of triangles. (3) It must be noted that of each existing thing there necessarily exists a certain cause on account of which it exists. (4) Finally, it must be noted that this cause on account of which some thing exists must either be contained in the very nature and definition of the existing thing (namely, because it belongs to its nature to exist), or it must exist outside it. Granted all this, it follows that if there exists in Nature a certain number of individuals, then there must necessarily exist a cause for the existence of just those individuals, and of neither more nor less. Suppose, for example, that there exist in the universe twenty men. (For the sake of greater clarity I assume that these exist at the same time, and that no man existed in Nature previously.) For us to give the reason why twenty men exist, it will not be enough to show the cause of human nature in general, but it will also be necessary to show the cause of the fact that neither more nor less than twenty men exist. For, by (3), there must necessarily exist a cause of the existence of each man. But this cause, by (2) and (3), cannot be contained in human nature itself, since the true definition of man does not involve the number twenty. So, by (4), the cause of the existence of these twenty men, and consequently of the existence of each one, must necessarily exist outside each one. Therefore, it must be concluded absolutely that everything of whose nature several individuals can exist must necessarily have an external cause of those individuals' existence. Now since (by what has already been shown in this Scholium) it belongs to the nature of substance to exist, its definition must involve necessary existence, and consequently its existence must be inferred from its definition alone. But from its definition (as we have already shown from (2) and (3)) there cannot follow the existence of several substances. It therefore follows necessarily from that definition that there exists only a unique substance of the same nature, as we set out to show.

Proposition 9

The more reality or being each thing has, the more attributes belong to it.

Demonstration. This is evident from Def. 4.

Proposition 10

Each attribute of one substance must be conceived through itself.

Demonstration. For an attribute is that which intellect perceives of substance, as constituting its essence (by Def. 4), and so (by Def. 3) it must be conceived through itself. QED.

Scholium

From this it is evident that, although two attributes are conceived as really distinct—that is, one without the help of the other—we cannot infer from this that they constitute two entities, or, two different substances. For it is of the nature of substance that each of its attributes is conceived through itself, since all the attributes that it has were always in it at the same time and one could not be produced by another, but each one expresses the reality, or, the being of substance. It is therefore far from absurd to ascribe several attributes to one substance. On the contrary, nothing in Nature is more clear than that each entity must be conceived under some attribute, and that the more reality or being it has, the more attributes it has which express both necessity (or, eternity) and infinity. Consequently, nothing is clearer than that an absolutely infinite being is necessarily to be defined (as we stated in Def. 6) as an entity which consists of infinite attributes, each of which expresses a certain eternal and infinite essence. But if anyone now asks by what sign we can recognize the diversity of substances, let him read the following propositions, which show that in the universe there exists only a unique substance, and that this is absolutely infinite. So the sign in question would be sought in vain.

Proposition 11

God—in other words a substance consisting of infinite attributes, each of which expresses eternal and infinite essence—necessarily exists.

Demonstration. If you deny this, conceive (if this can be done) that God does not exist. Therefore (by Ax. 7), his essence does not involve existence. But this (by Prop. 7) is absurd; therefore, God necessarily exists. QED.

ALTERNATIVE PROOF

To each thing there must be ascribed a cause or reason[18] both for its existence and for its non-existence. For example, if a triangle exists, a reason or cause of its existence must exist. But if it does not exist, there must also be a reason or cause which hinders it from existing, or, which negates its existence. This reason or cause must be contained either in the nature of the thing or outside it. For example, the reason why a square circle does not exist is indicated by its very nature; namely, in that its nature involves a contradiction. On the other hand, the reason why a substance exists follows from its nature alone, in that its nature involves existence (see Prop. 7). But the reason why a circle or a triangle exists or does not exist follows, not from their nature, but from the order of the whole of corporeal Nature. For from that it must follow, either that the triangle now exists necessarily, or that it is impossible that it should now exist. All this is self-evident. From this it follows that there exists necessarily that of which there is no reason or cause which hinders it from existing. If, therefore, there can be no reason or cause which hinders God from existing, or which negates his existence, then it must be inferred that God exists necessarily. But if such a reason or cause did exist, then it must exist either in God's nature or outside it, that is, in another substance of another nature. (For if it were of the same nature, then by that very fact it would be granted that God exists.) But a substance which was of another nature could have nothing in common with God (by Prop. 2), and so could neither affirm nor negate his existence. Since, therefore, the reason or cause which negates the divine existence cannot exist outside the divine nature, it must (if indeed God does not exist) necessarily be in the very nature of God, which would consequently involve a contradiction. But to affirm this of an entity which is absolutely infinite and supremely perfect is absurd. Therefore, neither in God nor outside God is there any cause or reason which negates his existence, and therefore God necessarily exists. QED.

ALTERNATIVE PROOF

To be able not to exist is a lack of power, and on the other hand to be able to exist is a power (as is self-evident). So if what now necessarily exists consists only of finite entities, finite entities are more powerful than an absolutely infinite entity. This (as is self-evident) is absurd; therefore, either nothing exists, or an absolutely infinite entity necessarily exists. But we ourselves exist, either in ourselves or in something else that exists necessarily (see Ax. 1 and Prop. 7). Therefore, an absolutely infinite entity, that is (by Def. 6) God, necessarily exists. QED.

Scholium

In this last demonstration I wanted to prove the existence of God a posteriori so that the demonstration is perceived more easily, and not on account of the fact that the existence of God does not follow a priori from the very same basis.[19] For since to be able to exist is a power, it follows that the more reality belongs to the nature of some thing, the more power of existence it has from itself. So it follows that an absolutely infinite entity, God, has from itself an absolutely infinite power of existing, and therefore exists absolutely. However, many people will perhaps not be able to see the force of this demonstration easily. This is because they have become accustomed to consider only those things that flow from external causes; and they see that, of these things, those which are made quickly, that is, which exist easily, also perish easily. On the other hand, they judge that those things are more difficult to make, that is, do not exist with such ease, to which more things belong. However, I have no need to show here, in order to free them from these prejudices, in what way the proposition 'What is quickly made quickly perishes' is true; nor, again, whether or not all things are equally easy with respect to the whole of Nature. It is sufficient to note only this: that I am speaking here, not of things which are produced by external causes, but only of substances, which (by Prop. 6) can be produced by no external cause. For with regard to things which are produced by external causes:

whether they consist of many parts or few, whatever perfection, i.e. reality,[20] they have is owed entirely to the power of the external cause. So their existence arises from the perfection of the external cause alone, and not from their own perfection. On the other hand, whatever perfection a substance has is owed to no external cause; so its existence too must follow solely from its nature, which is consequently nothing other than its essence.[21] Perfection, therefore, does not negate the existence of a thing, but on the contrary affirms it; imperfection, on the other hand, negates it. So we cannot be more certain of the existence of any thing than of the existence of an absolutely infinite, i.e. of a perfect, entity— that is, God. For since his essence excludes all imperfection and involves absolute perfection, by that very fact it removes all cause of doubt about his existence and gives supreme certainty about it. This, I believe, will be evident to anyone who gives only a little attention to the matter.

Proposition 12

No attribute of a substance can truly be conceived from which it follows that substance can be divided.[22]

Demonstration

For the parts into which a substance which is conceived in this way would be divided will either retain the nature of substance or they will not. If the first is assumed, then (by Prop. 8) each part will have to be infinite and (by Prop. 7)[23] the cause of itself, and (by Prop. 5) will have to consist of a different attribute. So several substances can be formed from one, which (by Prop. 6) is absurd. In addition, the parts (by Prop. 2) would have nothing in common with the whole which they constitute, and the whole (by Def. 4 and Prop. 10) could both exist and be conceived without its parts; and no one can doubt the absurdity of this. But if the second alternative is assumed—namely, that the parts will not retain the nature of substance—then it follows that when the whole substance is divided into equal parts, it will lose the nature of substance and cease to exist, which (by Prop. 7) is absurd.[24]

Proposition 13

An absolutely infinite substance is indivisible.

Demonstration. For if it were divisible, the parts into which it is divided will either retain the nature of an absolutely infinite substance or they will not. If the first is assumed, then there will exist several substances of the same nature, which (by Prop. 5) is absurd. If the second is assumed, then (as above)[25] absolutely infinite substance will be able to cease to exist, which (by Prop. 11) is also absurd.

Corollary

From this it follows that no substance, and consequently no corporeal substance[26] in so far as it is a substance, is divisible.

Scholium

The indivisibility of substance is understood more directly from just this: that the nature of substance cannot be conceived except as infinite, and that by a part of substance one can understand nothing other than a finite substance, which (by Prop. 8) implies an evident contradiction.

Proposition 14

Besides God no substance can exist or be conceived.

Demonstration. Since God is an absolutely infinite entity of which no attribute that expresses the essence of substance can be denied (by Def. 6), and since God necessarily exists (by Prop. 11), then if there were some substance besides God, that substance would have to be explained through some attribute of God. So there would exist two substances of the same attribute, which (by Prop. 5) is absurd. Therefore, no substance besides God can exist, and consequently it cannot also be conceived. For if it could be conceived, it would necessarily have to be conceived as existing; but this (by the first part of this demonstration) is absurd. Therefore, besides God no substance can exist or be conceived. QED.

Corollary 1

From this it follows most clearly, first, that God is unique, that is (by Def. 6), that there exists in the universe only one substance, and that it is absolutely infinite, as we have already hinted in the Scholium to Prop. 10.

Corollary 2

Secondly, it follows that an extended thing and a thinking thing are either attributes of God or (by Ax. 1) are affections of the attributes of God.

Proposition 15

Whatever exists exists in God, and nothing can exist or be conceived without God.

Demonstration. No substance exists or can be conceived besides God (by Prop. 14), that is (by Def. 3), a thing which is in itself and is conceived through itself. But modes (by Def. 5) can neither exist nor be conceived without substance; therefore they can exist solely in the divine nature, and can be conceived through that nature alone. But nothing exists besides substances and modes (by Ax. 1). Therefore, nothing can exist or be conceived without God. QED.

Scholium

Some people imagine God in the form of a man, consisting of body and mind, and as subject to passions.[27] But it has been satisfactorily established, from what has already been proved, how far these people stray from a true knowledge of God. But I pass them by; for all who have in any way contemplated the divine nature deny that God is corporeal. They also prove this very well from the fact that by 'body' we understand a quantity of any kind, having length, width, and depth, and limited by some definite shape, and it is impossible to say anything more absurd than this about God, namely an absolutely infinite entity. Sometimes, however, they show clearly (by other arguments by which they try to prove the same thing) that they try to remove corporeal, i.e. extended substance itself from the divine nature entirely, and they think that it has been created by God.[28] But they are evidently ignorant of the divine power by which it could have been created, which clearly shows that they do not understand what they themselves say. I, at all events, have demonstrated clearly enough, in my view (see Prop. 6, Coroll., and Prop. 8, Schol. 2), that no substance can be produced or created from something else. Further, we showed in Prop. 14 that besides God no substance can exist or be conceived, and from this we inferred[29] that extended substance is one of the infinite attributes of God. However, for the sake of a fuller explanation I will refute the arguments of my opponents, all of which come to the following. The first is that, in their opinion, corporeal substance, in so far as it is a substance, consists of parts. For this reason they deny that it can be infinite, and consequently can belong to God. They explain this by means of many examples, of which I will cite one or two. If (they say) corporeal substance is infinite, then let it be conceived to be divided into two parts; each part will be either finite or infinite. If the former, then the infinite will be composed of two finite parts, which is absurd. If the latter, then there is an infinite which is twice as large as another infinite, which is also absurd. Further, if an infinite quantity is measured by parts each of which equals one foot, it must consist of an infinity of such parts—as it must also do, if it is measured by parts each of which equals an inch. Consequently, one infinite number will be twelve times larger than another infinite number.[30] Finally: if from one point of a certain infinite quantity two lines, such as AB and AC, which are initially at a certain and determinate distance, are conceived as prolonged to infinity, then it is certain that the distance between AB AC is continuously increased, and from being determinate will finally become indeterminate. Since, therefore, these absurdities follow (they think) from the fact that an infinite quantity is supposed, they infer from this that corporeal substance must be finite, and consequently

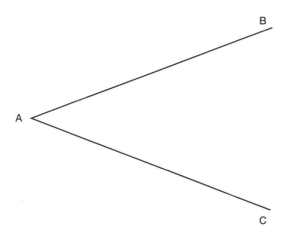

does not belong to the essence of God. A second argument is also sought from the supreme perfection of God. They say that since God is a supremely perfect entity, he cannot be acted upon. But corporeal substance can be acted upon, since it is divisible; it therefore follows that it does not belong to the essence of God.[31] These are the arguments which I find put forward by writers in their attempts to prove that corporeal substance is unworthy of the divine nature, and cannot belong to it. However, anyone who pays proper attention will see that I have already replied to these arguments. For they have their basis solely in this: that they assume corporeal substance to be composed of parts, which I have already (Prop. 12, together with Prop. 13, Coroll.) shown to be absurd. Further, anyone who is willing to think the matter over properly will see that all these absurdities (if indeed they are all absurd, of which I do not dispute at present) from which they want to infer that extended substance is finite are far from following from the fact that an infinite quantity is supposed. Rather, the absurdities follow from the fact that they suppose infinite quantity to be measurable, and to consist of finite parts. So from the absurdities which follow from this supposition they are able to conclude no more than that infinite quantity is not measurable, and that it cannot consist of finite parts. But this is the same as what we have already demonstrated above (Prop. 12, etc.). So the spear that they aim at us they are really hurling at themselves. If, therefore, they want to conclude from the absurdity to which they refer[32] that extended substance must be finite, then (if you please) they simply act like someone who, by virtue of the fact that he has imagined that a circle has the properties of a square, concludes that a circle does not have a centre from which all the lines to the circumference are equal. For in order to infer the finitude of corporeal substance—which can be conceived only as infinite, only as unique, and only as indivisible (see Props. 8, 5, and 12)—they conceive it to be composed of finite parts, and to be multiple and divisible. So also other people, after supposing a line to be composed of points, know how to devise many arguments to show that a line cannot be divided to infinity.[33] And indeed, it is no less absurd to assume that corporeal substance is composed of bodies, i.e. of parts, than to suppose that a body is composed of surfaces, surfaces of lines, and finally lines of points. All those who admit that true reason is infallible must admit this, and especially those who deny the existence of a vacuum. For if corporeal substance could be divided in such a way that its parts are really distinct, why could not one part be annihilated whilst the other parts remain interconnected, as before? And why should all the parts be adapted in such a way that no vacuum exists? It is certainly true of things which are really distinct from each other that one can exist and remain in its state without the other.[34] Since, therefore, no vacuum exists in Nature (a topic which I shall discuss elsewhere),[35] but all its parts must agree in such a way that a vacuum does not exist, it follows also that they cannot be really distinguished; that is, that corporeal substance, in so far as it is substance, cannot be divided. But if someone now asks why we are so inclined by nature to divide quantity, I reply that quantity is conceived by us in two ways; that is, abstractly, i.e. superficially—namely, as we imagine it—or as substance, which is done by the intellect alone. So if we pay attention to quantity as it is in the imagination—which we do often and with ease—it will be found to be finite, divisible, and composed of parts. But if we pay attention to it as it is in the intellect, and conceive it in so far as it is substance—which is done with great difficulty—then, as we have already demonstrated sufficiently, it will be found to be infinite, unique, and indivisible. This will be sufficiently clear to all those who know how to distinguish between the imagination and the intellect;[36] especially if one also pays attention to this, that matter is everywhere the same, and parts are not distinguished in it except in so far as we conceive matter as affected in various ways, from which it follows that its parts are distinguished only modally, and not really.[37] For example, we conceive water, in so far as it is water, to be divided, and its parts separated from each other. But we do not conceive it in this way in so far as it is corporeal substance; for in that respect it is neither separated nor divided. Further, water, in so far as it is water, comes into existence and is destroyed; but in so far as it is substance it neither comes into existence nor is destroyed. With this, I think that I have also replied to the second argument.[38] For that argument too is based on the assumption that matter, in so far as it is substance, is divisible and composed of parts. And even if this were not the case, I do not know why matter should be unworthy of the divine nature; for (by Prop. 14) there can exist no substance except God which could act on it. I assert that all things are in God, and that all things that happen happen solely through the laws of the infinite nature of God, and follow from the necessity of his essence (as I shall soon show).[39] So it cannot be said with any justification that God is acted upon by something else, or that extended substance is unworthy of the divine nature, even though it is supposed to be divisible, provided that it is granted to be eternal and infinite. But enough of these matters for the present.

Proposition 16

There must follow, from the necessity of the divine nature, infinite things in infinite ways (that is, all the things which can fall under an infinite intellect).

Demonstration. This Proposition must be evident to anyone who simply attends to the following. From a given definition of any thing the intellect infers several properties, which in truth follow necessarily from that definition (that is, the very essence of the thing); further, the intellect infers more properties, the more reality the definition of the thing expresses, that is, the more reality the essence of the thing defined involves. But since the divine nature has absolutely infinite attributes (by Def. 6), of which each expresses, in its own kind, infinite essence, there must necessarily follow from the necessity of its nature infinite things in infinite ways (that is, all the things which can fall under an infinite intellect). QED.

Corollary 1

From this it follows that God is the efficient cause[40] of all the things that can fall under an infinite intellect.

Corollary 2

It follows, secondly, that God is a cause through himself and not by accident.[41]

Corollary 3

It follows, thirdly, that God is absolutely the first cause.

Proposition 17

God acts from the laws of his nature alone, and is compelled by no one.

Demonstration. We have just shown in Prop. 16 that infinite things follow absolutely from the necessity of the divine nature alone, or (what is the same) from the laws of that nature alone. Further, we have demonstrated in Prop. 15 that nothing exists or can be conceived without God, but that all things exist in God. So nothing can exist outside God by which he is determined or compelled to act, and so God acts from the laws of his nature alone, and is compelled by no one. QED.

Corollary 1

It follows from this, first, that there is no cause which, either extrinsically or intrinsically, incites God to action, apart from the perfection of his own nature.

Corollary 2

It follows, secondly, that God alone is a free cause. For God alone exists by the necessity of his nature alone (by Prop. 11 and Coroll. 1 of Prop. 14), and acts by the necessity of his nature alone (by the preceding Proposition). So (by Def. 7) God alone is a free cause.

Scholium

Others think that God is a free cause on account of the fact that he can (so they think) bring it about that the things that we have declared to follow from his nature—that is, which are in his power—do not happen, or, are not produced by him. But this is the same as if they were to say that God can bring it about that it does not follow from the nature of a triangle that its three angles equal two right angles, or, that from a given cause an effect does not follow;[42] which is absurd. Further, I shall show later, without the help of this Proposition, that neither intellect nor will belong to the nature of God. I know that there are many who think that they can demonstrate that a supreme intellect and a free will belong to the nature of God; for they say that they know of nothing that they can ascribe to God which is more perfect than that which is a supreme perfection in us.[43] Further, although they conceive God as actually supremely intelligent, they do not believe that he can bring into existence everything that he actually understands; for they think that in that way they destroy God's power.[44] They say that if he were to create everything that is in his intellect, then he could create nothing further, which they believe to be inconsistent with God's omnipotence. So they have preferred to set up a God who is indifferent towards everything, and who creates only that which he decided to create by some absolute will. But I think that I have shown with sufficient clarity (see Prop. 16) that from the

Proposition 22

Whatever follows from some attribute of God in so far as it is modified by a modification which, through that same attribute, exists both necessarily and as infinite must also exist both necessarily and as infinite.[54]

Demonstration. The demonstration of this Proposition proceeds in the same way as the demonstration of the preceding Proposition.

Proposition 23

Every mode which exists both necessarily and as infinite must necessarily have followed either from the absolute nature of some attribute of God, or from some attribute modified by a modification which exists both necessarily and as infinite.

Demonstration. For a mode is in something else, through which it must be conceived (by Def. 5); that is (by Prop. 15), it is in God alone and can be conceived through God alone. If, therefore, a mode is conceived to exist necessarily and to be infinite, each one of these must necessarily be inferred, i.e. perceived, through some attribute of God, in so far as that is conceived to express infinity and necessity of existence, i.e. (what is the same, by Def. 8) eternity, that is (by Def. 6 and Prop. 19), in so far as it is considered absolutely. Therefore, a mode which exists both necessarily and as infinite must necessarily have followed from the absolute nature of some attribute of God, either immediately (on which, see Prop. 21) or by the mediation of some modification which follows from its absolute nature; that is (by the preceding proposition), which exists both necessarily and as infinite. QED.

Proposition 24

The essence of things produced by God does not involve existence.

Demonstration. This is evident from Definition 1. For that whose nature, considered in itself, involves existence is a cause of itself, and exists by the necessity of its own nature alone.

Corollary

It follows from this that God is not only the cause of things' beginning to exist, but is also the cause of their persevering in existence; or, to use Scholastic terminology, God is the cause of the being of things. For whether things do or do not exist, as long as we pay attention to their essence, we find it to involve neither existence nor duration. So their essence can be the cause of neither their existence nor their duration; the cause can only be God, to whose nature alone existence belongs (by Prop. 14, Coroll. 1).

Proposition 25

God is the efficient cause, not only of the existence of things, but also of their essence.

Demonstration. If you deny this, then God is not the cause of the essence of things, and so (by Ax. 4) the essence of things can be conceived without God. But this (by Prop. 15) is absurd. Therefore, God is also the cause of the essence of things. QED.

Scholium

This Proposition follows more clearly from Prop. 16. For it follows from this that both the essence and the existence of things must necessarily be inferred from the given divine nature, and (to put it briefly) in the sense in which God is called cause of himself, he is also to be called the cause of all things. This will be established yet more clearly by the following Corollary.

Corollary

Particular things are nothing other than the affections, i.e. the modes, of the attributes of God, by which the attributes of God are expressed in a certain and determinate way. The demonstration is evident from Prop. 15 and Def. 5.

Proposition 26

A thing which has been determined to operate in some way[55] was necessarily so determined by God; and that thing which was not determined by God cannot determine itself to operate.

Demonstration. That through which things are said to be determined to operate in some way is necessarily something positive (as is self-evident). So God, by the necessity of his nature, is the efficient cause of both a thing's essence and its existence (by Props. 25 and 16). This was the first thing to be proved. From this there also follows very clearly that which was put forward for proof in the second place. For if a thing which was not determined by God could determine itself, then the first part of this Proposition would be false; which, as we have shown, is absurd.

Proposition 27

A thing which was determined by God to operate in some way cannot render itself undetermined.

Demonstration. This Proposition is evident from Ax. 3

Proposition 28

Every particular thing, or, any thing which is finite and has a determinate existence, cannot exist or be determined to operate unless it is determined to existence and operation by another cause, which is also finite and has a determinate existence; and again, the latter cause also cannot exist or be determined to operation unless it is determined to existence and operation by another cause, which is also finite and has a determinate existence, and so on to infinity.

Demonstration. Whatever is determined to existence and operation was determined by God in this way (by Prop. 26 and Prop. 24, Coroll.). But that which is finite and has a determinate existence could not have been produced from the absolute nature of some attribute of God; for whatever follows from the absolute nature of some attribute of God is infinite and eternal (by Prop. 21). It must therefore have followed from God, or from some attribute of God, in so far as it is considered as affected by some mode; for nothing exists besides substance and its modes (by Ax. 1 and Defs. 3 and 5), and modes (by Prop. 25, Coroll.) are nothing other than the affections of the attributes of God. But it could not have followed from God, or from some attribute of his, in so far as it was affected by a modification which is eternal and infinite (by Prop. 22). It must therefore have followed from, or have been determined to existence and operation by, God or by some attribute of his, in so far as it is modified by a modification which is finite and has a determinate existence. This was the first thing to be proved. Then again, this cause, or, this mode (by the same reasoning by which we have just demonstrated the first part of this Proposition) must also have been determined by another, which also has a finite and determinate existence; and again this last cause (by the same reasoning) by another; and so on perpetually (by the same reasoning) to infinity. QED.

Scholium[56]

Since certain things must have been produced by God immediately, namely those which follow necessarily from his absolute nature, and other things through the mediation of these[57] (though these other things cannot exist or be conceived without God) it follows, first, that God is the absolutely proximate cause of the things produced by him immediately—absolutely, and not in its own kind, as people say. For the effects of God can neither exist nor be conceived without their cause (by Prop. 15 and Prop. 24, Coroll.). It follows, secondly, that God cannot properly be called the remote cause of particular things—except perhaps in order that we may distinguish them from the things which he produced immediately, or rather, which follow from his absolute nature. For by a remote cause we understand a cause such that it is in no way linked with its effect. But all the things that exist exist in God and depend on God in such a way that without him they can neither exist nor be conceived.

Proposition 29

In Nature there exists nothing contingent, but all things have been determined by the necessity of the divine nature to exist and operate in a certain way.

Demonstration. Whatever exists exists in God (by Prop. 15); but God cannot be called a contingent thing. For (by Prop. 11) he exists necessarily, but not contingently. Next, the modes of the divine nature have followed from it necessarily, but not contingently (by Prop. 16), and they do so either in so far as the divine nature is considered absolutely (by Prop. 21) or in so far as it is considered as determined to act in a certain way (by Prop. 28).[58] Further, God is the cause of these modes, not only in so far as they simply exist (by Prop. 24, Coroll.) but also (by Prop. 26) in so far as they are considered as determined to operate in some way. But if (by the same Proposition) they are not determined by God, it is impossible, and not contingent, that they should determine themselves. On the other hand (by Prop. 27) if they are determined by God, it is impossible, and not contingent, that they should render themselves undetermined. So all things are determined by the necessity of the divine nature not only to exist, but also to exist and operate in a certain way, and there exists nothing contingent. QED.

Scholium

Before I go any further, I wish to explain here—or rather to give a reminder—of what we are to understand by active and passive Nature.[59] For I judge that it has now been established by what has gone before that by 'active Nature' we are to understand that which is in itself and is conceived through itself, or, such attributes of substance as express eternal and infinite essence; that is (by Prop. 14, Coroll. 1, and Prop. 17, Coroll. 2), God, in so far as he is considered as a free cause. By 'passive Nature' I understand everything which follows from the necessity of the nature of God, or, of each of the attributes of God; that is, all the modes of the attributes of God, in so far as they are considered as things which are in God, and which can neither exist nor be conceived without God.

Proposition 30

The actual intellect, whether finite or infinite,[60] must grasp the attributes of God and the affections of God, and nothing else.

Demonstration. A true idea must agree with that of which it is the idea (by Ax. 6); that is (as is self-evident) that which is contained objectively[61] in the intellect must necessarily exist in Nature. But in Nature (by Prop. 14, Coroll. 1) there exists only one substance, namely God, and no other affections (by Prop. 15) than those which exist in God, and which (by the same Proposition) can neither exist nor be conceived without God. Therefore, the actual intellect, whether finite or infinite, must grasp the attributes of God and the affections of God, and nothing else. QED.

Proposition 31

The actual intellect, whether finite or infinite, must (just like will, desire, love,[62] etc.) be related to passive and not to active Nature.

Demonstration. For by intellect we understand (as is self-evident) not absolute thought, but only a certain mode of thinking, which differs from other modes, such as desire, love, etc. So (by Def. 5) it must be conceived through absolute thought; namely (by Prop. 15 and Def. 6), it must be conceived through some attribute of God, which expresses the eternal and infinite essence of thought, in such a way that it can neither exist nor be conceived without that attribute, and so (by Prop. 29, Schol.) it must, like the other modes of thinking, be related to passive and not to active Nature. QED.

Scholium

The reason why I speak here of actual intellect is not that I grant that any potential intellect exists, but that (since I desire to avoid all confusion) I wanted to speak only of what is perceived by us with the greatest clarity—namely, of understanding itself, than which we perceive nothing more clearly. For we can understand nothing that does not lead us to a more perfect knowledge of understanding.

Proposition 32

Will cannot be called a free cause, but can only be called a necessary cause.

Demonstration. Will is only a certain mode of thinking,[63] like the intellect; so (by Prop. 28) each volition cannot exist or be determined to operate unless it is determined by another cause, and that again by another, and so on to infinity. Now if will is supposed to be infinite, it must also be determined to existence and to operation by God, not in so far as he is an absolutely infinite substance, but in so far as he has an attribute which expresses the infinite and eternal essence of thought (by Prop. 23). So however the will is conceived—whether as finite or as infinite—it requires a cause by which it is determined to existence and to operation . So (by Def. 7) it cannot be called a free cause, but can only be called a cause that is necessary, or compelled. QED.

Corollary 1

From this it follows, first, that God does not operate by means of freedom of will.

Corollary 2

It follows, secondly, that will and intellect are related to the nature of God as are motion and rest, and, absolutely speaking, as are all natural things which (by Prop. 29) must be determined by God to exist and to operate in a certain way. For the will, like everything else, requires a cause by which it is determined to existence and to operation in a certain way. And although infinite things follow from a given will, i.e. intellect,[64] yet God cannot on this account be said to act by means of freedom of will, any more than he can be said to act by means of freedom of motion and rest on account of the things that follow from motion and rest (for infinite things follow from these as well). So will does not belong to the nature of God any more than other natural things do, but it is related to that nature in the same way as motion and rest, and all other things which we have shown to follow from the necessity of the divine nature and to be determined by it to existence and operation in a certain way.[65]

Proposition 33

Things could not have been produced by God in any other way, or in any other order, than that in which they were produced.

Demonstration. For all things have followed necessarily from the given nature of God (by Prop. 16), and were determined by the necessity of the nature of God to exist and to operate in a certain way (by Prop. 29). So if things of another nature could exist or be determined to operate in another way, so that the order of nature were different, then the nature of God as well could be other than what it now is. Consequently (by Prop. 11) that nature too must exist, and consequently there could exist two or more Gods, which (by Prop. 14, Coroll. 1) is absurd. Consequently, things could not have been produced by God in any other way or in any other order, etc. QED.

Scholium 1

Since I have just shown, more clearly than the light of noon, that nothing exists absolutely in things on account of which they may be called contingent, I want now to explain in a few words what we are to understand by 'contingent'. First, however, I will explain what we are to understand by 'necessary' and 'impossible'. A thing is called 'necessary', either in respect of its essence, or in respect of its cause. For the existence of some thing follows necessarily either from its essence and definition, or from a given efficient cause. Next, some thing is called 'impossible' from these causes again: namely, either because the thing's essence, i.e. definition, involves a contradiction, or because there exists no external cause which is determined to the production of such a thing. But a thing is called 'contingent' only with regard to a defect in our knowledge. For consider a thing whose essence we do not know to involve a contradiction, or of which we know well that its essence does not involve a contradiction, and yet we can affirm nothing with certainty about its existence, because the order of causes escapes us: this thing can never appear to us either as necessary or as impossible, and therefore we call it either contingent or possible.

Scholium 2

From what has gone before it follows clearly that things were produced by God with supreme perfection; for they have followed necessarily from a given most perfect nature. Nor does this accuse God of any imperfection, for it is his perfection that has made us affirm this. Indeed, from the contrary of this it would follow clearly (as I have just shown) that God is not supremely perfect. The reason is that if things had been produced in another way, then another nature must be ascribed to God, different from that which we were compelled to ascribe to him from a consideration of the most perfect entity. However, I do not doubt that many will reject this opinion as absurd, and will be unwilling to examine it closely. The cause of this is simply that they have become accustomed to ascribing to God a freedom—namely, an absolute will—which is far different from that which we (Def. 7) have established.[66] However, I also do not doubt that if they were willing to think about the matter, and consider properly the sequence of our demonstrations, they would entirely reject freedom of the kind that they now ascribe to God as being not only worthless, but also a major obstacle to knowledge. There is no need for me to repeat here what was said in Prop. 17, Schol. However, for the benefit of my opponents I will show further that even if it is granted that will belongs to the essence of God[67], it follows none the less from his perfection that things could not have been created by God in any other way or in any other order. It will be easy to show this if we consider first something that they themselves grant: namely, that it depends solely on the decree and the will of God that each thing is what it is. For otherwise God would not be the cause of all things. Next, we must consider the fact that all the decrees of God were enacted by him from eternity; for otherwise he would be accused of imperfection and inconstancy. But since there is no 'when', 'before', or 'after' in eternity, it follows from this—namely, from God's perfection—that God can never decree anything else, and never could have done so. In other words, it follows that God did not exist before his decrees, and cannot exist without them. But they will say that[68] even if it is supposed that God had made a different universe, or that he had decreed from eternity something different about Nature and its order, no imperfection would follow in God from this. However, if they say this, they concede at the same time that God could have changed his decrees. For if God had decreed something other than what he did decree about Nature and its order—that is, if he had willed and conceived something different about Nature—he would necessarily have had an intellect which is different from the one that he now has, and a will which is different from the one that he now has. And if it is permissible to ascribe to God a different intellect and a different will without any change in his essence and his perfection, then why should he not be able to change his decrees about created things now, whilst still remaining equally perfect? For his intellect and will concerning created things and their order is the same in respect of his essence and perfection, in whatever way it is conceived. Further, all the philosophers whom I have read concede that there is no potential intellect in God, but only actual intellect. But since both his intellect and his will are not distinguished from his essence, as they all concede as well, it follows from this too that if God had another actual intellect and another will, his essence would also necessarily have been different. Therefore (as I concluded at the outset) if things had been produced by God as different from what they now are, then the intellect and will of God, that is (as is conceded), his essence, must have been different, which is absurd.

Since, therefore, things could have been produced by God in no other way and in no other order, and since the fact that this is true follows from the supreme perfection of God, no sound reason can persuade us to believe that God was unwilling to create all the things that are in his intellect with the very same perfection which he understands them to have.[69] But, people will say, there is in things no perfection or imperfection; that which is in them on account of which they are called perfect or imperfect, and good or bad, depends solely on the will of God.[70] So, if God had willed it, he could have brought it about that what is now a perfection would have been a supreme imperfection, and conversely. But this is simply to state openly that God, who necessarily understands what he wills, could bring it about by his will that he understands things in a way which is other than that in which he does understand them; and this (as I have just shown) is a great absurdity. So I can turn the argument against them in the following way. All things depend on the power of God. So in order that things may be different, the will of God must necessarily also be different; but the will of God cannot be different (as we have just shown with the greatest clarity from the perfection of God). Neither, therefore, can things be different. I confess that this view, which subjects everything to a kind of indifferent will of God, and which asserts that all things depend on his good pleasure, is less far from the truth than that of those who assert that God does everything with the good in mind.[71] For the latter seem to posit something outside God, which does not depend on God, to which God looks as a kind of exemplar when he works, or at which he aims as if it were a fixed target. This is nothing other than to subject God to fate; and nothing can be said of God that is more absurd than this. For we have shown God to be the first and the sole free cause of both the essence and the existence of things. So there is no need for me to spend time on refuting this absurdity.

Proposition 34

The power of God is his essence.

Demonstration. For it follows simply from the necessity of the essence of God that God is the cause of himself (by Prop. 11) and (by Prop. 16 and its Corollary) of all things. Therefore, the power of God, by which he himself and all things exist and act, is his essence. QED.

Proposition 35

Whatever we conceive to be in the power of God necessarily exists.

Demonstration. For whatever is in the power of God must (by the preceding Proposition) be included in his essence in such a way that it follows necessarily from it, and so it necessarily exists. QED.

Proposition 36

Nothing exists from whose nature some effect does not follow.

Demonstration. Whatever exists expresses the nature, i.e. the essence, of God in a certain and determinate way (by Prop. 25, Coroll.). That is (by Prop. 34), whatever exists expresses in a certain and determinate way the power of God, which is the cause of all things, and so (by Prop. 16) some effect must follow from it.

Appendix

With this I have explained the nature and properties of God, such as that he necessarily exists; that he is unique; that he exists and acts solely by the necessity of his own nature; that he is the free cause of all things, and in what way; that all things exist in God, and depend on him in such a way that without him they can neither exist nor be conceived; and finally that all things were predetermined by God, not out of freedom of will, i.e. his absolute good pleasure, but from the absolute nature of God, i.e. his infinite power. Further, whenever an opportunity arose, I have tried to remove prejudices which could hinder the perception of my demonstrations. But since there still remain many prejudices which have had, and still have, the power to constitute a major obstacle to men's understanding of the interconnection of all things as I have explained it, I have thought it worth while here to summon these to the court of reason.[72] All the prejudices that I undertake to point out here depend on one fact: that men commonly suppose that all natural things act on account of an end, as they themselves do. Indeed they think it certain that God himself directs all things towards a certain end, for they say that God has made everything on account of man, and man in order that he might worship God.[73] This, therefore, I shall consider first. I shall seek first of all the cause of the fact that many people acquiesce in this prejudice, and that all people are inclined by nature to embrace it. Then I shall show that it is false, and finally how prejudices about good and bad, merit and wrongdoing, praise and blame, order and confusion, beauty and deformity, and other matters of this sort, have arisen from it.[74] However, this is not the place to deduce these from the nature of the human mind. It will be sufficient if I take as a basis here something which everyone must admit: namely, that all human beings are born ignorant of the causes of things, and that all have an appetite for seeking what is useful to them, and that they are conscious of this. For from this it follows, first, that human beings think themselves to be free in so far as they are conscious of their volitions and of their appetite, and do not even dream of the causes by which they are led to appetition and to will, since they are ignorant of them. It follows, secondly, that human beings do everything on account of an end; namely, on account of something that is useful, which they seek. From this it comes about that they always seek to know only the final causes of things that have been done, and when they have heard these they are satisfied, because they have no cause for future doubt. But if they cannot learn these final causes from another, nothing remains for them but to turn to themselves and to reflect on the ends by which they themselves are usually determined to similar things, and so they necessarily judge the mind of another from their own mind. Further, since they find, both inside and outside themselves, many means which contribute greatly to the procurement of what is useful to them—for example, eyes for seeing, teeth for chewing, vegetables and animals for food, the sun for light, the sea for breeding fish—it has come about that they consider all natural things as if they were means to what is useful for them. And since they know that these means were discovered and not made by them, they had reason to believe that there is someone else who made these means for their use. For after they had considered things as means, they could not believe that they themselves had made these things, but they had to infer, from the means that they themselves commonly made for themselves, that there exists some governor or governors of Nature, endowed with human freedom, who have taken care of everything for them, and have made everything for their use. And since they had never heard anything about the mind of these beings, they had to judge it from their own, and so they asserted that the gods arrange everything for the use of men, in order that they might bind men to them and be held by them in the highest honour. From this it came about that each person, in accordance with his own way of thinking, thought out different ways of worshipping God, so that God might love them above the rest, and direct the whole of Nature to the advantage of their blind desire and insatiable avarice. So this prejudice turned into a superstition, and put down deep roots in the mind, which was the cause of the fact that each person endeavoured mightily to understand and to explain the final causes of all things. But whilst they tried to show that Nature does nothing in vain[75] (that is, nothing that is not to the advantage of men), they seem to have shown simply that Nature and the gods are as mad as men. For just look at the way in which things have finally turned out! Among so many things in Nature which are advantageous they were bound to find many which are not, such as storms, earthquakes, diseases, etc., and they judged that these occurred because the gods were angry on account of the injuries that men had done to them, or, on account of faults that they had committed in worshipping them. And although experience cried out daily, and showed with an infinity of examples that advantages and disadvantages happen indiscriminately to the pious and the impious alike, they did not on this account cease from their inveterate prejudice. For it was easier for them to place this among other unknown things of whose use they were ignorant, and so to retain their present and inborn state of ignorance, rather than destroy that whole fabric and devise a new one. So they thought it certain that the judgements of the gods vastly surpass human comprehension; which would of itself have been sufficient to cause truth to be hidden from the human race for eternity, had not mathematics, which is concerned not with ends but solely with the essences and properties of figures, shown to human beings another standard of truth. Besides mathematics one could state other causes (which it is superfluous to list here) which could have brought it about that men took note of these common prejudices, and were led to the true knowledge of things.

With this, I have given a satisfactory explanation of what I promised in the first place.[76] I do not need many words in order to show now that Nature has no end which is pre-established for it, and that all final causes are nothing but human inventions. For I think that this has already been satisfactorily established—both from basic principles, and from the causes from which I showed this prejudice to have originated, as well as from Prop. 16 and the Corollaries of Prop. 32, and then again from all those passages in which I showed that all natural things proceed with a certain eternal necessity and with supreme perfection. However, I will add this point: that this doctrine of the end completely overturns Nature. For that which is really a cause it considers as an effect, and conversely. Then again, that which is prior in nature it makes posterior; and finally, that which is supreme and most perfect it makes most imperfect. For (omitting the first two, which are self-evident) it is established by Props. 21, 22, and 23 that that effect is the most perfect which is produced by God immediately, and that the more intermediate causes something needs in order to be produced, the more imperfect it is. But if the things which have been produced immediately by God were made in order that God might achieve his end, then necessarily the ultimate things, because of which the prior things were made, would be the most excellent of all. Then again, this doctrine takes away the perfection of God; for if God acts on account of an end, he necessarily desires something which he lacks. And although theologians and metaphysicians distinguish between the end of lack and the end of assimilation,[77] yet they admit that God did all things for his own sake and not on account of the things to be created. For they cannot point to anything before creation on account of which God acts, apart from God; and so they are necessarily compelled to admit that God lacked those things for which he wished to prepare the means, and that he desired them, as is self evident. Nor should one ignore here the fact that the supporters of this doctrine, who wished to show their ingenuity in assigning the ends of things, produced a new method of argument in order to prove this doctrine of theirs: namely, by a reduction, not to the impossible, but to ignorance, which shows that there was no other means of arguing for this doctrine. For example, if a stone fell off a roof on to someone's head and killed him, they will show in the following way that the stone fell in order to kill the man. They will say that unless the stone fell in this way, by the will of God, how could so many circumstances (for many circumstances often come together at the same time) occur by chance? Perhaps you will reply that this came about because the wind was blowing, and the man was walking in that particular direction. But (they will insist) why was the wind blowing at that time? Why was the man walking that way at the very same time? If you reply that the wind was blowing at that time because, after a period of calm weather, the sea began to toss on the previous day, and the man had been invited by a friend, they will again press you—for there is no end to questioning—by asking why the sea was tossing, and why the man had been invited for that particular time. So they will not cease to ask for the causes of causes, until you take refuge in the will of God, that is, the asylum of ignorance. Similarly, when they see the structure of the human body, they are amazed; and because they are ignorant of the causes of such great art, they conclude that it was constructed and established in such a way that one part does not damage another, not by the art of mechanics, but by divine or supernatural art. So it comes about that someone who seeks the true causes of miracles, and whose concern it is to understand natural things like a man of learning, and not to marvel at them like a fool, is commonly taken to be heretical and impious, and is proclaimed as such by those whom the mob adores as interpreters of Nature and of the gods.[78] For the latter know that if ignorance is removed, then the wonder which is their sole means of arguing and of protecting their authority is removed also. But I leave this aside, and pass to what I arranged to discuss here as my third topic.

After human beings had persuaded themselves that all the things that happen happen on account of them, they were bound to consider as most important in each thing that which was most useful to them, and to reckon as most excellent those things by which they were best affected. So they had to form the following notions, by which they explained the nature of things: namely, good, bad, order, confusion, hot, cold, beauty, and ugliness. Further, since they think themselves free, the following notions have arisen: namely, praise, blame, wrongdoing, and merit. I will describe the latter below,[79] after I have discussed human nature; however, I will briefly explain the former here. Everything that contributes to health and to the worship of God they have called 'good', and the opposite of these they have called 'bad'. And since those who do not understand the nature of things, but only imagine them, affirm nothing of things and take imagination for understanding, they therefore firmly believe that there is an order in things, ignorant as they are of things and of their own nature. For when things are so arranged that when they are represented to us by the senses we can easily imagine them, and consequently can recollect them easily, we call them well ordered; if the contrary is the case we call them badly ordered, or, confused. And since those things which we can easily imagine are more pleasant to us than others are, human beings prefer order to confusion— as if order were something in Nature besides its relation to our imagination—and say that God created everything in an orderly way. In this way they ascribe to God, in their ignorance, imagination; unless perhaps they want to say that God, out of regard for human imagination, arranged all things in an order in which they could most easily be imagined. Nor, perhaps, are they led to hesitate by the fact that an infinity of things are found that far surpass our imagination, and many things are found that confuse it because of its weakness. But enough of this. Then again, other concepts are nothing but ways of imagining, by which the imagination is affected in various ways, and yet they are considered by the ignorant as if they were important attributes of things.

This is because, as we have said already, the ignorant believe that all things have been made on their account, and they say that the nature of some thing is good or bad, healthy or putrid or corrupt, in accordance with the way in which they are affected by it. For example, if the motion which the nerves receive from objects which are represented through the eyes conduces to health, then the objects by which it is caused are called beautiful, but those which excite the opposite motion are called deformed. Then those that excite the sense through the nostrils are called fragrant or fetid, and those that excite the sense through the tongue are called sweet or bitter, tasty or insipid, and so on. Further, those that excite the sense through touch are called hard or soft, rough or smooth, and so on. Finally, those that excite the ears are said to produce noise, sound, or harmony. The last of these has so crazed human beings that they believed that God, too, is delighted by harmony; again, there were some philosophers who persuaded themselves that the movements of the heavenly bodies produce a harmony. All this shows sufficiently that each person has judged about things in accordance with the disposition of his brain, or rather that he has accepted the affections of the imagination as things. So it is not surprising (to note this in passing) that there have arisen among men the many controversies that we experience, from which scepticism has finally arisen. For although human bodies agree in many things, they also disagree in very many things, and so what seems good to one seems bad to another; what seems ordered to one seems confused to another; what is pleasant to one is unpleasant to another—and so with other things, which I pass by here, both because this is not the place at which to discuss these at length, and because everyone has sufficient experience of this. For everybody says that there are as many heads as there are opinions, that everyone is full of his own wisdom, and that as brains differ, so do tastes. These sayings show sufficiently that human beings judge about things in accordance with the disposition of their brain, and that they imagine things rather than understand them. For if they understood things, then those things (as mathematics bears witness) would at any rate convince them, even if they did not attract them.

So we see that all the notions by which the common people are accustomed to explain Nature are only modes of the imagination and that they indicate, not the nature of any thing, but only the constitution of the imagination. Since they have names which are as it were the names of entities which exist outside the imagination, I call them entities, not of reason, but of the imagination.[80] So all the arguments which people seek against us from similar notions can easily be repulsed. For many people tend to argue like this: if all things have followed from the necessity of the most perfect nature of God, how does it come about that so many imperfections have arisen in Nature?—for example, the fact that things go rotten and eventually become putrid; the deformity of things which produces nausea; confusion, badness, wrongdoing, and so on. But, as I have just said, they are easily refuted. For the perfection of things is to be estimated from their nature and power alone, nor are things more or less perfect on account of the fact that they delight or offend human senses, or that they assist human nature or are repugnant to it. But to those who ask why God did not create all men in such a way that they were governed only by the guidance of reason, I simply reply that this was because he did not lack the material for creating all things, from the highest to the lowest grade of perfection; or, to speak more properly, because the laws of his nature were so ample that they were sufficient for creating everything that can be conceived by an infinite intellect, as I have demonstrated in Prop. 16.

These are the prejudices that I undertook to note here. If any of this kind still remain, they can be corrected, with a little meditation, by anyone.

End of the First Part

PART TWO

ON THE NATURE AND ORIGIN[1] OF THE MIND

I pass now to an explanation of those things that necessarily had to follow from the essence of God, or, an eternal and infinite entity. Not, however, all of them; for we demonstrated in Prop. 16, Part 1, that from that essence there must follow infinite things in infinite ways. I shall explain only those things that can lead us, as it were by the hand, to a knowledge of the human mind and of its supreme blessedness.

Definitions

1. By body I understand a mode which expresses in a certain and determinate way the essence of God, in so far as he is considered as an extended thing. See Prop. 25, Coroll., Part 1.

2. I say that there belongs to the essence of a thing[2] that which, being given, the thing is necessarily posited, and which, being taken away, the thing is necessarily negated; or that without which a thing can neither exist nor be conceived, and conversely that which can neither exist nor be conceived without the thing.

3. By an idea I understand a conception[3] of the mind, which the mind forms on account of the fact that it is a thinking thing.

Explanation. I say 'conception' rather than 'perception',[4] because the word 'perception' seems to indicate that the mind is in a passive relation to an object; but 'conception' seems to express an action of the mind.[5]

4. By an adequate idea I understand an idea which, in so far as it is considered in itself without relation to its object, has all the properties, or, the intrinsic denominations, of a true idea.

Explanation. I say 'intrinsic' so that I may exclude what is extrinsic,[6] namely the agreement of the idea with that of which it is the idea.

5. Duration is the indefinite continuation of existing.

Explanation. I say 'indefinite', because it cannot be determined in any way by the nature of the existing thing, nor again by an efficient cause, which necessarily posits the existence of a thing and does not negate it.

6. By reality and perfection I understand the same.

7. By particular things I understand things which are finite and have a determinate existence. But if a number of individuals concur in one action in such a way that all are simultaneously the cause of one effect, then to this extent I consider all of them as one particular thing.

Axioms

1. The essence of man does not involve necessary existence; that is, it can come about by the order of Nature that this or that man exists just as much as that he does not exist.

2. Man thinks.

3. Modes of thinking, such as love, desire, or whatever emotions[7] of the mind are distinguished by name, do not exist unless there exists in the same individual the idea of the thing that is loved or desired, etc. But an idea can exist, even though there exists no other mode of thinking.

4. We sense a certain body to be affected in many ways.

5. We neither sense not perceive any particular things apart from bodies and modes of thinking.

For Postulates, see after Proposition 13.

Proposition 1

Thought is an attribute of God, or, God is a thinking thing.

Demonstration. Particular thoughts, i.e. this or that thought, are modes which express the nature of God in a certain and determinate way (by Prop. 25, Coroll., Part 1). There therefore belongs to God (by Def. 5, Part 1) an attribute, the conception of which involves all particular thoughts, through which they are also conceived. Thought, therefore, is one of the infinite attributes of God, which expresses the eternal and infinite essence of God (see Def. 6, Part 1), or, God is a thinking thing. QED.

Scholium

This Proposition is also evident from the fact that we can conceive an infinite thinking entity. For the more things an infinite entity can think, the more reality, i.e. the more perfection we conceive it to contain;[8] therefore, an entity which can conceive infinite things in infinite ways is necessarily infinite by its power of thinking. Since, therefore, we may conceive an infinite entity by attending to thought alone, thought (by Defs. 4 and 6, Part 1) is necessarily one of the infinite attributes of God, as we wished to prove.

Proposition 2

Extension is an attribute of God, or, God is an extended thing.

Demonstration. The demonstration of this Proposition proceeds in the same way as the demonstration of the preceding one.

Proposition 3

In God there necessarily exists an idea both of his essence and of all the things that follow necessarily from his essence.

Demonstration. For God (by Prop. 1, Part 2) can think infinite things in infinite ways, or (what is the same, by Prop. 16, Part 1), he can form an idea of his essence and of all the things that follow necessarily from it. But everything that is in God's power necessarily exists (by Prop. 35, Part 1); therefore, such an idea necessarily exists, and (by Prop. 15, Part 1) exists only in God. QED.

Scholium

The common people[9] understand by the power of God his free will and his right over all the things that exist; consequently, these things are commonly considered as contingent. For they say that God has the power of destroying everything, and of reducing it to nothing. Further, they very often compare the power of God with the power of kings. But we have refuted this view in Prop. 32, Corolls. 1 and 2, Part 1, and we showed in Prop. 16, Part 1, that God acts by the same necessity as that by which he understands himself; that is, just as it follows from the necessity of the divine nature that God understands himself (as all assert unanimously), so it follows with the same necessity that God does infinite things in infinite ways. Further, we showed in Proposition 34 of Part 1 that the power of God is simply the actual essence of God; so it is just as impossible for us to conceive that God does not act as it is impossible for us to conceive that God does not exist. If I were at liberty to pursue these matters further, I could also show here that that power which the common people attach to God is not only human power (which shows that God is conceived by the common people as a man, or as like a man) but also involves a lack of power. But I do not wish to discuss the same subject so many times. I simply ask the reader, again and again, to consider repeatedly what has been said about this in the first Part, from Proposition 16 to the end. For no one can see properly what I have in mind without taking great care not to confuse the power of God with the human power or right of kings.

Proposition 4

The idea of God, from which infinite things follow in infinite ways, can only be unique.

Demonstration. An infinite intellect grasps nothing apart from the attributes of God and his affections (by Prop. 30, Part 1). But God is unique (by Prop. 14, Coroll. 1, Part 1); therefore, the idea of God, from which infinite things follow in infinite ways, can only be unique. QED.

Proposition 5

The formal being[10] of ideas recognizes God as a cause only in so far as he is considered as a thinking thing, and not in so far as he is explained by another attribute. That is, the ideas both of the attributes of God and of particular things recognize as their efficient cause, not those things of which they are the ideas, i.e. the things perceived, but God himself, in so far as he is a thinking thing.

Demonstration. This is evident from Prop. 3 of this part. For there we concluded that God can form an idea of his essence, and of all the things that follow necessarily from it, simply from the fact that he is a thinking thing, and not from the fact that he is the object of his idea. Therefore, the formal being of ideas recognizes God as its cause, only[11] in so far as he is a thinking thing. This is demonstrated in another way, as follows. The formal being of ideas is a mode of thinking (as is self-evident); that is (by Prop. 25, Coroll., Part 1), a mode which expresses in a certain way the nature of God, in so far as he is a thinking thing. So (by Prop. 10, Part 1) it involves the conception of no other attribute of God, and consequently (by Ax. 4, Part 1) it is the effect[12] of no other attribute apart from thought. So the formal being of the ideas of God recognizes God as a cause only in so far as he is a thinking thing. QED.

Proposition 6

The modes of each attribute have God as a cause in so far as he is considered only under that attribute of which they are modes, and not in so far as he is considered under any other attribute.

Demonstration. For each attribute is considered through itself without any other (by Prop. 10, Part 1). So the modes of each attribute involve the concept of their own attribute, but not of another; and so (by Ax. 4, Part 1) they have God as a cause in so far as he is considered only under that attribute of which they are modes, and not in so far as he is considered under any other attribute. QED.

Corollary

It follows from this that the formal being of things which are not modes of thinking does not follow from the divine nature because it knew things first;[13] the things of which we have ideas follow from and are inferred from their attributes in the same way, and with the same necessity, as we have shown ideas to follow from the attribute of thought.

Proposition 7

The order and connection of ideas is the same as the order and connection of things.[14]

Demonstration. This is evident from Ax. 4, Part 1. For the idea of each thing that is caused depends on the knowledge of the cause of which it is an effect.

Corollary

It follows from this that God's power of thinking is the equal of his actual power of doing. That is, whatever follows formally from the infinite nature of God follows objectively[15] in God from the idea of God, in the same order and with the same connection.

Scholium[16]

Here, before we proceed any further, we must recall what we showed above:[17] namely, that whatever can be perceived by an infinite intellect as constituting the essence of substance belongs to a unique substance alone, and consequently that thinking substance and extended substance is one and the same substance, which is understood now under this and now under that attribute. So also a mode of extension and the idea of that mode is one and the same thing, but expressed in two ways—which some Hebrews[18] appear to have seen as if through a cloud, in asserting that God, the intellect of God, and the things understood by him are one and the same. For example, a circle existing in Nature[19] and the idea of the existing circle, which is also in God, is one and the same thing, which is explained through different attributes. So whether we conceive Nature under the attribute of extension, or under the attribute of thought, or under any other attribute whatsoever,[20] we shall find one and the same order, or, one and the same connection of causes; that is, we shall find that the same things follow reciprocally. Again, I said that God is the cause of (for example) the idea of a circle only in so far as he is a thinking thing, and of a circle only in so far as he is an extended thing, solely because the formal being of idea of the circle can be perceived only through some other mode of thinking as its proximate cause, and that again through another mode of thinking, and so on to infinity, so that as long as things are conceived as modes of thinking, we must explain the whole of Nature, i.e. the connection of causes, through the attribute of thought alone. Again, in so far as things are considered as modes of extension, the order of the whole of Nature must be explained through the attribute of extension alone; and I understand the same of the other attributes. So God is truly the cause of things as they are in themselves in so far as he consists of infinite attributes—something which I cannot explain more clearly at present.

Proposition 8

The ideas of particular things, i.e. of modes, that do not exist must be included in the infinite idea of God[21] in the same way as the formal essences of particular things, i.e. of modes, are contained in the attributes of God.

Demonstration. This proposition is evident from the preceding one, but is understood more clearly from the preceding Scholium.

Corollary

It follows from this that, as long as particular things exist only in so far as they are included in the attributes of God, their objective being, i.e. ideas, exist only in so far as the infinite idea of God exists; and when particular things are said to exist, not only in so far as they are included in the attributes of God, but also in so far as they are said to endure, their ideas will also include the existence through which they are said to endure.

Scholium

If anyone requires an example in order to have this matter explained more fully, I cannot of course provide one which explains adequately what I am discussing, since it is unique. However, I will try to illustrate it as far as possible. A circle is of such a nature that, for all the straight lines

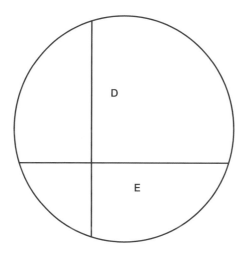

that intersect each other within it, the rectangles within their segments are equal to each other. So there are contained within a circle an infinity of rectangles that are equal to each other. However, none of these can be said to exist except in so far as the circle exists, nor again can the idea of any one of these rectangles be said to exist, except in so far as it is included in the idea of the circle. Let there now be conceived to exist, of this infinity of lines, just two, namely E and D. Clearly, the ideas of these also exist not only in so far as they are included solely in the idea of the circle, but also in so far as they involve the existence of these rectangles, by which it comes about that they are distinguished from the remaining ideas of the remaining rectangles.

Proposition 9

The idea of a particular thing that actually exists has God for a cause, not in so far as he is infinite, but in so far as he is considered as affected by another idea of a particular thing that actually exists, of which God is also the cause in so far as he is considered as affected by another, third idea, and so on to infinity.

Demonstration. The idea of a particular thing that actually exists is a particular mode of thinking, and is distinct from the rest (by the Coroll. and Schol. of Prop. 8, Part 2), and so it has as its cause God, in so far as he is solely a thinking thing (by Prop. 6, Part 2). But not (by Prop. 28, Part 1) in so far as he is a thing that thinks absolutely, but in so far as he is considered as affected by another mode of thinking; and of this also God is the cause in so far as he is affected by another mode, and so on to infinity. But (by Prop. 7, Part 2) the order and connection of ideas is the same as the order and connection of causes. Therefore, the cause of one particular idea is another idea, or, God in so far as he is considered as affected by another idea, and of this idea also God is the cause in so far as he is affected by another, and so on to infinity. QED.

Corollary

The knowledge of whatever happens in the particular object of any idea exists in God only in so far as he has the idea of that object.

Demonstration. The idea of whatever happens in the object of any idea exists in God (by Prop. 3, Part 2), not in so far as he is infinite, but in so far as he is considered as affected by another idea of a particular thing (by the preceding Proposition). But (by Prop. 7, Part 2) the order and connection of ideas is the same as the order and connection of things. Therefore, the knowledge of that which happens in some particular object will be in God only in so far as he has the idea of that object. QED.

Proposition 10

The being of substance does not belong to the essence of man; or, substance does not constitute the form of man.[22]

Demonstration. For the being of substance involves necessary existence (by Prop. 7, Part 1). If, therefore, the being of substance were to belong to the essence of man, then given that substance exists, man would necessarily exist (by Def. 2, Part 2), and consequently man necessarily exists, which (by Ax. 1, Part 2) is absurd. Therefore, etc. QED.

Scholium

This Proposition is also demonstrated from Prop. 5, Part 1, namely that there do not exist two substances of the same nature. For since several men can exist, it follows that that which constitutes the form of man is not the being of substance. Further, this Proposition is also evident from the remaining properties of substance, namely that it is by its nature infinite, immutable, indivisible, etc., as anyone can easily see.

Corollary

From this it follows that the essence of man is constituted by certain modifications of the attributes of God.

Demonstration. For the being of substance (by the preceding Proposition) does not belong to the essence of man. The essence of man, therefore (by Prop. 15, Part 1), is something that is in God, and which cannot exist or be conceived without God, or, it is (by Prop. 25, Coroll., Part 1) an affection, i.e. a mode, which expresses the nature of God in a certain and determinate way.

Scholium

Everyone must surely admit that without God, nothing can exist or be conceived. For everyone acknowledges that God is the unique cause of all things, in respect of both their essence and their existence; that is, God is the cause of things not only in respect of their coming into existence, as people say, but also in respect of their being.[23] However, several say that there belongs to the essence of some thing that without which the thing can neither exist nor be conceived; so they either believe that the essence of God belongs to the essence of created things, or they believe that created things can either exist or be conceived without God, or, what is more certain, they are not self-consistent. I believe that the cause of this was that they did not keep to the order of philosophizing. For the divine nature—which they ought to have contemplated before all things, since it is prior both in knowledge and in Nature—was believed by them to be last in the order of knowledge; further, the things which are called the objects of the senses were believed by them to be the first of all things.[24] The result of this was that while they contemplated natural things, they ignored the divine nature; and when they later directed their mind to the contemplation of the divine nature, they had to ignore their first fictions, on which they had built the knowledge of natural things, inasmuch as these could give them no help towards a knowledge of the divine nature. So it is not surprising that they often contradicted themselves. But I leave this aside. For my intention here was simply to explain why I did not say[25] that there belongs to the essence of a thing that without which the thing can neither exist nor be conceived. This was because particular things can neither exist nor be conceived without God; yet God does not belong to their essence. Instead of this I said that there necessarily constitutes the essence of a thing that which, being given, the thing is posited, and which, being taken away, the thing is negated; or that without which a thing can neither exist nor be conceived, and conversely that which can neither exist nor be conceived without the thing.

Proposition 11

The first thing that constitutes the actual being of the human mind is simply the idea of some particular thing which actually exists.

Demonstration. The essence of man (by the Corollary of the preceding

Proposition) is constituted by certain modes of the attributes of God; namely (by Axiom 2, Part 2), the modes of thinking. Of all these modes (by Axiom 3, Part 2), the idea is prior in nature, and this idea being given the other modes (namely, those to which the idea is prior in nature) must be in the same individual (by Axiom 3, Part 2). And so an idea is the first thing which constitutes the being of the human mind. But not the idea of a thing which does not exist. For then (by Prop 8, Coroll., Part 2) the idea itself could not be said to exist. The idea, then, will be the idea of a thing that actually exists. But it will not be the idea of an infinite thing; for an infinite thing (by Props. 21 and 22, Part 1) must always necessarily exist. But in the present case (by Ax. 1, Part 2) this is absurd; therefore, the first thing that constitutes the actual being of the human mind is the idea of a particular thing which actually exists. QED.

Corollary

From this it follows that the human mind is a part of the infinite intellect of God. Therefore, when we say that the human mind perceives this or that, we are simply saying that God—not in so far as he is infinite, but in so far as he is explained through the nature of the human mind, or, in so far as he constitutes the essence of the human mind—has this or that idea. And when we say that God has this or that idea, not only in so far as he constitutes the nature of the human mind, but also in so far as he has, simultaneously with the human mind, the idea of another thing, then we say that the human mind perceives the thing partially, i.e. inadequately.

Scholium

Here, without any doubt, my readers will be in trouble, and will think of many things that will bring them to a halt. For this reason I ask them to proceed slowly along with me, and not to judge these matters until they have read everything.[26]

Proposition 12

Whatever happens in the object of the idea constituting the human mind must be perceived by the human mind, or, there will necessarily exist in the human mind an idea of this thing. That is, if the object of the idea constituting the human mind is a body,[27] nothing can happen in that body which is not perceived by the mind.

Demonstration. For a knowledge of whatever happens in the object of each idea necessarily exists in God (by Prop. 9, Coroll., Part 2), in so far as he is conceived as affected by the idea of that object; that is (by Prop. 11, Part 2), in so far as he constitutes the mind of some thing. Therefore, a knowledge of whatever happens in the object of the idea constituting the human mind necessarily exists in God in so far as he constitutes the nature of the human mind; that is (by Prop. 11, Coroll., Part 2), the knowledge of this thing will necessarily be in the mind, or, the mind perceives it. QED.

Scholium

This Proposition is also evident, and is understood more clearly, from Prop. 7, Schol., Part 2, which see.

Proposition 13

The object of the idea constituting the human mind is the body,[28] or, a certain actually existing mode of extension, and nothing else.

Demonstration. For if the body were not the object of the human mind, the ideas of the affections of the body would be in God (by Prop. 9, Coroll., Part 2), not in so far as he constitutes our mind, but in so far as he constitutes the mind of another thing; that is (by Prop. 11, Coroll., Part 2), the ideas of the affections of the body would not be in our mind. But (by Ax. 4, Part 2) we do have ideas of the affections of the body. Therefore, the object of the idea constituting the human mind is the body, and indeed (by Prop. 11, Part 2) the actually existent body. Further, if there were some object of the mind besides the body, then (since, by Prop. 36, Part 1, nothing exists from which some effect does not follow) there must necessarily (by Prop. 12, Part 2) exist in our mind the idea of some effect of that object of the mind. But (by Ax. 5, Part 2) there is no idea of this. Therefore, the object of our mind is the existent body, and nothing else. QED.

Corollary

From this it follows that man consists of mind and body, and that the human body exists as we sense it.[29]

Scholium

From this we understand, not only that the human mind is united to the body, but also what is to be understood by the union of the mind and body. However, no one can understand this union adequately, i.e. distinctly, without a previous adequate knowledge of the nature of our body. For the things that we have shown so far are extremely general, and do not belong to human beings any more than to other individuals, all of which are animated, although in different degrees.[30] For there necessarily exists in God an idea of each thing, of which idea God is the cause, in the same way as he is the cause of the idea[31] of the human body; so whatever we have said of the idea of the human body must necessarily be said of the idea of each thing. But we also cannot deny that ideas differ among themselves as their objects do, and that one is superior to another and contains more reality, just as the object of one is superior to the object of another and contains more reality. So in order to determine how the human mind is different from the rest, and how it is superior to them, it is necessary for us (as we have said) to know the nature of that object, that is, the human body. However, I cannot explain this here, nor is it necessary for what I want to demonstrate. But I will say this in general: to the extent that some body is more capable than others of doing several things at the same time, or of being acted on at the same time, to that extent its mind is more capable than others of perceiving several things at the same time. Further, the more that the actions of one body depend on itself alone, and the less that other bodies co-operate with it in acting, the more the mind is capable of understanding distinctly. From this we can get to know the superiority of one mind over others, and also see the cause of the fact that we have only an extremely confused knowledge of our body, and many other things which I shall, in what follows, deduce from this. For this reason I thought it worth while to explain and demonstrate these matters more accurately, to which end it is necessary to state in advance a few things about the nature of bodies.

Axiom 1

All bodies either move or are at rest.

Axiom 2

Each body moves now more slowly, now more quickly.

Lemma 1[32]

Bodies are distinguished from each other in respect of motion and rest, speed and slowness, and not in respect of substance.

Demonstration. The first part of this I take to be self-evident. The fact that bodies are not distinguished from each other in respect of substance is evident both from Prop. 5 and Prop. 8 of Part 1, but more clearly from what has been said in Prop. 15, Schol., Part 1.

Lemma 2

All bodies agree in certain things.

Demonstration. For all bodies agree in these respects: that they involve the conception of one and the same attribute (by Def. 1, Part 2), and also that they can move now more quickly and now more slowly, and that they can now move and now be at rest absolutely.

Lemma 3

A body which is in motion or at rest must have been determined to motion or rest by another body, which was also determined to motion or rest by another, and that again by another, and so on to infinity.

Demonstration. Bodies (by Def. 1, Part 2) are particular things which (by Lemma 1) differ from each other in respect of motion and rest. So (by Prop. 28, Part 1) each must have been determined to motion or rest by another particular thing, namely (by Prop. 6, Part 2) by another body, which (by Ax. 1) also either moves or is at rest. But this again (for the same reason) could not move or be at rest unless it had been determined to motion or rest by another, and that again (for the same reason) by another, and so on to infinity. QED.

Corollary

From this it follows that a body in motion moves until it is determined to rest by another body, and a body at rest is at rest until it is determined by another to motion. This is also self-evident. For when I suppose that a body—for example, *A*—is at rest, and do not pay attention to other bodies in motion, I shall be able to say of the body *A* only that it is at rest. But if it happens later that the body *A* moves, this certainly could not have happened from the fact that it used to be at rest; for from that it could only have followed that the body *A* is at rest. If, on the other hand, it is supposed that *A* moves, then as long as we attend to *A* alone, we shall be able to affirm of it only that it moves. But if it later happens that *A* is at rest, that certainly could not have happened from the motion that it used to have; for from motion it could only follow that *A* moves. So its being at rest comes about by means of a thing which was not in *A*, namely an external cause by which it was determined to rest.

Axiom 1

All the ways in which a certain body is affected by another body follow from the nature of the affected body, and at the same time from the nature of the affecting body, in such a way that one and the same body is moved in various ways in accordance with the diversity of the nature of the bodies which move it, and, on the other hand, that different bodies are moved in various ways by one and the same body.

Axiom 2

When a body in motion impinges on another which is at rest, which it is unable to move, it is reflected, so that it continues to move, and the angle

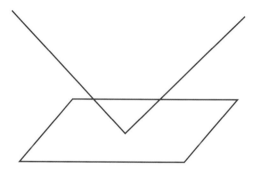

of the line of reflection with the plane of the body at rest, on which it impinges, will be equal to the angle which the line of incidence of motion makes with the same plane.[33]

So much concerning most simple bodies, namely, those which are distinguished from one another solely by motion and rest, speed and slowness. Let us now move upwards to composite bodies.

Definition

When a number of bodies of the same or of different magnitudes are constrained by others in such a way that they are in reciprocal contact with each other, or if they are moved with the same or different degrees of speed in such a way that they communicate their motions to each other in some fixed ratio, we shall say that those bodies are reciprocally united to each other. We shall also say that all such bodies simultaneously compose one body, i.e. an individual, which is distinguished from others by this union of bodies.

Axiom 3

In so far as the parts of an individual, or composite body, are in contact with each other with respect to their larger or smaller surfaces, they can be compelled to change their position with greater difficulty or more easily. Consequently, it can be brought about with greater difficulty or more easily that the individual assumes another shape. Therefore, I shall call those bodies whose parts are in contact with each other with respect to their large surfaces 'hard'; those whose parts are in contact with each other with respect to their small surfaces I shall call 'soft'; finally, those whose parts move among themselves I shall call 'fluid'.

Lemma 4

If certain bodies that belong to a body, i.e. an individual, which is composed of several bodies are removed, and at the same time as many other bodies of the same nature occupy their place, the individual will retain its nature as it did before, without any change of its form.

Demonstration. For bodies (by Lemma 1) are not distinguished in respect of substance, but that which constitutes the form of an individual consists in the union of bodies (by the preceding definition). But this (by hypothesis) is retained, even though there is a continuous change of bodies; therefore, the individual will retain its nature, in respect of both substance and mode, as it did before. QED.

Lemma 5

If the parts that compose an individual become larger or smaller, but in a proportion such that they all preserve towards each other the same ratio of motion and rest that they had before, the individual will in the same way retain its nature as before, without any change of form.

Demonstration. This is the same as that of the preceding Lemma.

Lemma 6

If certain bodies which compose an individual are compelled to change their motion from one direction to another, but in such a way that they can continue their own motions and communicate them to each other in the same ratio that they had before, the individual will in the same way retain its nature, without any change of form.

Demonstration. This is self-evident. For the individual is supposed to retain all that which we stated in its definition[34] to constitute its form.

Lemma 7

Further, an individual composed in this way will retain its nature whether it moves or is at rest as a whole, or whether it moves in this or that direction, provided that each part retains its motion, and communicates it to the others as before.

Demonstration. This is evident from its definition, to be seen before Lemma 4.

Scholium

From this, therefore, we see how a composite individual can be affected in many ways, though its nature is none the less preserved. Now, so far we have conceived an individual which is composed solely of bodies which are distinguished from each other only by motion and rest, speed and slowness; that is, which is composed of most simple bodies. But if we now conceive another individual, which is composed of several individuals of a diverse nature, we shall find that it can be affected in several other ways, though its nature is none the less preserved. For since each part of it is composed of several bodies, each part (by the preceding Lemma) will therefore be able, without any change of its nature, to move now more quickly and now more slowly, and consequently to communicate its motions to the rest more quickly or more slowly. But if we conceive further a third genus of individuals, composed of the members of this second genus, we shall find it able to be affected in many other ways, without any change of its form. And if in this way we proceed to infinity, we shall easily conceive the whole of Nature to be one individual,[35] whose parts—that is, all bodies—vary in infinite ways without any change of the whole individual. This, if it were my intention to discuss body in detail,[36] I ought to have explained and demonstrated more fully. But I have already said that my intention is different, and that I have mentioned what I have mentioned simply because I can easily deduce from it what I set out to demonstrate.

Postulates[37]

1. The human body is composed of very many individuals of a diverse nature, each of which is highly composite.

2. Of the individuals of which the human body is composed, some are fluid, some are soft, and some are hard.

3. The individuals that compose the human body, and consequently the human body itself, are affected in very many ways by external bodies.

4. The human body needs for its conservation very many other bodies, by which it is as it were continually regenerated.

5. When a fluid part of the human body is determined by an external body to impinge often on another soft part, it alters the latter's surface and as it were imprints on it certain traces of the external body that impels it.

6. The human body can move external bodies in very many ways, and dispose them in very many ways.

Proposition 14

The human body is capable of perceiving very many things, and the more so, the more its body can be disposed in several ways.

Demonstration. For the human body (by Posts. 3 and 6) is affected in very many ways by external bodies, and is disposed to affect external bodies in very many ways. But the human mind must perceive everything that happens in the human body (by Prop. 12, Part 2); therefore, the human mind is capable of perceiving very many things, and the more so, etc. QED.

Proposition 15

The idea which constitutes the formal being of the human mind is not simple, but is composed of very many ideas.

Demonstration. The idea which constitutes the formal being of the human mind is the idea of the body (by Prop. 13, Part 2), which (by Post. 1) is composed of very many extremely composite individuals. But there necessarily exists in God (by Prop. 8, Coroll., Part 2) the idea of each individual which composes the body; therefore (by Prop. 7, Part 2), the idea of the human body is composed of these very many ideas of the component parts. QED.

Proposition 16

The idea of any mode, by which the human body is affected by external bodies,[38] must involve the nature of the human body and at the same time the nature of the external body.

Demonstration. For all the modes by which some body is affected follow from the nature of the affected body, and at the same time from the nature of the affecting body (by Ax. 1 after Coroll., Lem. 3). Therefore, the idea of these modes (by Ax. 4, Part 1) necessarily involves the nature of each of these bodies, and so the idea of any mode by which the human body is affected by an external body involves the nature of the human body and of the external body. QED.

Corollary 1

From this it follows, first, that the human mind perceives the nature of very many bodies together with the nature of its own body.

Corollary 2

It follows, secondly, that the ideas that we have of external bodies indicate the constitution of our bodies rather than the nature of external bodies. I have explained this in the Appendix of Part One, with many examples.

Proposition 17

If the human body is affected by a mode which involves the nature of some external body,[39] the human mind will regard that same external body as actually existent, or as present to it, until the body is affected by an affection[40] which excludes the existence or presence of that body.

Demonstration. This is evident. For as long as the human body is affected in this way, so long will the human mind (by Prop. 12, Part 2) regard this affection of the body. That is (by the preceding Proposition), it will have the idea of an actually existing mode which involves the nature of the external body; that is, an idea which does not exclude the existence or presence of the external body, but affirms it. So the mind (by Coroll. 1 of the preceding Proposition) will regard the external body as actually existent, or as present, until it is affected, etc. QED.

Corollary

The mind will be able to regard, as if they were present, external bodies by which the human body was once affected, even though they neither exist nor are present.

Demonstration. While external bodies determine the fluid parts of the human body in such a way that they often impinge on the softer parts, they alter their surfaces (by Post. 5). From this it comes about (see Ax. 2 after Coroll., Lem. 3) that they are reflected from these in another way from that in which they were reflected previously, and also that afterwards, as the fluid parts impinge on these new surfaces by their own spontaneous motion, they are reflected in the same way as when they were impelled by external bodies towards those surfaces. Consequently, while they continue to move as they are reflected in this way, they affect the human body in the same way, of which the mind will again think (by Prop. 12, Part 2). That is (by Prop. 17, Part 2), the mind will again regard the external body as present, and will do so as often as the fluid parts of the human body impinge on the same surfaces by their own spontaneous motion. Consequently, although the external bodies by which the human body was once affected do not exist, the mind will regard them as present as often as this action of the body is repeated. QED.

Scholium

So from this we see how it can come about that we regard things that do not exist as if they were present to us, which often happens. It can come about that this happens from other causes, but for me to have shown one cause by which I could explain this matter is as satisfactory as if I had proved it through its true cause. However, I do not think that I have strayed far from the true cause, since all the postulates that I have assumed contain scarcely anything that is not established by experience, of which we may not doubt now that we have shown that the human body exists as we sense it[41] (see the Coroll. after Prop. 13, Part 2). Further (by the preceding Coroll. and Prop. 16, Coroll. 2, Part 2) we understand clearly the nature of the difference between the idea (say) of Peter, which constitutes the essence of the mind of Peter, and the idea of Peter which is in another man—say, Paul. For the former explains directly the essence of the body of Peter, and involves existence only as long as Peter exists. The latter, however, indicates the constitution of the body of Paul rather than the nature of Peter. Therefore, as long as that constitution of the body of Paul continues to exist, the mind of Paul will continue to regard Peter as present to itself, even though Peter does not exist.[42] Further, in order that we may retain some commonly used words, we shall call the affections of the human body, the ideas of which represent external bodies as if they were present to us, the 'images' of things, even though they do not reproduce the shapes of things.[43] And when the mind regards bodies in this way, we shall say that it 'imagines'.[44] Here, so that I may begin to indicate the nature of error, I would like you to note that the imaginations of the mind, regarded in themselves, contain no error; or, the mind does not err from the fact that it imagines. Rather, the mind errs only in so far as it is considered as lacking an idea which excludes the existence of those things which it imagines as present to it. For if the mind, whilst it imagines non-existent things as present to it, knew at the same time that those things do not really exist, it would ascribe this power of imagining to a virtue of its nature and not to a defect—especially if this faculty of imagining depended on its own nature alone, that is (by Def. 7, Part 1), if this faculty of imagining that the mind has were free.

Proposition 18

If the human body was once affected by two or more bodies at the same time, when the mind later imagines one of them it will immediately recollect the others as well.

Demonstration. The mind (by the preceding Coroll.) imagines something because of this: that the human body is affected and disposed by the traces of an external body in the same way as it was affected when certain of its parts were moved by the external body itself. But (by hypothesis) the body was so disposed at that time that the mind imagined two bodies at the same time. Therefore, the mind will now also imagine the two at the same time, and when the mind imagines either of the two, it will immediately recollect the other as well. QED.

Scholium

From this we clearly understand what memory[45] is. It is simply a certain interconnection of ideas which involve the nature of things which are outside the human body, and which occurs in the mind in accordance with the order and interconnection of the affections of the human body. I say, first, that the interconnection is of those ideas only which involve the nature of things which are outside the human body, and not of the ideas which explain the nature of those things. For there are indeed (by Prop. 16, Part 2) ideas of the affections of the human body which involve the nature both of this body and of external bodies. Secondly, I say that this interconnection occurs in accordance with the order and interconnection of the affections of the human body, in order that I may distinguish it from the interconnection of ideas which occurs in accordance with the order of the intellect, by which the mind perceives things through their primary causes, and which is the same in all human beings.

Further, from this we also understand clearly why the mind, from think-ing about one thing, at once falls to thinking of another thing which has no similarity to the first. So, for example, from thinking about the word 'pomum' ('apple') a Roman would at once proceed to thinking of the fruit, which has no similarity to the articulate sound and nothing in common with it, apart from the fact that the body of the same man was often affected by these two: that is, that the same man often heard the word 'pomum' whilst he looked at the fruit. So each person will proceed from one thought to another, in accordance with the way in which habit has arranged the images of things in his body. For a soldier, for example, on seeing the tracks of a horse in the sand, will at once proceed from thinking about a horse to thinking about a rider, and from that to think-ing about war, and so on. A countryman, on the other hand, will pro-ceed from thinking about a horse to thinking about a plough, a field, and so on; and so each person will, from one thought, light upon this thought or some other thought, in accordance with the various ways in which he has been accustomed to join and interconnect the images of things.

Proposition 19

The human mind does not know the human body, nor does it know that it exists, except through the ideas of the affections by which the body is affected.

Demonstration. For the human mind is the idea, i.e. the knowledge, of the human body[46] (by Prop. 13, Part 2), which (by Prop. 9, Part 2) is in God in so far as he is considered as affected by another idea of a particu-lar thing; or because (by Post. 4) the human body needs very many bodies, by which it is as it were continually regenerated, and the order and connection of ideas is (by Prop. 7, Part 2) the same as the order and connection of causes. This idea will be in God, in so far as he is con-sidered as affected by the ideas of very many particular things. God, therefore, has the idea of the human body, or, God knows the human body, in so far as he is affected by very many other ideas, and not in so far as he constitutes the nature of the human mind. That is (by Prop. 11, Coroll., Part 2), the human mind does not know the human body. But the ideas of the affections of the human body are in God in so far as he constitutes the nature of the human mind, or, the human mind perceives those affections (by Prop. 12, Part 2). Consequently (by Prop. 16, Part 2), it perceives the human body, and indeed (by Prop. 17, Part 2) as actually existing. Therefore, the human mind perceives the human body only to this extent.[47] QED.

Proposition 20

There exists also in God the idea, i.e. the knowledge, of the human mind, which follows in God in the same way, and is related to God in the same way, as the idea, i.e. the knowledge, of the human body.

Demonstration. Thought is an attribute of God (by Prop. 1, Part 2), and so (by Prop. 3, Part 2) there must also necessarily exist in God an idea both of thought and of all its affections, and consequently (by Prop. 11, Coroll., Part 2)[48] of the human mind also. Next, the existence in God of this idea, i.e. the knowledge of the mind, follows from God, not in so far as he is infinite, but in so far as he is affected by another idea of a particular thing (by Prop. 9, Part 2). But the order and connection of ideas is the same as the order and connection of causes (by Prop. 7, Part 2); it follows, therefore, that this idea, i.e. knowledge, of the mind is in God, and is related to God in the same way as the idea, i.e. the knowledge, of the body. QED.

Proposition 21

This idea of the mind is united to the mind in the same way as the mind itself is united to the body.

Demonstration. We have shown that the mind is united to the body from the fact that the body is the object of the mind (see Props. 12 and 13, Part 2). So, by that same reason, the idea of the mind must be united with its object, that is, with the mind itself, in the same way as the mind is united to the body. QED.

Scholium

This Proposition is understood much more clearly from what has been said in the Scholium to Proposition 7 of this Part. For there we showed that the idea of the body and the body—that is (by Prop. 13, Part 2) the mind and the body—are one and the same individual, which is conceived now under the attribute of thought and now under the attribute of extension. Therefore, the idea of the mind and the mind itself is one and the same thing which is conceived under one and the same attribute, namely that of thought. The idea of the mind and the mind itself, I say, follow in God with the same necessity from the same power of thinking. For in truth the idea of the mind, that is, the idea of an idea, is simply the form of an idea, in so far as this is considered as a mode of thinking, without relation to an object. For as soon as someone knows something, by that very fact he knows that he knows it, and at the same time he knows that he knows that he knows, and so on to infinity. But more of this later.[49]

Proposition 22

The human mind perceives, not only the affections of the body, but also the ideas of these affections.

Demonstration. The ideas of the ideas of affections follow in God in the same way, and are related to God in the same way, as the ideas of the affections. This is demonstrated in the same way as Proposition 20 of this Part. But the ideas of the affections of the body are in the human mind (by Prop. 12, Part 2); that is (by Prop. 11, Coroll., Part 2), they are in God in so far as he constitutes the essence of the human mind. Therefore, the ideas of these ideas will be in God, in so far as he has the knowledge, i.e. the idea, of the human mind. That is (by Prop. 21, Part 2), they will be in the human mind itself, which accordingly perceives not only the affections of the body, but also the ideas of those affections. QED.

Proposition 23

The mind does not know itself, except in so far as it perceives the ideas of the affections of the body.

Demonstration. The idea, i.e. the knowledge, of the mind (by Prop. 20, Part 2) follows in God in the same way, and is related to God in the same way, as the idea, i.e. the knowledge, of the body. But since (by Prop. 19, Part 2) the human mind does not know the human body, that is (by Prop. 11, Coroll., Part 2) the knowledge of the human body is not related to God in so far as he constitutes the nature of the human mind, neither is the knowledge of the mind related to God in so far as he constitutes the essence of the human mind. So (again by Prop. 11, Coroll., Part 2) to this extent the human mind does not know itself. Next, the ideas of the affections by which the body is affected involve the nature of the human body itself (by Prop. 16, Part 2); that is (by Prop. 13, Part 2), they agree with the nature of the mind. So the knowledge of these ideas will necessarily involve the knowledge of the mind. But (by the preceding Proposition) the knowledge of these ideas is in the human mind itself; therefore, to this extent alone the human mind knows itself. QED.

Proposition 24

The human mind does not involve an adequate knowledge of the parts that make up the human body.

Demonstration. The parts that make up the human body belong to the essence of that body only in so far as they communicate their motions to each other in some fixed ratio (see the Definition after Lemma 3, Coroll.), and not in so far as they can be considered as individuals without relation to the human body. For the parts of the human body (by Post. 1) are highly composite individuals, whose parts (by Lemma 4) can be separated from the human body whilst its nature and form are preserved,[50] and can communicate their motions (see Ax. 1 after Lemma 3) to other bodies in another ratio. So (by Prop. 3, Part 2) the idea, i.e. the knowledge, of each part will be in God, and indeed will be in God in so far as (by Prop. 9, Part 2) he is considered as affected by another idea of a particular thing, which particular thing (by Prop. 7, Part 2) is prior in the order of Nature to the part itself. Further, the same must be said of each part of the individual that makes up the human body; so the knowledge of each part that makes up the human body is in God in so far as he affected by very many ideas of things, and not in so far as he has the idea of the human body alone—that is (by Prop. 13, Part 2), the idea that constitutes the nature of the human mind. So (by Prop. 11, Coroll., Part 2) the human mind does not involve an adequate knowledge of the parts that make up the human body. QED.

Proposition 25

The idea of any affection of the human body does not involve an adequate knowledge of an external body.

Demonstration. We have shown (see Prop. 16, Part 2) that an idea of an affection of the human body involves the nature of an external body to the extent that the external body determines the human body in some fixed way. But in so far as the external body is an individual which is not related to the human body, the idea, i.e. the knowledge, of it is in God (by Prop. 9, Part 2) in so far as God is considered as affected by the idea of another thing, which (by Prop. 7, Part 2) is prior in nature to the external body. Therefore, an adequate knowledge of an external body is not in God in so far as he has the idea of an affection of the human body, or, the idea of an affection of the human body does not involve an adequate knowledge of an external body. QED.

Proposition 26

The human mind perceives no external body as actually existing, except through the ideas of the affections of its body.

Demonstration. If the human body is in no way affected by some external body, then (by Prop. 7, Part 2) neither is the idea of the human body, that is (by Prop. 13, Part 2), the human mind, affected in any way by the idea of the existence of that body; or, it does not perceive in any way the existence of that external body. But in so far as the human body is affected in some way by some external body, to that extent (by Prop. 16, Part 2, together with its first Corollary) it perceives the external body. QED.

Corollary

In so far as the human mind imagines an external body, to that extent it does not have an adequate knowledge of it.

Demonstration. When the human mind regards external bodies through the ideas of the affections of its body, we say that it imagines (see Prop. 17, Schol., Part 2). Further, the human mind (by the preceding Proposition) cannot imagine external bodies as actually existing in another way. So (by Prop. 25, Part 2) in so far as the human mind imagines external bodies, it does not have an adequate knowledge of them. QED.

Proposition 27

The idea of any affection of the human body does not involve an adequate knowledge of the human body itself.[51]

Demonstration. Any idea of any affection of the human body involves the nature of the human body to the extent that the human body is considered as affected in some fixed way (see Prop. 16, Part 2). But in so far as the human body is an individual which can be affected in many other ways, then its idea, etc.[52] See the Demonstration of Prop. 25, Part 2.

Proposition 28

The ideas of the affections of the human body, in so far as they are related to the human mind alone, are not clear and distinct,[53] but confused.

Demonstration. For the ideas of the affections of the human body involve the nature both of external bodies and of the human body itself (by Prop. 16, Part 2); nor must they involve the nature of the human body alone, but they must also involve the nature of its parts. For its affections are modes (Post. 3) by which the parts of the human body, and consequently the whole body, is affected. But (by Props. 24 and 25, Part 2) the adequate knowledge of external bodies, like that of the parts that make up the human body, is not in God in so far as he is considered to be affected by the human mind, but is in him in so far as he is considered to be affected by other ideas. Therefore, the ideas of these affections, in so far as they are related to the human mind alone, are like consequences without premises, that is (as is self-evident) they are confused ideas.[54] QED.

Scholium

The idea which constitutes the nature of the human mind, considered in itself alone, is demonstrated in the same way not to be clear and distinct; as also is the idea of the human mind, and the ideas of the ideas of the affections of the human body, in so far as they are related to the mind alone. This can easily be seen by anyone.

Proposition 29

The idea of the idea of any affection of the human body does not involve an adequate knowledge of the human mind.

Demonstration. For an idea of an affection of the human body does not (by Prop. 27, Part 2) involve an adequate idea of the body itself, or, it does not express its nature adequately. That is (by Prop. 13, Part 2) it does not agree adequately with the nature of the mind. So (by Axiom 6, Part 1) the idea of this idea does not express adequately the nature of the human mind, or, does not involve an adequate knowledge of it. QED.

Corollary

From this it follows that the human mind, whenever it perceives things through the common order of Nature, has an adequate knowledge neither of itself, nor of its body, nor of external bodies, but only a confused and mutilated knowledge. For the mind does not know itself except in so far as it perceives the ideas of the affections of the body (by Prop. 23, Part 2). But (by Prop. 19, Part 2) it does not perceive its body except through the ideas of those affections, through which alone (by Prop. 26, Part 2) it also perceives external bodies. So in so far as it has these ideas it has an adequate knowledge neither of itself (by Prop. 29, Part 2), nor of its body (by Prop. 27, Part 2), nor of external bodies (by Prop. 25, Part 2), but only (by Prop. 28, Part 2, together with its Scholium) a mutilated and confused knowledge. QED.

Scholium

I say expressly that the mind has an adequate knowledge neither of itself, nor of its body, nor of external bodies, but only a confused[55] knowledge, whenever it perceives things through the common order of Nature; that is, whenever it is determined externally, namely by its fortuitous contact with things, to regard this or that, and not whenever it is determined internally, namely by the fact that it regards several things at the same time, to an understanding of their agreements, differences, and oppositions. For as often as it is determined internally in this or in some other way, it regards things clearly and distinctly, as I shall show below.[56]

Proposition 30

We can have only an extremely inadequate knowledge of the duration of our body.

Demonstration. The duration of our body does not depend on its essence (by Ax. 1, Part 2), nor again on the absolute nature of God (by Prop. 21, Part 1). It is determined (by Prop. 28, Part 1) to existence and operation by such causes as are also determined by others to existence and operation in a certain and determinate way, and these again by others, and so on to infinity. Therefore, the duration of our body depends on the common order of Nature and on the constitution of things. But an adequate knowledge of the way in which things are constituted exists in God in so far as he has the ideas of all things, and not in so far as he has the idea of the human body alone (by Prop. 9, Coroll., Part 2). So the knowledge of the duration of our body is extremely inadequate in God, in so far as he is considered to constitute only the nature of the human mind, that is (by Prop. 11, Coroll., Part 2), this knowledge is extremely inadequate in our mind. QED.

Proposition 31

We can have only an extremely inadequate knowledge of the duration of particular things that are outside us.

Demonstration. For each particular thing (for example, the human body) must be determined by another particular thing to existence and operation in a certain and determinate way; and this again must be determined by another, and so on to infinity (by Prop. 28, Part 1). However, in the previous Proposition we demonstrated, from this common property of particular things, that we can have only an extremely inadequate knowledge of the duration of our body; therefore, this same thing must be inferred concerning the duration of particular things, namely that we can have only an extremely inadequate knowledge of it. QED.

Corollary

From this it follows that all particular things are contingent and corruptible. For we can have no adequate knowledge of their duration (by the preceding Proposition), and this is what we are to understand (see

Prop. 33, Schol. 1, Part 1) by the contingency and the possibility of the corruption of things. For (by Prop. 29, Part 1) this is just what a contingent thing is.

Proposition 32

All ideas, in so far as they are related to God, are true.

Demonstration. For all ideas which are in God agree entirely with those things of which they are the ideas (by Prop. 7, Coroll., Part 2) and so (by Ax. 6, Part 1) they are all true. QED.

Proposition 33

There is nothing positive in ideas on account of which they are called false.

Demonstration. If you deny this, then conceive (if this can be done) a positive mode of thinking which constitutes the form of error, i.e. of falsity. This mode of thinking cannot be in God (by the preceding Proposition); but it can neither exist nor be conceived outside God (by Prop. 15, Part 1). So nothing positive can exist in ideas, on account of which they are called false. QED.

Proposition 34

Every idea which is absolute, i.e. adequate and perfect, in us is true.

Demonstration. When we say that there exists in us an idea which is adequate and perfect, we are simply saying (by Prop. 11, Coroll., Part 2) that an adequate and perfect idea exists in God, in so far as he constitutes the essence of our mind. Consequently (by Prop. 32, Part 2), we are simply saying that such an idea is true. QED.

Proposition 35

Falsity consists in the privation of knowledge which inadequate, i.e. mutilated and confused, ideas involve.

Demonstration. There exists nothing positive in ideas which constitutes the form of falsity (by Prop. 33, Part 2). But falsity cannot consist in absolute privation (for minds, not bodies, are said to err and to be deceived); nor again can it consist in absolute ignorance, for to be ignorant and to err are different. So it consists in the privation of knowledge which the inadequate knowledge of things, or, inadequate and confused ideas, involve. QED.

Scholium

In the Scholium to Prop. 17 of this Part I explained the way in which error consists in the privation of knowledge, but to give a fuller explanation of this matter I will give an example. It is this. Men are deceived in that they think themselves free, an opinion which consists simply in the fact that they are conscious of their actions and ignorant of the causes by which those actions are determined. This, therefore, is their idea of liberty: that they know no cause of their actions. For when they assert that human actions depend on the will, these are just words, of which they have no idea. They are all ignorant of what the will is and how it moves the body, and those who boast otherwise and invent dwelling-places and habitations for the soul tend to evoke laughter or disgust.[57] So also, when we see the sun, we imagine it to be about two hundred feet distant from us; an error which consists, not in this imagination alone, but in the fact that whilst we imagine the sun in this way we are ignorant of its true distance and of the cause of this imagination. For even after we get to know that the sun is distant from us by over six hundred diameters of the earth[58] we shall still imagine it to be close at hand. For we imagine the sun to be so close, not because we are ignorant of its true distance, but because an affection of our body involves the essence of the sun in so far as the body is affected by the sun.

Proposition 36

Inadequate and confused ideas follow with the same necessity as adequate, i.e. clear and distinct, ideas.

Demonstration. All ideas are in God (by Prop. 15, Part 1) and in so far as they are related to God they are true (by Prop. 32, Part 2) and adequate (by Prop. 7, Coroll., Part 2). So no ideas are inadequate or confused except in so far as they are related to the particular mind of someone (on this, see Props. 24 and 28, Part 2). So all ideas, both adequate and inadequate, follow with the same necessity (by Prop. 6, Coroll., Part 2). QED.

Proposition 37

That which is common to all things (see Lemma 2 above) and which is equally in the part and in the whole constitutes the essence of no particular thing.

Demonstration. If you deny this, then conceive (if this can be done) that this constitutes the essence of some particular thing—say, the essence of *B*. Therefore (by Def. 2, Part 2), it can neither exist nor be conceived without *B*. But this is contrary to the hypothesis; therefore, it does not belong to the essence of *B*, nor does it constitute the essence of another particular thing. QED.

Proposition 38

Those things which are common to all things, and are equally in the part and in the whole, can only be conceived adequately.

Demonstration. Let *A* be something which is common to all bodies, and which is equally in the part of any body and in the whole. I assert that *A* can only be conceived adequately. For the idea of it (by Prop. 7, Coroll., Part 2) will necessarily be adequate in God, both in so far as he has the idea of the human body and in so far as he has the ideas of its affections, which (by Props. 16, 25, and 27, Part 2) partially involve the nature both of the human body and of external bodies. That is (by Props. 12 and 13, Part 2), this idea will necessarily be adequate in God in so far as he constitutes the human mind, or, in so far as he has ideas which are in the human mind. The mind, therefore (by Prop. 11, Coroll., Part 2), necessarily perceives *A* adequately, both in so far as it perceives itself and in so far as it perceives its own or any external body; nor can *A* be conceived in another way. QED.

Corollary

From this it follows that there are certain ideas, i.e. notions, which are common to all human beings.[59] For (by Lem. 2) all bodies agree in some things, which (by the preceding Proposition) must be conceived adequately, i.e. clearly and distinctly, by all.

Proposition 39

There will be an adequate idea in the mind of that which is common to, and a property of, the human body and certain external bodies by which the human body is often affected, and which is equally in the part and in the whole of any of these.[60]

Demonstration. Let A be that which is common to, and a property of, the human body and certain external bodies, and which is equally in the human body and in those external bodies, and which, finally, is equally in the part of any external body and in the whole. There will necessarily exist in God an adequate idea of A (by Prop. 7, Coroll., Part 2), both in so far as he has the idea of the human body and also in so far as he has the ideas of the assumed external bodies. Let it now be assumed that the human body is affected by an external body through that which it has in common with it, that is, by A. The idea of this affection will involve the property A (by Prop. 16, Part 2), and so (again by Prop. 7, Coroll., Part 2) the idea of this affection, in so far as it involves the property A, will be adequate in God in so far as he is affected by the idea of the human body, that is (by Prop. 13, Part 2) in so far as he constitutes the nature of the human mind. So (by Prop. 11, Coroll., Part 2) this idea is also adequate in the human mind. QED.

Corollary

From this it follows that the human body is the more capable of perceiving several things adequately, the more things its body has in common with other bodies.

Proposition 40

Whatever ideas follow in the mind from ideas which are adequate in it are also adequate.

Demonstration. This is evident. For when we say that an idea in the human mind follows from ideas which are adequate in it, we simply say (by Prop. 11, Coroll., Part 2) that an idea exists in the divine intellect of which God is the cause, not in so far as he is infinite, nor in so far as he is affected by the ideas of very many particular things, but only in so far as he constitutes the essence of the human mind.

Scholium 1

With this I have explained the cause of the notions which are called 'common',[61] and which are the bases of our reasoning. There exist other causes of certain axioms, i.e. notions, which it would be useful to explain by this method of ours,[62] for from these causes it would be established which notions are more useful than others, and which on the other hand are of scarcely any use. Then again it would be established which notions are common, and which are clear and distinct only to those who do not labour under prejudices,[63] and which finally are badly based. Further, it would be established from what source those notions which are called 'second',[64] and consequently the axioms which are based on them, have derived their origin, and other related matters on which I have meditated in the past. But since I have set these aside for another treatise,[65] and so that I do not create aversion by discussing this matter at undue length, I have decided to pass these by. However, so that I do not omit any of these matters which it is necessary to know, I will briefly add the causes from which the so-called 'transcendental' terms,[66] such as entity, being, and something, have derived their origin. These terms arise from the fact that the human body, in that it is limited, is capable of forming distinctly within itself at the same time only a certain number of images (I have explained what an image is in Prop. 17, Schol., Part 2). If this number is exceeded, these images will begin to be confused, and if the number of images which the body is capable of forming distinctly within itself at the same time is greatly exceeded, all the images will be entirely confused with one another. As this is the case, it is evident (from Prop. 17, Coroll. and from Prop. 18, Part 2) that the human mind will be able to imagine distinctly at the same time as many bodies as the images which can be formed in its body at the same time. But when the images in the body are entirely confused, then the mind also will imagine all the bodies confusedly without any distinction and as it were under one attribute, namely under the attribute of being, thing, etc. This can also be deduced from the fact that images do not always have the same strength, and from other analogous causes which it is unnecessary to explain here, for it is sufficient for the end at which we are aiming to consider just one. For they all come to this: that these terms stand for ideas that are in the highest degree confused. Those notions that are called 'universal', such as man, horse, dog, etc., have arisen from similar causes: namely, because there are found in the human body at the same time so many images of (for example) men that they surpass the power of imagination—not completely, but to such an extent that the mind cannot imagine the small differences that particular things have (namely the colour, magnitude, etc. of each) and their determinate number, and imagines distinctly only that in which they all agree in so far as the body is affected by them. For the body, as it was affected by each particular thing, was affected most by that in which they all agree. This the mind expresses by the word 'man', and it predicates it of an infinity of particulars; for, as we have said, it is unable to imagine the determinate number of the particulars. It must be noted that these notions are not formed by everyone in the same way, but that they vary in each person in accordance with the thing by which the body was affected more often, and which the mind imagines or recollects more easily. For example, those who have more often regarded with admiration the stature of men will understand by the name 'man' an animal of erect stature, whereas those who have been accustomed to regard something else will form another common image of man: namely, that man is an animal that laughs, a biped without feathers, or a rational animal.[67] So also concerning the rest: each person, in accordance with the disposition of his body, will form universal images of things. So it is not strange that so many controversies have arisen among philosophers who wanted to explain natural things solely by the images of things.

Scholium 2

From all that has been said above it is clearly evident that we perceive many things and form universal notions:[68] first, from particular things, represented to us through the senses in a way that is mutilated, confused, and without intellectual order (see Prop. 29, Coroll., Part 2). Consequently, I have been accustomed to call such perceptions 'knowledge from inconstant experience'.[69] Secondly, from signs—for example, from the fact that on hearing or reading certain words we recollect things and form of them certain ideas which are similar to those through which we imagine the things (see Prop. 18, Schol., Part 2). In what follows, I shall call each of these ways of regarding things 'knowledge of the first kind', 'opinion', or 'imagination'. Third and last, from the fact that we have common notions and adequate ideas of the properties of things (see

Prop. 38, Coroll., Prop. 39 and Coroll., and Prop. 40, Part 2). This I shall call 'reason' and 'knowledge of the second kind'. Besides these two kinds of knowledge there is, as I shall show in what follows, a third kind, which we will call 'intuitive knowledge'. This kind of knowledge proceeds from an adequate idea of the formal essence of some of the attributes of God to an adequate knowledge of the essence of things. I will illustrate all these by a single example. One is given, for example, three numbers, and one is required to find a fourth number which shall be to the third as the second is to the first. Merchants will not hesitate to multiply the second by the third and divide the product by the first: either because they have not yet forgotten what they heard from their teacher without any proof, or because they have often had experience of it in the case of very simple numbers, or by the force of the demonstration of Prop. 19 of Book 7 of Euclid, namely from the common property of proportionals. But in the case of very simple numbers there is no need of these. For example, given that the numbers are 1, 2, and 3, everyone will see that the fourth proportional number is 6; and we see this much more clearly because we infer the fourth number from the very ratio that we see with one intuition that the first has to the second.

Proposition 41

Knowledge of the first kind is the sole cause of falsity, but knowledge of the second and third kind is necessarily true.

Demonstration. We said in the preceding Scholium that there belong to the first kind of knowledge all those ideas which are inadequate and confused, and so (by Prop. 35, Part 2) this knowledge is the sole cause of falsity. Then we said that there belong to the second and third kinds of knowledge those ideas which are adequate, and so (by Prop. 34, Part 2) such knowledge is necessarily true. QED.

Proposition 42

Knowledge of the second and third kind, and not of the first, teaches us to distinguish the true from the false.

Demonstration. This Proposition is self-evident. For someone who knows how to distinguish between the true and the false must have an adequate idea of the true and the false; that is (by Prop. 40, Schol. 2, Part 2), he must know the true and the false by either the second or the third kind of knowledge.

Proposition 43

Someone who has a true idea knows at the same time that he has a true idea, and cannot doubt about the truth of the matter.[70]

Demonstration. An idea that is true in us is one which is adequate in God, in so far as he is explained through the nature of the human mind (by Prop. 11, Coroll., Part 2). Let us therefore assume that there exists in God, in so far as he is explained through the nature of the human mind, an adequate idea *A*. There must also necessarily exist in God an idea of this idea, which is related to God in the same way as the idea *A* (by Prop. 20, Part 2, the demonstration of which is universal). But the idea *A* is assumed to be related to God in so far as he is explained through the nature of the human mind; therefore, the idea of the idea *A* must also be related to God in the same way, that is (again by Prop. 11, Coroll., Part 2), this adequate idea of the idea *A* will be in the very mind that has the adequate idea *A*. So a person who has an adequate idea, i.e. who (by Prop. 34, Part 2) knows a thing truly, must at the same time have an adequate idea, i.e. a true knowledge, of his knowledge. That is (as is self-evident) he must at the same time be certain.[71] QED.

Scholium

In the Scholium of Proposition 21 of this Part I explained what the idea of an idea is; but it is to be noted that the previous Proposition is clear enough of itself. For no one who has a true idea is ignorant of the fact that a true idea involves the highest certainty; for to have a true idea simply means knowing a thing perfectly, or, in the best way. Nor, indeed, can anyone doubt of this matter, unless he thinks that an idea is something mute like a picture on a panel and not a mode of thinking, namely understanding itself. And who, I ask, can know that he understands some thing, unless he first understands the thing? That is, who can know that he is certain of some thing, unless he is first certain of that thing? Then, what can exist which is clearer and more certain as a standard of truth than a true idea? Clearly, just as light manifests both itself and the darkness, so truth is the standard both of itself and of falsity. With this, I think that I have replied to the following questions: namely, whether, if a true idea is distinguished from a false idea solely in so far as it is said to agree with that of which it is the idea, it will have no more reality or perfection than a false idea, since they are distinguished only by an extrinsic denomination;[72] consequently, whether a man who has true ideas will have no more reality or perfection than a man who has only false ideas. Then, how does it come about that men have false ideas? And finally, how can someone know that he has ideas which correspond to those things of which they are the ideas? To these questions, I say, I think that I have already replied. For as to what concerns the difference between a true and a false idea: it has been established by Prop. 35, Part 2, that the former is related to the latter as an entity to a non-entity. The causes of falsity I have explained with the greatest clarity, from Proposition 19 up to Proposition 35, with its Scholium. From these it is also evident how a man who has true ideas differs from a man who has only false ideas. Finally, as to what concerns the last question—namely, how a man can know that he has an idea which agrees with that of which it is the idea—I have just shown, more than sufficiently, that this arises solely from the fact that he has an idea which agrees with that of which it is the idea, or, because truth is its own standard. In addition to this, our mind, in so far as it perceives things truly, is a part of the infinite intellect of God (by Prop. 11, Coroll., Part 2), and so it is as necessary that the clear and distinct ideas of the mind are as true as that the ideas of God are true.

Proposition 44

It is of the nature of reason to regard things, not as contingent, but as necessary.

Demonstration. It is of the nature of reason to perceive things truly (by Prop. 41, Part 2), namely (by Ax. 6, Part 1) as they are in themselves; that is (by Prop. 29, Part 1), not as contingent, but as necessary. QED.

Corollary 1

From this it follows that it depends solely on the imagination that we regard things, in respect of both the past and the future, as contingent.

173 *Scholium*

I will explain in a few words how this comes about. We showed above (Prop. 17, Part 2, with its Corollary) that even though things do not exist, the mind always imagines them as present to it unless causes arise which exclude their present existence. Then we showed (Prop. 18, Part 2) that if the human body was once affected simultaneously by two external bodies, when the mind later imagines one or other of these it will immediately recollect the other as well—that is, it will regard both as present to it—unless causes arise which exclude their present existence. Further, no one doubts that we also imagine time from the fact that we imagine some bodies to move more slowly or more quickly than, or at the same speed as, others. So let us suppose a boy who yesterday first saw Peter in the morning, Paul at noon, and Simon in the evening, and today saw Peter again in the morning. From Proposition 18, Part 2, it is evident that as soon as he sees the morning light he will immediately imagine the sun traversing the same part of the heaven that he saw it doing on the previous day—i.e. he will imagine the whole day—and that he will imagine Peter simultaneously with the morning, Paul with noon, and Simon with the evening. That is, he will imagine the existence of Paul and Simon in relation to a future time. On the other hand, if he sees Simon in the evening, he will relate Paul and Peter to past time, namely by imagining them simultaneously with past time. He will do this the more constantly, the more often he has seen them in this particular order. But if it ever happens that on some other evening he sees Jacob instead of Simon, then on the following morning he will imagine with the evening now Simon and now Jacob, but not both together. For he is supposed to have seen, simultaneously with the evening, just one of the two and not both together. So his imagination will waver, and together with the future evening he will imagine now this one and now that one; that is, he will regard neither of them as certainly, but each of them as contingently, in the future. This wavering of the imagination will be the same if the imagination is of things which we regard in the same way with relation to the past or to the present; consequently, we shall imagine things as contingent both with relation to the present and the past or future.

Corollary 2

It is of the nature of reason to perceive things under a certain species of eternity.[73]

Demonstration. It is of the nature of reason to regard things as necessary and not as contingent (by the preceding Proposition). It perceives this necessity of things truly (by Prop. 41, Part 2), that is (by Ax. 6, Part 1), as it is in itself. But (by Prop. 16, Part 1) this necessity of things is the very necessity of the eternal nature of God; therefore, it is of the nature of reason to perceive things under this species of eternity. Add to this that the bases of reason are the notions which (by Prop. 38, Part 2) explain those things which are common to all, and which (by Prop. 37, Part 2) explain the essence of no particular thing, and which must therefore be conceived without any temporal relation, but under a certain species of eternity. QED.

Proposition 45

Each idea of any body, or of any particular thing that actually exists, necessarily involves the eternal and infinite essence of God.

Demonstration. The idea of a particular thing that actually exists necessarily involves both the essence and the existence of the thing (by Prop. 8, Coroll., Part 2). But particular things (by Prop. 15, Part 1) cannot be conceived without God, but because (by Prop. 6, Part 2) they have God as a cause in so far as he is considered under the attribute of which the things themselves are modes, the ideas of these things (by Ax. 4, Part 1) must necessarily involve the conception of their attribute. That is (by Def. 6, Part 1), they must necessarily involve the eternal and infinite essence of God. QED.

Scholium

By existence here I do not understand duration, that is, existence in so far as it is conceived abstractly and as a certain species of quantity. For I am speaking of the very nature of existence, which is ascribed to particular things on account of the fact that infinite things follow in infinite ways from the eternal necessity of the nature of God (see Prop. 16, Part 1). I am, I say, speaking of the very existence of particular things, in so far as they are in God. For although each one is determined by another particular thing to exist in a certain way, yet the force by which each one perseveres in existing[74] follows from the eternal necessity of the nature of God. On this matter, see Prop. 24, Coroll., Part 1.

Proposition 46

179 The knowledge of the eternal and infinite essence of God which each idea involves is adequate and perfect.

180 *Demonstration.* The demonstration of the preceding Proposition is universal, and whether a thing is considered as a part or as a whole, its idea, whether this is of the whole or of a part, involves the eternal and infinite essence of God (by the preceding Proposition). Consequently, that which provides a knowledge of the eternal and infinite essence of God is common to all, and is equally in the part and in the whole, and so (by Prop. 38, Part 2) this knowledge will be adequate. QED.

Proposition 47

181 The human mind has an adequate knowledge of the eternal and infinite essence of God.

182 *Demonstration.* The human mind has ideas (by Prop. 22, Part 2) by which (by Prop. 23, Part 2) it perceives itself, its body (by Prop. 19, Part 2), and (by Prop. 16, Coroll. 1, and Prop. 17, Part 2) external bodies as actually existing. So (by Props. 45 and 46, Part 2) it has an adequate knowledge of the eternal and infinite essence of God. QED.

Scholium

183 From this we see that the infinite essence of God, and its eternity,[75] are known to all. Since all things are in God and are conceived through God, it follows that we can deduce from this knowledge very many things which we know adequately, and so form that third kind of knowledge of which we spoke in Proposition 40, Scholium 2 of this Part, and of whose excellence and usefulness we shall have occasion to speak in Part Five. That people do not have an equally clear idea of God as they do of the common notions arises from the fact that they cannot imagine God as they can imagine bodies, and that they have linked the name 'God' to the

images of things that they are accustomed to see. This is something that people can hardly avoid, since they are continually affected by external bodies. And indeed, many errors consist solely in the fact that we do not apply names correctly to things. For when someone says that the lines that are drawn from the centre of a circle to its circumference are unequal, he certainly understands by a circle, then at any rate, something other than mathematicians do. So also when people make mistakes in a calculation, they have in their mind numbers which are different from those which are on paper. So if you consider their mind, they do not err; however, they seem to err because we think that they have in their mind the numbers that are on the paper. If this were not the case, we would in no way believe that they are erring—just as I did not believe to have been in error a certain man whom I recently heard shouting that his yard had flown into his neighbour's hen; for his mind seemed to be perfectly evident to me. Many controversies arise from this, namely because people do not explain their mind correctly, or because they interpret badly the mind of someone else. For in fact, whilst people contradict each other most, their thoughts are either the same or different,[76] with the result that what they think to be another's errors and absurdities are not really such.

Proposition 48

There is in the mind no absolute, i.e. no free, will, but the mind is determined to will this or that by a cause, which is again determined by another, and that again by another, and so on to infinity.

Demonstration. The mind is a certain and determinate mode of thinking (by Prop. 11, Part 2), and so (by Prop. 17, Coroll. 2, Part 1) it cannot be the free cause of its actions, or, it cannot have an absolute faculty of willing and being unwilling, but must be determined to will this or that (by Prop. 28, Part 1) by a cause, which is also determined by another, and this again by another, etc. QED.

Scholium

In the same way as this it is demonstrated that there exists in the mind no absolute faculty of understanding, desiring, loving, etc. From this it follows that these and similar faculties are either utterly fictitious, or are nothing but metaphysical entities, i.e. universals,[77] which we are accustomed to form from particulars. The result of this is that intellect and will are related to this and that idea, or to this and that volition, in the same way as stoneness is related to this and that stone, or humanity to Peter and Paul. I have explained in the Appendix of Part One why it is that people think themselves free; however, before I proceed further, it must be noted here that I understand by will the faculty of affirming and denying, but not desire. I understand, I repeat, the faculty by which the mind affirms or denies what is true or what is false, and not the desire by which the mind desires things or has an aversion to them.[78] But now that we have demonstrated that these faculties are universal notions, which are not distinguished from the particulars from which we form them, we must inquire whether volitions themselves are anything other than the ideas of things. We must inquire, I say, whether there is in the mind any affirmation and negation other than that which an idea involves, in so far as it is an idea. On this matter, see the following Proposition, and also Def. 3, Part 2, so that thinking is not confused with picturing.[79] For I understand by ideas, not images, such as those which are formed in the bottom of the eye and, if you wish, in the middle of the brain, but the conceptions of thought.

Proposition 49

There is in the mind no volition, or, no affirmation and negation, apart from that which an idea involves in so far as it is an idea.

Demonstration. There is in the mind (by the preceding Proposition) no absolute faculty of willing and being unwilling; there exist in it only particular volitions, namely this and that affirmation, and this and that negation. Let us therefore conceive some particular volition, namely the mode of thinking by which the mind affirms that the three angles of a triangle are equal to two right angles. This affirmation involves the conception, i.e. the idea, of a triangle; that is, it cannot be conceived without the idea of a triangle. For if I say that A must involve the conception of B, it is the same as if I say that A cannot be conceived without B. Further, this affirmation (by Ax. 3, Part 2) cannot exist without the idea of a triangle. This affirmation, therefore, can neither exist nor be conceived without the idea of a triangle. Again, this idea of a triangle must involve the affirmation that its three angles are equal to two right angles. Therefore, and vice versa, this idea of a triangle can neither exist nor be conceived without this affirmation, and so (by Def. 2,

Part 2) this affirmation belongs to the essence of the idea of a triangle, and is nothing apart from that essence. What we have said of this volition is also to be said (since we chose it at random) of any volition whatsoever, namely, that it is nothing apart from an idea. QED.

Corollary

Will and intellect are one and the same.

Demonstration. Will and intellect are simply particular volitions and ideas (by Proposition 48, Part 2, and its Scholium). But a particular volition and a particular idea (by the preceding Proposition) are one and the same; therefore, will and intellect are one and the same. QED.

Scholium

With this we have refuted a common supposition about the cause of error.[80] We showed above[81] that falsity consists solely in the privation which mutilated and confused ideas involve. So a false idea, in so far as it is false, does not involve certainty. So when we say that a man accepts what is false, and does not doubt about it, we do not therefore say that he is certain; we say only that he does not doubt, or that he accepts what is false, because there are no causes that bring it about that his imagination fluctuates. On this, see the Scholium of Proposition 44, Part 2. Therefore, as long as a man is supposed to cling to what is false, we shall never say that he is certain. For by certainty we understand something positive (see Prop. 43, Part 2, and its Scholium), but not the privation of doubt. But by the privation of certainty we understand falsity. However, for a fuller explanation of the preceding Proposition there remain a number of warnings that must be given. Then it remains for me to reply to objections that can be brought against this doctrine of ours; and finally, so that I may remove all doubt, I thought it worth while to indicate some benefits of this doctrine. I say 'some benefits'; for the chief ones will be understood better from what we shall say in Part Five.

I begin, therefore, with the first, and I warn my readers that they should distinguish accurately between an idea, i.e. a conception of the mind, and the images of things, which we imagine. Then it is necessary that they should distinguish between ideas and the words by which we signify things. For these three—namely, images, words, and ideas—are either entirely confused by many, or are not distinguished by them with sufficient accuracy, or with sufficient care. Therefore, they are entirely ignorant of this doctrine of ours concerning the will, which it is utterly necessary to know, both for speculative purposes and for the wise conduct of life. For those who think that ideas consist of images, which are formed in us through the impact of bodies, persuade themselves that the ideas of things of which we can form no similar image are not ideas, but only figments which we form by a free decision of the will. They therefore regard ideas as if they were mute pictures on a panel,[82] and preoccupied with this prejudice they do not see that an idea, in so far as it is an idea, involves affirmation or negation. Then again, those who confuse words with an idea, or with the affirmation that an idea involves, suppose that they can will the opposite of what they think,[83] when they affirm or deny by words alone something that is the opposite of what they think. But these prejudices can easily be cast off by anyone who attends to the nature of thought, which is far from involving the concept of extension, and who understands clearly that an idea (since it is a mode of thinking) consists neither in an image of some thing nor in words. For the essence of words and images is constituted solely by corporeal motions, which are far from involving the concept of thought.

These few warnings about these matters are sufficient, so I proceed to the objections mentioned above. The *first*[84] of these objections is that people think that it has been established that the will is more widely extended than the intellect,[85] and so is different from it. The reason why they think that the will is more widely extended than the intellect is this. They say that they experience that they do not need, for assenting to an infinity of things that we do not perceive, a faculty of assent—i.e. of affirmation and negation—which is greater than that which we now have; but that they do need a greater faculty of understanding. Therefore, the will is distinguished from the intellect, because the latter is finite and the former is infinite. *Secondly*, it can be objected to us that experience seems to teach nothing more clearly than that we can suspend our judgement, so that we do not assent to things that we perceive.[86] This is confirmed by the fact that no one is said to be deceived in so far as he perceives something, but only in so far as he assents or dissents. For example, someone who imagines a winged horse does not therefore grant that a winged horse exists; that is, he is not deceived unless he grants at the same time that a winged horse exists. So experience seems to teach nothing more clearly than that the will, i.e. the faculty of assent, is free and different from the faculty of understanding.

Thirdly, it can be objected that one affirmation does not seem to contain more reality than another. That is, we seem not to need more power to affirm that something that is true is true than we need to affirm that something that is false is true. But we perceive that one idea has more reality, i.e. perfection, than another; for the more that some objects are more excellent than others, the more their ideas are more perfect than other ideas.[87] A difference between will and intellect seems to be established by this. *Fourthly*, it can be objected that if a man did not operate out of freedom of will, what will happen if he is in equilibrium, like Buridan's ass?[88] Will he perish of hunger and thirst? If I grant this, I may seem to be thinking of an ass, or a statue of a man, and not a man; but if I deny it, then the man will determine himself, and consequently he has the faculty of moving and of doing whatever he wills. Perhaps other objections can be brought besides these; but since I am not bound to force upon my readers whatever anyone can dream, I shall trouble myself to reply only to the objections listed, and as briefly as I can. In response to the *first* objection, I say that I grant that will is more widely extended than the intellect, if by intellect they understand only clear and distinct ideas. But I deny that will is more widely extended than perceptions, or, the faculty of conceiving. Nor indeed do I see why the faculty of willing should be called infinite rather than the faculty of sensing; for just as we can affirm, by the same faculty of willing, an infinity of things (one after the other; for we cannot affirm an infinity of things at the same time), so also we can sense, i.e. perceive, an infinity of bodies (one after the other) by the same faculty of sensing. But what if they say that there is an infinity of things that we cannot perceive? I reply that we cannot reach these by any thought, and consequently by any faculty of willing. But they say that if God wanted to bring it about that we should perceive these things as well, he would have had to give us a greater faculty of perceiving than he did, but not a greater faculty of willing. This is the same as if they were to say that if God wanted to bring it about that we should understand an infinity of other entities, it would be necessary that he should give us, in order that we should grasp this infinity of entities, a greater intellect than he gave us, but not a more universal idea of an entity. For we have shown that will is a universal entity, i.e. an idea by which we explain all particular volitions, that is, what is common to all of them. Since, therefore, they believe that this common, i.e. universal, idea of all volitions is a faculty, it is by no means remarkable if they say that this faculty is extended to infinity, beyond the limits of the intellect. For something universal is asserted equally of one, many, and an infinity of individuals. I reply to the *second* objection by denying that we have a free power of suspending judgement. For when we say that someone suspends judgement, we simply say that he sees that he does not perceive a thing adequately. Suspense of judgement, therefore, is really perception, and not free will. So that this may be clearly understood, let us conceive a boy imagining a winged horse, and perceiving nothing else. Since this imagination involves the existence of the horse (by Prop. 17, Coroll., Part 2) and the boy perceives nothing that takes away the existence of the horse, he will necessarily regard the horse as present, nor will he be able to doubt of its existence, even though he is not certain of it. We experience this daily in dreams, and I do not believe that there is anyone who thinks that, whilst he is dreaming, he has a free power of suspending his judgement about that of which he dreams, and of bringing it about that he does not dream what he dreams he sees. Nevertheless, it happens that even in dreams we suspend judgement, namely when we dream that we are dreaming. Further, I grant that nobody is deceived in so far as he perceives; that is, I grant that the imaginations of the mind, considered in themselves, involve no error (see Prop. 17, Schol., Part 2). But I deny that a man affirms nothing in so far as he perceives. For what is it to perceive a winged horse, other than to affirm wings of a horse? For if the mind were to perceive nothing other than a winged horse, it would regard the horse as present to it, and would have no cause of doubt about its existence and no faculty of dissent, unless its imagination of the winged horse were joined to an idea which takes away the existence of that horse, or because it perceives that the idea of the winged horse that it has is inadequate. Then it will either necessarily negate the existence of the horse, or it will necessarily doubt it. With this I think that I have replied to the *third* objection: namely, by saying that the will is something universal, which is predicated of all ideas, and that this only means what is common to all ideas, namely affirmation. Consequently, the adequate essence of affirmation, in so far as it is conceived so abstractly, must be in each idea, and in this way only is it the same in all; but not in so far as it is regarded as constituting the essence of an idea, for to that extent particular affirmations differ among themselves just as much as the ideas do. For example, the affirmation that the idea of a circle involves differs from the affirmation that the idea of a triangle involves as much as the idea of a circle differs from the idea of a triangle. Further, I deny absolutely that we need an equal power of thinking to affirm that something that is true is true as we do to affirm that something that is false is true. For these two affirmations, if you regard the mind, are related to each other as an entity to a non-entity; for there is nothing positive in ideas which constitutes the form of falsity (see Prop. 35 and its Schol., Part 2, and Prop. 47, Schol., Part 2). Consequently, one must note here especially how easily we are deceived when we confuse universals with particulars, and entities of reason and abstractions with real things. Finally, as to what concerns the *fourth* objection, I say that I grant entirely that a man placed in such a state of equilibrium (namely, a man who perceives nothing but hunger and thirst, and food and drink such that they are equally distant from him) will perish of hunger and thirst. But if people ask me whether such a man is not to be regarded as an ass rather than as a man, I reply that I do not know; just as I also do not know how we are to regard a man who hangs himself, and how we are to regard children, fools, and madmen, etc.

It now remains to indicate how much the knowledge of this doctrine benefits our life, which we shall see easily from what follows. First, it benefits us in so far as it teaches us to act solely in accordance with the command of God and to be participants in the divine nature, and the more so as we perform actions which are more perfect, and the more we understand God. This doctrine, therefore, besides the fact that it makes the mind entirely calm, has the further benefit that it teaches us in what our supreme happiness, or, our blessedness, consists: namely, solely in the knowledge of God, from which we are led to do only those things which love and piety advise. From this we clearly understand how far those people stray from a true appraisal of virtue who expect to be honoured by God with the highest rewards for their virtue and their good actions, as though for their supreme servitude—as if virtue and the service of God were not happiness itself, and supreme freedom.[89] Secondly, our doctrine benefits us in so far as it teaches us how we must conduct ourselves with regard to matters of fortune, or, matters that are not in our power: that is, matters which do not follow from our nature. It teaches us to expect and to bear with a calm mind both faces of fortune, since all things follow from the eternal decree of God with the same necessity as it follows from the essence of a triangle that its three angles are equal to two right angles. Thirdly, this doctrine contributes to social life, in so far as it teaches us to hate no one, to despise no one, to deride no one, to be angry with no one, and to envy no one.[90] It also contributes to social life in so far as it teaches us that each one should be content with what he has and should help his neighbour, not from effeminate pity, bias, or superstition, but solely from the guidance of reason, as time and circumstances demand, as I shall show in the Fourth Part.[91] Fourthly, and lastly, this doctrine contributes greatly to society in general, in so far as it teaches us how citizens are to be governed and led: namely, not so that they should be slaves, but so that they should do freely what is the best. With this, I have fulfilled what I promised to do in this Scholium, and with this I bring to an end this Second Part. I think that, in this Part, I have explained the nature of the human mind and its properties at sufficient length and (as far as the difficulty of the subject allows) with sufficient clarity. Further, I think that I have set down things such that from them there can be inferred much that is excellent, extremely useful, and necessary to know, as will be established in part from what follows.

End of the Second Part

PART THREE

ON THE ORIGIN AND NATURE
OF THE EMOTIONS[1]

Preface

Most of those who have written about the emotions and about men's way of living seem not to discuss natural things, which follow the common laws of Nature; rather, they seem to discuss things that are outside Nature. Indeed, they seem to conceive the place of man in Nature as being like an empire within an empire. For they believe that man disturbs the order of Nature rather than that he follows it, that he has an absolute power over his actions, and that he is determined by himself alone. Further, they ascribe the cause of human impotence and inconstancy, not to the common power of Nature, but to some defect or other in human nature, which they accordingly lament, laugh at, condemn, or (as happens most often) denounce, and the person who can revile the impotence of the human mind most eloquently or most cleverly is regarded as if he were divine. There were some outstanding men (to whose labour and industry we confess ourselves much indebted) who wrote many excellent things about the right way of living, and gave to mortals some counsels that were full of prudence; but no one, as far as I know, has determined the nature and strength of the emotions, and what the mind can do by way of moderating them. I know, indeed, that the famous Descartes—even though he also believed that the mind has an absolute power over its actions[2]—tried to explain human emotions through their primary causes, and at the same time to show a way by which the mind could rule absolutely over the emotions. But, in my opinion at any rate, all that he did was show the keenness of his great intellect, as I shall show in its proper place.[3] For I want to return to those who prefer to denounce or laugh at the emotions and actions of human beings, rather than understand them. To these people it will doubtless seem extraordinary that I should undertake to treat the faults and follies of human beings in a geometrical way, and should want to demonstrate by sure reason what they proclaim to be contrary to reason, and to be empty, absurd, and horrible. But my argument is this. Nothing happens in Nature which can be ascribed to a defect in it. For Nature is always the same and everywhere is one, and its virtue and power of acting is the same. That is, the laws of Nature and the rules in accordance with which all things happen and are changed from one form into another are everywhere and always the same; and therefore there must also be one and the same way of understanding the nature of things of any kind—namely, by the universal laws and rules of Nature. Therefore, the emotions of hatred, anger, envy, etc., considered in themselves, follow from the same necessity and virtue of Nature as do all other particular things. Consequently, they recognize certain causes by which they are understood, and they have certain properties which are equally worthy of knowledge as are the properties of any other thing by whose contemplation alone we are delighted. So I shall discuss the nature and strength of the emotions, and of the power of the mind over them, by the same method as that by which I discussed God and the mind in preceding parts, and I shall discuss human actions and appetites just as if the inquiry concerned lines, planes, or bodies.

Definitions

1. I call that an adequate cause whose effect can be clearly and distinctly perceived through itself. I call that an inadequate, or, a partial, cause whose effect cannot be understood through itself alone.

2. I say that we act when something occurs either in us or outside us of which we are the adequate cause; that is (by the preceding Definition), when there follows from our nature,[4] either in us or outside us, something that can be understood clearly and distinctly through that nature alone. Conversely, I say that we are passive when something occurs in us, or when something follows from our nature, of which we are only a partial cause.

3. By emotion I understand the affections of the body by which the body's power of acting is increased or diminished, helped or hindered, and at the same time the ideas of these affections.

If, therefore, we can be the adequate cause of one of these affections, then I understand by the emotion an action; otherwise, I understand it to be a passion.

Postulates

1. The human body can be affected in many ways by which its power of acting is increased or diminished, and also in other ways which make its power of acting neither greater nor smaller.

This postulate, i.e. axiom, depends on Post. 1 and Lem. 5 and Lem. 7 following Prop. 13, Part 2.[5]

2. The human body can undergo many changes, and yet retain the impressions, i.e. the traces, of objects (see Post. 5, Part 2), and consequently the same images of things. (For the definitions of these, see Prop. 17, Schol., Part 2.)

Proposition 1

Our mind sometimes acts, but sometimes is passive; namely, in so far as it has adequate ideas, so far it necessarily acts, and in so far as it has inadequate ideas, so far it is necessarily passive.

Demonstration. In every human mind, some of the ideas are adequate but others are mutilated and confused (by Prop. 40, Schol., Part 2). The ideas which are adequate in someone's mind are adequate in God in so far as he constitutes the essence of that mind (by Prop. 11, Coroll., Part 2), and those which are inadequate in the mind are also adequate in God (by the same Corollary), not in so far as he constitutes solely the essence of that mind, but also in so far as he contains in himself at the same time the minds of other things. Further, from any given idea some effect must necessarily follow (by Prop. 36, Part 1), of which effect God is the adequate cause (see Def. 1, Part 3), not in so far as he is infinite, but in so far as he is considered as affected by that given idea (see Prop. 9, Part 2). But in the case of an effect of which God is the cause in so far as he is affected by an idea which is adequate in someone's mind, that same mind is the adequate cause of this effect (by Prop. 11, Coroll., Part 2). Therefore, our mind (by Def. 2, Part 3), in so far as it has adequate ideas, necessarily acts; which was the first thing to be proved. Further: in the case of whatever follows necessarily from an idea which is adequate in God, not in so far as he constitutes the mind of one man alone, but in so far as he has in himself the ideas of other things simultaneously with the mind of that man, the mind of that man (again by Prop. 11, Coroll., Part 2) is not the adequate, but the partial cause of this. Therefore (by Def. 2,

Part 3), the mind, in so far as it has inadequate ideas, is necessarily passive, which was the second thing to be proved. Therefore, our mind, etc. QED.

Corollary

From this it follows that our mind is liable to more passions the more inadequate ideas it has, and conversely that it performs more actions the more adequate ideas it has.

Proposition 2

The body cannot determine the mind to thinking, nor can the mind determine the body to motion or to rest, or to anything else (if there is anything else).

Demonstration. All the modes of thinking have God as a cause in so far as he is a thinking thing, and not in so far as he is explained by another attribute (by Prop. 6, Part 2). Therefore, that which determines the mind to thinking is a mode of thinking and not of extension, that is (by Def. 1, Part 2), it is not a body; which was the first thing to be proved. Next, the motion and rest of a body must arise from another body, which was also determined to motion or rest by another; and in absolute terms,[6] whatever arises in a body must have arisen from God in so far as he is considered as affected by some mode of extension, and not in so far as he is considered as affected by some mode of thinking (again by Prop. 6, Part 2). That is, it cannot arise from the mind, which (by Prop. 11, Part 2) is a mode of thinking; which was the second thing to be proved. Therefore, the body cannot determine the mind, etc. QED.

Scholium

This is understood more clearly from what was said in the Scholium of Prop. 7, Part 2: namely, that the mind and the body is one and the same thing which is conceived now under the attribute of thought and now under the attribute of extension. From this it comes about that the order, i.e. the interconnection, of things is one, whether Nature is conceived under this or that attribute, and consequently that the order of the actions and passions of our body is simultaneous in nature with the order of the actions and passions of the mind. This is also evident from the way in which we have demonstrated Prop. 12, Part 2. However, although the situation is such that no reason for doubt remains, I find it hard to believe that men can be led to weigh these things calmly in their mind, unless I confirm the matter by experience—so firmly are they persuaded that the body now moves and now is at rest simply at the command of the mind, and that it does very many things that depend solely on the mind's will and ingenuity. For no one has so far determined what the body can do; that is, experience has so far taught no one what the body can do and what it cannot do by the laws of Nature alone, in so far as Nature is considered as corporeal only, without being determined by the mind. For no one so far has had such an accurate knowledge of the structure of the body that he can explain all its functions; to say nothing of the many things that are observed in the lower animals which far exceed human sagacity, and of the fact that sleepwalkers do many things in their sleep that they would not dare to do whilst awake. This shows sufficiently that the body can, by virtue of the laws of its own nature, do many things at which its mind is astonished. Then again, no one knows by what method or by what means the mind moves the body, or how many degrees of motion it can give the body, or with what speed the mind can move it. It follows from this that when men say that this or that action of the body has its origin in the mind, which has mastery over the body, they do not know what they are saying, and do nothing but confess with specious words that they are blithely ignorant of the true cause of that action. But they will say that, whether or not they know by what means the mind moves the body, yet they experience the fact that, unless the human mind were capable of making plans, the body would be inert. Then again, they will say that it is in the power of the mind alone both to speak and to be silent, and many other things which they therefore believe to depend on the decree of the mind. But as to the first of these: I ask them whether experience does not also teach that if, on the other hand, the body is inert, the mind is at the same time incapable of thinking. For when the body is at rest in sleep, the mind remains asleep at the same time, and does not have the power of making plans that it has when it is awake. Further, I believe that everyone has experienced the fact that the mind is not always equally capable of thinking about the same object, but just as the body is more capable of having the image of this or that object excited in it, so the mind is more capable of considering this or that object. But, they will say, it cannot happen that there can be deduced solely from the laws of Nature, in so far as it is conceived as corporeal alone, the causes of buildings, pictures, and things of this kind, which come into existence only by human skill; nor is the human body capable of building some temple unless it is determined by and guided by the mind. But I have already shown[7] that they themselves do not know of what the body is capable, or what can be deduced simply from a consideration of its nature, and that they experience many things to occur from the laws of Nature alone which they would never have believed to have been able to occur without the direction of the mind—such as the things that sleepwalkers do in their sleep, which they themselves marvel at when they are awake. I add here the very structure of the human body, which far exceeds in ingenuity all the things that are manufactured by human skill: to say nothing of the fact that, as I have shown above,[8] infinite things follow from Nature, under whatever attribute it is considered. As to the second point: certainly, human affairs would be much happier if it were equally in the power of man both to be silent and to speak. But experience teaches us more than sufficiently that men have nothing less in their power than their tongue, or than the restraint of their appetites. This has brought it about that many believe that we do freely only those things which we pursue casually, since the desire for these things can easily be restrained by the memory of another thing which we often recall; but that we are far from doing freely those things which we pursue with great emotion, and which cannot be calmed by the memory of something else. However, unless they had experience of the fact that we often do things which we later regret, and that we often (namely, when we are harassed by contrary emotions) see the better and follow the worse,[9] nothing would hinder them from believing that we do everything freely. So an infant believes that it desires milk freely, an angry boy believes that he seeks revenge freely, and a timid man believes that he seeks flight freely. Then again, a drunkard believes that he says by a free decree of the mind things that, when sober, he wishes that he had not said; so also a madman, a garrulous woman, a boy, and many others of this sort believe that they speak by a free decree of the mind, when in fact they cannot hold back their urge to speak. So experience, no less clearly than reason, teaches us that men believe themselves to be free by virtue of this cause alone: that they are conscious of their actions and ignorant of the causes by which they are determined.[10] It also teaches us that the decrees of the mind are simply the appetites themselves, which therefore vary in accordance with the varied disposition of the body. For each person regulates everything in accordance with his emotion, and those who are harassed by contrary emotions do not know what they want, but those who are harassed by no emotion are easily driven this way and that way. All this clearly shows that both the decree of the mind, and the appetite and the determination of the body, are simultaneous in nature, or rather are one and the same thing which, when it is considered under the attribute of thought and is explained through it, we call a decree, and when it is considered under the attribute of extension and is deduced from the laws of motion and rest, we call a determination. This will appear still more clearly from what is now to be said. For there is something else that I want to be noted here first of all: namely, that we can do nothing from a decree of the mind unless we recollect it. For example, we cannot speak a word unless we recollect it. Next, it is not in the free power of the mind either to recollect some thing or to forget it. So this alone is believed to be in the power of the mind: namely that we can, by a free decree of the mind alone, either be silent about or speak of a thing which we recollect. However, when we dream that we speak, we believe that we speak by a free decree of the mind; but we do not speak, or if we do speak, this comes about by a spontaneous motion of the body. Then again we dream that we conceal certain things from men, and that we do so by the same decree of the mind as that by which, when we are awake, we remain silent about what we know. Finally, we dream that we do certain things by a decree of the mind that we would not dare to do whilst we were awake. So I would like to know whether there are in the mind two kinds of decree: one consisting of the decrees of fantasy, and the other consisting of free decrees. But if one is not disposed to be as insane as this, then it must necessarily be conceded that this decree of the mind, which is believed to be free, is not distinguished from the imagination, i.e. from the memory, and is simply the affirmation which an idea necessarily involves, in so far as it is an idea (see Prop. 49, Part 2). So these decrees of the mind arise in the mind with the same necessity as the ideas of things that actually exist. Therefore, those people who believe that they speak, or are silent, or do anything by a free decree of the mind, dream with their eyes open.

Proposition 3

The actions of the mind arise from adequate ideas alone, but passions depend on inadequate ideas alone.

Demonstration. The first thing that constitutes the essence of the mind is simply the idea of a body that actually exists (by Props. 11 and 13, Part 2).

This idea (by Prop. 15, Part 2) is composed of many others, of which some (by Prop. 38, Coroll., Part 2) are adequate, but some (by Prop. 29, Coroll., Part 2) are inadequate. Therefore, whatever follows from the nature of the mind, and of which the mind is the proximate cause[11] through which it must be understood, must necessarily follow from either an adequate or an inadequate idea. But in so far as the mind (by Prop. 1, Part 3) has inadequate ideas, so far it is necessarily passive; therefore, the actions of the mind follow solely from adequate ideas, and accordingly the mind is passive only because it has inadequate ideas. QED.

Scholium

So we see that passions are not related to the mind except in so far as it has something that involves negation, or, in so far as it is considered as a part of Nature, which cannot be perceived clearly and distinctly through itself and without others. I could show by this reasoning that the passions are related to particular things in the same way that they are related to the mind, and cannot be perceived in any other way; but my intention is to speak of the human mind alone.

Proposition 4

Nothing can be destroyed except by an external cause.

Demonstration. This proposition is self-evident, for the definition of each thing affirms, but does not deny, the essence of the thing; or, it posits, but does not negate, the essence of the thing. Whilst, therefore, we attend to the thing itself alone, but not to external causes, we shall be able to find nothing in it which can destroy it. QED.

Proposition 5

Things are of a contrary nature, that is, they cannot be in the same subject, in so far as one can destroy the other.

Demonstration. For if they could be consistent with each other, or be in the same subject at the same time, then there could exist in the same subject something that could destroy it, which (by the preceding Proposition) is absurd. Therefore things, etc. QED.

Proposition 6

Each thing, in so far as it is in itself, endeavours to persevere in its being.[12]

Demonstration. For particular things are modes, by which the attributes of God are expressed in a certain and determinate way (by Prop. 25, Coroll., Part 1). That is (by Prop. 34, Part 1), they are things which express in a certain and determinate way the power of God, by which God exists and acts. Nor does any thing have in itself something by which it could be destroyed, or, which negates its existence (by Prop. 4, Part 3), but on the contrary it is opposed to everything which can negate its existence (by the preceding Proposition), and so it endeavours, as far as it can and is in itself, to persevere in its being. QED.

Proposition 7

The endeavour by which each thing endeavours to persevere in its being is nothing other than the actual essence of the thing.[13]

Demonstration. From the given essence of each thing, certain things necessarily follow (by Prop. 36, Part 1), nor can things do anything other than that which necessarily follows from their determinate nature (by Prop. 29, Part 1). So the power, i.e. the endeavour, of each thing by which, either alone or with others, it either acts or endeavours to act—that is (by Prop. 6, Part 3) the power, i.e. the endeavour, by which it strives to persevere in its being—is nothing other than the given, i.e. the actual, essence of the thing. QED.

Proposition 8

The endeavour by which each thing strives to persevere in its being involves, not a finite, but an indefinite, time.

Demonstration. For if it involved a limited time, which determined the duration of the thing,[14] then it would follow, simply from the power by which the thing exists, that the thing could not exist after that limited time, but must then be destroyed. But this (by Prop. 4, Part 3) is absurd. Therefore, the endeavour by which the thing exists does not involve a definite time, but on the contrary this endeavour involves an indefinite time, since (again by Prop. 4, Part 3) if it is not destroyed by an external cause, it will always continue to exist with the same power by which it exists now. QED.

Proposition 9

The mind, both in so far as it has clear and distinct ideas and in so far as it has confused ideas, endeavours to persevere in its being for an indefinite duration, and is conscious of this endeavour.

Demonstration. The essence of the mind is constituted by both adequate and inadequate ideas (as we showed in Prop. 3, Part 3). So (by Prop. 7, Part 3) it endeavours to persevere in its being in so far as it has both the former and the latter, and also (by Prop. 8, Part 3) it does so for an indefinite duration. But the mind (by Prop. 23, Part 2) is necessarily conscious of itself through the ideas of the affections of the body; therefore (by Prop. 7, Part 3), it is conscious of its endeavour. QED.

Scholium

This endeavour, when it is related to the mind alone, is called 'will',[15] but when it is related to the mind and body simultaneously, it is called 'appetite'. Appetite, therefore, is nothing other than the very essence of man, from the nature of which there necessarily follow those things that contribute to his preservation, and so man is determined to do these things. Further, there is no difference between appetite and desire, except that desire is usually related to men in so far as they are conscious of their appetite,[16] and so it can be defined as follows: 'Desire is appetite together with a consciousness of the appetite'. So it is established from all this that we do not endeavour, will, seek after,[17] or desire something because we judge it to be good, but on the contrary we judge something to be good because we endeavour, will, seek after, or desire it.

Proposition 10

An idea which excludes the existence of our body cannot exist in our mind, but is contrary to it.[18]

Demonstration. Whatever can destroy our body cannot exist in it (by Prop. 5, Part 3), and so an idea of that thing cannot exist in God in so far as he has the idea of our body (by Prop. 9, Coroll., Part 2). That is (by

Props. 11 and 13, Part 2), the idea of that thing cannot exist in our mind; but on the contrary, since (by Props. 11 and 13, Part 2) the first thing that constitutes the essence of the mind is the idea of a body that actually exists, the first and principal feature of our mind is (by Prop. 7, Part 3) the endeavour to affirm the existence of our body. So an idea that negates the existence of our body is contrary to our mind, etc. QED.

Proposition 11

Whatever increases or diminishes, helps or hinders,[19] our body's power of acting, the idea of that same thing increases or diminishes, helps or hinders, our mind's power of thinking.

Demonstration. This proposition is evident from Prop. 7, Part 2, or again from Prop. 14, Part 2.

Scholium

So we see that the mind can undergo great changes, and pass now to a greater and now to a lesser perfection. These passions explain to us the emotions of pleasure and pain.[20] Therefore, by 'pleasure' I shall understand in what follows 'the passion by which the mind passes to a greater perfection',[21] and by 'pain' I shall understand 'the passion by which the mind passes to a lesser perfection'. Further, I call the emotion of pleasure, in so far as it is related simultaneously to the mind and the body, either 'titillation' or 'joy'; the emotion of pain I shall call either 'anguish' or 'melancholy'.[22] It must be noted that titillation and anguish are related to a man in so far as one part of him is affected more than another, but joy and melancholy are related to a man in so far as all his parts are affected equally. I have explained what desire is in the Scholium of Prop. 9 of this Part, and besides these three[23] I recognize no other primary emotion; for I will show in what follows that the other emotions arise from them. But before I proceed any further, I wish to explain here more fully Proposition 10 of this Part, so that it may be understood more clearly how an idea is contrary to an idea.

In the Scholium of Proposition 17, Part 2, we showed that the idea that constitutes the essence of the mind involves the existence of the body as long as the body itself exists. Then from what we showed in Prop. 8, Coroll., Part 2 and its Scholium, it follows that the present existence of our mind depends on this alone: that the mind involves the actual existence of the body. Finally, we showed that the power of the mind, by which it imagines and recollects things, also depends (see Prop. 17, and Prop. 18 and Scholium, Part 2) on the fact that it involves the actual existence of the body. From this it follows that the present existence of the mind and its power of imagining is negated as soon as the mind ceases to affirm the present existence of the body. But the cause on account of which the mind ceases to affirm this existence of the body cannot be the mind itself (by Prop. 4, Part 3), nor can the cause be the fact that the body ceases to exist. For (by Prop. 6, Part 2) the cause on account of which the mind affirms the existence of the body is not the fact that the body has begun to exist; and therefore, by the same reasoning, it does not cease to affirm the existence of its body because the body ceases to exist. Rather (by Prop. 8, Part 2) this arises from another idea, which excludes the present existence of our body, and consequently of our mind, and which is therefore contrary to the idea which constitutes the essence of our mind.[24]

Proposition 12

The mind endeavours, as far as it can, to imagine those things which increase or help the body's power of acting.

Demonstration. As long as the human body is affected in a way which involves the nature of some external body, so long the human mind will regard that body as present (by Prop. 17, Part 2). Consequently (by Prop. 7, Part 2), as long as the human mind regards some external body as present, that is (by Prop. 17, Schol., Part 2), imagines it, so long the human body is affected in a way which involves the nature of that external body. So as long as the mind imagines those things which increase or help our body's power of acting, so long the body is affected in ways which increase or help its power of acting (see Post. 1, Part 3). So long, consequently (by Prop. 11, Part 3), the mind's power of thinking is increased or helped, and therefore (by Prop. 6 or Prop. 9, Part 3) the mind endeavours, as far as it can, to imagine those things. QED.

Proposition 13

When the mind imagines things that diminish or hinder the body's power of acting, it endeavours, as far as it can, to recollect that which excludes the existence of these things.

Demonstration. As long as the mind imagines something of this sort, so long the power of the mind and the body is diminished or hindered (as we demonstrated in the preceding Proposition). Nevertheless, it will imagine this thing until the mind imagines something else which excludes the thing's present existence (by Prop. 17, Part 2). That is (as we have just shown) the power of the mind and the body is diminished or hindered until the mind imagines something else, which excludes the existence of this thing. So (by Prop. 9, Part 3) the mind will, as far as it can, endeavour to imagine or recollect that which excludes the existence of this thing. QED.

Corollary

From this it follows that the mind is averse to imagining those things which diminish or hinder its own power, and the power of the body.

Scholium

From this we clearly understand what love and hatred are. Namely, love is simply pleasure, with the accompaniment of the idea of an external cause, and hatred is simply pain, with the accompaniment of the idea of an external cause.[25] We see, further, that the person who loves necessarily endeavours to have present and to preserve the thing that he loves; on the other hand, the person who hates endeavours to remove and destroy the thing that he hates. But all these matters will be discussed more fully in what follows.

Proposition 14

If the mind was once affected by two emotions simultaneously, when it is later affected by either of these it will also be affected by the other.

Demonstration. If the human body was once affected by two bodies simultaneously, when the mind later imagines either of these it will immediately recollect the other (by Prop. 18, Part 2). But the mind's imaginations indicate the emotions of our bodies, rather than the nature of external bodies (by Prop. 16, Coroll. 2, Part 2). Therefore, if the body, and consequently the mind (see Def. 3, Part 3), was once affected by two emotions simultaneously,[26] when it is later affected by one or other of these it will also be affected by the other. QED.

Proposition 15

Any thing can by accident be the cause of pleasure, pain, or desire.

Demonstration. Let it be assumed that the mind is affected simultaneously by two emotions: one which neither increases nor diminishes its power of acting, and another which either increases or diminishes it (see Post. 1, Part 3). It is evident from the preceding Proposition that when the mind is later affected by the former as its true cause, which (by hypothesis) through itself neither increases or diminishes its power of thinking, it will immediately be affected by the latter also, which increases or diminishes its power of thinking, that is (by Prop. 11, Schol., Part 3), it will be affected by pleasure or pain. So the thing will be the cause of pleasure or pain, not through itself, but by accident. In the same way it can easily be shown that that thing can by accident be the cause of desire. QED.[27]

Corollary

From the mere fact that we have contemplated some thing with the emotion of pleasure or pain, of which it is not the efficient cause, we are able to love it or hate it.

Demonstration. For from this fact alone it comes about (by Prop. 14, Part 3) that when the mind later imagines this thing, it is affected by the emotion of pleasure or pain; that is (by Prop. 11, Schol., Part 3), that the power of the mind and the body is increased or diminished, etc. Consequently, it comes about (by Prop. 12, Part 3) that the mind either desires to imagine it (by Prop. 13, Coroll., Part 3) or is averse to it; that is (by Prop. 13, Schol., Part 3), that it loves it or hates it. QED.

Scholium

From this we understand how it can happen that we can love or hate something without any cause that is known to us, but simply out of what is called 'sympathy' or 'antipathy'. To this one must also relate those objects that affect us with pleasure or pain simply from the fact that they have something similar to objects that usually affect us with these emotions, as I shall show in the next Proposition. I know that the authors who first introduced the terms 'sympathy' and 'antipathy'[28] meant to indicate by them certain occult qualities of things;[29] nevertheless, I think that it is permissible for us to understand by them known or manifest qualities.

Proposition 16

From the mere fact that we imagine a thing to have something that is similar to an object which is accustomed to affect our mind with pleasure or pain, we shall love or hate the thing, even though that in respect of which it is similar to the object is not the efficient cause of these emotions.

Demonstration. We have (by hypothesis) regarded in the object itself, with the emotion of pleasure or pain, that which is similar to the object; and so (by Prop. 14, Part 3) when the mind is affected by its image, it will immediately be affected by the latter or the former emotion. Consequently, the thing which we perceive to have this will (by Prop. 15, Part 3) be by accident the cause of pleasure or of pain. So (by the preceding Corollary) although that in respect of which it is similar to the object is not the efficient cause of these emotions, yet we shall love or hate the thing. QED.

Proposition 17

If we imagine a thing which is accustomed to affect us with the emotion of pain to have something which is similar to another thing, which is accustomed to affect us with an equally great emotion of pleasure, we shall simultaneously love and hate the same thing.

Demonstration. For this thing (by hypothesis) is through itself the cause of pain, and (by Prop. 13, Schol., Part 3) in so far as we imagine it with this emotion, we hate it. Further, in so far as we imagine it to have besides something which is similar to another thing, which is accustomed to affect us with an equally great emotion of pleasure, we shall (by the preceding Proposition) love it with a pleasurable effort that is equally great; and so we shall simultaneously love and hate the same thing. QED.

Scholium

This disposition of the mind, which arises out of two contrary emotions, is called a 'wavering of the mind',[30] which is related to an emotion as doubt is related to the imagination (see Prop. 44, Schol., Part 2). Wavering of mind and doubt do not differ from one another, except in respect of more and less. But it must be noted that in the preceding Proposition I deduced these fluctuations of the mind from causes which are respectively the cause of one emotion through itself, and the cause of another emotion by accident. I did this because in this way they could be deduced more easily from what precedes, and not because I deny that fluctuations of the mind generally arise from an object which is the efficient cause of each emotion. For the human body (by Post. 1, Part 2) is composed of very many individuals of a diverse nature, and so (by Axiom 1 after Lemma 3, following Prop. 13, Part 2) it can be affected by one and the same body in very many different ways. Conversely, because one and the same thing can be affected in many ways, it can also affect one and the same part of the body in many different ways. From this we can easily conceive that one and the same object can be the cause of many contrary emotions.

Proposition 18

A man is affected by the image of a past or future thing with the same emotion of pleasure or pain as he is by the image of a present thing.[31]

Demonstration. As long as a man is affected by the image of some thing, he will regard the thing as present, even though it does not exist (by Prop. 17 and its Coroll., Part 2). He will not imagine it as past or as future, except in so far as the image is joined to the image of past or future time (see Prop. 44, Schol., Part 2). Consequently, the image of the thing, considered in itself alone, is the same whether it is related to future or past time, or to the present. That is (by Prop. 16, Coroll. 2, Part 2), the disposition of the body, i.e. the emotion, is the same, whether the image is of a past or future thing, or of a present thing. So the emotion of pleasure or of pain is the same, whether the image is of a past or future thing, or of a present thing. QED.

Scholium 1

Here, I call a thing past or future in so far as we have been affected by it, or will be affected by it: for example, in so far as we have seen it or will see it, it has reinvigorated us or will reinvigorate us, it has harmed us or will harm us, etc. For in so far as we imagine it in this way, so far we affirm its existence, that is, the body is affected by no emotion which excludes the existence of the thing, and so (by Prop. 17, Part 2) the body is affected by the image of that thing in the same way as if the thing itself were present. However, it commonly happens that those who have experienced many things waver as long as they regard a thing as future or past, and usually doubt about the outcome of a matter (see Prop. 44, Schol., Part 2). From this it comes about that the emotions which arise from similar images of things[32] are not so constant, but are commonly disturbed by the images of other things, until men become more certain about the outcome of a matter.

Scholium 2

From what has just been said we understand what hope, fear, confidence, despair, delight, and remorse[33] are. For hope is simply an inconstant pleasure which has arisen from the image of a thing that is future or past, about whose outcome we are in doubt. Fear, on the contrary, is an inconstant pain, which has also arisen from the image of a thing that is doubtful. If doubt is removed from these emotions, then hope becomes confidence and fear becomes despair: namely, pleasure or pain which has arisen from the image of a thing which we have feared or hoped. Next, delight is pleasure which has arisen from the image of a thing in the past, of whose outcome we have been in doubt. Finally, remorse is a pain which is opposed to delight.

Proposition 19

Someone who imagines that what he loves is destroyed will feel pain; but if he imagines that it is preserved, he will feel pleasure.

Demonstration. The mind endeavours, as far as it can, to imagine those things which increase or help the body's power of acting (by Prop. 12, Part 3); that is (by Prop. 13, Schol., Part 3), things that it loves. But the imagination is helped by those things which posit the existence of a thing, and on the other hand is hindered by those things which exclude the existence of a thing (by Prop. 17, Part 2).[34] Therefore, the images of things which posit the existence of the thing that is loved help the endeavour of the mind by which it endeavours to imagine the thing that is loved; that is (by Prop. 11, Schol., Part 3), they affect the mind with pleasure. On the other hand, those things that exclude the existence of the thing that is loved hinder this same endeavour of the mind; that is (by the same Scholium), they affect the mind with pain. So someone who imagines that what he loves is destroyed will feel pain, etc. QED.

Proposition 20

Someone who imagines that what he hates is destroyed will feel pleasure.

Demonstration. The mind (by Prop. 13, Part 3) endeavours to imagine those things which exclude the existence of things by which the body's power of acting is diminished or hindered. That is (by the Scholium of the same Proposition), it endeavours to imagine those things which exclude the existence of the things which it hates. So the image of a thing which excludes the existence of that which the mind hates helps this endeavour of the mind; that is (by Prop. 11, Schol., Part 3), it affects the mind with pleasure. So someone who imagines that what he hates is destroyed will feel pleasure. QED.

Proposition 21

Someone who imagines that what he loves is affected with pleasure or pain will also be affected with pleasure or pain, and each of these emotions will be greater or less in the lover as each is greater or less in the thing loved.

Demonstration. The images of things (as we have demonstrated in Prop. 19, Part 3) which posit the existence of the thing that is loved help the endeavour of the mind by which it endeavours to imagine the thing that is loved. But pleasure posits the existence of the thing that feels pleasure, and the more so, the more the emotion of pleasure is greater; for (by Prop. 11, Schol., Part 3) it is a transition to a greater perfection. There-fore, the image in the lover of the pleasure of the thing that is loved helps the endeavour of his mind; that is (by Prop. 11, Schol., Part 3), it affects the lover with pleasure, and with a pleasure that is greater, the greater this emotion will have been in the thing that is loved. This was the first thing to be proved. Then, in so far as a thing is affected with pain, to that extent it is destroyed, and the more so the more it is affected with a greater pain (again by Prop. 11, Schol., Part 3). So (by Prop. 19, Part 3) someone who imagines that what he loves is affected with pain will also be affected with pain, and with a pain that is the greater, the greater this emotion will have been in the thing loved. QED.

Proposition 22

If we imagine someone to affect with pleasure a thing that we love, we shall be affected with love towards him. If, on the other hand, we imagine him to affect it with pain, we shall on the contrary be affected with hatred towards him.

Demonstration. Someone who affects with pleasure or pain a thing that we love also affects us with pleasure or pain, if we imagine the thing that we love to be affected with that pleasure or pain (by the preceding Proposition). But this pleasure or pain is supposed to exist in us with the accompaniment of the idea of an external cause; therefore (by Prop. 13, Schol., Part 3), if we imagine someone to affect with pleasure or pain a thing that we love, we shall be affected with love or hatred towards him. QED.

Scholium

Proposition 21 explains to us what compassion is: we can define it as 'pain which arises from another's harm'. I do not know with what name we are to call pleasure which arises from another's harm. We shall call love towards a person who has done good to another 'favour'; on the other hand, hatred towards a person who has done harm to another we shall call 'indignation'. Finally, it must be noted that we do not pity only a thing which we have loved (as we showed in Proposition 21), but that we also pity that towards which we have previously had no emotion, provided that (as I shall show below)[35] we judge it to be like us. So we shall also favour someone who has done good to a thing that is like us, and on the other hand we shall be indignant towards someone who has harmed a thing that is like us.

Proposition 23

Someone who imagines what he hates to be affected with pain will feel pleasure; if on the contrary he imagines it to be affected with pleasure he will feel pain. Each of these emotions will be greater or less as its contrary is greater or less in that which he hates.

Demonstration. In so far as a hateful thing is affected with pain, so far it is destroyed, and the more so, the greater the pain with which it is affected (by Prop. 11, Schol., Part 3). Therefore, someone who (by Prop. 20, Part 3) imagines a thing which he hates to be affected with pain will on the contrary be affected with pleasure, and with a pleasure that is greater, the greater the pain with which the hateful thing is imagined to be affected. This was the first thing to be proved. Then, pleasure posits the existence of the thing that feels pleasure (again by Prop. 11, Schol., Part 3), and the more so, the greater the pleasure is conceived to be. If someone imagines a person whom he hates to be affected with pleasure, this imagination (by Prop. 13, Part 3) will hinder his own endeavour, that is (by Prop. 11, Schol., Part 3), the person who hates will be affected with pain, etc. QED.

Scholium

This pleasure can hardly be firm, and without any conflict of mind. For (as I shall soon show, in Prop. 27) in so far as a man imagines that a thing which is like him is affected with the emotion of pain, so far he must feel pain; and conversely if he imagines it to be affected with pleasure. Here, however, we are discussing hatred only.

Proposition 24

If we imagine someone to affect with pleasure a thing which we hate, we shall also be affected with hatred towards him. If, on the other hand, we imagine him to affect the same thing with pain, we shall be affected with love towards him.

Demonstration. This Proposition is demonstrated in the same way as Prop. 22, Part 3.

Scholium

These and similar emotions of hatred are related to envy, which, accordingly, is simply hatred in so far as it is considered as disposing a man in such a way that he rejoices in another's harm, and is pained by another's good.

Proposition 25

We endeavour to affirm everything about ourselves and about a thing loved that we imagine to affect us or the thing loved with pleasure; conversely, we endeavour to negate everything that we imagine to affect us or the thing loved with pain.

Demonstration. That which we imagine to affect the thing loved with pleasure or pain affects us with pleasure or pain (by Prop. 21, Part 3). But our mind (by Prop. 12, Part 3) endeavours as far as it can to imagine those things that affect us with pleasure, that is (by Prop. 17 and its Coroll., Part 2), it endeavours to regard them as present. Conversely (by Prop. 13, Part 3), our mind endeavours to exclude the existence of the things that affect us with pain. Therefore, we endeavour to affirm everything about ourselves and about the thing loved that we imagine to affect us or the thing loved with pleasure, and conversely. QED.

Proposition 26

We endeavour to affirm about a thing which we hate everything that we imagine to affect the thing with pain, and conversely to negate that which we imagine to affect it with pleasure.

Demonstration. This Proposition follows from Prop. 23, just as the preceding Proposition follows from Prop. 21, Part 3.

Scholium

From this we see that it easily comes about that a man has too high an opinion of himself and of the thing loved, and too low an opinion of a thing that he hates. This imagination, when it regards the man who thinks too highly of himself, is called 'pride'. It is a kind of madness, since the proud man has a waking dream that he can do all those things that he attains only in his imagination, and therefore regards them as if they were real and exults in them as long as he cannot imagine the things that exclude the existence of these things and determine his own power of acting. Pride, therefore, is pleasure which arises from the fact that a man has too high an opinion of himself. Next, pleasure which arises from the fact that a man has too high an opinion of someone else is called 'esteem', and finally the pleasure that arises from the fact that a man has too low an opinion of someone else is called 'scorn'.[36]

Proposition 27

From the fact that we imagine to be affected with some emotion a thing which is like us, and towards which we have previously had no emotion, we are affected with a similar emotion.[37]

Demonstration. The images of things are the affections of the human body whose ideas represent external bodies as if they were present to us (by Prop. 17, Schol., Part 2); that is (by Prop. 16, Part 2), whose ideas involve the nature of our body and at the same time the present nature of the external body. If, therefore, the nature of the external body is similar to the nature of our body, then the idea of the external body that we imagine involves an affection of our body that is like the affection of the external body. Consequently, if we imagine someone who is like us to be affected with some emotion, this imagination will express an affection of our body[38] which is similar to this emotion. So from the fact that we imagine some thing that is like us to be affected with some emotion, we are affected with a similar emotion. But if we hate a thing which is like us, to that extent (by Prop. 23, Part 3) we shall be affected, along with the emotion, with an emotion which is contrary to its emotion, and not similar. QED.[39]

Scholium

This imitation of the emotions, when it is related to pain, is called 'compassion' (on which, see Prop. 22, Schol., Part 3). When it is related to desire it is called 'emulation', which accordingly is nothing other than the desire of some thing, which is produced in us from the fact that we imagine others who are like us to have the same desire.

Corollary 1

If we imagine someone towards whom we have had no emotion to affect with pleasure a thing which is like us, we will be affected with love towards him. If, on the other hand, we imagine him to affect the thing with pain, we shall be affected with hatred towards him.

Demonstration. This is demonstrated from the previous Proposition in the same way that Prop. 22, Part 3, is demonstrated from Prop. 21.

Corollary 2

Although the misery of a thing that we pity affects us with pain, we cannot on this account hate the thing.

Demonstration. For if we could hate it on account of this, then (by Prop. 23, Part 3) we would feel pleasure at its pain, which is contrary to the hypothesis.

Corollary 3

We shall endeavour, as far as we can, to free from its misery a thing which we pity.

Demonstration. That which affects with pain a thing which we pity affects us with a similar pain (by the preceding Proposition). So we shall endeavour (by Prop. 13, Part 3) to bring about everything that negates the existence of that thing, or, which destroys it; that is (by Prop. 9, Schol., Part 3), we shall seek to destroy it, or, we shall be determined to its destruction. So we shall endeavour to free from its misery a thing which we pity. QED.

Scholium

This will, i.e. this appetite for doing good, which arises from the fact that we pity a thing on which we want to confer a benefit, is called 'benevolence', which is therefore simply desire which has arisen from compassion. Concerning love and hatred towards a person who has done good or ill to a thing which we imagine to be like us, see Prop. 22, Schol., Part 3.

Proposition 28

We endeavour to promote the coming into existence of everything that we imagine to lead to pleasure; but that which we imagine to be opposed to this, i.e. to lead to pain, we endeavour to remove or destroy.

Demonstration. We endeavour, as far as we can, to imagine that which we imagine to lead to pleasure (by Prop. 12, Part 3); that is (by Prop. 17, Part 2), we shall endeavour as far as we can to regard it as present, i.e. as actually existing. But the mind's endeavour, i.e. its power of thinking, is equal to and simultaneous in nature with the body's endeavour, i.e. its power of acting (as follows clearly from Prop. 7, Coroll., and Prop. 11, Coroll., Part 2). Therefore, we endeavour absolutely that it shall exist, or (what is the same, by Prop. 9, Schol., Part 3), we seek and strive for it; which was the first thing to be proved. Then, if we imagine the destruction of that which we believe to be the cause of pain, that is (by Prop. 13, Schol., Part 3), that which we hate, we shall feel pleasure (by Prop. 20, Part 3); and so (by the first part of this Demonstration) we shall endeavour to destroy it, i.e. (by Prop. 13, Part 3) to remove it from us so that we do not regard it as present. This was the second thing to be proved. Therefore, we endeavour to promote, etc. QED.

Proposition 29

We shall also endeavour to do everything which we imagine men (understand here and in the following Propositions, men towards whom we have no emotion) to view with pleasure, and on the other hand we shall be averse to doing that to which we imagine men to be averse.

Demonstration. From the fact that we imagine men to love or hate something, we shall love or hate the same thing (by Prop. 27, Part 3); that is (by Prop. 13, Schol., Part 3) we shall by that very fact feel pleasure or pain at its presence. So (by the preceding Proposition) we shall endeavour to do everything which we imagine men to love, i.e. to view with pleasure, etc. QED.

Scholium

This endeavour to do, and also to abstain from doing, something, the sole cause of which is that we may please men, is called 'ambition', especially when we endeavour so eagerly to please the mob that, in doing or abstaining from doing, some things, we harm ourselves or someone else; otherwise it is usually called 'politeness'.[40] The pleasure with which we imagine the action of another, by which he has endeavoured to please us, I call 'praise'; the pain with which we turn away from his action I call 'blame'.

Proposition 30

If someone has done something which, he imagines, affects others with pleasure, he will be affected with pleasure accompanied with the idea of himself as cause, or, he will regard himself with pleasure. If, on the other hand, he has done something which, he imagines, affects others with pain, he will on the contrary regard himself with pain.

Demonstration. Someone who imagines that he affects others with pleasure or pain will by that very fact (by Prop. 27, Part 3) be affected with pleasure or pain. But since a man (by Props. 19 and 23, Part 2) is conscious of himself through the affections by which he is determined to act, the person who has done something which, he imagines, affects others with pleasure will be affected with pleasure accompanied by the consciousness of himself as cause, or, he will regard himself with pleasure, and conversely. QED.

Scholium

Since love (by Prop. 13, Schol., Part 3) is pleasure with the accompaniment of the idea of an external cause, and hatred is pain, also with the accompaniment of the idea of an external cause, this pleasure and this pain will be species of love and hatred. But since love and hatred are related to external objects, we shall refer to these emotions by other names. We shall call pleasure, accompanied by the idea of an internal[41] cause, 'glory',[42] and the pain that is the contrary of this we shall call 'shame'. It must be understood here that the pleasure or pain arises from the fact that a man believes himself to be praised or blamed; otherwise I shall call pleasure, accompanied by the idea of an internal cause, 'self-contentment', and the pain that is the contrary of this I shall call 'repentance'. Further, since it can come about (by Prop. 17, Coroll., Part 2) that the pleasure with which someone imagines himself to affect others is only imaginary, and (by Prop. 25, Part 3) each person endeavours to imagine everything that, he imagines, affects him with pleasure, it can easily happen that a person who glorifies himself[43] is proud and imagines that he is pleasing to everyone, when in fact he is annoying to everyone.

Proposition 31

If we imagine someone to love or desire or hate something that we ourselves love, desire, or hate, by that very fact we shall love etc. the thing more steadfastly. But if we imagine him to be averse to that which we love, or conversely, then we shall undergo a wavering of the mind.

Demonstration. From the mere fact that we imagine someone to love something, we shall love the thing (by Prop. 27, Part 3). But we are assuming that we love the thing without this, so there is added to that love a new cause by which it is fostered. So by this fact we shall love more steadfastly that which we love. Then, from the fact that we imagine someone to be averse to something, we shall be averse to it (by the same Proposition). But if we suppose that we love the thing at the same time, then we shall at the same time love and be averse to this thing, or (see Prop. 17, Schol., Part 3), we shall undergo a wavering of the mind. QED.

Corollary

From this and from Prop. 28, Part 3, it follows that each person endeavours as far as he can to bring it about that each person loves what he loves, and hates what he hates. Hence the words of the poet:

> As lovers let us hope and fear alike;
> Unfeeling is the man who loves what the other leaves.[44]

Scholium

This endeavour to bring it about that everyone shall approve of what a man loves or hates is in fact ambition (see Prop. 29, Schol., Part 3). So we see that each person, by his nature, desires other people to live in accordance with his own way of thinking; and when all people seek this equally they are equally an obstacle to one another, and when all want to be praised, i.e. loved[45] by all, they hate each other.

Proposition 32

If we imagine that someone enjoys some thing that only one person can possess, we shall endeavour to bring it about that he does not possess that thing.

Demonstration. From the mere fact that we imagine someone to enjoy something, we shall (by Prop. 27 and Coroll. 1, Part 3) love this thing, and will desire to enjoy it. But (by hypothesis) we imagine that there stands in the way of this pleasure the fact that the possessor enjoys this thing; therefore (by Prop. 28, Part 3), we shall endeavour to bring it about that he does not possess the thing. QED.

Scholium

So we see that the nature of men is in general so constituted that they pity those who fare badly and envy those who fare well, and (by the preceding Proposition) with a hatred that is the greater, the more they love a thing that they imagine another to possess. We see next that, from the same property of human nature from which it follows that men feel pity, it follows also that they are envious and ambitious. Finally, if we are willing to consult experience, we find that it teaches all these things, especially if we attend to the earlier years of our life. For we find by experience that boys, since their body is as it were constantly in a state of equilibrium, laugh or cry from the sole fact that they see others laugh or cry, that they immediately want to imitate whatever else they see others do, and finally that they want for themselves all the things by which they imagine other people are pleased. This is because, as we have said[46], the images of things are the affections of the human body, i.e. the modes by which the human body is affected by external causes, and is disposed to do this or that.

Proposition 33

When we love a thing which is like ourselves,[47] we endeavour as far as we can to bring it about that it loves us in return.

Demonstration. We endeavour as far as we can to imagine above all others a thing that we love (by Prop. 12, Part 3). If therefore the thing is like us, we shall endeavour (by Prop. 29, Part 3) to affect it, above all others, with pleasure; or, we shall endeavour as far as we can to bring it about that the thing that we love is affected with pleasure, with the accompaniment of the idea of ourselves; that is (by Prop. 13, Schol., Part 3), that it loves us in return. QED.

Proposition 34

The greater the emotion towards us with which we imagine the thing we love to be affected, the more we shall feel glory.

Demonstration. We endeavour (by the preceding Proposition) as far as we can to bring it about that the thing that we love loves us in return; that is (by Prop. 13, Schol., Part 3), that the thing that is loved is affected with pleasure, with the accompaniment of the idea of ourselves. So the greater the pleasure with which we imagine the thing that we love to be affected because of us, the more this endeavour is helped; that is (by Prop.11, Part 3, together with its Scholium) the greater the pleasure with which we are affected. But when we feel pleasure on account of the fact that we have affected with pleasure someone else who is similar to us, then we regard ourselves with pleasure (by Prop. 30, Part 3); therefore, the greater the emotion towards us with which we imagine the thing we love to be affected, the greater the pleasure with which we regard ourselves, or (by Prop. 30, Schol., Part 3), the more we shall feel glory. QED.

Proposition 35

If someone imagines that a thing that he loves joins someone else to himself with a bond of friendship[48] that is the same as or closer than that by which he alone possessed the thing, he will be affected with hatred towards the thing loved, and will envy the other person.

Demonstration. The greater the love with which someone imagines that the thing that he loves is affected towards him, the more (by the previous Proposition) he will feel glory; that is (by Prop. 30, Schol., Part 3), the more he will feel pleasure. So (by Prop. 28, Part 3) he will endeavour, as far as he can, to imagine that the thing that he loves is bound to him as closely as possible. This endeavour, i.e. this appetite, is strengthened if he imagines someone else to desire the same thing for himself (by Prop. 31, Part 3). But this endeavour, i.e. this appetite, is assumed to be hindered by the image of the thing loved, accompanied by the image of the person whom the thing loved joins to itself. Therefore (by Prop. 11, Schol., Part 3), by this very fact the man will be affected with pain, with the accompaniment of the idea of the beloved thing as its cause, and simultaneously with the image of the other person. That is (by Prop. 13, Schol., Part 3), he will be affected with hatred towards the thing loved, and at the same time towards the other person (by Prop. 15, Coroll., Part 3), whom (by Prop. 23, Part 3) he will consequently envy, because he takes pleasure in the thing loved. QED.

Scholium

This hatred towards a thing that is loved, joined with envy, is called 'jealousy'. Jealousy, therefore, is simply a wavering of the mind which has arisen from love and hatred together, with the accompaniment of the idea of another person who is envied. Further, this hatred towards a thing that is loved will be the greater in accordance with the pleasure with which the jealous person used to be affected by the reciprocal love of the thing loved, and also in accordance with the emotion with which he was affected towards the person who, he imagines, joins the thing to himself. For if he hated him, then by that very fact he will (by Prop. 24, Part 3) hate the thing loved, because he imagines that thing to affect with pleasure that which he hates, and also (by Prop. 15, Coroll., Part 3) from the fact that he is compelled to join the image of the thing that is loved with the image of the person whom he hates. The latter consideration commonly holds in the case of love for a woman. For a man who imagines that the woman he loves is prostituting herself to another will not only feel pain from the fact that his own appetite is hindered; he will also be averse to her because he is compelled to link the image of the thing that he loves with the genitals and excrement of another. Finally, there is the additional fact that the jealous man is not received by his beloved with the same countenance as that with which she used to receive him. This is another cause of the lover's pain, as I shall now show.

Proposition 36

Someone who recollects a thing from which he once received pleasure desires to possess it under the same circumstances as when he first received pleasure from it.

Demonstration. Whatever a man saw at the same time as a thing which gave him pleasure will (by Prop. 15, Part 3) be by accident a cause of pleasure. So (by Prop. 28, Part 3) he will desire to possess all this together with the thing that gave him pleasure; or, he will desire to possess the thing under the same circumstances as when he first received pleasure from it. QED.

Corollary

So if the lover discovers that one of these circumstances is missing, he will feel pain.

Demonstration. For in so far as he finds that some circumstance is missing, to that extent he imagines something that excludes the existence of the thing. But since, on account of his love, he is desirous of that thing, i.e. that circumstance (by the preceding Proposition), he will therefore (by Prop. 19, Part 3) feel pain in so far as he imagines it to be missing. QED.

Scholium

This pain, in so far as it concerns the absence of that which we love, is called 'regret'.

Proposition 37

The desire which arises on account of pleasure or pain, and on account of hatred or love, is greater as the emotion is greater.

Demonstration. Pain (by Prop. 11, Schol., Part 3) diminishes or hinders a man's power of acting, that is (by Prop. 7, Part 3), it diminishes or hinders the endeavour by which a man endeavours to persevere in his being. So (by Prop. 5, Part 3) it is contrary to this endeavour; and whatever a man affected with pain endeavours to do is to remove that pain. But (by the definition of pain) the greater a pain is, the greater must be the part of a man's power of acting to which it is opposed. Therefore, the greater a pain is, the greater is the power of acting with which a man will endeavour to remove the pain; that is (by Prop. 9, Schol., Part 3), the greater is the desire, i.e. the appetite, with which he will endeavour to remove the pain. Then because (again by Prop. 11, Schol., Part 3) pleasure increases or helps a man's power of acting, it is easily demonstrated in the same way that a man who is affected with pleasure desires nothing other than to preserve it, and with a desire that is greater, the greater the pleasure is. Finally, since hatred and love are emotions of pain or pleasure, it follows in the same way that the endeavour, appetite, or in other words the desire that arises on account of hatred or love will be the greater in proportion to the hatred or love. QED.

Proposition 38

If someone begins to hate a thing loved in such a way that the love is entirely destroyed, then (the cause of the hatred being equal)[49] his hatred for it will be greater than if he had never loved it, and it will be the greater, the greater his love had previously been.

Demonstration. For if someone begins to hate a thing which he loves, more of his appetites will be hindered than if he had never loved it. For love (by Prop. 13, Schol., Part 3) is pleasure, which a man endeavours to conserve as far as he can (by Prop. 28, Part 3): namely (by the same Scholium), by regarding the loved thing as present and (by Prop. 21, Part 3) by affecting it with pleasure as far as he can. This endeavour (by the preceding Proposition) is greater, the greater his love is, as is his endeavour of bringing it about that the thing loved shall love him (see Prop. 33, Part 3). But these endeavours are hindered by hatred towards the thing loved (by Prop. 13, Coroll., and Prop. 23, Part 3). Therefore, the lover (by Prop. 11, Schol., Part 3) will be affected with pain from this same cause, and the more so, the greater his love was. That is, besides the pain which was the cause of the hatred, another will arise from the fact that he loved the thing, and consequently he will regard the thing loved with a greater emotion of pain. That is (by Prop. 13, Schol., Part 3), he will pursue it with greater hatred than if he had not loved it, and his hatred for it will be greater, the greater his love had been. QED.

Proposition 39

Someone who hates somebody will endeavour to do him harm, unless he is afraid that from this a greater harm will arise for himself; and conversely, someone who loves somebody will by the same law endeavour to do good to him.

Demonstration. To hate someone is (by Prop. 13, Schol., Part 3) to imagine someone as the cause of pain; so (by Prop. 28, Part 3) someone who hates somebody will endeavour to remove or destroy him. But if he fears from this something more painful, or (what is the same), a greater harm for himself, and thinks that he can avoid this by not inflicting on the person he hates the harm that he was considering, then (again by Prop. 28, Part 3) he will desire to abstain from harming him. He will do so (by Prop. 37, Part 3) with an endeavour that is greater than the endeavour of doing harm by which he was possessed, and this will therefore prevail, which is what we wished to show. The demonstration of the second part proceeds in the same way; therefore, someone who hates somebody, etc. QED.

Scholium

By 'good' I understand here[50] every sort of pleasure, and also whatever leads to pleasure, and especially that which satisfies a desire, whatever that may be. By 'bad'[51] I understand every sort of pain, and especially that which frustrates a desire. For we showed above (in Prop. 9, Schol., Part 3) that we do not desire anything because we judge it to be good, but that on the contrary we call it 'good' because we desire it, and that consequently we call 'bad' that to which we are averse. Therefore, it is in accordance with his own emotion that each person judges, i.e. estimates, what is good, what is bad, what is better, what is worse, and finally what is the best or what is the worst. So, for example, a miser judges that abundance of money is the best, and lack of it is the worst. An ambitious man desires nothing as much as glory, and on the other hand fears nothing as much as shame. Then, nothing is more pleasant to an envious man than the unhappiness of another, and nothing is more irksome than someone else's happiness. So each person, in accordance with his own emotion, judges some thing to be good or bad, useful or useless. For the rest, emotion which so disposes a man that he does not want what he wants, or wants what he does not want, is called 'timidity', which is accordingly nothing other than fear, is so far as a man is disposed by it to avoid by a lesser harm one which he judges to be in the future (see Prop. 28, Part 3).[52] But if the harm that he fears is shame, then timidity is called 'bashfulness'. Finally, if the desire to avoid a future harm is hindered by timidity concerning another harm in such a way that a man does not know which he wants, this fear is called 'consternation', especially if each of the harms feared is very great.

Proposition 40

Someone who imagines himself to be hated by some person, and believes that he has given him no cause of hatred, will hate that person in return.

Demonstration. Someone who imagines some person to be affected with hatred will by that very fact also be affected with hatred (by Prop. 27, Part 3), that is (by Prop. 13, Schol., Part 3), with pain, with the accompaniment of the idea of an external cause. But he himself (by hypothesis) imagines no cause of this pain apart from the person who hates him. Therefore, from the fact that he imagines himself to be hated by some person, he will be affected with pain, with the accompaniment of the idea of the person who hates him, or (by the same Scholium), he will hate that person. QED.

Scholium

But if someone imagines that he has given a just cause of hatred, then (by Prop. 30 and its Schol., Part 3) he will be affected with shame. But this (by Prop. 25, Part 3) rarely happens. Further, this reciprocal hatred can also arise from the fact that hatred is followed by the endeavour to do harm to the person who is hated (by Prop. 39, Part 3). Therefore, someone who imagines himself to be hated by some person will imagine that person to be the cause of some harm, i.e. of pain. So he will be affected with pain, i.e. with fear,[53] with the accompaniment of the idea of the person who hates him as its cause; that is, he will hate that person, as stated above.

Corollary 1

Someone who imagines that a person whom he loves is affected with hatred towards him will be tormented with hatred and love at the same time. For in so far as he imagines that he is hated by that person, he is determined (by the previous Proposition) to hate the person in return. But (by hypothesis) he loves the person nevertheless, and so he is harassed by hatred and love at the same time.

Corollary 2

If anyone imagines that harm has been inflicted on him out of hatred by someone towards whom he has previously had no emotion, he will at once endeavour to repay that harm.

Demonstration. Someone who imagines that some person is affected with hatred towards him will (by the previous Proposition) hate that person, and (by Prop. 26, Part 3) he will endeavour to bring about everything that can affect that person with pain, and will strive (by Prop. 39, Part 3) to inflict it on the person. But (by hypothesis) the first thing of this kind that he imagines is the harm that was inflicted on him; therefore, he will at once endeavour to inflict it on the person in question. QED.

Scholium

The endeavour to inflict harm on a person whom we hate is called 'anger'; the endeavour to repay harm that has been inflicted on us is called 'revenge'.

Proposition 41

If anyone imagines that he is loved by somebody, and does not believe that he has provided any cause of this (something that can happen, by Prop. 15, Coroll., and Prop. 6, Part 3), he will love that person in return.

Demonstration. This Proposition is demonstrated in the same way as the preceding one; see also the Scholium of that Proposition.

Scholium

If anyone believes that he has provided a just cause of love, then (by Prop. 30, Part 3 and its Scholium) he will feel glory. This (by Prop. 25, Part 3) happens quite often, and is the contrary of that which we said to happen when someone imagines that he is hated by somebody (see the Scholium of the preceding Proposition). Further, this reciprocal love, and consequently (by Prop. 39, Part 3) the endeavour to do good to someone who loves us, and (again by Prop. 39, Part 3) who endeavours to do good to us, is called 'gratefulness', or, 'gratitude'. So it is evident that men are much more ready to take revenge than to repay a benefit.[54]

Corollary

Someone who imagines that he is loved by somebody he hates will be harassed by hatred and love at the same time. This is demonstrated in the same way as the first Corollary of the preceding Proposition.

Scholium

But if hatred prevails, he will try to inflict harm on the person by whom he is loved. This emotion is called 'cruelty' especially if the person who loves is believed to have provided no common cause of hatred.

Proposition 42

Someone who, moved by love or by the hope of glory, has conferred a benefit on somebody will feel pain if he sees that the benefit is received with ingratitude.

Demonstration. Someone who loves some thing which is like himself endeavours, as far as he can, to bring it about that he is loved by that thing in turn (by Prop. 33, Part 3). Therefore, someone who has conferred a benefit on somebody out of love does this by the desire by which he is bound of being loved in return, that is (by Prop. 34, Part 3), by the hope of glory, i.e. (by Prop. 30, Schol., Part 3) of pleasure. So (by Prop. 12, Part 3) he will endeavour, as far as he can, to imagine this cause of glory, i.e. to regard it as actually existing. But (by hypothesis) he imagines something else, which excludes the existence of that cause; therefore (by Prop. 19, Part 3) he will feel pain at this. QED.

Proposition 43

Hatred is increased by reciprocal hatred, and conversely can be destroyed by love.

Demonstration. If someone imagines that a person whom he hates is affected with hatred towards him, then by that very fact (by Prop. 40, Part 3) there arises a new hatred whilst (by hypothesis) the first one still lasts. But if on the contrary he imagines the person to be affected with love towards him, then in so far as he imagines this he regards himself (by Prop. 30, Part 3) with pleasure, and (by Prop. 29, Part 3) will endeavour to please the person in question. That is (by Prop. 41, Part 3), he endeavours not to hate him, and not to affect him with any pain. This endeavour will (by Prop. 37, Part 3) be greater or smaller in proportion to the emotion from which it arises. So if it is greater than the emotion which arises from hatred, and by which he endeavours to affect with pain the thing which he hates (by Prop. 26, Part 3), it will prevail over this emotion and will remove the hatred from his mind. QED.

Proposition 44

Hatred which is entirely conquered by love passes over into love, and the love is greater on this account than if hatred had not preceded it.

Demonstration. This proceeds in the same way as Prop. 38, Part 3. For the person who begins to love a thing which he hated, or, which he used to regard with pain, feels pleasure by the very fact that he loves. Further, to the pleasure that love involves (see its definition in Prop. 13, Schol., Part 3) there is also added the pleasure that arises from the fact that the endeavour to remove the pain that hatred involves is greatly helped (as we showed in Proposition 37, Part 3); this is accompanied, as its cause, by the idea of the person who was hated.

Scholium

Although this is so, no one will endeavour to hate some thing, or to inflict pain on it, so that he may enjoy this greater pleasure; that is, no one will want to inflict harm on himself in the hope of recovery, nor will he desire to become ill in the hope of convalescing. For each person will always endeavour to preserve his own being, and to remove pain as far as he can. But if on the contrary it could be conceived that a man can want to hate somebody so that he may later have greater love for the person, then he will always want to hate the person. For the greater the hatred was, the greater will the love be, and so he will always desire the hatred to be greater and greater. From the same cause a man will endeavour to be more and more ill, so that he may later enjoy more pleasure from the restoration of his health; and so he will always endeavour to be ill, which (by Prop. 6, Part 3) is absurd.

Proposition 45

If anyone imagines that a person who is like him is affected with hatred towards a thing which is like him and which he himself loves, he will hate that person.

Demonstration. For the thing that is loved hates the person who hates it (by Prop. 40, Part 3); so the lover who imagines a person to hate the thing that he loves, by that very fact imagines the thing that is loved to be affected with hatred, that is (by Prop. 13, Schol., Part 3) with pain. Consequently (by Prop. 21, Part 3), he feels pain, together with the idea of the person who hates the thing loved as the cause of the pain; that is (by Prop. 13, Schol., Part 3), he will hate that person. QED.

Proposition 46

If anyone has been affected with pleasure or pain by someone who belongs to a group or nation that is different from his own, and this is accompanied by the idea of that person, under the universal name of that group or nation, as its cause, then he will love or hate not only the person in question, but all the members of that group or nation.

Demonstration. The demonstration of this is evident from Proposition 16, Part 3.

Proposition 47

Pleasure which arises from the fact that we imagine a thing that we hate to be destroyed, or to be affected with some other harm, does not arise without some pain of mind.

Demonstration. This is evident from Proposition 27, Part 3. For in so far as we imagine a thing which is like us to be affected with pain, to that extent we feel pain.

Scholium

This Proposition can also be demonstrated from Prop. 17, Coroll., Part 2. For as often as we recollect a thing, even though it does not exist actually, yet we regard it as present and the body is affected in the same way.

Therefore, in so far as the memory of the thing hated[55] flourishes, to that extent a man is determined to regard the thing with pain. This determination is hindered, whilst the image of the thing still remains, by the memory of the things which exclude its existence, but it is not removed. So the man feels pleasure only in so far as this determination is hindered, and from this it comes about that this pleasure, which arises from the harm that is suffered by the thing that we hate, is repeated as often as we recollect this thing. For, as we have said, when the image of the thing is excited, then since it involves the existence of the thing in question, it determines the man to regard it with the pain with which he used to regard it when it existed. But since he has joined to the image of this thing others which exclude the existence of the thing, this determination to pain is immediately hindered, and the man feels pleasure again—and as often as this repetition takes place. This is the cause of the fact that men feel pleasure as often as they recollect some past harm, and why they enjoy recounting the dangers from which they have been liberated. For when they imagine some danger, they regard it as if it were still in the future, and are determined to fear it. This determination is once again hindered by the idea of liberty, which (since they have been liberated from danger) they have joined to the idea of this danger. This idea makes them feel safe once again, and so they once again feel pleasure.

Proposition 48

Love and hatred towards (for example) Peter is destroyed if the pain which the latter, and the pleasure which the former, involves is joined to the idea of another cause; also, each of the two is diminished in so far as we imagine Peter not to have been the sole cause of either.

Demonstration. This is evident simply from the definition of love and of hate (on which see Prop. 13, Schol., Part 3). For pleasure is called love for Peter, and pain is called hatred for Peter, on account of this alone: that Peter is considered to be the cause of the latter or of the former emotion. So if this is removed, either wholly or in part, then the emotion towards Peter is wholly or partially diminished. QED.

Proposition 49

Love and hatred towards a thing which we imagine to be free must each be greater (the cause being equal) than love and hatred towards a thing which we imagine to be necessary.

Demonstration. A thing which we imagine to be free must (by Def. 7, Part 1) be perceived through itself and without any others. If therefore we imagine the same thing to be the cause of pleasure or of pain, then by that very fact (by Prop. 13, Schol., Part 3) we shall love it or hate it, and (by the preceding Proposition) with the greatest love or hatred that can arise from the given emotion. But if we imagine as necessary a thing which is the cause of the same emotion, then (again by Def. 7, Part 1) we shall imagine it not to be the sole cause of the emotion, but to be a cause in conjunction with others. Therefore (by the preceding Proposition), the love and hatred towards it will be less. QED.

Scholium

From this it follows that men have greater love or hatred towards each other than towards other things because they think themselves free; to which one must add the imitation of the emotions, on which see Props. 27, 34, 40, and 43, Part 3.

Proposition 50

Any thing can be a cause by accident of hope or of fear.

Demonstration. This Proposition is demonstrated in the same way as Prop. 15, Part 3; which see, together with Prop. 18, Schol. 2,[56] Part 3.

Scholium

Things which are causes by accident of hope or of fear are called 'good or bad omens'. Further, in so far as these omens are the cause of hope or fear, then to that extent they are the cause of pleasure or pain (by the definition of hope and fear, Prop. 18, Schol. 2, Part 3). Consequently (by Prop. 15, Coroll., Part 3), to that extent we love or hate them, and (by Prop. 28, Part 3) we endeavour to use them as means towards the things which we hope for, or to remove them as obstacles or as causes of fear. Further, from Proposition 25, Part 3, it follows that we are so constituted by nature that we believe readily the things which we hope for and reluctantly the things which we fear, and that our opinions of these things are too high or too low. From these there have arisen the superstitions by which men are everywhere harassed. For the rest, I do not think it worth while to show here the waverings of mind which arise out of hope and fear. This is because it follows simply from the definitions of these emotions that hope does not exist without fear, nor fear without hope (as we shall explain more fully in due course);[57] also because in so far as we hope for or fear something, to that extent we love it or hate it, and so whatever we have said about love and hatred can easily be applied by anyone to hope and fear.

Proposition 51

Different men can be affected by one and the same object in different ways, and one and the same man can be affected in different ways by one and the same object at different times.

Demonstration. The human body (by Post. 3, Part 2) is affected in very many ways by external bodies. Therefore, two men can be affected in different ways at the same time, and so (by Axiom 1 following Lemma 3, which follows Prop. 13, Part 2) they can be affected in different ways by one and the same object. Next (by the same Postulate) the human body can be affected now in this way and now in another, and consequently (by the same Axiom) it can be affected in different ways by one and the same object at different times. QED.

Scholium

So we see that it can come about that what one person loves another hates; that what one person fears another does not fear; that one and the same person now loves what he previously hated, and now dares to do what he previously feared, and so on. Then, because each person judges in accordance with his own emotion what is good and what is bad, and what is better and what is worse (see Prop. 39, Schol., Part 3), it follows that men can vary both in judgement and in emotion. (We have shown in Prop. 13, Schol., Part 2,[58] that this can happen, even though the human mind is a part of the divine intellect.) From this it comes about that when we compare people with one another, we distinguish them solely by a difference of emotions, and that we call some intrepid and some timid, and call others by some other name. For example, I shall call 'intrepid' a man who despises harm that I usually fear; and if, further, I pay attention to the fact that his desire of doing harm to someone he hates and good to someone he loves is not hindered by the fear of harm by which I am usually restrained, then I shall call him 'bold'. Then again, that person will seem timid to me who fears harm that I usually despise; and if, further, I pay attention to the fact that his desire is hindered by a fear of harm that cannot restrain me, then I shall say that he is cowardly—and everyone will judge in this way. Finally, I have spoken of the nature of man and of the inconstancy of his judgement, such as the fact that he often judges about things from emotion alone, and that the things that he believes to make for pleasure or pain, and which he therefore (by Prop. 28, Part 3) endeavours to promote or to remove, are often merely imaginary—to say nothing of the other things that we have shown in the Second Part about the uncertainty of things. From this we readily conceive that a man can often be the cause both of his feeling pain and of his feeling pleasure, or, that he is affected both by pain and by pleasure, with the accompaniment of the idea of himself as cause. So we readily understand what repentance and self-contentment are. For repentance is pain, with accompaniment of the idea of oneself as cause, and self-contentment is pleasure, with the accompaniment of the idea of oneself as cause.[59] These emotions are extremely strong, because men believe themselves to be free. (See Prop. 49, Part 3.)

Proposition 52

We shall not regard an object which we have previously seen together with others, or which we imagine to have nothing but what is common to several things, as long as one which we imagine to have something that is particular to it.

Demonstration. As soon as we imagine an object that we have seen simultaneously with others, we shall immediately recollect the others also (by Prop. 18, Part 2; see also its Scholium). So from regarding one we shall immediately proceed to regard another. The same holds in the case of an object which we imagine to have nothing but what is common to several things. For by that very fact we suppose that we regard in it nothing that we have not seen previously together with other things. But when we suppose that we imagine in some object something particular to it that we have never seen before, we are simply saying that the mind, whilst it regards that object, has in itself nothing else which it can

proceed to regard as a result of regarding that object; and so it is determined to regard that object alone. Therefore, we shall not regard an
object, etc. QED.

Scholium

This affection of the mind, i.e. the imagination of a particular thing in so
far as it exists alone in the mind, is called 'wonder'. If it is evoked by an
object which we fear, it is called 'consternation', since wonder at some
harm holds the man who is suspended in its exclusive contemplation in
such a way that he is not able to think of other things by which he could
avoid that harm. But if that at which we wonder is someone's prudence
or industry, or something of this sort, since in this respect we regard him
as far exceeding us, then the wonder is called 'veneration'; otherwise, if
we wonder at someone's anger, envy, etc., it is called 'horror'. Then, if
we wonder at the prudence, industry, etc. of someone whom we love, by
that very fact (by Prop. 12, Part 3) the love will be greater, and we call this
love that is joined to wonder, i.e. to veneration, 'devotion'. We can also
conceive hatred, hope, confidence, and other emotions to be joined to
wonder after this fashion, and so we shall be able to deduce more emotions than those which are commonly indicated by means of accepted
terms. From this it is evident that the names of the emotions were
invented more from their common use than from an accurate knowledge of them.[60]
    To wonder there is opposed 'contempt', of which the usual cause is
this. Because we see that someone wonders at, loves, or fears, etc. some
thing, or because a thing appears at first sight to be like things that we
wonder at, love, or fear, etc., we are determined (by Prop. 15 and Coroll.,
and Prop. 27, Part 3) to wonder at, love, or fear, etc. that thing. But if as a
result of the presence of the thing, or of a more accurate scrutiny of it,
we are compelled to deny of it everything that can be a cause of wonder,
love, or fear, etc., then the mind remains determined (as a result of the
presence of the thing) to think of those things that are not in the object
rather than those that are. Usually, however, the presence of the object
leads the mind to think above all of the things that are in it. Further, just
as devotion arises from wonder at a thing that we love, so does derision
arise from contempt of a thing that we hate or fear; again, disdain arises
from the contempt of foolishness, just as veneration arises from wonder
at prudence. Finally, we can conceive love, hope, glory, and other emotions to be joined to contempt, and from this we can deduce other

emotions besides, which again we do not usually distinguish from others by any particular term.

Proposition 53

When the mind thinks of itself and of its power of acting, it feels pleasure, and the more so, the more distinctly it imagines itself and its power of acting.

Demonstration. A man does not know himself except through the affections of his body and the ideas of these affections (by Props. 19 and 23, Part 2). Therefore, when it happens that the mind can think of itself, by that very fact it is supposed to make a transition to a greater perfection, that is (by Prop. 11, Schol., Part 3), to be affected with pleasure, and the more so, the more distinctly it can imagine[61] itself and its power of acting. QED.

Corollary

This pleasure is fostered more and more, the more a man imagines that he is praised by others. For the more that he imagines that he is praised by others, the greater is the pleasure with which he imagines himself to affect others, and this pleasure is accompanied with the idea of himself (by Prop. 29, Schol., Part 3). So (by Prop. 27, Part 3) he himself is affected with more pleasure, with the accompaniment of the idea of himself. QED.

Proposition 54

The mind endeavours to imagine only those things which posit its power of acting.

Demonstration. The endeavour of the mind, i.e. its power, is the essence of the mind itself (by Prop. 7, Part 3). But the essence of the mind (as is self-evident) affirms only what the mind is and can do, and not what it is not and cannot do. So it endeavours to imagine only that which affirms, i.e. posits, its power of acting. QED.

Proposition 55

When the mind imagines its lack of power, it thereby feels pain.

Demonstration. The essence of the mind affirms only what the mind is and can do; or, it is of the nature of the mind to imagine only those things that posit its power of acting (by the preceding Proposition). So when we say that the mind, whilst it thinks of itself, imagines its lack of power, we simply say that whilst the mind endeavours to imagine something that posits its power of acting, its endeavour is hindered, or (by Prop. 11, Schol., Part 3), it feels pain.

Corollary

This pain is fostered more and more if the mind imagines itself to be blamed by others. This is demonstrated in the same way as the Corollary of Prop. 53 of this Part.

Scholium

This pain, accompanied by the idea of our weakness, is called 'humility'; the pleasure which arises from thinking of ourselves is called 'self-love', or 'self-contentment'.[62] And since the latter is repeated as often as a man thinks of his virtues, i.e. his power of acting,[63] it comes about from this that everyone exults in talking about his own deeds, and in boasting of his strength, both of body and of mind, and that this is a cause of men's annoyance with one another. From this it also follows that men are by nature envious (see Prop. 24, Schol., and Prop. 32, Schol., Part 3), or, that they delight in[64] the weakness of their equals, and on the other hand feel pain because of their virtue. For as often as anyone imagines his actions, he is affected with pleasure (by Prop. 53, Part 3), and the more so, the more he imagines his actions to express more perfection and imagines them more distinctly, that is (by what has been said in Prop. 40, Schol. 1, Part 2), the more he can distinguish them from others, and can think of them as particular things. So everyone will delight most from thinking about himself when he thinks of something in himself that he negates of others. But if he relates that which he affirms of himself to the universal idea[65] of man or animal, he will not delight as much; on the contrary, he will feel pain if he imagines his actions to be weaker in comparison with the actions of others. This pain (by Prop. 28, Part 3) he will endeavour to remove, by misinterpreting the actions of his equals, or by embellishing his own actions as far as he can. It is therefore evident that men are inclined by nature to hatred and to envy. To this one must add their education. For parents commonly encourage their children to be virtuous simply by the stimulus of honour and envy. However, perhaps some doubt remains, on the ground that we often admire the virtues of men, and venerate the men themselves. To remove this I will add the following Corollary.

Corollary

No one envies the virtue of another unless that other is an equal.

Demonstration. Envy is hatred (see Prop. 24, Schol., Part 3), or (by Prop. 13, Schol., Part 3), pain; that is (by Prop. 11, Schol., Part 3), an affection by which a man's power of acting, i.e. his endeavour, is hindered. But a man (by Prop. 9, Schol., Part 3) neither endeavours nor desires to do anything apart from that which can follow from his given nature. Therefore, a man will desire to predicate of himself no power of acting, i.e. (what is the same) no virtue, which is peculiar to the nature of another and foreign to his own. So his desire cannot be hindered, that is (by Prop. 11, Schol., Part 3), he himself cannot feel pain from the fact that he thinks of some virtue in someone who is unlike himself, and consequently he will be unable to envy him. However, he can envy his equal, who is supposed to be of the same nature as himself. QED.

Scholium

When, therefore, we said above, in Prop. 52, Schol., Part 3, that we venerate a man on account of the fact that we admire his prudence, bravery, etc., this comes about (as is evident from the Proposition itself) because we imagine these virtues to be peculiar to him and not to be common to our nature. So we shall not envy him for them, any more than we envy trees for their height, or lions for their bravery, etc.

Proposition 56

There are as many species of pleasure, pain, and desire, and consequently of each emotion which is composed of these (such as wavering of the mind) or which is derived from these (namely love, hatred, hope, fear, etc.) as there are species of objects by which we are affected.

Demonstration. Pleasure and pain, and consequently the emotions which are composed of or derived from these, are passions (by Prop. 11, Schol., Part 3)[66]. But we (by Prop. 1, Part 3) are necessarily passive, in so far as we have inadequate ideas, and only in so far as we have them (by Prop. 3, Part 3) are we passive. That is (by Prop. 40, Schol., Part 2), we necessarily are passive only in so far as we imagine, or (see Prop. 17, Part 2, and its Scholium), in so far as we are affected by an emotion which involves the nature of our body and of an external body. Therefore, the nature of each passion must necessarily be explained in such a way that the nature of the object by which we are affected is expressed. For the pleasure which arises from an object (say, A) involves the nature of the object A, and the pleasure which arises from object B involves the nature of the object B, and so these two emotions of pleasure are different in nature, because they arise from causes of a different nature. So also the emotion of pain which arises from one object is different in nature from the pain which arises from another cause. The same is to be understood of love, hatred, hope, fear, wavering of the mind, etc., and so there necessarily exist as many species of pleasure, pain, love, hatred, etc. as there are species of objects by which we are affected. But desire[67] is the very essence, i.e. the nature, of each person, in so far as that nature is conceived as determined (see Prop. 9, Schol., Part 3) to do something by any given disposition of the person. Therefore, in so far as anyone is affected, by external causes, with this or that species of pleasure, pain, love, hatred, etc., that is, in so far as his nature is constituted in this or that way, then it is necessary that his desire varies, and that the nature of one desire must differ from that of another as much as the emotions, from which each one arises, differ among themselves. So there exist as many species of desire as there are species of pleasure, pain, love, etc., and consequently (by what has just been shown) as many as there are species of objects by which we are affected. QED.

Scholium

Noteworthy species of the emotions (which, by the preceding Proposition, must be very many) are luxury, drunkenness, lust, avarice, and ambition. These are simply concepts of love or of desire, which explain the nature of each of these emotions by the objects to which they are related. For by luxury, drunkenness, lust, avarice, and ambition we simply understand the uncontrolled love of or desire for feasting, drinking, sexual intercourse, wealth, and glory. Further, these emotions, in so far as we distinguish them from others solely by the object to which they are related, have no opposite. For temperance, sobriety, and chastity, which we commonly oppose to luxury, drunkenness, and lust respectively, are not emotions, i.e. passions.[68] Rather, they indicate the power of the mind, which controls these emotions. For the rest, I cannot explain here the remaining species of the emotions (for they are as many as are the species of their objects), nor is it necessary that I should do so even if I could. For it is sufficient for our purpose—namely, the determination of the strength of the emotions, and the power of the mind over them—to have a general definition of each emotion. It is sufficient, I say, for us to understand the common properties[69] of the emotions and of the mind, so that we can determine what and how great is the power of the mind in controlling and restraining the emotions. So although there is a great difference between this and that emotion of love, hatred, or desire—e.g. between love towards children and towards a wife—yet it is not necessary for us to grasp these differences, nor to investigate any further the origin and nature of the emotions.[70]

Proposition 57

Any emotion of each individual differs from the emotion of another only in so far as the essence of one differs from the essence of the other.

Demonstration. This Proposition is evident from Axiom 1, after Lemma 3, Prop. 13, Schol., Part 2. However, we will demonstrate it from the definitions of the three primitive emotions.

All the emotions are related to desire, pleasure, and pain, as is shown by the definitions that we have given of them. But desire is the nature, i.e. the essence, of each thing (see its definition in Prop. 9, Schol., Part 3); therefore, the desire of each individual differs from the desire of another only in so far as the nature, i.e. the essence, of one differs from the essence of another. Next, pleasure and pain are passions[71] by which the power, i.e. the endeavour, of each thing to persevere in its being is increased or diminished, helped or hindered (by Prop. 11 and its Scholium, Part 3). But by the endeavour to persevere in one's being, in so far as it is related to the mind and the body simultaneously, we understand appetite and desire (see Prop. 9, Schol., Part 3). Therefore, pleasure and pain are desire, i.e. appetite, in so far as it is increased or diminished, helped or hindered, by external causes;[72] that is (by the same Scholium), it is the very nature of each individual. So the pleasure or pain of each thing differs from the pleasure or pain of another only in so far as the nature, i.e. the essence, of the one differs from the essence of the other. Consequently, any emotion of each individual differs from the emotion of another etc. QED.

Scholium

From this it follows that the emotions of what are called the 'irrational' animals (for we can in no way doubt that the beasts feel, now that we have got to know the origin of the mind) differ from the emotions of men only in so far as their nature differs from human nature. Horse and man are indeed led by the lust of procreation, but the former is led by equine lust and the latter by human lust. So also the lusts and appetites of insects, fishes, and birds must differ from one another. Therefore, although each individual lives content with, and delights in, that nature of his by which he is constituted, yet the life with which each one is content, and the delight that he has, is nothing other than the idea, i.e. the soul, of each individual. So the delight of the one differs in nature from that of another only in so far as the essence of one differs from the essence of the other. Finally—something that I wanted to note here in passing—it follows from the preceding Proposition that there is also no small difference between the delight with which (for example) the drunkard is led and the delight which the philosopher possesses. So much for the emotions which are related to a man in so far as he is passive. It remains for me to add a few things about the emotions which are related to him in so far as he acts.

Proposition 58

Besides the pleasure and the desire which are passions, there exist other emotions of pleasure and desire which are related to us in so far as we act.

Demonstration. When the mind conceives itself and its power of acting, it feels pleasure (by Prop. 53, Part 3); however, the mind necessarily thinks of itself when it conceives a true, i.e. an adequate, idea (by Prop. 43, Part 2). But the mind conceives certain adequate ideas (by Prop. 40, Schol. 2,

Part 2); therefore, it also feels pleasure in so far as it conceives adequate ideas, that is (by Prop. 1, Part 3) in so far as it acts. Next, the mind endeavours to persevere in its being both in so far as it has clear and distinct ideas and in so far as it has confused ideas (by Prop. 9, Part 3). But by endeavour we understand (by Prop. 9, Schol., Part 3) desire; therefore, desire is also related to us in so far as we understand, or (by Prop. 1, Part 3), in so far as we act. QED.

Proposition 59

Among all the emotions which are related to the mind in so far as it acts, there are none apart from those which are related to pleasure or desire.[73]

Demonstration. All emotions are related to desire, pleasure, or pain, as is shown by the definitions that we have given of them. But by pain we understand that the mind's power of thinking is diminished or hindered[74] (by Prop. 11 and its Scholium, Part 3); and so in so far as the mind feels pain, to that extent its power of understanding, that is, its power of acting (by Prop. 1, Part 3), is diminished or hindered. So no emotion of pain can be related to the mind in so far as it acts, but only emotions of pleasure and of desire, which (by the preceding Proposition) are to that extent also related to the mind. QED.

Scholium

All the actions which follow from emotions which are related to the mind in so far as it understands, I relate to fortitude, which I divide into courage and nobility. For by 'courage' I understand 'the desire by which each person endeavours to preserve his being in accordance with the dictate of reason alone', and by 'nobility' I understand 'the desire by which each person, in accordance with the dictate of reason alone, endeavours to help other men and join them to him in friendship'. So those actions which aim only at the advantage of the agent I relate to courage, and those which also aim at the advantage of another I relate to nobility. Therefore, temperance, sobriety, presence of mind in danger, etc. are species of courage, but modesty,[75] clemency, etc. are species of nobility. With this I think that I have explained, and displayed through their first causes, the chief emotions and waverings of the mind which arise from the compounding of the three primitive emotions, namely desire, pleasure, and pain. From this it is evident that we are driven to and fro by external causes in many ways, and that we toss like the waves of the sea when they are driven by opposing winds, ignorant of our fortune and of our fate. I said that I have shown only the chief conflicts of the mind, and not all that can exist; for we can easily show (proceeding in the same way as above) that love is joined to repentance, disdain, and shame, etc. Indeed I believe that, from what has already been said, it will be clear to everyone that the emotions can be combined with one another in so many ways, and so many variations will arise from this, that one cannot set bounds to them by any number. But it is sufficient for my purposes to have enumerated the chief emotions only; for the others that I have omitted would satisfy curiosity rather than be of any use. However, one thing remains to be noted about love. It happens very often that, while we are enjoying a thing which we were seeking, our body acquires, as a result of this enjoyment, a new disposition by which it is determined in another way and other images of things are excited in it, and at the same time the mind begins to imagine and to desire other things. For example, when we imagine something that usually delights us by its taste, we desire to enjoy it, i.e. to eat it. But as long as we enjoy it in this way, the stomach is filled, and our body is disposed in another way. If, therefore, whilst the body has this different disposition, the image of the same food is stimulated by the presence of the actual food, and consequently the endeavour, i.e. the desire, to eat it is also stimulated, this new disposition will be opposed to the original desire, i.e. endeavour. Consequently, the presence of the food which we used to seek will be offensive to us, and this is what we call satiety and disgust. For the rest, I have omitted the external affections of the body which are observed in the emotions, such as trembling, pallor, sobbing, laughter, etc., because these are related to the body alone without any relation to the mind. Finally, some things must be noted about the definitions of the emotions; accordingly I will repeat these definitions here in a systematic way,[76] and will insert such observations as are required in each case.

Definitions of the Emotions

1. Desire[77] is the very essence of man, in so far as it is conceived as determined to do something from some given affection of itself.

Explanation. We said above in the Scholium of Proposition 9 of Part 3 that desire is appetite together with a consciousness of the appetite, and that desire is the very essence of man in so far as it is determined to do those things that contribute to his preservation. But in the same Scholium I gave warning of the fact that I really do not recognize any difference between human appetite and desire. For whether a man is conscious of his appetite or not, the appetite remains one and the same. So, in order not to seem to commit a tautology, I was unwilling to define desire by means of appetite, but took care to define desire in such a way as to take together all the endeavours of human nature which we indicate by the name of appetite, will, desire, or impulse. For I could have said that desire is the very essence of man, in so far as it is conceived as determined to do something; but from this definition (by Prop. 23, Part 2) it would not follow that the mind can be conscious of its desire, i.e. its appetite. Therefore, in order that I might include the cause of this consciousness, it was necessary (by the same Proposition) to add, 'in so far as it is conceived as determined to do something from some given affection of itself'. For by an affection of human essence we understand any disposition of that essence, whether it is innate, whether it is conceived through the attribute of thought alone or of extension alone, or whether finally it is related to both at the same time. Here, therefore, I understand by the name 'desire' all human endeavours, impulses, appetites, and volitions, which vary in accordance with the disposition of the same man, and which are often so opposed to each other that a man is dragged in different directions and does not know where to turn.

2. Pleasure[78] is man's transition from a lesser to a greater perfection.

3. Pain[79] is man's transition from a greater to a lesser perfection.

Explanation. I say 'transition'; for pleasure is not perfection itself. For if man were born with the perfection to which he makes a transition, he would possess it without the emotion of pleasure. This is more clearly evident from the emotion of pain, which is the opposite of pleasure. For no one can deny that pain consists in a transition to a lesser perfection, and not in that lesser perfection itself, for a man cannot feel pain in so far as he shares in some perfection. Nor can we say that pain consists in the privation of a greater perfection; for privation is nothing, whereas the emotion of pain is an act, which cannot therefore be anything other than the act of transition to a lesser perfection, that is, the act by which a man's power of acting is diminished or hindered (see Prop. 11, Schol., Part 3). For the rest, I omit the definitions of joy, titillation, melancholy, and anguish, since these are related to the body in particular,[80] and are only species of pleasure or pain.

4. Wonder[81] is the imagination of some thing, in which the mind remains fixed because this particular imagination has no connection with others. See Prop. 52, with its Scholium.

Explanation. In the Scholium of Prop. 18, Part 2, I showed the cause of the fact that the mind, from regarding one thing, proceeds immediately to the thought of another thing: namely, because the images of these things are interconnected, and are so arranged that one follows the other. This, however, cannot be conceived when the image of the thing is new; in those circumstances the mind will be occupied in regarding the same thing until it is determined by other causes to think of other things. So, considered in itself, the imagination of a new thing is of the same nature as other imaginations, and because of this I do not count wonder as one of the emotions.[82] Nor do I see any cause for doing so, since this distraction of the mind arises from no positive cause which distracts the mind from other things, but only on account of the fact that there is an absence of a cause which would explain why the mind is determined, after regarding one thing, to think of others. I therefore recognize (as I noted in Prop. 11, Schol., Part 3) only three primitive, i.e. primary, emotions: namely, pleasure, pain, and desire. I have mentioned wonder simply because it has been the practice for certain emotions which are derived from the three primitive ones to be referred to by other names when they are related to objects at which we wonder. This same reason also moves me to add a definition of contempt.

5. Contempt[83] is the imagination of some thing which touches the mind so little that the mind is moved by the presence of the thing to imagine what is not in the thing rather than what is in it. See Prop. 52, Schol., Part 3.

I pass over here the definitions of veneration and disdain, since, as far as I know, no emotions derive their name from them.

6. Love[84] is pleasure, with the accompaniment of the idea of an external cause.

Explanation. This definition expresses clearly enough the essence of love; for the definition given by those authors who define love as the will of the lover to join himself with the loved thing[85] expresses, not the essence of love, but a property of it. Further, since these authors did not perceive the essence of love satisfactorily, they were unable to have any clear conception of its property, and so it has come about that their definition has been judged by everyone to be extremely obscure. But it must be noted that when I say that it is a property of the lover to will to join himself with the loved thing, I do not understand by 'will' consent, or a deliberation of the mind, i.e. a free decree (for I have demonstrated this to be fictitious in Prop. 48, Part 2). Nor, again, do I understand the lover's desire to join himself with the loved thing when it is absent, or of continuing in its presence when it is at hand; for love can be conceived without the latter or the former desire. Rather, by 'will' I understand the contentment that there is in the lover on account of the presence of the loved thing, by which the pleasure of the lover is strengthened, or at any rate fostered.

7. Hatred[86] is pain, with the accompaniment of the idea of an external cause.

Explanation. What is to be noted here is easily perceived from what has been said in the Explanation of the preceding Proposition. See also the Scholium of Prop. 13, Part 3.

8. Propensity is pleasure, with the accompaniment of the idea of some thing which is by accident the cause of the pleasure.

9. Aversion is pain, with the accompaniment of the idea of some thing which is by accident the cause of the pain. On these matters, see the Scholium of Prop. 15, Part 3.[87]

10. Devotion[88] is love for a person at whom we wonder.

Explanation. We showed in Proposition 52, Part 3, that wonder arises from the novelty of a thing. If, therefore, it happens that we often imagine a thing at which we wonder, we shall cease to wonder at it. So we see that the emotion of devotion easily degenerates into simple love.

11. Derision[89] is pleasure that has arisen from the fact that we imagine, in a thing that we hate, the presence of something that we despise.[90]

Explanation. In so far as we despise a thing that we hate, to that extent we deny existence of it (see Prop. 52, Schol., Part 3), and to that extent (by Prop. 20, Part 3) we feel pleasure. But since we assume that a man hates that which he derides, it follows that this pleasure is not firm. See Prop. 47, Schol., Part 3.

12. Hope[91] is an inconstant pleasure, which has arisen from the idea of a thing that is future or past, about whose outcome we are in some doubt.

13. Fear is an inconstant pain, which has arisen from the idea of a thing

that is future or past, about whose outcome we are in some doubt. See on these matters Prop. 18, Schol.2, Part 3.

Explanation. From these definitions it follows that there is no hope without fear, and no fear without hope. For someone who is suspended in hope, and is doubtful about the outcome of some thing, is supposed to imagine something that excludes the existence of a future thing, and so to that extent to feel pain (by Prop. 19, Part 3); consequently, whilst he is suspended in hope he is supposed to fear that the thing will happen. On the other hand, the person who is in a state of fear, that is, who is doubtful about the outcome of a thing that he hates, also imagines something that excludes the existence of that thing, and so (by Prop. 20, Part 3) he feels pleasure, and consequently to that extent he hopes that it will not happen.

14. Confidence is pleasure which has arisen from the idea of a future or a past thing, about which the cause of doubt has been removed.

15. Despair is pain which has arisen from the idea of a future or of a past thing, about which the cause of doubt has been removed.

Explanation. So confidence arises from hope, and despair arises from fear, when the cause of doubt about the outcome of the matter has been removed. This comes about because a man imagines a future or a past thing to be at hand, and regards it as present; or because he imagines other things which exclude the existence of those things that instilled doubt in him. For although (by Prop. 31, Coroll., Part 2) we can never be certain about the outcome of particular things, yet it can happen that we do not doubt about the outcome. For we have shown (see Prop. 49, Schol., Part 2) that it is one thing not to doubt about a thing, and another to be certain about the thing. So it can come about that, as a result of the image of a past or future thing, we are affected with the same emotion of pleasure or pain as we are as a result of the image of a present thing, as we demonstrated in Prop. 18, Part 3—which see, together with its Scholia.

16. Delight[92] is pleasure, with the accompaniment of the idea of a past thing which turned out in a way contrary to one's fear.

17. Remorse[93] is pain, with the accompaniment of the idea of a past thing which turned out in a way contrary to one's hope.

18. Compassion[94] is pain, with the accompaniment of the idea of harm which has happened to another whom we imagine to be like us. See Prop. 22, Schol., and Prop. 27, Schol., Part 3.

Explanation. Between compassion and pity[95] there seems to be no differ-ence, except perhaps that compassion regards a particular emotion, and pity a disposition.

19. Favour[96] is love towards someone who has benefited another.

20. Indignation is hatred towards someone who has done harm to another.

Explanation. I know that these names mean something else in common usage. But my purpose is to explain, not the meaning of words, but the nature of things,[97] and to refer to them by terms whose common mean-ing is not entirely at variance with the meaning in which I wish to use them. Let this single warning be enough. For the rest, for the cause of these emotions, see Prop. 27, Coroll. 1, and Prop. 22, Schol., Part 3.

21. Esteem[98] is thinking too highly of someone on account of love.

22. Scorn is thinking too little of someone on account of hatred.

Explanation. So esteem is an effect, i.e. a property, of love, and scorn is an effect, i.e. a property, of hatred. Consequently, 'esteem' can also be defined as 'love, in so far as it affects a man in such a way that he thinks too highly of the thing that is loved', and on the other hand 'scorn' can be defined as 'hatred, in so far as it affects a man in such a way that he thinks too little of the thing that he hates'. On these, see Prop. 26, Schol., Part 3.

23. Envy[99] is hatred in so far as it affects a man in such a way that he feels pain at the happiness of another and, on the other hand, rejoices in another's harm.

Explanation. To envy there is commonly opposed pity, which can there-fore (despite the usual meaning of the word) be defined as follows:

24. Pity[100] is love in so far as it affects a man in such a way that he rejoices at another's good, and on the other hand feels pain at another's harm.

Explanation. Concerning envy, see Prop. 24, Schol., and Prop. 32, Schol., Part 3. The preceding emotions of pleasure and pain are those which are accompanied by the idea of an external thing, either as a cause through itself or as a cause by accident.[101] From these I proceed to other emo-tions, which are accompanied by the idea of an internal thing as a cause.

25. Self-contentment[102] is pleasure which has arisen from the fact that a man thinks of himself and of his power of acting.

26. Humility[103] is pain which has arisen from the fact that a man thinks of his lack of power, i.e. his weakness.

Explanation. Self-contentment is opposed to humility, in so far as by the former we understand pleasure which arises from the fact that we think of our power of acting; but in so far as we also understand by it pleasure with the accompaniment of the idea of some deed that we believe that we have done from a free decree of the mind, then it is opposed to repentance, which I define as follows:

27. Repentance is pain with the accompaniment of the idea of some deed that we believe that we have done from a free decree of the mind.

Explanation. We have shown the causes of these emotions in Prop. 51, Schol., and Prop. 53, Prop. 54, and Prop. 55 and Scholium, Part 3. Concerning a free decree of the mind, see Prop. 35, Schol., Part 2. Here it must also be noted that it is not remarkable that all the acts that are usually called 'wicked' are followed by pain, and those which are called 'right' are followed by pleasure. For we easily understand, from what has been said above, that this depends on education above all. For parents, by condemning the former acts and often reproving their children because of them, and on the other hand by recommending and praising the latter, have brought it about that feelings of pain are joined to the former and feelings of pleasure to the latter. This is also confirmed by experience. For custom and religion are not the same for all men, but on the contrary things that are sacred for some men are unholy for others, and things that are honourable for some men are base for others. Therefore, each person will either repent of some deed or glory in it, in accordance with the way in which he has been educated.

28. Pride[104] is thinking too highly of oneself on account of love of oneself.

Explanation. Pride, therefore, differs from esteem, in that the latter is related to an external object, but pride is related to a man himself, in so far as he thinks too highly of himself. However, just as esteem is an effect of love, so is pride an effect or a property of self-love; accordingly it can also be defined as 'love of oneself, i.e. self-contentment, in so far as it affects a man in such a way that he thinks too highly of himself' (see Prop. 26, Schol., Part 3). This emotion has no opposite. For no one thinks too little of himself on account of hatred of himself; indeed, no one thinks too little of himself in so far as he imagines that he cannot do this or that. For whatever a man imagines that he cannot do, he imagines necessarily; and by this imagination he is so disposed that he really cannot do what he imagines that he cannot do. For as long as a man imagines that he cannot do this or that, so long he is not determined to do it, and consequently it is impossible for him to do it over that period. However, if we pay attention to those things that depend on opinion alone, we shall be able to conceive it possible that a man thinks too little of himself. For it can happen that someone, whilst he sadly contemplates his weakness, imagines that he is disparaged by everyone, whilst other people are thinking of nothing less than of disparaging him. Further, a man can think too little of himself if he negates of himself in the present something of which he is uncertain that is related to a future time; for example, if he says that he can conceive nothing certain, and can desire or do etc. nothing but what is wicked or base. Again, we can say that someone thinks too little of himself when we see that, as a result of excessive fear of shame, he dare not do what is dared by others who are equal to him. This emotion, therefore, we can oppose to pride; I will call it 'self-abasement',[105] for just as pride arises from self-contentment, so self-abasement arises from humility. Accordingly I define it as follows:

29. Self-abasement is thinking too little of oneself on account of pain.

Explanation. We are often accustomed to oppose humility to pride; but then we are paying attention rather to the effects of each than to their nature. For we are accustomed to call that person proud who glorifies himself excessively (see Prop. 30, Schol., Part 3), who recounts only his own virtues and other people's defects, who wants to take precedence over everyone, and who, finally, proceeds with the solemnity and in the dress that is usual among those who are placed far above him. On the other hand, we call that man humble who often blushes, who confesses his own faults and recounts the virtues of others, who gives way to everyone, and who, finally, walks with a bowed head and neglects his dress. For the rest, these emotions—namely, humility and self-abasement—are very rare. For human nature, considered in itself, strives against these emotions as far as it can (see Props. 13 and 54, Part 3); consequently, those who are believed to be most self-abasing and humble are often most ambitious and envious.

30. Glory[106] is pleasure, with the accompaniment of the idea of some action of ours which we imagine others to praise.

31. Shame[107] is pain, with the accompaniment of the idea of some action which we imagine others to blame.

Explanation. On these, see the Scholium of Prop. 30, Part 3. Here one must note a difference that exists between shame and bashfulness.[108] For shame is pain which follows a deed of which one is ashamed; but bashfulness is fear, i.e. the fear of shame, by which a man is restrained from doing something base. It is usual to oppose shamelessness to bashfulness, although shamelessness is not truly an emotion, as I shall show in its proper place.[109] But (as I have already noted) the names of emotions have regard to usage rather than to Nature.[110] With this I have dealt with the emotions of pleasure and pain that I proposed to explain. So I proceed to those which I relate to desire.

32. Regret[111] is the desire, i.e. the appetite of possessing some thing, which is fostered by the memory of the thing and is at the same time restrained by the memory of other things which exclude the existence of that thing.

Explanation. When we recollect something (as I have already said many times)[112] we are by that very fact disposed to think of it with the same emotion as we would if the thing were present; but whilst we are awake this disposition, i.e. this endeavour, is often restrained by the images of things which exclude the existence of the thing that we recollect. So when we remember a thing which affects us with some kind of pleasure, by that very fact we endeavour to think of it as present with the same emotion of pleasure. This endeavour is immediately hindered by the memory of things which exclude its existence. Therefore, regret is really pain, which is opposed to that pleasure which arises from the absence of the thing which we hate, on which see Prop. 47, Schol., Part 3. But since the name 'regret' seems to concern desire, I therefore relate this emotion to the emotions of desire.

33. Emulation[113] is the desire of some thing, which is produced in us from the fact that we imagine others to have the same desire.

Explanation. We say that a man who flees because he sees others flee, or who is afraid because he sees others to be afraid, or again the man who, because he sees another to have burned his hand, draws his hand towards himself and moves his body as if his own body were burned—such a man, we say, imitates the emotion of another, but does not emulate it. This is not because we know one cause of imitation and another of emulation, but because it has become usual to call emulous only that man who imitates what we judge to be honourable, useful, or pleasant. For the rest, see, on the cause of emulation, Prop. 27 and its

Scholium, Part 3. As to why envy is usually linked with this emotion, see Prop. 32 and its Scholium, Part 3.

34. Gratefulness, i.e. gratitude,[114] is the desire, i.e. the zeal, displayed by love, by which we endeavour to benefit a man who, with an equal emotion of love, has benefited us. See Prop. 39, together with the Scholium of Prop. 41, Part 3.

35. Benevolence[115] is the desire of doing good to someone whom we pity. See Prop. 27, Schol., Part 3.

36. Anger[116] is the desire by which, as a result of hatred, we are incited to do harm to the person whom we hate. See Prop. 39, Part 3.

37. Revenge is the desire by which, as a result of reciprocal hatred, we are driven to inflict harm on someone who, with an equal emotion, has inflicted harm on us. See Prop. 40, Coroll. 2 of Part 3, with its Scholium.

38. Cruelty, i.e. savagery,[117] is the desire by which someone is led to inflict harm on someone we love, or whom we pity.

Explanation. To cruelty there is opposed clemency, which is not a passion, but a power of the mind[118] by which a man controls anger and revenge. 250

39. Timidity[119] is the desire to avoid by a lesser harm a greater harm which we fear. See Prop. 39, Schol., Part 3.

40. Boldness[120] is the desire by which someone is led to do something which involves a danger which his equals are afraid to undergo.

41. Cowardliness is asserted of the man whose desire is hindered by the fear of a danger which his equals dare to undergo.

Explanation. So cowardliness is simply the fear of some harm that most people do not usually fear, and for this reason I do not relate it to the emotion of desire. However, I wanted to explain it here, because in so far as we pay attention to desire, cowardliness is genuinely opposed to the emotion of boldness.

42. Consternation[121] is asserted of the person whose desire to avoid harm is hindered by wonder at the harm which he fears.

Explanation. So consternation is a kind of cowardice. But because consternation arises from a double fear, it can be more conveniently defined as 'a fear which keeps a man either stunned or hesitant in such a way that he cannot remove a harm'. I say 'stunned', in so far as we understand this desire to remove a harm to be hindered by wonder; I say 'hesitant', in so far as we conceive that desire to be hindered by the fear of another harm, which torments him equally, as a result of which he does not know which of the two he should remove. On these matters, see Prop. 39, Schol., and Prop. 52, Schol., Part 3. On cowardliness and boldness, see Prop. 51, Schol., Part 3.

43. Politeness,[122] i.e. modesty, is the desire of doing those things that please men and of not doing those things that displease them.

44. Ambition is the unrestrained desire of glory.

Explanation. Ambition is the desire by which all the emotions (by Props. 27 and 31, Part 3) are fostered and strengthened, and so this emotion can hardly be overcome. For as long as a man is held by any desire, he is at the same time necessarily held by this desire. 'Every excellent man', says Cicero,[123] 'is led by glory above all. Even philosophers inscribe their name on the books which they write about the need to scorn glory, etc.'

45. Luxury[124] is the uncontrolled desire, or also the love, of feasting.

46. Drunkenness is the uncontrolled desire and love of drinking.

47. Avarice is the uncontrolled desire and love of wealth.

48. Lust is the desire and love of sexual intercourse.

Explanation. Whether this desire of sexual intercourse is controlled or not, it is usually called 'lust'. Further, these five emotions (as I pointed out in Prop. 56, Schol., Part 3) do not have opposites. For modesty is a kind of ambition (on which, see Prop. 29, Schol., Part 3); again, I have already noted [125] that temperance, sobriety, and chastity indicate a power of the mind, and not a passion. And although it can happen that a man who is avaricious, ambitious, or timid can abstain from excess of food, drink, and sexual intercourse, yet avarice, ambition, and timidity are not the opposites of luxury, drunkenness, or lust. For an avaricious man often wishes to gorge himself on someone else's food and drink. Again, an ambitious man will moderate himself in nothing, provided that he hopes to keep it secret, and if he lives among the drunken and the lustful, then, precisely because he is ambitious, he will be more inclined to these vices. Finally, a timid man does what he does not want. For even if he casts his wealth into the sea to escape death, he still remains avaricious; and if a lustful man is pained at not being able to carry on his usual way of life, he does not on this account cease to be lustful. In absolute terms, these emotions do not so much concern the acts of feasting, drinking, etc., as the appetite and the love itself. Nothing, therefore, can be opposed to these emotions apart from nobility and courage,[126] on which I will speak in what follows.

The definitions of jealousy[127] and of other waverings of the mind I pass over in silence, both because they arise from the combination of the emotions which I have already defined, and also because most of them have no names, which shows that it is enough for practical purposes just to know them in general. For the rest it is clear, from the definitions of the emotions that I have explained, that all the emotions spring from desire, pleasure, or pain; or rather, that there are no emotions apart from these three, which are customarily called by various names on account of their relations and extrinsic denominations.[128] If we are now ready to pay attention to these primitive emotions, and to what has been said above about the nature of the mind, we shall be able to give the following definition of the emotions, in so far as they are related to the mind alone:

General Definition of the Emotions

An emotion that is called a passive state[129] of the mind is a confused idea, by which the mind affirms of its body, or of any part of its body, a greater or less force of existing than before, and which being given, the mind itself is determined to thinking this rather than that.

Explanation. I say first that an emotion, i.e. a passion of the mind, is a 'confused idea'. For we have shown (see Prop. 3, Part 3) that the mind is passive only in so far as it has inadequate, i.e. confused, ideas. I then say, 'by which the mind affirms of its body, or of any part of its body, a greater or less force of existing than before'. For all the ideas of bodies that we have indicate rather the actual constitution of our body (by Prop. 16, Coroll. 2, Part 2) than the nature of an external body. But the idea that constitutes the form of the emotion must indicate or express the constitution of the body, or of some part of it—a constitution which the body, or some part of it, has from the fact that its power of acting, i.e. its force of existing, is increased or diminished, helped or hindered. But it must be noted that when I say 'a greater or less force of existing than before', I do not understand that the mind compares the present constitution of the body with a past one, but that the idea that constitutes the form of the emotion affirms something of the body, which genuinely involves more or less reality than before. And since the essence of the mind consists (by Props. 11 and 13, Part 2) in the fact that it affirms the actual existence of its body, and we understand by perfection the very essence of a thing, it therefore follows that the mind makes a transition to a greater or less perfection when it happens to affirm of its body, or of some part of it, that which involves more or less reality than before. When, therefore, I said above that the mind's power of thinking is increased or diminished, I simply wanted it to be understood that the mind has formed an idea of its body, or of some part of it, which expresses more or less reality than it had affirmed of its body. For the excellence of ideas, and the actual power of thinking, is estimated from the excellence of the object. I added finally, 'and which being given, the mind itself is determined to thinking this rather than that' so that I might express, besides the nature of pleasure and pain, which is explained by the first part of the definition, the nature of desire as well.

End of the Third Part

PART FOUR

ON HUMAN SERVITUDE, OR, ON THE STRENGTH OF THE EMOTIONS

Preface

Human lack of power in controlling and restraining the emotions I call 'servitude'. For a man who is subject to the emotions is not his own master, but is mastered by fortune, whose power over him is such that he is often compelled, even though he sees what is better for himself,[1] to follow what is worse. I propose in this Part to demonstrate the cause of this matter, and also to demonstrate what goodness or badness the emotions have. But before I begin, I will add a few prefatory remarks about perfection and imperfection, and about good and bad.

Someone who has completed something that he has decided to make will say that that thing is 'perfect'.[2] And not only will he say this, but so will everyone who rightly knows, or believes that he knows, the mind and the aim of the producer of that piece of work. For example, if someone sees some piece of work (which I assume not yet to be complete) and knows that the aim of its producer is to build a house, he will say that the house is imperfect; conversely, he will call it perfect as soon as he sees that it has been carried through to the end that the producer has resolved to give to it. But if he sees some piece of work whose like he has never seen, and does not know the mind of the producer, he cannot know whether it is perfect or imperfect. This seems to have been the original meaning of these words. But after men began to form universal ideas and to think out exemplars[3] of houses, buildings, towers, etc., and began to prefer some exemplars to others, then it came about that each person called that thing 'perfect' which he saw to agree with the universal idea which he had formed of a thing of that kind; conversely, he called that thing 'imperfect' which he saw not to agree closely with the exemplar that he had conceived, even though, in the opinion of the producer, it was evidently finished. Nor does there seem to be any other reason why natural things, which are not made by the human hand, are also commonly called perfect or imperfect. For men are accustomed to form universal ideas both of natural and of artificial things, which they treat as exemplars and which they believe that Nature (which, they think, does nothing except for the sake of some end) looks towards and sets before itself as exemplars. So when they see something to occur in Nature which does not agree closely with the exemplar that they have conceived of a thing of that kind, then they believe that Nature itself has failed, or has erred, and has left the thing imperfect. So we see that men have formed the custom of calling natural things perfect or imperfect more out of prejudice than from a genuine knowledge of them. For we have shown in the Appendix of the First Part that Nature does not act for an end; for the eternal and infinite entity that we call God, i.e. Nature,[4] acts by the same necessity as that by which he exists. For we have shown (Prop. 16, Part 1) that he acts out of the same necessity of nature as that by which he exists. Therefore, the reason, i.e. the cause, why God or in other words Nature acts, and the reason why he exists, is one and the same. Therefore, just as he does not exist for the sake of any purpose, neither does he act for the sake of any purpose, but just as he has no principle or end of existing, so he has no principle or end of acting. What is called a 'final cause'[5] is simply human appetite, in so far as it is conceived as if it were a principle, i.e. a primary cause of some thing. For example, when we say that habitation was the final cause of this or that house, then we simply understand the fact that a man, from the fact that he imagined the advantages of domestic life, had an appetite for building a house. So habitation, in so far as it is considered as a final cause, is simply this particular appetite, which is actually an efficient cause which is considered as primary because men are usually ignorant of the causes of their appetites. For, as I have often said already,[6] they are conscious of their actions and of their appetites, but ignorant of the causes by which they are determined to have an appetite for something. The further common assertions that Nature is sometimes deficient, or errs, and produces things that are imperfect, I count among the fabrications that I discussed in the Appendix of the First Part.[7] Really, therefore, perfection and imperfection are merely ways of thinking, namely notions which we are accustomed to form from the fact that we compare with each other individuals which are of the same species or genus. This was the cause of my saying above (Def. 6, Part 2) that by reality and perfection I understand the same. For we are accustomed to reduce all the individuals of Nature to one genus, which is called 'most general'—namely, to the notion of being,[8] which belongs to all individuals of Nature absolutely. So in so far as we reduce all the individuals of Nature to this genus, and compare them with each other and find some to have more being, i.e. reality, than others, to that extent we call some more perfect than others. Further, in so far as we ascribe to them something that involves negation, such as limit, end, lack of power, etc., to that extent we call them imperfect. This is because they do not affect our mind to a equal degree as those which we call perfect, and not because there is lacking in them something that is their own, or because Nature has made a mistake. For to the nature of a thing there belongs only that which follows from the necessity of the nature of an efficient cause, and whatever follows from the necessity of the nature of an efficient cause is necessarily produced.

As to what concerns good and bad, these also indicate nothing positive in things considered in themselves, and are simply ways of thinking, i.e. notions which we form from the fact that we compare things with one another. For one and the same thing can at the same time be good, bad, and indifferent. For example, music is good to someone who is melancholy, bad to a mourner, but neither good nor bad to someone who is deaf. However, although this is how things are, we must retain these names. For since we desire to form an idea of man, as an exemplar of human nature towards which we may look, it will be useful for us to retain these words in the sense which I have stated. So in what follows I shall understand by 'good' that which we know with certainty to be a means by which we may approach more and more closely that exemplar of human nature which set before ourselves.[9] By 'bad' I shall understand that which we know with certainty to hinder us from reaching that exemplar. Then we shall say that men are more or less perfect as they approach this exemplar more or less. For it must be especially noted that when I say that someone passes from a lesser to a greater perfection, and conversely, I do not understand that he is changed from one essence, i.e. one form, into another. (For a horse, for example, is as much destroyed if it is changed into a man as if it is changed into an insect.) Rather, we conceive someone's power of acting to be increased or diminished in so far as this is understood through his own nature. Finally, by perfection in general I shall, as I have said, understand reality; that is, the essence of each thing in so far as it exists and operates in a certain way, no attention being paid to its duration. For no particular thing can be said to be more perfect because it has persevered in existing for a longer time. For the duration of things cannot be determined by their essence, since the essence of things involves no certain and determinate time of existence, but each thing—whether it is more or less perfect—will always be able to persevere in existing with the same force with which it begins to exist, such that all are equal in this matter.

Definitions

1. By good I shall understand that which we know with certainty to be useful to us.

2. By bad I shall understand that which we know with certainty to hinder us from possessing something good.

On these, see the preceding Preface, towards the end.

3. I call particular things contingent in so far as, whilst we attend to their essence alone, we find nothing that necessarily posits their existence or necessarily excludes it.

4. I call particular things possible in so far as, whilst we attend to the causes from which they must be produced, we do not know whether the causes are determined to the production of these things.

In Prop. 33, Schol. 1, Part 1, I drew no distinction between possible and contingent, because it was not necessary there to distinguish between them with accuracy.

5. I shall, in what follows, understand by contrary emotions those which draw a man in different directions, even though they are of the same genus—such as luxury and avarice, which are species of love—and are contraries, not by nature, but by accident.

6. What I understand by an emotion towards a thing which is future, present, or past, I have explained in Prop. 18, Scholia 1 and 2, Part 3.

However, this must be noted as well: that just as in the case of distance of place, so also we cannot distinctly imagine distance of time beyond a certain limit. That is to say: we are accustomed to imagine all objects which are more than two hundred feet distant from us—i.e. whose distance from the place in which we are exceeds that which we imagine distinctly—as equally distant from us, and as if they were in the same plane.[10] Similarly, all objects whose time of existence is distant from the present by a longer interval than that which we usually imagine distinctly, we imagine to be equally distant from the present, and we relate them as it were to one moment of time.

7. By the end for the sake of which we do something I understand appetite.[11]

8. By virtue and power I understand the same; that is (by Prop. 7,

Part 3), virtue, in so far as it is related to man, is the very essence, i.e. the nature, of man, in so far as he has the power of doing certain things which can be understood through the laws of his nature alone.

Axiom

There exists no particular thing in the universe such that there does not exist another thing which is more powerful than it, but given any particular thing there exists another which is more powerful than it and by which it can be destroyed.

Proposition 1

Nothing positive that a false idea has is removed by the presence of what is true, in so far as it is true.

Demonstration. Falsity consists solely in the privation of knowledge that inadequate ideas involve (by Prop. 35, Part 2), and they themselves have nothing positive on account of which they are called false (by Prop. 33, Part 2); on the contrary, in so far as they are related to God, they are true (by Prop. 32, Part 2). If, therefore, something positive that a false idea has were removed by the presence of what is true, in so far as it is true, then a true idea would be removed by itself, which (by Prop. 4, Part 3) is absurd. Therefore, nothing positive, etc. QED.

Scholium

This Proposition is understood more clearly from Prop. 16, Coroll. 2, Part 2. For an imagination is an idea which indicates the present constitution of the body rather than the nature of an external body—not distinctly, indeed, but confusedly—from which it comes about that the mind is said to err. For example, when we see the sun, we imagine it to be about two hundred feet distant from us.[12] In this we are deceived, as long as we are ignorant of its true distance. But when the sun's distance is known, the error is removed, but not the imagination, that is, an idea of the sun which explains the sun's nature only in so far as the body is affected by it. So, although we know its true distance, we nevertheless imagine it to be close to us. For, as we said in Prop. 35, Schol., Part 2, we imagine the sun to be so close, not because we are ignorant of its true distance, but because the mind conceives the magnitude of the sun in so far as the body is affected by it. In the same way, when the rays of the sun, falling on the surface of water, are reflected to our eyes, we imagine the sun as if it were in the water, even though we know its true position. And in the same way the other imaginations by which the mind is deceived—whether they indicate the natural constitution of the body, or an increase or diminution of its power of acting—are not contrary to what is true, and do not vanish together with its presence. It does indeed happen that, when we falsely fear some harm, the fear vanishes when we hear a true report; but on the other hand it also happens that when we fear a harm that will certainly come, the fear also vanishes when we hear a false report. So imaginations do not vanish with the presence of what is true, in so far as it is true; they vanish because of the occurrence of other imaginations, stronger than they are, which exclude the present existence of the things that we imagine, as we have shown in Prop. 17, Part 2.

Proposition 2

We are passive in so far as we are a part of Nature which cannot be conceived through itself, without others.

Demonstration. We are said to be passive when something happens in us of which we are only a partial cause (by Def. 2, Part 3); that is (by Def. 1, Part 3), something that cannot be deduced from the laws of our nature alone. We are therefore passive in so far as we are a part of Nature which cannot be conceived through itself, without others. QED.

Proposition 3

The force by which a man perseveres in existence is limited, and is infinitely surpassed by the power of external causes.

Demonstration. This is evident from the Axiom of this Part. For given a man, there is also given something else—say, *A*—more powerful than the man; and given *A* there is given something else, say, *B*, more powerful than *A*, and so on to infinity. Therefore, the power of a man is bounded by the power of another thing, and is infinitely surpassed by the power of external causes.

Proposition 4

It cannot happen that a man is not a part of Nature and can undergo no changes apart from those that can be understood through his nature alone, and of which he is the adequate cause.

Demonstration. The power by which particular things, and consequently a man, preserve their being is the power of God, i.e. of Nature (by Prop. 24, Coroll., Part 1); not in so far as it is infinite, but in so far as it can be explained by actual human essence (by Prop. 7, Part 3). So the power of a man, in so far as it is explained through his actual essence, is a part of the infinite power, that is, of the essence (by Prop. 34, Part 1) of God, i.e. of Nature. This was the first thing to be proved. Then, if it could happen that a man can undergo no changes apart from those that can be understood through the nature of man alone, then it would follow (by Props. 4 and 6, Part 3) that he could not perish, but would necessarily exist always. This must follow from a cause whose power is either finite or infinite; namely, either solely from the power of a man, who would be capable of averting from himself the other changes which can arise from external causes, or from the infinite power of Nature, by which all particular things are so directed that a man can undergo no changes other than those which serve for his preservation. But the first is absurd (by the preceding Proposition, whose demonstration is universal, and can be applied to all particular things). Therefore, if it could happen that a man should suffer no changes, apart from those that can be understood through the nature of man alone, and consequently (as we have just shown) that he should necessarily always exist, this must follow from the infinite power of God. Consequently (by Prop. 16, Part 1), the order of the whole of Nature, in so far as it is conceived under the attributes of extension and thought, would have to be deduced from the necessity of the divine nature, in so far as it is considered as affected by the idea of some man. So it would follow (by Prop. 21, Part 1) that a man would be infinite, which (by the first part of this Demonstration) is absurd. So it cannot happen that a man should suffer no other changes apart from those of which he is the adequate cause. QED.

Corollary

From this it follows that a man is necessarily always subject to passions, and follows and obeys the common order of Nature, and complies with it as much as the nature of things demands.

Proposition 5

The force and the growth of each passion and its perseverance in existing is defined, not by the power by which we endeavour to persevere in existing, but by the power of an external cause compared with our own.

Demonstration. The essence of a passion cannot be explained by our essence alone (by Defs. 1 and 2, Part 3); that is (by Prop. 7, Part 3), the power of a passion cannot be defined by the power by which we endeavour to persevere in our being, but (as was shown in Prop. 16, Part 2) it must necessarily be defined by the power of an external cause compared with our own. QED.

Proposition 6

The force of some passion, i.e. of some emotion, can so surpass the other actions, i.e. the power, of a man that the emotion adheres stubbornly to the man.

Demonstration. The power and the growth of each passion, and its perseverance in existing, is defined by the power of an external cause compared with our own (by the preceding Proposition), and so (by Prop. 3, Part 4) it can exceed the power of a man, etc. QED.

Proposition 7

An emotion can neither be restrained nor removed except by an emotion which is contrary to and stronger than the one which is to be restrained.

Demonstration. An emotion, in so far as it is related to the mind,[13] is an idea by which the mind affirms of its body a greater or less force of existing than before (by the General Definition of the Emotions, to be found at the end of Part Three). When, therefore, the mind is harassed by some emotion, the body is simultaneously affected by an affection by which its power of acting is increased or diminished. Further, this affection of the body (by Prop. 5, Part 4) receives from its cause the force of persevering in its being; accordingly, this can neither be restrained nor removed except by a corporeal cause (by Prop. 6, Part 2) which affects the body with an affection which is contrary to it (by Prop. 5, Part 3) and stronger than it (by the Axiom of Part 4). And so (by Prop. 12, Part 2) the mind will be affected by the idea of an affection which is stronger than, and contrary to, the former one, that is (by the General Definition of the Emotions), the mind will be affected by an emotion which is stronger than and contrary to the former one, which excludes or removes the existence of the former one. Therefore, an emotion can neither be removed nor restrained, except by an emotion which is contrary to and stronger than it. QED.

Corollary

An emotion, in so far as it is related to the mind, can neither be restrained nor removed except by the idea of an affection of the body which is contrary to and stronger than the affection through which we are acted upon.[14] For an emotion by which we are acted upon can neither be restrained nor removed except by an emotion which is stronger than and contrary to it (by the preceding Proposition); that is (by the General Definition of the Emotions) except by the idea of an affection of the body which is stronger than and contrary to the affection by which we are acted upon.

Proposition 8

The knowledge of good and bad is simply the emotion of pleasure or pain, in so far as we are conscious of it.[15]

Demonstration. We call that good or bad which is either helpful, or an obstacle, to us in the preservation of our being (by Def. 1 and Def. 2, Part 4), that is (by Prop. 7, Part 3) which increases or diminishes, helps or hinders, our power of acting. So (by the definitions of pleasure and pain in Prop. 11, Schol., Part 3) in so far as we perceive something to affect us with pleasure or pain, we call it good or bad, and so the knowledge of good and bad is simply the idea of pleasure or pain, which necessarily follows from the emotion of pleasure or pain itself (by Prop. 22, Part 2). But this idea is united to the emotion in the same way that the mind is united to the body (by Prop. 21, Part 2): that is (as was shown in the Scholium of the same Proposition), this idea is not really distinguished from the emotion itself, i.e. (by the General Definition of the Emotions) from the idea of an affection of the human body, except in conception alone. Therefore, this knowledge of good and bad is simply the emotion itself, in so far as we are conscious of it. QED.

Proposition 9

An emotion, whose cause we imagine to be with us at present, is stronger than if we imagine the cause not to be with us.

Demonstration. An imagination is an idea by which the mind regards a thing as present (see its definition in Prop. 17, Schol., Part 2), but which indicates the constitution of the human body rather than the nature of the external thing (by Prop. 16, Coroll., Part 2). Therefore (by the General Definition of the Emotions), an emotion is an imagination, in so far as it indicates the constitution of the body. But an imagination (by Prop. 17, Part 2) is more intense as long as we imagine nothing that excludes the present existence of the external thing; therefore, an emotion, whose cause we imagine to be with us at present, is also more intense, i.e. stronger, than if we imagine the cause not to be with us. QED.

Scholium

When I said above in Prop. 18, Part 3, that, as a result of the image of a future or a past thing, we are affected by the same emotion as if the thing which we imagine were present, I gave express warning that this is true in so far as we attend only to the image of the thing; for that is of the same nature, whether or not we have imagined things as present. But I did not deny that it is made weaker when we regard other things, which are present to us, which exclude the present existence of a future thing. I neglected to give this warning then, because I had resolved to discuss the strength of the emotions in this Part.

Corollary

The image of a future or of a past thing—that is, of a thing which we regard with relation to a future or a past time, the present being excluded—is, other things being equal, weaker than the image of a present thing. Consequently, an emotion towards a future or a past thing is, other things being equal, milder than an emotion towards a present thing.

Proposition 10

We are more intensely affected towards a future thing that we imagine to come into existence soon than if we imagine its time of existence to be further away from the present. Again, we are more intensely affected by the memory of a thing which we imagine to have ceased to exist not long ago than if we imagine it to have ceased to exist long ago.

Demonstration. For in so far as we imagine a thing to come into existence soon, or to have ceased to exist not long ago, by that very fact we imagine something that excludes the present existence of the thing less than if we were to imagine that its future time of existence is further away from the present, or that it had ceased to exist long ago (as is self-evident). So (by the preceding Proposition) to that extent we shall be more intensely affected towards it. QED.

Scholium

From our observations on Definition 6 of Part 4, it follows that we are affected in an equally mild way towards objects that are distant from the present by a larger interval of time than we can determine by imagining it, even though we understand that they are distant from each other by a long interval of time.

Proposition 11

An emotion towards a thing which we imagine as necessary is, other things being equal, more intense than one towards a thing which is either possible or contingent, i.e. not necessary.

Demonstration. In so far as we imagine some thing to be necessary, to that extent we affirm its existence, and conversely we negate its existence when we imagine it as not necessary (by Prop. 33, Schol. 1, Part 1). Therefore (by Prop. 9, Part 4), an emotion towards a necessary thing is, other things being equal, more intense than one towards a thing which is not necessary. QED.

Proposition 12

An emotion towards a thing which we know not to exist at present and which we imagine as possible is, other things being equal, more intense than one towards a contingent thing.

Demonstration. In so far as we imagine a thing as contingent, we are not affected by the image of any other thing which posits the existence of the thing (by Def. 3, Part 4). On the contrary, we imagine (according to the hypothesis) certain things which exclude its present existence. But in so far as we imagine a thing to be possible in the future, to that extent we imagine certain things which posit its existence (by Def. 4, Part 4); that is (by Prop. 18, Part 3),[16] things which foster hope or fear. So an emotion towards a possible thing is more violent. QED.

Corollary

An emotion towards a thing which we know not to exist at present, and which we imagine as contingent, is much milder than if we imagine the thing to be with us at present.

Demonstration. An emotion towards a thing which we imagine to exist at present is more intense than if we were to imagine it as future (by Prop. 9, Coroll., Part 4), and is much more violent than if we were to imagine that future time as very distant[17] from the present (by Prop. 10, Part 4). So the emotion towards a thing whose time of existing we imagine to be far distant from the present is much milder than if we were to imagine it as present; nevertheless, it is (by the preceding Proposition) more intense than if we were to imagine the same thing as contingent. So an emotion towards a contingent thing is much milder than if we imagine the thing to be with us at present. QED.

Proposition 13

An emotion towards a contingent thing which we know not to exist at present is, other things being equal, milder than an emotion towards a past thing.

Demonstration. In so far as we imagine a thing as contingent, we are not affected by the image of any other thing that posits the existence of the thing (by Def. 3, Part 4). On the contrary, we imagine (by hypothesis) certain things that exclude its present existence. But in so far as we imagine it with relation to a past time, to that extent we are supposed to imagine something that brings it back to the memory, or, that excites an image of the thing (see Prop. 18, Part 2, together with its Scholium), and which therefore to that extent brings it about that we regard the thing as if it were present (by Prop. 17, Coroll., Part 2). So (by Prop. 9, Part 4) an emotion towards a contingent thing which we know not to exist at present is, other things being equal, milder than an emotion towards a past thing. QED.

Proposition 14

A true knowledge of good and bad cannot, in so far as it is true, restrain any emotion; it can do so only in so far as it is considered as an emotion.

Demonstration. An emotion is an idea by which the mind affirms of the body a greater or less force of existing than it did before (by the General Definition of the Emotions). So (by Prop. 1, Part 4) it has nothing positive that can be removed by the presence of what is true; consequently, a true knowledge of good and bad, in so far as it is true, cannot restrain any emotion. But if, in so far as it is an emotion (see Prop. 8, Part 4), it should be stronger than the emotion that is to be restrained, to that extent alone (by Prop. 7, Part 4) it will be able to restrain the emotion. QED.

Proposition 15

The desire which arises from a true knowledge of good and bad can be destroyed or restrained by many other desires which arise from the emotions by which we are harassed.

Demonstration. From a true knowledge of good and bad, in so far as this (by Prop. 8, Part 4) is an emotion, there necessarily arises a desire (by Def. 1 of the Emotions), which is the greater as the desire from which it arises is greater (by Prop. 37, Part 3). But since this desire (by hypothesis) arises from the fact that we understand something truly, it follows in us in so far as we act (by Prop. 3, Part 3). So it must be understood through our essence alone (by Def. 2, Part 3), and consequently (by Prop. 7, Part 3) its force and its growth must be defined by human power alone. Now, the desires which arise from the emotions by which we are harassed are also the greater as these emotions are more violent, and so their force and growth (by Prop. 5, Part 4) must be defined by the power of external causes, which, if compared with ours, exceeds our power indefinitely (by Prop. 3, Part 4). So the desires which arise from similar emotions can be more violent than one which arises from a true knowledge of good and bad, and therefore (by Prop. 7, Part 4) they can restrain or destroy it. QED.

Proposition 16

The desire which arises from a true knowledge of good and bad can, in so far as this knowledge regards the future, be more easily restrained or destroyed by a desire of things which are pleasing at present.

Demonstration. An emotion towards a thing which we imagine to be future is milder than one which is towards a thing which is present (by Prop. 9, Coroll., Part 4). But a desire which arises from a true knowledge of good and bad can—even though this knowledge concerns things which are good at present—be destroyed or restrained by some chance desire (by the preceding Proposition, whose demonstration is universal). Therefore, the desire which arises from this knowledge can, in so far as it regards the future, be more easily destroyed, etc. QED.

Proposition 17

The desire which arises from a true knowledge of good and bad, in so far as this concerns contingent things, can be much more easily restrained by a desire of things which are present.

Demonstration. This Proposition is demonstrated from Prop. 12, Coroll., Part 4, in the same way as the preceding Proposition.

Scholium

By this I think that I have shown the cause of the fact that men are moved by opinion rather than by true reason, and why a true knowledge of good and bad excites disturbances of the mind, and often submits to every kind of lust. From this there arises the saying of the poet,[18] 'I see and approve the better; I follow the worse.' The author of Ecclesiastes seems to have had the same in mind when he said, 'He that increaseth knowledge increaseth sorrow.'[19] I do not say this in order that I may infer from it that being ignorant is preferable to having knowledge, or that the intelligent man is in no way different from the fool in respect of the control of the emotions. Rather, I say this because it is necessary to know both the power and the lack of power of our nature, so that we can determine what reason can do and what it cannot do in controlling the emotions, and I have said that in this Part I shall deal solely with human lack of power. For I have decided to discuss separately the power of reason over the emotions.

Proposition 18

The desire which arises from pleasure is, other things being equal, stronger than the desire which arises from pain.

Demonstration. Desire (by Def. 1 of the Emotions) is the very essence of man, that is (by Prop. 7, Part 3), the endeavour by which a man endeavours to persevere in his being. Therefore, the desire which arises from pleasure is (by the definition of pleasure: see Prop. 11, Schol., Part 3) helped or increased by the emotion of pleasure itself; on the other hand, the desire which arises from pain is (by the same Scholium) diminished or hindered. So the force of the desire which arises from pleasure must be defined by human power and at the same time by the power of an external cause; but that which arises from pain must be defined by human power alone, and therefore the former is stronger than the latter. QED.

Scholium

In these few Propositions I have explained the causes of human lack of power and lack of constancy, and why men do not obey the precepts of reason. It now remains for me to show what it is that reason prescribes to us, and what emotions agree with the rules of human reason and what on the other hand are contrary to them. But before I begin to demonstrate this by our detailed geometrical method, I want first to state the dictates of reason briefly, so that everyone can perceive my views more easily. Since reason demands nothing that is contrary to Nature, it therefore demands that each person should love himself, should look for what is useful to him (which is truly useful), should seek everything that truly leads a man to greater perfection, and, in absolute terms, that everyone, in so far as he is in himself, should endeavour to preserve his being. This, indeed, is as necessarily true as it is true that the whole is greater than its part (see Prop. 4, Part 3).[20] Then, since virtue (by Def. 8, Part 4) is simply acting from the laws of one's own nature, and since no one (by Prop. 7, Part 3) endeavours to preserve his being except from the laws of his own nature, from this it follows, first, that the basis of virtue is the endeavour to preserve one's own being and that happiness consists in the fact that a man is able to preserve his being. Secondly, it follows that virtue is to be sought on its own account, and that there exists nothing which is more excellent or more useful to us on account of which virtue must be sought. Thirdly, it follows that those who kill themselves are weak-minded, and are overcome by external causes which are repugnant to their nature. Further, it follows from Postulate 4 of Part 2 that we can never bring it about that we need nothing outside ourselves to preserve our being and that we live in such a way that we have no dealings with things which are outside us; it follows also that, if we also consider our mind, then our intellect would be more imperfect if the mind were alone, and understood nothing apart from itself. Therefore, there exist many things outside us that are useful to us and which, consequently, are to be sought. Of these, none can be conceived as more excellent than those which agree entirely with our nature. For if (for example) two individuals of the same nature are joined with each other, they constitute an individual which is twice as powerful as either. Nothing, therefore, is more useful to man than man. I mean by this that men can ask for nothing that is more efficacious for the preservation of their being than that all men should agree in everything in such a way that the minds and bodies of all should as it were constitute one mind and one body, and that all should simultaneously endeavour, as far as they can, to preserve their own being, and that all should simultaneously look for the common advantage of all. From this it follows that men who are governed by reason—that is, men who, under the guidance of reason, look for what is useful to them—seek for themselves nothing that they do not desire for the rest of human beings, and so they are just, faithful, and honourable.[21]

These are the dictates of reason, which I have decided to state here in a few words, before I begin to demonstrate them in an order that is more detailed. I did this so that I might, if possible, gain the attention of those who believe that the principle that each person is bound to look for what is useful to him is the basis of impiety, and not of virtue and of piety.[22] So now that I have shown briefly that the situation is the opposite of this, I proceed to demonstrate the same thing in the way by which we have so far proceeded.

Proposition 19

Each person, by the laws of his nature, necessarily either seeks or is averse to what he judges to be good or bad.

Demonstration. The knowledge of good and bad (by Prop. 8, Part 4) is the emotion of pleasure or pain, in so far as we are conscious of it. Therefore (by Prop. 28, Part 3), each person necessarily seeks what he judges to be good and conversely is averse to what he judges to be bad. But this appetite is simply the essence, i.e. the nature, of man (by the definition of appetite in Prop. 9, Schol., Part 3, and Def. 1 of the Emotions). Therefore, each person, by the laws of his nature, necessarily either seeks or is averse to, etc. QED.

Proposition 20

The more each person endeavours to look for what is useful to him, that is, to preserve his being, and is able to do this, the more he is endowed with virtue. Conversely, in so far as each person neglects what is useful to him, that is, neglects to preserve his being, to that extent he is lacking in power.

Demonstration. Virtue is human power itself, which is defined by the essence of man alone (by Def. 8, Part 4); that is (by Prop. 7, Part 3), which is defined solely by the endeavour by which a man endeavours to persevere in his being. The more, therefore, each person endeavours to preserve his being, and is able to do so, the more he is endowed with virtue; consequently (by Props. 4 and 6, Part 3), in so far as he neglects to preserve his being, to that extent he is lacking in power. QED.

Scholium

No one, therefore, neglects to seek what is useful to himself, i.e. to preserve his being, unless he is overcome by causes which are external to him and contrary to his nature. No one, I say, refuses food or kills himself out of the necessity of his nature; he does so because he is compelled by external causes. This can happen in many ways. Someone may kill himself if he is compelled by another, who twists the right hand which happens to be holding a sword, and compels him to direct the sword towards his own heart. Or again, he may kill himself because, like

Seneca,[23] he is compelled by the order of a tyrant to open his own veins; that is, because he desires to avoid a greater evil by a lesser. Finally, he may do so because hidden external causes so dispose his imagination and affect his body that it takes on a nature that is contrary to the one that it previously had, and of which an idea cannot exist in the mind (by Prop. 10, Part 3). But that a man, by the necessity of his own nature, should endeavour not to exist or should endeavour to be changed into another form is as impossible as that something should come from nothing, as anyone can see with a little thought.

Proposition 21

No one can desire to be blessed,[24] to act well, and to live well without at the same time desiring to be, to act, and to live, that is, actually to exist.

Demonstration. The demonstration of this Proposition, or rather the thing itself, is self-evident, and is also evident from the definition of desire. For (by Def. 1 of the Emotions) the desire of living, acting, etc. blessedly, i.e. well, is the very essence of man; that is (by Prop. 7, Part 3) it is the endeavour by which each person endeavours to preserve his own being. Therefore, no one can desire, etc. QED.

Proposition 22

No virtue can be conceived as prior to this—namely, the endeavour to preserve oneself.

Demonstration. The endeavour to preserve itself is the very essence of a thing (by Prop. 7, Part 3). If, therefore, some other virtue could be conceived as prior to this one, namely to this endeavour, then (by Def. 8, Part 4) the essence of a thing would be conceived as prior to itself, which (as is self-evident) is absurd. Therefore, no virtue, etc. QED.

Corollary

The endeavour to preserve oneself is the first and unique basis of virtue. For nothing else can be conceived as prior to this principle (by the preceding Proposition) and (by Prop. 21, Part 4) no virtue can be conceived without it.

Proposition 23

A man, in so far as he is determined to do something by the fact that he has inadequate ideas, cannot be said absolutely to act from virtue; he can only be said to do so in so far as he is determined by the fact that he understands.

Demonstration. In so far as a man is determined to do something by the fact that he has inadequate ideas, to that extent (by Prop. 1, Part 3) he is passive, that is (by Defs. 1 and 2, Part 3), he does something that cannot be perceived through his essence alone; that is (by Def. 8, Part 4), which does not follow from his virtue. But in so far as he is determined to do something by the fact that he understands, to that extent (again by Prop. 1, Part 3) he acts, that is (by Def. 2, Part 3), he does something which is perceived through his essence alone, or (by Def. 8, Part 4), which follows adequately from his virtue. QED.

Proposition 24

In our case, to act absolutely in accordance with virtue is simply to act, live, and preserve one's being (these three mean the same) in accordance with the guidance of reason, and on the basis of looking for what is useful to oneself.

Demonstration. To act absolutely in accordance with virtue is (by Def. 8, Part 4) simply to act in accordance with the laws of one's nature. But we act solely in so far as we understand (by Prop. 3, Part 3). Therefore, in our case, to act in accordance with virtue is simply to act, live, and preserve one's being in accordance with the guidance of reason, and (by Prop. 22, Coroll., Part 4) on the basis of looking for what is useful to oneself. QED.

Proposition 25

No one endeavours to preserve his being for the sake of another thing.

Demonstration. The endeavour by which each thing endeavours to persevere in its being is defined solely by the essence of the thing itself (by Prop. 7, Part 3), and it follows necessarily, given that essence alone and not from the essence of another thing (by Prop. 6 Part 3), that each person endeavours to preserve his being. This Proposition is also evident from Prop. 22, Coroll., Part 4. For if a man were to endeavour to preserve his being for the sake of another thing, then that thing would (as is self-evident) be the primary foundation of his virtue, which (by the above-mentioned Corollary) is absurd. Therefore, no one endeavours, etc. QED.

Proposition 26

Whatever we endeavour to do in accordance with reason is simply to understand; nor does the mind, in so far as it uses reason, judge to be useful to itself anything except that which leads to understanding.

Demonstration. The endeavour to preserve itself is simply the essence of a thing (by Prop. 7, Part 3), which, in so far as it exists as such, is conceived to have a force of perseverance in existing (by Prop. 6, Part 3) and of doing those things that follow necessarily from its given nature (see the definition of appetite in Prop. 9, Schol., Part 3). But the essence of reason is simply our mind, in so far as it understands clearly and distinctly (see its definition in Prop. 40, Schol. 2, Part 2). Therefore (by Prop. 40, Part 2), whatever we endeavour to do in accordance with reason is simply to understand. Further, since this endeavour of the mind by which the mind, in so far as it reasons, endeavours to preserve its being is simply understanding (by the first part of this Proposition), this endeavour to understand (by Prop. 22, Coroll., Part 4) is the primary and the sole basis of virtue, nor (by Prop. 25, Part 4) shall we endeavour to understand things for the sake of any end. On the contrary, the mind, in so far as it reasons, will be able to conceive as good for itself only that which leads to understanding (by Def. 1, Part 4). QED.

Proposition 27

We know with certainty to be good or bad nothing but that which truly leads to understanding, or which can hinder us from understanding.

Demonstration. In so far as it reasons, the mind seeks simply to understand, nor does it judge to be useful to itself anything except that which leads to understanding (by the preceding Proposition). But the mind (by Props. 41 and 43, Part 2, and also the Scholium of the latter Proposition) does not have any certainty about things, except in so far as it has adequate ideas; or, what is the same by Prop. 40, Schol. 2, Part 2, in so far as it reasons. Therefore, we know with certainty to be good only that which truly leads to understanding, and consequently we know to be bad only that which can hinder us from understanding. QED.

Proposition 28

The highest good of the mind is the knowledge of God, and the highest virtue of the mind is to know God.

Demonstration. The highest thing that the mind can understand is God, that is (by Def. 6, Part 1) an entity that is absolutely infinite and without which (by Prop. 15, Part 1) nothing can exist or be conceived. So (by Props. 26 and 27, Part 4) the highest thing that is useful for the mind, or (by Def. 1, Part 4), its highest good, is the knowledge of God. Further, the mind acts only in so far as it understands (by Props. 1 and 3, Part 3), and to that extent alone (by Prop. 23, Part 4) it can be said absolutely that it acts from virtue. Therefore, the absolute virtue of the mind is to understand. But the highest thing that the mind can understand is God (as we have demonstrated just now); therefore, the highest virtue of the mind is to understand, i.e. to know, God.

Proposition 29

Any particular thing whose nature is entirely different from ours can neither help nor hinder our power of acting, and in absolute terms no thing can be good or bad for us unless it has something in common with us.

Demonstration. The power of each particular thing by which it exists and acts, and consequently (by Prop. 10, Coroll., Part 2) the power of man, is determined only by another particular thing (by Prop. 28, Part 1), whose nature (by Prop. 6, Part 2) must be understood through the same attribute through which human nature is conceived. Therefore, our power of acting, in whatever way it is conceived, can be determined, and consequently helped or hindered, by the power of another particular thing which has something in common with us, and not by the power of a thing whose nature is entirely different from ours. And since we call that thing good or bad which is the cause of pleasure or pain (by Prop. 8, Part 4), that is (by Prop. 11, Schol., Part 3), which increases or diminishes, helps or hinders, our power of acting, therefore a thing whose nature is entirely different from ours can be neither good nor bad for us. QED.

Proposition 30

No thing can be bad through that which it has in common with our nature; but in so far as a thing is bad for us, to that extent it is contrary to us.

Demonstration. We call that bad which is the cause of pain (by Prop. 8, Part 4), that is (by the definition of pain in Prop. 11, Schol., Part 3), which diminishes or restrains our power of acting. If, therefore, some thing were bad through that which it has in common with us, then that thing could diminish or restrain that which it has in common with us, which (by Prop. 4, Part 3) is absurd. No thing, therefore, can be bad for us through that which it has in common with us, but on the contrary in so far as it is bad, that is (as we have shown just now), in so far as it can diminish or restrain our power of acting, to that extent (by Prop. 5, Part 3) it is contrary to us. QED.

Proposition 31

In so far as some thing agrees with our nature, to that extent it is necessarily good.

Demonstration. For in so far as some thing agrees with our nature, it cannot be bad (by the preceding Proposition). Therefore, it will necessarily be either good or indifferent. If one assumes the latter—namely, that it is neither good nor bad—then (by the Axiom[25] of this Part) there will follow from its nature nothing that serves for the preservation of our nature, that is (by hypothesis) which serves for the preservation of the nature of the thing itself. But that is absurd (by Prop. 6, Part 3); therefore, in so far as it agrees with our nature, it will necessarily be good. QED.

Corollary

From this it follows that, the more some thing agrees with our nature, the more it is useful to us, that is, the more it is good; conversely, the more some thing is useful to us, to that extent it agrees more with our nature. For in so far as it does not agree with our nature, it will necessarily be either different from our nature, or contrary to it. If it is different, then (by Prop. 29, Part 4) it can neither be good nor bad; but if it is contrary, then it will also be contrary to that which agrees with our nature, that is (by the preceding Proposition) contrary to good, i.e. it will be bad. Nothing, therefore, can be good except in so far as it agrees with our nature, and so the more some thing agrees with our nature, the more it is useful, and conversely. QED.

Proposition 32

In so far as men are liable to passions, to that extent they cannot be said to agree in nature.

Demonstration. Those things that are said to agree in nature are understood to agree in power (by Prop. 7, Part 3), but not in lack of power, i.e. negation, and consequently (see Prop. 3, Schol., Part 3) not in passion either. Therefore, in so far as men are liable to passions, they cannot be said to agree in nature. QED.

Scholium

The matter is also self-evident. For anyone who says that white and black agree solely in that neither is red affirms absolutely that white and black agree in nothing. So also if someone says that a stone and a man agree solely in this, that each is finite, or lacking in power, or does not exist by the necessity of its own nature, or finally is surpassed indefinitely by the power of external causes—such a person affirms in general that a stone and a man agree in nothing. For those things that agree in negation alone, i.e. in that which they do not have, really agree in nothing.

Proposition 33

Men can be discrepant in nature in so far as they are harassed by emotions which are passions, and to that extent one and the same man is variable and inconstant.

Demonstration. The nature, i.e. the essence, of the emotions cannot be explained solely through our essence, i.e. our nature (by Defs. 1 and 2, Part 3); it must be defined by the power, that is (by Prop. 7, Part 3), by the nature, of external causes, compared with ours. From this it comes about that there are as many species of each emotion as there are species of the objects by which we are affected (see Prop. 56, Part 3), and that men are affected in different ways by one and the same object (see Prop. 51, Part 3) and to that extent are discrepant in nature; and finally that one and the same man (again by Prop. 51, Part 3) is affected towards the same object in various ways, and to that extent is variable, etc. QED.

Proposition 34

As far as men are harassed by emotions which are passions they can be contrary to one another.

Demonstration. A man, for example Peter, can be the cause of Paul's feeling pain, on account of the fact that he has something which is similar to a thing that Paul hates (by Prop. 16, Part 3), or on account of the fact that Peter alone possesses some thing that Paul himself also loves (see Prop. 32, Part 3, together with its Scholium), or on account of other causes (for the chief of these, see Prop. 55, Schol., Part 3). So from this it will come about (by Def. 7 of the Emotions) that Paul hates Peter, and consequently it will easily come about (by Prop. 40, Part 3, together with its Scholium) that, conversely, Peter hates Paul, and so (by Prop. 39, Part 3) that they endeavour to harm one another, that is (by Prop. 30, Part 4), that they are contrary to one another. But the emotion of pain is always a passion (by Prop. 59, Part 3); therefore, men, in so far as they are harassed by emotions which are passions, can be contrary to one another. QED.

Scholium

I said that Paul hates Peter because the former imagines that the latter possesses a thing that Paul himself also loves. From this it appears at first sight to follow that these two, from the fact that they love the same thing, and consequently from the fact that they agree in nature, are damaging to one another. So it might appear that, if this is true, then Propositions 30 and 31 of Part 4 are false. However, if we are willing to consider the matter impartially, we shall see that all these things are entirely consistent. For these two men are irksome to one another, not in so far as they agree in nature, that is, in so far as each one loves the same thing, but in so far as they differ from one another. For in so far as each one loves the same thing, the love of each is fostered (by Prop. 31, Part 3);

that is (by Def. 6 of the Emotions) the pleasure of each is fostered. Therefore, it is far from being the case that, in so far as they love the same thing and agree in nature, they are irksome to one another. The cause of this matter is, as I have said, simply that they are supposed to disagree in nature. For we are supposing that Peter has the idea of a loved thing that he now possesses, and that Paul on the other hand has the idea of a loved thing that he has lost. From this it comes about that the latter is affected with pain and the former is affected with pleasure, and to that extent they are contrary to one another. And we can easily show in this way that the other causes of hatred depend solely on the fact that men differ in nature, and do not depend on that in which they agree.

Proposition 35

In so far as men live in accordance with the guidance of reason, to that extent alone they always necessarily agree in nature.

Demonstration. In so far as men are harassed by emotions which are passions, they can be different in nature (by Prop. 33, Part 4) and contrary to one another (by the preceding Proposition). But men are said to act only in so far as they live in accordance with the guidance of reason (by Prop. 3, Part 3), and so whatever follows from human nature, in so far as it is defined by reason, must (by Def. 2, Part 3) be understood through human nature alone, as its proximate cause. But everyone, in accordance with the laws of his nature, seeks that which he judges to be good, and endeavours to remove that which he judges to be bad (by Prop. 19, Part 4); further, that which we judge in accordance with the dictate of reason to be good or bad is necessarily good or bad (by Prop. 41, Part 2). Therefore, men, in so far as they live in accordance with the guidance of reason, to that extent alone necessarily do those things that are necessarily good for human nature, and consequently for each man; that is (by Prop. 31, Coroll., Part 4), that agree with the nature of each man. So men also necessarily always agree among themselves in so far as they live in accordance with the guidance of reason. QED.

Corollary 1

There exists in Nature no particular thing that is more useful to a man than a man who lives in accordance with the guidance of reason. For that is most useful to a man which agrees most with his nature (by Prop. 31, Coroll., Part 4); that is (as is self-evident), a man. But a man acts absolutely in accordance with the laws of his nature when he lives in accordance with the guidance of reason (by Def. 2, Part 3), and to that extent alone he necessarily always agrees with the nature of another man (by the preceding Proposition); therefore, there exists among particular things nothing that is more useful to a man than a man, etc. QED.

Corollary 2

Men are most useful to one another when each man looks most for what is useful to himself. For the more that each person looks for what is useful to himself and endeavours to preserve himself, the more he is endowed with virtue (by Prop. 20, Part 4),[26] or, what is the same (by Def. 8, Part 4), he is endowed with a greater power of acting in accordance with the laws of his nature, that is (by Prop. 3, Part 3) of living in accordance with the guidance of reason. But men are said to agree most in nature when they live in accordance with the guidance of reason (by the preceding Proposition); therefore (by the preceding Corollary), men will be most useful to one another when each one looks most for what is useful to himself. QED.

Scholium

What we have just shown is also confirmed by daily experience with so many and such striking examples that 'Man is a god to man' has become a proverb. But it rarely happens that men live in accordance with the guidance of reason; rather, the position with regard to them is that for the most part they are envious of and irksome to one another. Nevertheless, they can hardly endure a solitary life, with the result that the definition that man is a social animal[27] has been very attractive to many. And indeed the situation is that much more benefit than harm arises from the common society of men. So let satirists laugh at human affairs as much as they like, let theologians denounce them, and let the melancholy, as much as they can, praise an uncultivated and boorish life, and let them condemn men and admire the beasts. Men will find by experience that they can procure what they need much more easily by mutual help, and that they can avoid the dangers that threaten them everywhere only by joining their forces—to say nothing of the fact that it is much more excellent, and worthy of our knowledge, to study the deeds of men rather than those of the beasts. But I will discuss these matters in greater detail elsewhere.

Proposition 36

The highest good of those who follow virtue is common to all, and all can enjoy it equally.

Demonstration. To act from virtue is to act in accordance with the guidance of reason (by Prop. 24, Part 4), and whatever we endeavour to do in accordance with reason is to understand (by Prop. 26, Part 4). So (by Prop. 28, Part 4) the highest good of those who follow virtue is to know God; a good which (by Prop. 47, Part 2 and its Scholium) is common to all men, and which can be possessed equally by all men, in so far as they are of the same nature. QED.

Scholium

Suppose that someone asks, 'What if the highest good of those who follow virtue were not common to all? Would it not follow, as above (see Prop. 34, Part 4), that men who live in accordance with the guidance of reason, that is (by Prop. 35, Part 4), men in so far as they agree in nature, would be contrary to one another?' Let him take this as a reply: that it arises, not by accident, but from the very nature of reason, that the highest good of man is common to all. This is because it is deduced from the very essence of man, in so far as it is defined by reason, and because a man could neither exist nor be conceived, if he did not have the power of enjoying this highest good. For (by Prop. 47, Part 2) it belongs to the essence of the human mind that it has an adequate knowledge of the eternal and infinite essence of God.

Proposition 37

The good which each person who follows virtue seeks for himself he also desires for all other men, and the more so, the more he has a greater knowledge of God.

Demonstration. Men are most useful to a man in so far as they live in accordance with the guidance of reason (by Prop. 35, Coroll. 1, Part 4), and so (by Prop. 19, Part 4) we shall, in accordance with the guidance of reason, necessarily endeavour to bring it about that men live in accordance with the guidance of reason. But the good which each person who lives in accordance with the dictate of reason—that is (by Prop. 24, Part 4), each person who follows virtue—seeks for himself is to understand (by Prop. 26, Part 4). Therefore, the good which each person who follows virtue seeks for himself he will also desire for all other men. Next, desire, in so far as it is related to the mind, is the very essence of the mind (by Def. 1 of the Emotions); but the essence of the mind consists in knowledge (by Prop. 11, Part 2), which involves the knowledge of God (by Prop. 47, Part 2), and without which (by Prop. 15, Part 1) it can neither exist nor be conceived. So the more the essence of the mind involves a greater knowledge of God, the greater also will be the desire by which he who follows virtue desires for another a good which he seeks for himself. QED.

ALTERNATIVE PROOF

A man who seeks for himself, and loves, a good will love that good more constantly if he sees that others love it (by Prop. 31, Part 3). So (by the Corollary of the same Proposition) he will endeavour that all others shall love it; and since this good (by the preceding Proposition) is common to all, and all can enjoy it, he will (by the same reason) endeavour that all shall enjoy it, and (by Prop. 37, Part 3) the more so, the more he enjoys this good. QED.

Scholium 1

The person who, from emotion alone, endeavours to bring it about that all others love what he loves, and that all others should live in accordance with his way of thinking, acts from impulse[28] alone, and so is hateful—especially to those who are pleased by other things, and who consequently desire and endeavour with the same impulse that all others should live in accordance with their way of thinking. Then, since the highest good that men desire from emotion is often of such a kind that one person alone can possess it, it comes about that people who love are not consistent, and that whilst they enjoy singing the praises of the thing that they love, they are afraid of being believed. But the person who endeavours to lead all others by reason is not led by impulse, but acts humanely and benevolently, and is self-consistent in the highest degree. Further: whatever we desire and do of which we are the cause in so far as we have an idea of God, i.e. in so far as we know God, I relate to 'religion'. The desire of doing good, which is generated in us by the fact that we live in accordance with the guidance of reason I call 'piety'. Then, the desire by which a man who lives in accordance with the guidance of reason is bound to join all others with him in friendship I call 'probity'. I call that 'honourable' which is praised by men who live in accordance with the guidance of reason, and on the other hand I call that 'base' which is repugnant to the formation of friendship. Besides this, I have also shown what the foundations of a commonwealth[29] are. Further, the difference between true virtue and lack of power is easily perceived from what has been said above. The difference is that true virtue is nothing other than living solely in accordance with the guidance of reason; so lack of power consists in this alone, that a man suffers himself to be led by things which are outside him, and is determined to do those things which are demanded by the constitution of external things, and not those which are demanded by his own nature, considered in itself alone. This is what I promised, in the Scholium of Prop. 18 of this Part, that I would demonstrate. From this it is evident that the law against slaughtering animals is based more on empty superstition and effeminate pity than on sound reason.[30] The principle of seeking what is useful to us teaches us the necessity of uniting with men, but not with the beasts, or with things whose nature is different from human nature; we have the same right over them that they have over us. Indeed, since the right of each thing is defined by the virtue, i.e. the power, of each thing, we have much more right over the beasts than they have over men.[31] I do not deny that the beasts have feelings, but I do deny that it is impermissible, on this account, for us to consult our own advantage, and to use them as we wish and to treat them in such a way as is more convenient for us. This is because they do not agree with us in nature, and their emotions are different in nature from human emotions (see Prop. 57, Schol., Part 3). It remains for me to explain what is just, what is unjust, what is wrongdoing, and finally what merit is. On these, see the Scholium that follows.

Scholium 2

In the Appendix of the First Part I promised to explain[32] what praise and blame, merit and wrongdoing, just and unjust are. As to what concerns praise and blame, I have explained these in Proposition 29, Scholium, Part 3; this is now the place to speak of the rest. But first I must say a few things about the natural and the civil state of man.

Each person exists by the highest right of Nature, and consequently each person, by the highest right of Nature, does what follows with necessity from his own nature. So it is by the highest right of Nature that each person judges what is good and bad, considers in accordance with his own way of thinking what is useful to him (see Props. 19 and 20, Part 4), revenges himself (see Prop. 40, Coroll. 2, Part 3), and endeavours to preserve that which he loves and to destroy that which he hates (see Prop. 28, Part 3). Now if men lived in accordance with the guidance of reason, each one (by Prop. 35, Coroll. 1, Part 4) would possess this right of his without any harm to another. But because men are liable to emotions (by Prop. 4, Coroll., Part 4) which far exceed human power, i.e. virtue (by Prop. 6, Part 4), they are often drawn in different directions (by Prop. 33, Part 4) and are contrary to one another (by Prop. 34, Part 4) whilst they lack mutual aid (by Prop. 35, Schol., Part 4). In order, therefore, that men can live in harmony and help one another, it is necessary that they should give up their natural right and make each other mutually confident that they will do nothing that could harm someone else. The way that this can come about—namely, that men, who are necessarily subject to the emotions (by Prop. 4, Coroll., Part 4) and are inconstant and changeable (by Prop. 33, Part 4), can make each other mutually confident and can have trust in one another—is evident from Proposition 7, Part 4, and Proposition 39, Part 3. From these it is evident that no emotion can be restrained except by an emotion which is stronger than and contrary to the one that is to be restrained, and that each person abstains from doing harm by the fear of a greater harm. By this law, therefore, a society can be made lasting, provided that it assumes for itself the right that everyone has of revenging himself and of judging about good and bad, and that it therefore has the power of prescribing a common way of life and of passing laws, and of strengthening these, not by reason, which (by Prop. 17, Schol., Part 4) cannot restrain the emotions, but by threats. This society, strengthened by laws and by the power of preserving itself, is called a 'commonwealth', and those who are defended by its right[33] are called 'citizens'. From this we easily understand that there exists nothing in a state of Nature which is universally agreed to be good or bad. This is because each person who is in a state of Nature consults his own advantage only, and decides what is good or bad in accordance with his own way of thinking and in so far as he regards his own advantage only, and is bound by no law to obey anyone but himself. So wrongdoing cannot be conceived in a natural state. However, it can be conceived in a civil state, where it is decided by common consent what is good or bad, and where each person is bound to obey the commonwealth. Wrongdoing, therefore, is simply disobedience, which accordingly is punished only by the right of the commonwealth, and on the other hand obedience to the commonwealth is considered to be merit, since by that very fact a man is judged to be worthy of enjoying the benefits of a commonwealth. Then again, in a natural state no one is by common consent the master of some thing, nor does there exist in Nature anything which can be said to belong to this man and not to that, but all things belong to all men. Therefore, in a state of Nature, there can be conceived no will of assigning to each man his own,[34] or of taking away from anyone what is his own. That is, in a state of Nature there occurs nothing that can be called just or unjust; however, this does occur in a civil state, where it is decided by common consent what belongs to this person or to that. From this it is evident that just and unjust, wrongdoing and merit, are extrinsic notions,[35] and not attributes that explain the nature of the mind. But this is enough about these matters.

Proposition 38

That which so disposes the human body that it can be affected in many ways, or which makes it capable of affecting external bodies in many ways, is useful to man; and it is the more useful, the more it makes the body more capable of being affected in many ways, and of affecting other bodies in many ways. Conversely, that thing is harmful that makes the body less capable of these things.

Demonstration. The more the body is made more capable of these things, the more the mind is made more capable of perceiving (by Prop. 14, Part 2). So that which disposes the body in this way, and makes it capable of these things, is necessarily good, i.e. useful (by Props. 26 and 27, Part 4), and it is the more useful, the more it can make the body more capable of these things. Conversely (by the converse of Prop. 14, Part 2, and by Props. 26 and 27, Part 4), it is harmful if it makes the body less capable of these things. QED.

Proposition 39

Those things that bring about the preservation of the ratio of motion and rest that the parts of the human body have to one another are good;

on the other hand, those things are bad that bring it about that the parts of the human body have another ratio of motion and rest to one another.

Demonstration. The human body needs for its conservation very many other bodies (by Post. 4, Part 2). But that which constitutes the form of the human body consists in the fact that its parts communicate their motions to one another in a certain way (by the Definition preceding Lemma 4, following Prop. 13, Part 2). Therefore, the things that bring about the preservation of the ratio of motion and rest that the parts of the human body have to one another preserve the form of the human body. Consequently, they bring it about (by Posts. 3 and 6, Part 2) that the human body can be affected in many ways and can affect external bodies in many ways, and so (by the preceding Proposition) they are good. Then again, those things that bring it about that the parts of the human body maintain another ratio of motion and rest bring it about (by the same Definition in Part 2)[36] that the human body takes on another form. That is (as is self-evident, and as we noted at the end of the Preface of this Part), they bring it about that the human body is destroyed, and consequently that it is made wholly incapable of being able to be affected in very many ways, and therefore (by the preceding Proposition) they are bad. QED.

Scholium

How much these things can be harmful or helpful to the mind will be explained in the Fifth Part. Here it must be noted that I understand the body to have died when its parts are so disposed that they maintain a different ratio of motion and rest to one another. For I am not so bold as to deny that the human body, whilst retaining the circulation of the blood and other features on account of which a body is thought to live, can nevertheless be changed into another nature which is very different from its own. For no reason compels me to assert that the body does not die unless it is turned into a corpse; indeed, experience seems to speak in favour of something else. For it happens sometimes that a man suffers such changes that it is not easy for me to say that he is the same. For example, I have heard of a certain Spanish poet[37] who was stricken with disease, and although he recovered from it, he was so forgetful of his past life that he did not believe that the dramatic poems and tragedies that he had written were his own, and could indeed have been taken for a grown-up infant if he had forgotten his native language. And if this seems incredible, what shall we say of infants? A man of mature years thinks their nature to be so different from his that he could be persuaded that he was never an infant, unless he had made a conjecture about himself from the example of others. But I prefer to leave these matters undecided, rather than provide the superstitious with material for raising new questions.

Proposition 40

Those things that contribute to a common society of men, or, which bring it about that men live in harmony, are useful; on the other hand, those things are bad that introduce discord into the commonwealth.

Demonstration. For those things that bring it about that men live in harmony bring it about at the same time that they live in accordance with the guidance of reason (by Prop. 35, Part 4), and so (by Props. 26 and 27, Part 4) they are good; on the other hand (for the same reason), those things are bad that stir up discords. QED.

Proposition 41

Pleasure is not directly bad, but good; pain, on the other hand, is directly bad.[38]

Demonstration. Pleasure (by Prop. 11, Part 3, together with its Scholium) is an emotion by which the body's power of acting is increased or helped; pain, on the other hand, is an emotion by which the body's power of acting is diminished or hindered. And so (by Prop. 38, Part 4) pleasure is directly good, etc. QED.

Proposition 42

Joy cannot be excessive, but is always good, and on the other hand melancholy is always bad.

Demonstration. Joy (see its Definition in Prop. 11, Schol., Part 3) is pleasure which, in so far as it is related to the body, consists in the fact that all parts of the body are equally affected. That is (by Prop. 11, Part 3), it consists in the fact that the body's power of acting is increased or helped, in such a way that all its parts maintain the same ratio of motion and rest to one another. And so (by Prop. 39, Part 4) joy is always good, and cannot be excessive. But melancholy (see its Definition in the same Scholium of Prop. 11, Part 3) is pain which, in so far as it is related to the body, consists in the fact that the body's power of acting, absolutely speaking, is diminished or hindered. So (by Prop. 38, Part 4) it is always bad. QED.

Proposition 43

Titillation can be excessive, and bad; however, anguish can be good to the extent that titillation, i.e. pleasure, is bad.

Demonstration. Titillation is pleasure which, in so far as it is related to the body, consists in the fact that one or several of the body's parts are affected more than others (see the definition of titillation in Prop. 11, Schol., Part 3). The power of this emotion can be so great that it surpasses all other emotions of the body (by Prop. 6, Part 4) and adheres stubbornly to it, and so hinders the body from being capable of being affected in very many other ways, and so (by Prop. 38, Part 4) it can be bad. Next, anguish, which is on the other hand pain, cannot be good when considered in itself alone (by Prop. 41, Part 4). But since its strength and growth is defined by the power of an external cause compared with our own power (by Prop. 5, Part 4), we can consider infinite degrees and kinds of the strength of this emotion (by Prop. 3, Part 4). So we can conceive it to be such that it can restrain titillation, with the result that it is not excessive, and to that extent (by the first part of this Proposition) can bring it about that the body is not made less capable, and therefore to that extent it will be good. QED.

Proposition 44

Love and desire can be excessive.

Demonstration. Love (by Def. 6 of the Emotions) is pleasure, with the accompaniment of the idea of an external cause. Therefore, titillation (by Prop. 11, Schol., Part 3), with the accompaniment of the idea of an external cause, is love; and so love (by the preceding Proposition) can be excessive. Next, desire is the greater, the more that the emotion from which it arises is greater (by Prop. 37, Part 3). Therefore, just as an emotion (by Prop. 6, Part 4) can surpass all the other actions of a man, so also the desire which arises from this emotion can surpass all other desires, and therefore can have the same excess that, in the preceding Proposition, we showed titillation to have. QED.

Scholium

Joy, which I have said to be good, is more easily conceived than observed. For the emotions by which we are harassed every day are for the most part related to some part of the body which is affected more than the rest of its parts. Accordingly, the emotions are for the most part excessive, and detain the mind in the sole contemplation of one object in such a way that it cannot think of other things. And although men are liable to many emotions, and so one seldom finds people who are always harassed by one and the same emotion, yet there are those to whom one and the same emotion clings stubbornly. For we see that men are sometimes affected by one object in such a way that, although it is not present to them, yet they believe that they have it before them; and when this happens to a man who is not asleep, we say that he is delirious or insane. Nor are those believed to be less insane who burn with love and who dream night and day of no one but their lady-love or a courtesan; for they usually excite laughter. But when a miser thinks of nothing else but profit, or money, and an ambitious man thinks of nothing else but glory, etc., they are not thought to be delirious, because they are usually irksome, and are thought to be worthy of hatred. But in fact avarice, ambition, lust, etc. are species of delirium, even though they are not numbered among the diseases.

Proposition 45

Hatred can never be good.

Demonstration. We endeavour to destroy a man whom we hate (by Prop. 39, Part 3); that is (by Prop. 37, Part 4), we endeavour to do something which is bad. Therefore, etc. QED.

Scholium

Note that here, and in what follows, I understand by 'hatred' only hatred towards human beings.

Corollary 1

Envy, derision, contempt, anger, revenge, and the rest of the emotions that are related to hatred, or arise from it, are bad, which is also evident from Prop. 39, Part 3, and Prop. 37, Part 4.

Corollary 2

Whatever we desire from the fact that we are affected with hatred is base and unjust in the commonwealth. This is also evident from Prop. 39, Part 3, and from the definitions of base and of unjust in Prop. 37, Schol., Part 4.

Scholium

I recognize a great difference between derision (which I said in Corollary 1 to be bad) and laughter. For laughter, like jesting, is pure pleasure, and so, provided that it is not excessive, it is good in itself (by Prop. 41, Part 4). Indeed, nothing but gloomy and sad superstition prohibits enjoyment. For why is it more acceptable to get rid of hunger and thirst than to dispel melancholy? This is my reasoning, and this is what I have resolved. No deity, and nobody else unless he is envious, is pleased by my lack of power and my misfortune, nor does he ascribe to our virtue our tears, sobs, fear, and other things of this kind, which are signs of an impotent mind. On the contrary, the more we are affected by pleasure, the greater the perfection to which we pass; that is, the more it is necessary that we participate in the divine nature. So it is a feature of a wise man that he makes use of things and delights in them as much as he can (though not to the point of disgust, for that is not to feel delight). It is, I say, a feature of a wise man that he renews and refreshes himself with moderate and pleasant food and drink, and also with scents, the beauty of plants in bloom, dress, music, sports, the theatre, and other things of this sort, of which everyone can make use without harming anyone else. For the human body is composed of very many bodies of a different nature, which constantly need new and varied food, so that the whole body is equally capable of all the things which can follow from its nature, and consequently so that the mind also is equally capable of understanding many things at the same time. So this way of living agrees very well both with our principles and with common practice. Therefore, this way of living is above all others the best, and is to be commended in all ways;

nor is there any need to discuss these matters more clearly or in greater detail.

Proposition 46

Someone who lives in accordance with the guidance of reason endeavours, as far as he can, to repay the hatred, anger, contempt, etc. that another has for him with love, i.e. with nobility.

Demonstration. All emotions of hatred are bad (by Coroll. 1 of the preceding Proposition); so someone who lives in accordance with the guidance of reason will endeavour, as far as he can, to bring it about that he is not harassed by emotions of hatred (by Prop. 19, Part 4). Consequently (by Prop. 37, Part 4), he will endeavour to bring it about that no other person suffers the same emotions. But hatred is increased by reciprocal hatred, and on the other hand can be extinguished by love (by Prop. 43, Part 3) in such a way that hatred passes over into love (by Prop. 44, Part 3). Therefore, a man who lives in accordance with the guidance of reason endeavours, as far as he can, to repay another's hatred etc. with love; that is, with nobility (see the definition of this in Prop. 59, Schol., Part 3). QED.

Scholium

A person who wants to avenge injuries by reciprocal hatred lives miserably. On the other hand, the person who tries to overcome hatred with love fights cheerfully and serenely; he resists many men just as easily as one, and is very little in need of fortune's help. Those whom he overcomes give way cheerfully, not because of a lack of strength, but because of an increase in strength. All these things follow so clearly solely from the definitions of love and of the intellect that there is no need to demonstrate them in detail.

Proposition 47

The emotions of hope and fear cannot be good through themselves.

Demonstration. The emotions of hope and fear do not exist without pain. For fear (by Def. 13 of the Emotions) is pain, and hope (see the Explanation of Defs. 12 and 13 of the Emotions) does not exist without fear. Therefore (by Prop. 41, Part 4), these emotions cannot be good through themselves, but are good only in so far as they can restrain an excess of pleasure (by Prop. 43, Part 4). QED.

Scholium

To this one must add that these emotions indicate a defect of knowledge and the mind's lack of power, and that because of this, confidence, despair, delight, and remorse are signs of an impotent mind. For although confidence and delight are emotions of pleasure, yet they pre-suppose that pain—namely, hope and fear—have preceded them. So the more we endeavour to live in accordance with the guidance of reason, the more we endeavour to depend less on hope and to free ourselves from fear, to control fortune as much as we can, and to direct our actions by the sure counsel of reason.

Proposition 48

The emotions of esteem and scorn are always bad.

139 *Demonstration.* For these emotions (by Defs. 21 and 22 of the Emotions) are repugnant to reason, and so (by Props. 26 and 27, Part 4) they are bad. QED.

Proposition 49

Esteem easily makes proud the man who is esteemed.

Demonstration. If we see that someone thinks too highly of us on account of love we shall easily feel glory (by Prop. 41, Schol., Part 3), or, we shall be affected with pleasure (by Def. 30 of the Emotions), and we shall easily believe the good that we hear stated of us (by Prop. 25, Part 3). So we shall think too highly of ourselves on account of love, that is (by Def. 28 of the Emotions), we shall easily become proud. QED.

Proposition 50

Compassion, in a man who lives in accordance with the guidance of reason, is bad through itself and useless.

Demonstration. For compassion (by Def. 18 of the Emotions) is pain, and therefore (by Prop. 41, Part 4) is bad through itself. But the good which follows from it, namely that we endeavour to free from his misery the man whom we pity (by Prop. 27, Coroll. 3, Part 3), we desire to do solely in accordance with the dictate of reason (by Prop. 37, Part 4); nor can we do anything that we know with certainty to be good except in accordance with the dictate of reason alone (by Prop. 27, Part 4). So compassion, in a man who lives in accordance with the guidance of reason, is bad through itself and useless. QED.

Corollary

From this it follows that a man who lives in accordance with the dictate of reason endeavours, as far as he can, not to be touched by compassion.

Scholium

He who knows that all things follow from the necessity of the divine nature and in accordance with the eternal laws and rules of Nature will certainly find nothing that is worthy of hatred, laughter,[39] or contempt, nor will he pity anyone. Rather he will, as far as human virtue goes, endeavour (as the saying goes) to act well and rejoice.[40] Further, the person who is easily touched by the emotion of compassion, and is moved by the misery or tears of another, often does something which he later regrets: both because we do, as a result of emotion, nothing that we know with certainty to be good, and because we are easily deceived by false tears. Here, I am expressly speaking of a man who lives in accordance with the guidance of reason. For he who is moved neither by reason nor by compassion to help others is rightly called inhuman, for (by Prop. 27, Part 3) he seems to be unlike a human being.

Proposition 51

Favour is not repugnant to reason, but can agree with it and arise from it.

Demonstration. For favour is love towards a person who has benefited another (by Def. 19 of the Emotions) and so it can be related to the mind in so far as the latter is said to act (by Prop. 59, Part 3); that is (by Prop. 3, Part 3) in so far as it understands, and therefore it agrees with reason, etc. QED.

ALTERNATIVE PROOF

The person who lives in accordance with the guidance of reason desires for another the good that he seeks for himself (by Prop. 37, Part 4). Therefore, from the fact that he sees someone doing good to another, his own endeavour of doing good is helped, that is (by Prop. 11, Schol., Part 3) he will feel pleasure. This (by hypothesis) is accompanied by the idea of the man who did good to another, and therefore (by Def. 19 of the Emotions) he favours him. QED.

Scholium

Indignation, as defined by us (see Def. 20 of the Emotions) is necessarily bad (by Prop. 45, Part 4); but it is to be noted that when the supreme power, from the desire that binds it of protecting peace, punishes a citizen who has injured another, I do not say that it is indignant with the citizen. For it is not stimulated by hatred to ruin the citizen, but is moved by piety to punish him.[41]

Proposition 52

Self-contentment can arise from reason, and only that contentment which arises from reason is the highest that can exist.

Demonstration. Self-contentment is pleasure that arises from the fact that a man contemplates himself and his power of acting (by Def. 25 of the Emotions). But a man's true power of acting, i.e. his virtue, is reason itself (by Prop. 3, Part 3), which the man contemplates clearly and distinctly (by Props. 40 and 43, Part 2). Therefore, self-contentment arises from reason. Next, whilst a man contemplates himself, he perceives nothing clearly and distinctly, i.e. adequately, apart from those things that follow from his own power of acting (by Def. 2, Part 3), that is (by Prop. 3, Part 3), which follow from his power of understanding. So it is only from this contemplation that there arises the highest contentment that can exist. QED.

Scholium

Self-contentment is indeed the highest thing that we can hope for. For (as we showed in Prop. 25, Part 4) no one endeavours to preserve his being for the sake of some end; and because this contentment is more and more fostered and strengthened by praise (by Prop. 53, Coroll., Part 3), and conversely (by Prop. 55, Coroll., Part 3) is more and more disturbed by blame, we are led by glory most of all, and can hardly endure a life that is accompanied by blame.

Proposition 53

Humility is not a virtue, or, it does not arise from reason.

Demonstration. Humility is a pain which arises from the fact that a man contemplates his lack of power (by Def. 26 of the Emotions). But in so far as a man knows himself by true reason, to that extent he is assumed to understand his essence, that is (by Prop. 7, Part 3) his power. Therefore, if a man, whilst he contemplates himself, perceives some lack of power in himself, this is not by virtue of the fact that he understands himself, but (as we showed in Prop. 55, Part 3) it is by virtue of the fact that his power of acting is hindered. But if we suppose that a man conceives his lack of power from the fact that he understands something more powerful than himself, by the knowledge of which he determines his power of acting, then we conceive simply that the man understands himself distinctly, i.e. (by Prop. 26, Part 4) that his power of acting is helped. Therefore, humility, i.e. pain which arises from the fact that a man contemplates his lack of power, does not arise from true contemplation, i.e. reason, and it is not a virtue but a passion. QED.

Proposition 54

Repentance is not a virtue, or, it does not arise from reason, but the man who repents of what he has done is twice as wretched, i.e. twice as impotent.

Demonstration. The first part of this is demonstrated in the same way as the preceding Proposition. The second part is evident from the mere definition of this emotion (see Def. 27 of the Emotions). For the man suffers himself to be overcome, first, by a wrong desire, and then by pain. QED.

Scholium

Because men rarely live in accordance with the dictate of reason, these two emotions—namely, humility and repentance, and besides these, hope and fear—bring more advantage than harm. So, since we have to err,[42] it is better to err in that direction. For if men who are impotent in mind were all equally proud, and were ashamed of nothing and feared nothing, by what bonds could they be joined together and restrained? The mob terrifies, unless it is afraid.[43] For this reason it is not surprising that the prophets, who looked to the common advantage and not to that of a few, recommended humility, repentance, and reverence so much. And indeed, those who are liable to these emotions can be led much more easily than others, so that they finally live in accordance with the guidance of reason, that is, so that they are free and enjoy the life of the blessed.

Proposition 55

The greatest pride, or the greatest self-abasement, is the greatest ignorance of oneself.

Demonstration. This is evident from Defs. 28 and 29 of the Emotions.

Proposition 56

The greatest pride, or the greatest self-abasement, indicates the greatest impotence of mind.

Demonstration. The primary basis of virtue is to preserve one's own being (by Prop. 22, Coroll., Part 4), and to do so in accordance with the guidance of reason (by Prop. 24, Part 4). Therefore, the man who is ignorant of himself is ignorant of the basis of all virtues, and consequently is ignorant of all virtues. Next, to act in accordance with virtue is simply to act in accordance with the guidance of reason (by Prop. 24, Part 4), and the person who acts in accordance with the guidance of reason must necessarily know that he does so (by Prop. 43, Part 2). So the person who is most ignorant of himself, and consequently (as we have already shown) of all the virtues, acts least in accordance with virtue; that is (as is evident from Def. 8, Part 4), he is extremely impotent in mind. So (by the preceding Proposition) the greatest pride, or the greatest self-abasement, indicates the greatest impotence of mind. QED.

Corollary

From this it follows with the greatest clarity that those who are proud and those who abase themselves are most subject to the emotions.

Scholium

However, self-abasement can be corrected more easily than pride, for the latter is an emotion of pleasure and the former is an emotion of pain; so (by Prop. 18, Part 4) the latter is stronger than the former.

Proposition 57

The proud man loves the presence of parasites, i.e. of flatterers, but hates the presence of the noble.[44]

Demonstration. Pride is pleasure that arises from the fact that a man thinks too highly of himself (by Defs. 28 and 6 of the Emotions). This opinion the proud man will endeavour to foster as much as he can (see Prop. 13, Schol., Part 3). So proud men will love the presence of parasites or flatterers (I have omitted their definitions, as these people are too well known), and will flee from the presence of the noble, who think of them in a fitting way. QED.

Scholium

It would take too long to list here all the evils of pride, since the proud are liable to all the emotions, but to none less than the emotions of love and pity. But I must by no means be silent about the fact that a person who thinks too little of all others is also called proud, and so in this sense pride is to be defined as the pleasure that arises from a false opinion whereby a man thinks he is above all others. Further, self-abasement, which is the contrary of such pride, is to be defined as pain which arises from a false opinion whereby a man thinks that he is beneath all others. Granted this, we easily understand that a proud man is necessarily envious (see Prop. 55, Schol., Part 3), that he hates most those who are praised most on account of their virtues, and that his hatred of them is not easily be overcome by love or by kindness (see Prop. 41, Schol., Part 3). We also easily understand that he takes pleasure solely in the presence of those who humour his impotence of mind, and make a madman out of a fool.

Although self-abasement is the contrary of pride, yet the person who abases himself is closest to the proud man. For since his pain arises from the fact that he judges his own lack of power from the power, i.e. the virtue, of others, his pain will be alleviated—that is, he will feel pleasure—if his imagination is occupied by the contemplation of the defects of others; hence the proverb 'It is a comfort to the unhappy to have had fellows in misery'. Conversely, he will feel pain the more he believes that he is beneath all others. The result of this is that no people are more prone to envy than those who abase themselves, and that they endeavour above all to observe the deeds of men in order to carp at them rather than to correct them. So, in the end, they praise nothing but self-abasement, and glory in it—but in such a way that they still appear to abase themselves. These things follow from this emotion as necessarily as it follows from the nature of a triangle that its three angles are equal to two right angles. I have already said that I call these and similar emotions bad, in so far as I pay attention solely to what is useful to human beings. But the laws of Nature regard the common order of Nature, of which man is a part—something that I decided to note in passing, so that no one should think that I am recounting here the defects and the absurd deeds of human beings, and not that I wanted to demonstrate the nature and the properties of things. For, as I said in the Preface of Part Three, I consider the emotions of human beings and their properties in the same way as I consider other natural things. And indeed human emotions indicate, if not human power and artifice, at any rate the power and artifice of Nature, no less than many other things which we admire and by whose contemplation we are delighted. I now proceed to note those things about the emotions which either bring advantage to human beings or inflict harm on them.

Proposition 58

Glory is not repugnant to reason, but can arise from it.

Demonstration. This is evident from Def. 30 of the Emotions, and from the definition of 'honourable' in Prop. 37, Schol. 1, Part 4.

Scholium

What is called 'vainglory' is self-contentment which is fostered solely by the opinion of the mob; and when that ceases, so does the contentment itself, that is (by Prop. 52, Schol., Part 4), the highest good that each person loves. From this it comes about that, day by day and with anxious care, the person who glories in the esteem of the mob strives, acts, and experiments in order to preserve his fame. For the mob is variable and inconstant, and so fame, unless it is preserved, quickly vanishes. Indeed, since all vainglorious people desire to gain the applause of the mob, each one readily plays down the reputation of another, as a result of which— since the strife concerns what is reckoned to be the highest good—there arises an immense desire to crush one another by whatever means, and the person who finally emerges as victor feels more glory for having done harm to another than for having benefited himself. So this glory, i.e. this contentment, is indeed vain; for it is valueless.

What has to be noted about shame is easily gathered from what we have said about pity and repentance. Here I add only this: that as in the case of compassion, so shame, although it is not a virtue, is good in so far as it indicates that there is in the man who blushes with shame the desire of living honourably; just as anguish is good in so far as it indicates that the damaged part has not yet putrefied. Therefore, although a man who is ashamed of something that he has done is indeed miserable, yet he is more perfect than a shameless man, who has no desire to live honourably.

This is what I undertook to note about the emotions of pleasure and pain. As to what concerns desires, these are good or bad in so far as they arise from good or bad emotions. But all of them, in so far as they are generated in us by emotions which are passions, are in fact blind (as is easily inferred from what we have said in Prop. 44, Schol., Part 4), and they would not be of any use if men could easily be led to live in accordance with the dictate of reason alone. I will now briefly show this.

Proposition 59

To all the actions to which we are determined by an emotion which is a passion, we can be determined by reason, without that emotion.

Demonstration. To act in accordance with reason is simply (by Prop. 3 and Def. 2, Part 3) to do those things that follow from the necessity of our nature, considered solely in itself. But pain is bad to the extent that it diminishes or hinders (by Prop. 41, Part 4) this power of acting; therefore, we can be determined by this emotion to no action which we could not perform if we were led by reason. Further, pleasure is bad to the extent that it hinders a man from being capable of action (by Props. 41 and 43, Part 4), and so again we can be determined to no action which we could not perform if we were led by reason. Finally, in so far as pleasure is good, to that extent it agrees with reason (for it consists in the fact that a man's power of acting is increased or helped), nor is it a passion except in so far as a man's power of acting is not increased to such an extent that it conceives adequately itself and its actions (by Prop. 3, Part 3, together with its Scholium). Therefore, if a man who is affected by pleasure is led to so much perfection that he conceives adequately himself and his actions, he is capable, indeed more capable, of the same actions to which he is already determined by emotions which are passions. But all the emotions are related to pleasure, pain, or desire (see the Explanation of Def. 4 of the Emotions), and desire (by Def. 1 of the Emotions) is simply the endeavour of acting itself. Therefore, to all the actions to which we are determined by an emotion which is a passion, we can be determined by reason, without that emotion. QED.

ALTERNATIVE PROOF

Any action is said to be bad in so far as it arises from the fact that we are affected by hatred, or by some bad emotion (see Prop. 45, Coroll. 1, Part 4). But no action, considered in itself alone, is good or bad (as we showed in the Preface of this Part), but one and the same action is now good and now bad. Therefore (by Prop. 19, Part 4), we can be led by reason to the same action which is now bad, or, which arises from some bad emotion. QED.

Scholium

These matters are explained more clearly by an example. The action of striking, in so far as it is considered physically, and we attend solely to the fact that a man raises his arm, clenches his fist, and violently moves the whole arm downwards, is a virtue which is conceived in accordance with the structure of the human body. So if a man, moved by anger or hatred, is determined to clenching his fist or moving his arm, this happens (as we showed in Part Two) because one and the same action can be joined to any images of things. So we can be determined to one and the same action both by the images of things that we conceive confusedly, and by those that we conceive clearly and distinctly. It is therefore evident that every desire, which arises from an emotion which is a passion, would be of no use if men could be led by reason. We now see why we call 'blind' the desire which arises from an emotion which is a passion.

Proposition 60

The desire arising from pleasure or pain which is related to one or several, but not to all, parts of the body, takes no account of the advantage of the whole man.

Demonstration. Let it be assumed, for example, that part A of a body is so strengthened by the force of some external body that it prevails over the remaining parts (by Prop. 6, Part 4). This part will not endeavour to lose its strength in order that the other parts of the body may perform their functions. For then it must have the strength, i.e. the power, to let go its own strength, which (by Prop. 6, Part 3) is absurd. So that part, and consequently (by Props. 7 and 12, Part 3) the mind also, will endeavour to preserve that state, and so the desire that arises from such a state of pleasure takes no account of the whole. But if on the other hand it is supposed that the part A is restrained in such a way that the other parts prevail, it is demonstrated in the same way that neither does the desire that arises from pain take account of the whole. QED.

Scholium

Therefore, since pleasure is for the most part (by Prop. 44, Schol., Part 4) related to one part of the body, we usually desire to preserve our being without taking any account of our health as a whole. Further, the desires by which we are bound most of all (by Prop. 9, Coroll., Part 4) take account only of the present, but not of the future.

Proposition 61

Desire which arises from reason cannot be excessive.

Demonstration. Desire (by Def. 1 of the Emotions) is, considered absolutely, the very essence of man, in so far as this is conceived as determined in any way to do something. So the desire which arises from reason, that is (by Prop. 3, Part 3), the desire which is generated in us in so far as we act, is the very essence, i.e. nature, of man, in so far as it is conceived as determined to do those things that are conceived adequately solely through the essence of man (by Def. 2, Part 3). So if this desire could be excessive, then human nature, considered in itself alone, could exceed itself; i.e. it could do more than it can do, which is a manifest contradiction. Therefore, this desire cannot be excessive. QED.

Proposition 62

In so far as the mind conceives things in accordance with the dictate of reason, it is equally affected whether the idea be of a thing that is future, past, or present.

Demonstration. Whatever the mind conceives when it is led by reason it conceives under the same species of eternity, i.e. of necessity (by Prop. 44, Coroll. 2, Part 2), and it is affected with the same certainty (by Prop. 43, Part 2, with its Scholium). Therefore, whether the idea be of a thing that is future, past, or present, the mind conceives the thing with the same necessity, and is affected with the same certainty. Further, whether the idea is of a thing that is future, past, or present, it will nevertheless be equally true (by Prop. 41, Part 2); that is (by Def. 4, Part 2), it will always have the same properties of an adequate idea. So in so far as the mind conceives things in accordance with the dictate of reason it is affected in the same way, whether the idea be of a thing that is future, past, or present. QED.

Scholium

If we could have an adequate knowledge of the duration of things and could determine by reason their times of existence, we would regard things that are future and present with the same emotion, and the mind would desire a good that it conceives as future just as if it were present. Consequently (as we shall soon demonstrate),[45] it would necessarily neglect a lesser present good in favour of a greater future good, and it would be far from seeking something that is good at present but is the cause of some future harm. But (by Prop. 31, Part 2) we can have only an extremely inadequate knowledge of the duration of things, and we can determine the times of existence of things (by Prop. 44, Schol., Part 2) by the imagination alone, which is not equally affected by the image of a thing that is present and of a thing that is future. From this it comes about that the true knowledge of good and bad that we have is only abstract, i.e. universal, and that the judgements that we make about the order of things and of the connection of causes, so that we can determine what is good or bad for us at present, is imaginary rather than real. So it is not surprising if the desire that arises from the knowledge of good and bad, in so far as this looks towards the future, can easily be restrained by the desire of things that are pleasing at present. On this, see Prop. 16, Part Four.

Proposition 63

The person who is led by fear, and who does good in order that he may avoid what is bad, is not led by reason.

Demonstration. All the emotions which are related to the mind in so far as it acts, that is (by Prop. 3, Part 3), which are related to reason, are simply the emotions of pleasure and desire (by Prop. 59, Part 3), and so (by Def. 13 of the Emotions) the person who is led by fear, and does what is good out of fear of what is bad, is not led by reason. QED.

Scholium

The superstitious, who know how to reprove vices rather than how to teach virtues, and who strive, not to lead people by reason, but to restrain them by fear in such a way that they flee what is bad rather than love the virtues, simply intend all other people to be as miserable as they are, and so it is not surprising that they are for the most part irksome and hateful to human beings.

Corollary

By the desire that arises from reason we follow what is good directly, and avoid indirectly what is bad.

Demonstration. For the desire that arises from reason can arise solely from the emotion of pleasure, which is not a passion (by Prop. 59, Part 3), that is, from pleasure, which cannot be excessive (by Prop. 61, Part 4). It cannot, however, arise from pain, and therefore this desire (by Prop. 8, Part 4) arises from knowledge of what is good, and not from knowledge of what is bad. Therefore, in accordance with the guidance of reason we seek what is good directly, and to that extent we avoid what is bad. QED.

Scholium

This Corollary is explained by the example of a sick man and a healthy man. The sick man eats what he dislikes from the fear of death, but the healthy man takes pleasure in his food, and so he enjoys life better than if he were to fear death, and desired to avoid it directly. In the same way, a judge who condemns a guilty man to death, not from hatred or anger, etc., but solely from a love of the public safety, is led by reason alone.

Proposition 64

The knowledge of what is bad is inadequate knowledge.

Demonstration. The knowledge of what is bad is (by Prop. 8, Part 4) pain, in so far as we are conscious of it. But pain is a transition to a lesser perfection (by Def. 3 of the Emotions), which therefore cannot be explained through the essence of man (by Props. 6 and 7, Part 3). Therefore (by Def. 2, Part 3), it is a passion, which (by Prop. 3, Part 3) depends on inadequate ideas, and consequently (by Prop. 29, Part 2) the knowledge of it, namely the knowledge of what is bad, is inadequate. QED.

Corollary

From this it follows that if the human mind had only adequate ideas, it would form no notion of bad.

Proposition 65

In accordance with the guidance of reason, we shall follow the greater of two goods and the lesser of two evils.

Demonstration. The good that hinders us from enjoying a greater good is in fact bad; for good and bad (as we showed in the Preface of this Part) are asserted of things in so far we compare them with one another, and (for the same reason) a lesser evil is in fact good. Therefore (by Prop. 63, Coroll., Part 4),[46] in accordance with the guidance of reason we shall seek, i.e. follow, only the greater good and the lesser evil. QED.

Corollary

In accordance with the guidance of reason, we shall follow the lesser evil as the greater good, and we shall disregard the lesser good which is the cause of greater evil. For the evil which is here called lesser is in fact good, and the good conversely is bad; therefore (by Prop. 63, Coroll., Part 4), we shall seek the former and disregard the latter. QED.

Proposition 66

In accordance with the guidance of reason, we shall seek a greater future good in preference to a lesser present one, and a lesser present evil in preference to a greater future one.[47]

Demonstration. If the mind could have an adequate knowledge of a future thing, it would be affected with the same emotion towards the future thing as towards a present thing (by Prop. 62, Part 4). Therefore, in so far as we pay attention to reason itself (as we assume that we are doing in this Proposition), the situation is the same whether the greater good or evil is supposed to be future or present. Therefore (by Prop. 65, Part 4), we shall seek a greater future good in preference to a lesser present one, etc. QED.

Corollary

In accordance with the guidance of reason, we shall seek a lesser present evil which is the cause of a greater future good, and we shall disregard a lesser present good which is the cause of a greater future evil. This Corollary is related to the preceding Proposition in the same way as Prop. 65, Coroll., is related to Prop. 65 itself.

Scholium

If, therefore, these things are compared with what we have shown about the strength of the emotions in this Part, up to Proposition 18, we shall easily see what a difference there is between the man who is led by emotion alone, i.e. by opinion,[48] and the man who is led by reason. For the former, whether he wills it or not, does things of which he is extremely ignorant; but the latter follows no one's way of life but his own, and does only those things that he knows to be of primary importance in life, and which he therefore desires most. Therefore, I call the former a slave, and the latter a free man, about whose way of thinking and manner of life I propose to note a few additional points.

Proposition 67

A free man thinks of nothing less than of death, and his wisdom is a meditation, not on death, but on life.

Demonstration. A free man, that is, one who lives in accordance with the dictate of reason alone, is not led by the fear of death (by Prop. 63, Part 4) but desires what is good directly (by the Corollary of the same Proposition). That is (by Prop. 24, Part 4), he desires to act, live, and preserve his being on the basis of seeking his own advantage, and so he thinks of nothing less than of death, but his wisdom is a meditation on life. QED.

Proposition 68

If men were born free, they would form no conception of good and bad as long as they were free.

Demonstration. I have said that that man is free who is led by reason alone; therefore, he who is born free and remains free has only adequate ideas, and therefore he has no conception of bad (by Prop. 64, Coroll., Part 4), and consequently (since good and bad are correlative) he does not have a conception of good. QED.

Scholium

It is evident from Prop. 4, Part 4, that the hypothesis of this proposition is false, and can be conceived only in so far as we pay attention to human nature alone, or rather to God, not in so far as he is infinite, but in so far as he is only the cause of a man's existence. This, and other things that we have now demonstrated, seem to have been indicated by Moses in his story of the first man. For in that story no power of God is conceived other than that by which he created man, that is, the power by which he consulted the advantage of the man alone. Therefore, the story is told that God forbade the free man to eat of the tree of the knowledge of good and evil, and that as soon as he ate of the tree he immediately feared death rather than desired to live. Then, when the man had discovered a wife, who agreed very much with his own nature, he knew that there could be nothing in Nature that could be more useful to him; but after he believed the beasts to be like himself, he began at once to imitate their emotions (see Prop. 27, Part 3) and to lose his liberty.[49] This liberty was later recovered by the Patriarchs, led by the spirit of Christ, that is, by the idea of God, on which alone it depends that a man is free, and that the good that he desires for himself he desires for all other men, as we have demonstrated above (by Prop. 37, Part 4).

Proposition 69

The virtue of a free man is seen to be equally great in avoiding as in overcoming dangers.

Demonstration. An emotion cannot be restrained or removed except by a contrary and stronger emotion (by Prop. 7, Part 4). But blind boldness[50] and fear are emotions which can be conceived to be equally great (by Props. 5 and 3, Part 4). Therefore, an equally great virtue of the mind, i.e. fortitude (see its definition in Prop. 59, Schol., Part 3), is required for restraining boldness as is required for restraining fear. That is (by Defs. 40 and 41 of the Emotions) a free man avoids dangers by the same virtue of mind as that by which he attempts to overcome them. QED.

Corollary

In a free man, therefore, timely flight is held to show as much courage as is fighting; or, a free man chooses flight with the same courage, i.e. presence of mind, as he chooses battle.

Scholium

What courage is, or what I understand by it,[51] I have explained in Prop. 59, Schol., Part 3. By 'danger' I understand everything that can be the cause of something bad, namely of pain, hatred, discord, etc.

Proposition 70

The free man who lives among the ignorant tries, as far as he can, to refuse their benefits.

Demonstration. Each person judges what is good in accordance with his own way of thinking (see Prop. 39, Schol., Part 3); therefore, an ignorant man who has conferred some benefit on another person will value it in accordance with his own way of thinking, and if he sees that it is valued less by the person to whom it is given, he will feel pain (by Prop. 42, Part 3). But a free man strives to join all other men to himself in friendship (by Prop. 37, Part 4), and not to repay men with similar benefits in accordance with their emotions, but to lead himself and all others with the free judgement of reason, and to do only those things that he knows to be of the first importance. Therefore, a free man, so that he is not hated by the ignorant, and so that he may obey, not their appetite, but reason alone, will endeavour to decline their benefits as far as he can. QED.

Scholium

I say, 'as far as he can'. For although men are ignorant, they are still men, who can provide human help—than which there is nothing more excellent—in need. So it often happens that it is necessary to accept a benefit from them, and consequently to congratulate them in accordance with their way of thinking. Further, one must exercise caution even when declining benefits, so that we do not seem to despise them, or to be afraid of repaying them on account of avarice, and so, whilst we flee their hatred, by that very fact we cause offence. So, in declining benefits, one must take account of what is useful and honourable.

Proposition 71

Only free men are very grateful to one another.

Demonstration. Only free men are very useful to one another, are joined to one another by the greatest necessity of friendship (by Prop. 35, Part 4, and its first Corollary), and endeavour to do good to one another with equal loving zeal (by Prop. 37, Part 4). So (by Def. 34 of the Emotions) only free men are very grateful to one another. QED.

Scholium

The gratitude that men who are led by blind desire display to one another is for the most part a business matter, or rather a snare, rather than gratitude. Further, ingratitude is not an emotion; however, ingratitude is base, because it indicates for the most part that a man is affected with excessive hatred, anger, pride, or avarice, etc. For a man who does not know how to repay gifts because of stupidity is not ungrateful; much less so is someone who is not moved by the gifts of a courtesan to serve her lust, nor by the gifts of a thief to conceal his thefts, or something similar. On the contrary, this man shows that he has a constant mind, in that he does not allow himself to be bribed by any gifts to destroy himself or the community.

Proposition 72

A free man never acts deceitfully, but always in good faith.[52]

Demonstration. If a free man, in so far as he is free, were to do something deceitfully, he would do it in accordance with the dictate of reason (for only in that respect do we call him free). So to act deceitfully would be a virtue (by Prop. 24, Part 4) and consequently (by the same Proposition) it would be more advantageous for each person to act deceitfully in order to preserve his own being. That is (as is self-evident), it would be more advantageous for men to agree only in words, but in fact to be opposed to one another, which (by Prop. 31, Coroll., Part 4) is absurd. Therefore, a free man, etc. QED.

Scholium

If it is now asked, 'What if a man could, by a breach of faith, free himself from the immediate danger of death; would not reason always advise him to break faith, in order that he may preserve his being?', the answer will be the same: that if reason were to advise him in this way, it would advise all men to do the same. So reason would always advise men to agree with one another, to join forces, and to have common laws, in bad faith only—that is, not really to have common laws; which is absurd.

Proposition 73

A man who is led by reason is more free in a commonwealth, where he lives in accordance with a common decree, than in solitude, where he obeys only himself.

Demonstration. A man who is led by reason is not led to obedience by fear (by Prop. 63, Part 4), but in so far as he endeavours to preserve his being in accordance with the dictate of reason—that is (by Prop. 66, Schol., Part 4), in so far as he endeavours to live freely—he desires to have regard for a common life and a common advantage (by Prop. 37, Part 4). Consequently (as we showed in Prop. 37, Schol. 2, Part 4), he desires to live in accordance with the common decree of the commonwealth. Therefore, a man who is led by reason desires to abide by the common laws of a commonwealth, in order that he may live more freely. QED.

Scholium

These and similar things that I have demonstrated about the true freedom of man are related to fortitude, that is (by Prop. 59, Schol., Part 3) to courage and nobility. I do not think it worth while to demonstrate here, one by one, all the properties of fortitude, and much less to demonstrate that a free man hates no one, is angry with no one, envies no one, is indignant with no one, despises no one, and is far from being proud. For these, and all the things that relate to true life and religion,[53] are easily demonstrated from Props. 37 and 46 of this Part: namely, that hatred is to be conquered by love, and that each person who is led by reason desires that the good that he seeks for himself should also exist for others. There is the further point, which we noted in Prop. 50, Schol., Part 4, and elsewhere, that the man of fortitude considers this above all: that all things follow from the necessity of the divine nature, and that therefore whatever he thinks to be irksome and bad, and whatever besides seems impious, horrible, unjust, and base arises from the fact that he conceives the things themselves in a distorted, mutilated, and confused way. Because of this he endeavours above all to conceive things as they are in themselves and to remove the obstacles to true knowledge, such as hatred, anger, envy, derision, pride, and other things of this sort that we have noted in what precedes. And so, as far as he can, he endeavours (as we have said)[54] to act well and rejoice. In the next Part I shall demonstrate the extent to which human virtue can attain these things, and what it can do.

Appendix

What I have said in this Part about the right way of living has not been arranged in such a way that it can be seen at a glance; rather, it has been demonstrated in a scattered fashion, according to the ease with which I could deduce one thing from another. I have therefore decided to put my views together here, and to arrange them in sections.

1. All our endeavours, i.e. desires, follow from the necessity of our nature in such a way that they can either be understood through that nature alone, as its proximate cause, or else in so far as we are a part of Nature, a part which cannot be conceived adequately through itself and apart from other individuals.

2. The desires which follow from our nature in such a way that they can be understood through it alone are those which are related to the mind in so far as it is conceived as consisting of adequate ideas. The other desires are related to the mind only in so far as it conceives things inadequately—things whose force and growth must be defined, not by human power, but by the power of things that are outside us. Therefore, the former are rightly called actions, and the latter, passions; for the former always indicate our power and the latter our impotence and mutilated knowledge.

3. Our actions, that is, those desires which are defined by human power, i.e. by reason, are always good, but the rest of our desires can be both good and bad.

4. In life, therefore, it is useful above all to perfect our intellect, i.e. reason, as far as we can, and in this one thing the supreme happiness, i.e. the blessedness, of man consists. For blessedness is simply the content-ment of mind that arises from the intuitive knowledge of God,[55] and to perfect the intellect is simply to understand God, the attributes of God, and the actions that follow from the necessity of his nature. Therefore, the ultimate end of the person who is led by reason, that is, the supreme desire by which he strives to control all other desires, is that by which he is led to conceive adequately himself and all things which can come within the range of his understanding.

5. There is, therefore, no rational life without understanding, and things are good only in so far as they help a man to enjoy the life of the mind, which is defined by the understanding. But on the other hand, those things that impede a man from being able to perfect his reason and enjoy a rational life—these things alone we assert to be bad.

6. But since all the things of which a man is the efficient cause are necessarily good, nothing that is bad can happen to a man except from external causes: namely, in so far as he is a part of the whole of Nature, whose laws human nature is compelled to obey, and to which he is compelled to adapt himself in almost an infinity of ways.

7. It cannot happen that man is not a part of Nature, and does not follow its common order. However, if he dwells among individuals which are such that they agree with the nature of man, by that very fact a man's power of acting is helped and fostered. But if, on the other hand, he lives among individuals which are such that they are far from agreeing with his nature, he will hardly be able to adapt himself to them without a great change in himself.

8. Whatever exists in the universe which we judge to be bad, i.e. which can impede us from being able to exist and to enjoy a rational life, we are entitled to remove from us in a way that seems to be safest. On the other hand, whatever exists that we judge to be good, i.e. to be useful for preserving our being and enjoying a rational life, we are entitled to take for our use and to employ in any way; and absolutely speaking each person is entitled, by the highest right of nature, to do what he judges to contribute to his own advantage.

9. Nothing can agree more with the nature of a thing than the rest of the individuals of the same species. So (by Section 7) there is nothing that exists that is more useful to a man for the preservation of his own being and the enjoyment of a rational life than a man who is led by reason. Again, since we know of no particular thing that is more excellent than a man who is led by reason, each person can give no greater display of the power of his skill and ingenuity than in educating men in such a way that they finally live in accordance with their own rule of reason.

10. In so far as men are brought into relation with each other by envy or by some emotion of hatred, to that extent they are opposed to one another, and consequently they are to be the more feared the more they can do than the rest of the individuals of Nature.

11. But minds are conquered, not by arms, but by love and nobility.

12. It is in the highest degree useful to men to join together their ways of life and to bind themselves with those bonds by which they may more easily make one being out of all of them, and, absolutely speaking, to do those things that serve for the strengthening of friendships.

13. But for these matters, skill and vigilance are required. Men are varied (for few are those who live in accordance with the prescript of

reason), yet for the most part they are envious and more inclined to revenge than to pity. So it needs remarkable power of mind to bear with each man in accordance with his own way of thinking, and to restrain oneself from imitating their emotions. On the other hand, those who know how to carp at men, and to reprove vices rather than to teach virtues, and not to strengthen the minds of men but to crush them— these people are irksome to themselves and to all others. The result of this is that many people, on account of excessive impatience of mind and a false zeal for religion, have preferred to live among the beasts rather than among men: just as boys or adolescents, unable to endure calmly the reproaches of their parents, take refuge in military service and choose the disadvantages of war and the rule of a tyrant in preference to the comforts of home and paternal admonition, and endure the imposition of any burden on themselves provided that they avenge themselves on their parents.

14. Although, therefore, men on the whole arrange everything in accordance with their lust, yet from their common society there follow many more advantages than disadvantages. Therefore, it is better to bear calmly the injuries inflicted by human beings, and to try to apply those measures that lead to the formation of concord and friendship.

15. The things that produce concord are those that are related to justice, fairness, and honour. For men bear with reluctance, not only what is unjust and injurious, but also what is regarded as base, i.e. the fact that someone spurns the accepted customs of the commonwealth. But for the formation of love, those things are necessary above all that regard religion and piety: on which, see Prop. 37, Scholia 1 and 2, Prop. 46, Schol., and Prop. 73, Schol., Part 4.

16. Concord often comes about as a result of fear, without good faith. Further, fear also arises from impotence of mind and therefore is not relevant to the use of reason; neither, again, is compassion, though it often seems to present an appearance of piety.

17. Men are also overcome by liberality: especially those who do not possess that by which they can acquire what is necessary for sustaining life. However, to bring help to each indigent person far exceeds the strength and the resources of a private man; for the wealth of a private man is by a long way unequal to supplying this. Further, the ability of one man is too limited for him to be able to join all men in friendship with him; therefore, the care of the poor falls upon society as a whole, and looks to the common advantage only.

18. In accepting benefits and returning thanks one's concern must be entirely different; on this, see Prop. 70, Schol., and Prop. 71, Schol., Part 4.

19. Further, meretricious love—that is, lust for generation that arises from beauty, and in absolute terms all love that recognizes some cause other than freedom of mind—easily passes into hatred; unless, what is worse, it is a form of madness, and then discord rather than concord is fostered.[56] See Prop. 31, Coroll., Part 3.

20. As to what concerns marriage, it is certain that this agrees with reason, if the desire of sexual intercourse is not engendered by beauty alone, but also by the love of begetting children and educating them wisely; and also if the love of each person, namely of the man and the woman, has as its cause, not beauty alone, but above all the freedom of the mind.

21. Flattery also produces concord, but it does so by the detestable offence of servitude, or by perfidy; for none are more taken in by flattery than are the proud, who want to be first, but are not.

22. There is in self-abasement a false appearance of piety and religion. And although self-abasement is the contrary of pride, yet the man who abases himself is closest to the proud man: see Prop. 57, Schol., Part 4.

23. Shame contributes to concord only in those things that cannot be concealed. Further, because shame itself is a species of pain, it does not concern the use of reason.

24. The remaining emotions of pain with respect to men are directly opposed to justice, fairness, honour, piety, and religion, and although indignation seems to bear before itself some semblance of fairness, yet one lives without law in a place where each person is allowed to judge the deeds of another, and assert either his own right or that of another.

25. Modesty, that is, the desire of pleasing men which is determined by reason, is related to piety (as we showed in Prop. 37, Schol. 1, Part 4). But if it arises from emotion, it is ambition, i.e. the desire by which men, under the false image of piety, often stir up discord and sedition. For the person who desires to help all others, either by counsel or by act, so that they may enjoy the highest good together, will strive above all to strengthen their love for him; not, however, to bring them into a state of wonder, so that a branch of learning may derive its name from him, or in absolute terms to provide other causes of envy. Again, in everyday conversations he will avoid referring to human vices, and will take care to speak only sparingly of human impotence. But he will speak at length of human virtue, i.e. power, and of the way in which it can be perfected, so that men may endeavour as far as they can to live in accordance with the

prescript of reason, moved, not by fear or by aversion, but by the emotion of pleasure alone.

26. Apart from men, we know of no particular thing in Nature in whose mind we can delight, and which we can join with us in friendship or in some kind of association. So a consideration of our advantage does not require us to conserve any thing that exists in Nature apart from human beings; rather, it teaches us to preserve, destroy, or adapt it in any way to our advantage, in accordance with its various uses.

27. The chief advantage that we derive from things that are outside us, besides the experience and knowledge that we acquire from the fact that we observe them and change them from one form into another, is the preservation of the body. For this reason, those things are useful above all that are able to feed and nourish the body in such a way that all its parts can perform their functions correctly. For the more the body is capable of being able to be affected in many ways, and of affecting external bodies in many ways, the more the mind is capable of thinking (see Props. 38 and 39, Part 4). But there seem to be very few things of this sort in Nature; so to feed the body as is required, it is necessary to use many foods of different natures. For the human body is composed of very many parts of different natures, which need continuous and varied food in order that the whole body may be equally capable of all the things that can follow from its nature, and consequently in order that the mind also may be equally capable of conceiving many things.

28. But the strength of any one person would hardly be enough to provide this, unless men exchanged services. Money has provided a short way to all these things, as a result of which its image tends to occupy the minds of the multitude very much, because they can hardly imagine any kind of pleasure unless it is accompanied by the idea of money as its cause.

29. But this is a fault only of those who seek money, not from need or on account of the necessities of life, but because they have learned the arts of gain by which they puff themselves up haughtily. For the rest, they feed their body in the customary way, but sparingly, because they believe that as much of their goods as they spend on the preservation of their body, they lose. But those who know the true use of money, and limit their wealth simply to what they need, live content with little.

30. Since, therefore, those things are good that help the parts of the body to perform their functions, and since pleasure consists in the fact that the power of a man, in so far as he consists of mind and body, is helped or increased, it follows that all the things that bring pleasure are

good. On the other hand, however, things do not act with the end of affecting us with pleasure, and their power of acting is not governed in accordance with our advantage, and finally pleasure is for the most part related to one part of the body in particular. For the most part, therefore, unless reason and vigilance assist one, the emotions of pleasure, and consequently the desires that spring from them as well, are excessive. Further, when we follow an emotion, we count as primary that which is pleasing at present, and cannot estimate future things with an equable emotion of the mind. See Prop. 44, Schol., and Prop. 60, Schol., Part 4.

31. But superstition, on the other hand, seems to think that that is good which brings pain, and on the other hand that that is bad which brings pleasure. But, as we have said before (see Prop. 45, Schol., Part 4), no one who is not envious is pleased by my lack of power and my misfortune. For the more we are affected with greater pleasure, the more we pass to a greater perfection, and consequently the more we participate in the divine nature; nor can pleasure which is controlled by a true regard for our advantage ever be bad. But the person who is led by fear, and who does what is good in order that he may avoid what is bad, is not led by reason.

32. But human power is extremely limited and is infinitely surpassed by the power of external causes, and so we do not have an absolute power of adapting to our use things that are outside us. However, we shall bear calmly the things that happen to us that are contrary to what is demanded by a regard for our advantage, if we are conscious of the fact that we have performed our function,[57] that the power that we have could not have extended itself so far that we could have avoided them, and that we are a part of the whole of Nature, whose order we follow. If we understand this clearly and distinctly, then that part of us which is defined by understanding, that is, the better part of us, will be wholly content with this and will endeavour to persevere in this contentment. For in so far as we understand, we can seek nothing apart from what is necessary, nor, in absolute terms, can we be contented except with what is true. So in so far as we understand this correctly, the endeavour of the better part of us agrees with the order of the whole of Nature.

End of the Fourth Part

PART FIVE

ON THE POWER OF THE INTELLECT, OR, ON HUMAN FREEDOM

Preface

I pass eventually to the remaining Part of the *Ethics*, which is about the method, i.e. the way, which leads to freedom. In this Part, therefore, I shall treat of the power of reason, by showing what is the power over the emotions of reason itself, and then what the freedom of the mind, i.e. blessedness, is. From this we shall see how much more powerful the wise man is than the ignorant. However, the question of how and in what way the intellect must be perfected, and by what art one must care for the body so that it may perform its function correctly, is not relevant here; for the latter concerns medicine and the former, logic. Here, therefore, as I have said, I shall treat solely of the power of the mind, i.e. of reason; above all I shall show how great and of what kind is its rule over the passions in respect of retraining and controlling them. For we have already demonstrated that we do not have an absolute rule over them.[1] The Stoics, however, thought that the emotions depend absolutely on our will, and that we can have absolute rule over them. But they were compelled to admit by the protest of experience—though not from their own principles—that no small amount of practice and study are necessary to restrain and control the emotions. Someone has tried to show this (if I remember aright) by the example of two dogs, one of them a house dog and the other a hunting dog, arguing that he was able by practice to accustom the house dog to hunt, and the hunting dog to stop chasing hares. Descartes was strongly in favour of this view. For he held that the soul, i.e. the mind, is united above all to a certain part of the brain, namely that which is termed the pineal gland,[2] by the help of which the mind senses all the movements which are excited in the body, together with external objects, and which the mind can move in various ways simply because it wills to do so. This gland, he held, is suspended in the middle of the brain in such a way that it can be moved by a very small motion of the animal spirits. He also held that this gland is suspended in the middle of the brain in as many different ways as the different ways in which the animal spirits impinge on it; and further, that there are impressed on the gland as many different traces as there are different external objects that propel the animal spirits towards it. From this it comes about that if, by the will of the soul that moves it in different ways, the gland is suspended in the way in which it was once suspended by the spirits which were agitated in this or that way, then the gland will propel and determine the animal spirits in the same way as that in they were previously repelled by the similar suspension of the gland. Further, he held that each act of will[3] of the mind is united by nature to a certain movement of the gland. For example, if someone has the will to look at a remote object, this act of the will brings it about that the pupil is dilated. But if he thinks solely of the dilation of the pupil, it will be of no advantage to him to have the will to do this. For Nature has not joined, to the will to dilate or contract the pupil, the movement of the gland that serves to impel the animal spirits towards the optic nerve in a way that is suitable for dilating or contracting it; rather, it has joined the movement to the will to look at remote or near objects. Finally, he held that, even though each movement of this gland seems to be connected by Nature to particular thoughts of ours from the beginning of our life, yet it can be joined to others by habit; this he tries to prove in article 50 of Part 1 of *The Passions of the Soul*. From this he infers that there is no soul so weak that it cannot, when well directed, acquire an absolute power over its passions. For these, as he defines them, are 'the perceptions, or the sensations, or the disturbances of the soul, which are related to it in particular, and which (NB) are produced, preserved and strengthened by some movement of the spirits' (see article 27, Part 1, *The Passions of the Soul*).[4] But we can join to any act of will any movement of the gland, and consequently of the spirits, and the determination of the will depends solely on our power. If, therefore, we determine our will by certain and firm judgements, in accordance with which we want to direct the actions of our life, and join to these judgements the movements of the passions that we want to have, then we shall acquire an absolute rule over our passions. This, as far as I understand it from his own words, is the opinion of this celebrated man—an opinion which I would hardly believe to have been put forward by so great a man, had it been less acute. Indeed, I can hardly wonder enough that a philosopher who firmly asserted that he would deduce nothing except from principles that are self-evident, and that he would affirm nothing except what he perceived clearly and distinctly, and who reproved the Scholastics so many times because they wanted to explain obscure matters by occult qualities,[5] should put forward a hypothesis that is more occult than any occult quality. What, I ask, does he understand by the union of mind and body? What clear and distinct conception does he have of thought which is very closely united to some tiny portion of quantity? I certainly wish that he had explained this union by its proximate cause. But he conceived the mind to be so distinct from the body that he could not assign any particular cause either for this union or for the mind itself, but it was necessary for him to have recourse to the cause of the whole universe, that is, to God. Then I would like to know how many degrees of motion the mind can contribute to that pineal gland, and with how much force it can keep it suspended. For I do not know whether this gland is moved around more slowly or more quickly by the mind than by the animal spirits. I also do not know whether the movements of the passions which we have joined closely to firm judgements cannot be separated from those judgements again by corporeal causes; from which it would follow that, although the mind has firmly resolved to oppose dangers, and has joined to this decree the motions of boldness, yet when the danger is in sight, the gland is suspended in such a way that the mind cannot think of anything but flight. And indeed, since there is no ratio of will to motion, there is also no comparison between the power, i.e. the strength, of the mind and of the body, and consequently the strength of the latter can in no way be determined by the strength of the former. To this one must add the fact that this gland is not found to be situated in the middle of the brain in such a way that it can be moved around so easily and in so many ways, and that not all the nerves are extended as far as the cavities of the brain. Finally, I omit everything that he says about the will and its freedom, since I have shown more than sufficiently that this is false. Therefore, since, as I have shown above, the power of the mind is determined by the understanding alone, we shall determine the remedies for the emotions—which, I believe, everyone experiences, but does not observe accurately, or see distinctly—by the power of the mind alone, and from it we shall deduce everything that regards its blessedness.

Axioms

1. If, in the same subject, two contrary emotions are excited, a change

will necessarily have to take place, either in each or in one alone, until they cease to be contrary.

2. The power of an effect is determined by the power of its cause, in so far as its essence is explained or defined through the essence of its cause.

This Axiom is evident from Proposition 7, Part 3.

Proposition 1

Just as the thoughts and ideas of things are arranged and interconnected in the mind, so the affections of the body, i.e. the images of things, are arranged and interconnected in the body in exactly the same way.

Demonstration. The order and connection of ideas is the same (by Prop. 7, Part 2) as the order and connection of things, and conversely the order and connection of things is the same (by Prop. 6, Coroll., and Prop. 7, Part 2) as the order and connection of ideas. Therefore, just as the order and connection of ideas in the mind takes place in accordance with the order and interconnection of the affections of the body (by Prop. 18, Part 2), so, conversely (by Prop. 2, Part 3), the order and connection of the affections of the body takes place just as thoughts and the ideas of things are arranged and interconnected in the mind. QED.

Proposition 2

If we remove a disturbance of the mind, i.e. an emotion, from the thought of an external cause, and join that disturbance of the mind to other thoughts, then the love or hatred towards the external cause, as well as the waverings of the mind[6] that arise from these emotions, will be destroyed.

Demonstration. For that which constitutes the form of love or of hatred is pleasure or pain, with the accompaniment of the idea of an external cause (by Defs. 6 and 7 of the Emotions). Therefore, when this has been removed, the form of love or of hatred is removed at the same time, and so these emotions are destroyed, together with those which arise from them. QED.

Proposition 3

An emotion which is a passion ceases to be a passion as soon as we form a clear and distinct idea of it.

Demonstration. An emotion which is a passion is a confused idea (by the General Definition of the Emotions). So if we form a clear and distinct idea of the emotion, this idea will be distinguished from the emotion itself, in so far as it is related to the mind alone, only by reason (by Prop. 21, Part 2, together with its Scholium); and so (by Prop. 3, Part 3) the emotion will cease to be a passion. QED.

Corollary

Therefore, an emotion is more in our power, and the mind suffers less from it, the more it is known to us.

Proposition 4

There is no affection of the body of which we cannot form some clear and distinct conception.

Demonstration. Those things that are common to all can be conceived only adequately (by Prop. 38, Part 2) and so (by Prop. 12, Part 2, and by Lemma 2 following Prop. 13, Schol., Part 2) there is no affection of the body of which we cannot form some clear and distinct conception. QED.

Corollary

It follows from this that there is no emotion of which we cannot form some clear and distinct conception. For an emotion is an idea of an affection of the human body (by the General Definition of the Emotions), which therefore (by the preceding Proposition) must involve some clear and distinct conception.

Scholium

Since nothing exists from which some effect does not follow (by Prop. 36, Part 1), and since we understand clearly and distinctly whatever follows from an idea which is adequate in us; (by Prop. 40, Part 2), it follows from this that each person has the power of understanding clearly and distinctly himself and his emotions—if not absolutely, at any rate in part—and consequently of bringing it about that he suffers less from them. We must therefore give particular attention to knowing each emotion clearly and distinctly, as far as is possible, so that in this way the mind may be determined by its emotion to thinking of those things that it clearly and distinctly perceives and with which it is entirely content, and so that the emotion itself is separated from the thought of an external cause and is joined to true thoughts. From this it will come about that not only are love, hatred, etc. destroyed (by Prop. 2, Part 5), but also that the appetites, i.e. the desires, that usually arise from such an emotion cannot be excessive (by Prop. 61, Part 4). For it must be noted above all that it is one and the same appetite through which a man is said both to act and to be acted on. For example, we have shown that human nature is so established that each person tries to bring it about that all others shall live in accordance with his way of thinking (Prop. 31, Coroll., Part 3). Now this appetite, in a man who is not led by reason, is a passion which is called ambition, and does not differ greatly from pride; on the other hand, in a man who lives in accordance with the dictate of reason it is an action, i.e. a virtue, which is called piety (see Prop. 37, Schol. 1, Part 4, and the second Demonstration of the same Proposition). In this way all the appetites, i.e. desires, are passions only in so far as they arise from inadequate ideas, and the same desires are ascribed to virtue in so far as they are excited or generated by adequate ideas. For all the desires by which we are determined to do something can arise both from adequate and from inadequate ideas (see Prop. 59, Part 4). And (to return from my digression) no remedy for the emotions which depends on our power can be found which is more excellent than this one: namely, the remedy that consists in a true knowledge of them. For, as we have shown above (by Prop. 3, Part 3), there exists no other power of the mind than the power of thinking and of forming adequate ideas.

Proposition 5

16 An emotion towards a thing which we imagine simply, and not as necessary, possible, or contingent, is (other things being equal) greatest of all.

17 *Demonstration.* An emotion towards a thing which we imagine to be free is greater than that towards a thing which is necessary (by Prop. 49, Part

3), and consequently even greater than that towards one which we imagine as either possible or contingent (by Prop. 11, Part 4). But to imagine some thing as free can be nothing other than to imagine the thing simply, whilst we are ignorant of the causes by which it was determined to act (by that which we showed in Prop. 35, Schol., Part 2). Therefore, an emotion towards a thing which we imagine simply is, other things being equal, greater than that towards a thing which is necessary, possible, or contingent, and consequently is the greatest emotion. QED.

Proposition 6

In so far as the mind understands all things as necessary, so far it has a greater power over the emotions, or, it suffers less from them.

Demonstration. The mind understands all things to be necessary (by Prop. 29, Part 1), and to be determined to existing and operating by an infinite connection of causes (by Prop. 28, Part 1). So to that extent (by the preceding Proposition) it brings it about that it suffers less from the emotions which arise from them, and (by Prop. 48, Part 3) it is less affected towards them. QED.

Scholium

The more this knowledge—namely, the knowledge that things are necessary—concerns particular things which we imagine more distinctly and more vividly, the greater is this power of the mind over the emotions. This is also supported by experience. For we see that pain at the loss of some good is mitigated as soon as the man who has lost it considers that that good could not in any way have been preserved. So also we see that no one pities an infant because it cannot speak, walk, or reason, and finally because it lives for so many years as if it were unconscious of itself. But if most people were born adult, and only one or two were born as infants, then each person would pity infants, because he would regard infancy not as a natural and necessary thing, but as a defect or error of Nature. We could note several other things of this kind.

Proposition 7

If one considers time, the emotions which arise from or are excited by reason are more powerful than those which are related to particular things which we regard as absent.

Demonstration. We do not regard some thing as absent as a result of the emotion by which we imagine it, but as a result of the fact that the body is affected by some emotion which excludes the existence of that thing (by Prop. 17, Part 2)[7]. So the emotion which is related to a thing which we regard as absent is not of a nature such that it surpasses all the remaining actions and power of a man (on which, see Prop. 6, Part 4), but on the contrary it is of a nature such that it can in some way be restrained by those affections which exclude the existence of its external cause (by Prop. 9, Part 4). But an emotion which arises from reason is necessarily related to the common properties of things (see the definition of reason in Prop. 40, Schol. 2, Part 2), which we always regard as present (for there can be nothing that excludes their present existence) and which we always imagine in the same way (by Prop. 38, Part 2). So such an emotion always remains the same, and consequently (by Axiom 1, Part 5) the emotions which are contrary to it, and which are not fostered by their external causes, will need to accommodate themselves to it more and more until they are no longer contrary, and to that extent the emotion which arises from reason is more powerful. QED.

Proposition 8

The more an emotion is excited by several causes which occur simultaneously, the greater it is.

Demonstration. Several simultaneous causes can do more than if they were fewer (by Prop. 7, Part 3), and so (by Prop. 5, Part 4) the more an emotion is excited by several causes simultaneously, the stronger it is. QED.

Scholium

This Proposition is also evident from Axiom 2, Part 5.

Proposition 9

An emotion which is related to several different causes, which the mind contemplates simultaneously with the emotion itself, is less harmful, and we suffer less through it and are less affected towards each cause, than another equally great emotion that is related to fewer causes, or to one cause alone.

Demonstration. An emotion is bad, i.e. harmful, only in so far as the mind is hindered by it from being able to think (by Props. 26 and 27, Part 4). So an emotion by which the mind is determined to regard several objects simultaneously is less harmful than another equally great emotion which detains the mind in the contemplation of fewer objects, or of one object alone, in such a way that it cannot think of others. This was the first thing to be proved. Next, since the mind's essence, that is (by Prop. 7, Part 3), its power, consists solely in thinking (by Prop. 11, Part 2), the mind suffers less through an emotion by which it is determined to contemplate several things simultaneously than through an equally great emotion which keeps the mind occupied in the contemplation of fewer objects, or of one object alone. This was the second thing to be proved. Finally, this emotion (by Prop. 48, Part 3), in so far as it is related to several external causes, is less towards each of them. QED.

Proposition 10

As long as we are not harassed by emotions which are contrary to our nature, we have the power of arranging and interconnecting the affections of the body in accordance with the order of the intellect.

Demonstration. The emotions which are contrary to our nature, that is (by Prop. 30, Part 4), which are bad, are bad in so far as they hinder the mind from understanding (by Prop. 27, Part 4). Therefore, as long as we are not harassed by emotions which are contrary to our nature, the power of the mind, by which it endeavours to understand things, is not hindered (by Prop. 26, Part 4); so long, therefore, it has the power of forming clear and distinct ideas, and of deducing some ideas from others (see Prop. 40, Schol. 2, and Prop. 47, Schol., Part 2). So long, consequently (by Prop. 1, Part 5), we have the power of arranging and interconnecting the affections of the body in accordance with the order of the intellect. QED.

Scholium

By this power of correctly arranging and interconnecting the affections of the body we can bring it about that we are not easily affected by bad emotions. For (by Prop. 7, Part 5) a greater force is required to restrain emotions which are arranged and interconnected in accordance with the order of the intellect than to restrain those that are uncertain and inconstant. The best we can do, therefore, as long as we do not have a perfect knowledge of our emotions, is to conceive a right way of living, i.e. fixed rules of life, that are certain,[8] and to commit these to memory and apply them constantly to particular things that often meet us in life, so that in this way our imagination is widely affected by them and they are always at hand. For example, among the fixed rules of life we have stated (see Prop. 46, Part 4, with its Scholium) that hatred is to be conquered by love, i.e. by nobility, but is not to be repaid with reciprocal hatred. But so that we may have this precept of reason always at hand when it is required, we need to think of and often meditate upon the common injuries of human beings, and how and in what way they are best warded off by nobility. For in this way we shall join the image of the injury to the imagination of this rule, and (by Prop. 18, Part 2) it will always be at hand when an injury is inflicted on us. But if we also had at hand a rational account of our true advantage, and also of the good that follows from mutual friendship and a shared society, as well as of the fact that the highest self-contentment arises from a right way of living (by Prop. 52, Part 4), and that men, like all other things, act by the necessity of Nature—if we had all this at hand, then the injury, or the hatred that commonly arises from this, will occupy a very small part of the imagination, and will easily be overcome. If the anger that commonly arises from the greatest injuries is not so easily overcome, yet it will be overcome, though not without some wavering of the mind, in a much shorter space of time than if we had not premeditated on these things in this way, as is evident from Props. 6, 7, and 8 of this Part. We must think in the same way of courage in putting aside fear; namely, we must enumerate and often imagine the common dangers of life, and how they can best be avoided and overcome by presence of mind and by fortitude. But it must be noted that, in arranging our thoughts and images, we must always (by Prop. 63, Coroll., Part 4, and Prop. 59, Part 3) pay attention to the things that are good in each thing, so that in this way we are always determined to act by the emotion of pleasure. For example, if someone sees that he pursues glory too much, let him think of its right use and to what end it is to be pursued and by what means it can be acquired; but not of its misuse and of the vanity and inconstancy of men, or other things of this sort of which no one thinks unless his mind is unhealthy. For ambitious men afflict themselves with such thoughts most of all when they despair of obtaining the honour that they seek, and, whilst they vomit up their anger, they want to appear wise. So it is certain that those people are most desirous of glory who exclaim most about its misuse and about the vanity of the world. Nor is this peculiar to the ambitious, but it is common to all people to whom fortune is unfavourable and who are weak in mind. For a poor man who is also greedy talks endlessly about the misuse of money and the vices of the rich—by which he does nothing but afflict himself and show to other people that he resents not only his own poverty, but also the wealth of others. So, again, those men who have been badly received by their mistress think of nothing but the inconstancy of women, their deceit-fulness, and the rest of their often proclaimed faults, all of which they immediately forget as soon as they are received by their mistress again. So the person who tries to control his emotions and his appetites simply from the love of freedom will, as far as he can, strive to know the virtues and their causes, and to fill his mind with the delight that arises from a true knowledge of them. But he will be far from striving to contemplate the vices of men, and to decry men and to rejoice in a false show of freedom. The person who will observe these things diligently (and they are not difficult) and will make use of them will in a short space of time be able to direct most of his actions in accordance with the rule of reason.

Proposition 11

In so far as some image is related to several things, the more frequent it is, i.e. the more often it flourishes, and occupies the mind more.

Demonstration. For in so far as an image, i.e. an emotion, is related to several things, the more causes there are by which it can be excited and fostered, all of which the mind (by hypothesis) regards simultaneously as a result of the emotion. So the emotion is the more frequent, i.e. it flourishes more often, and (by Prop. 8, Part 5) it occupies the mind more. QED.

Proposition 12

Images of things are more easily joined to images that are related to things that we understand clearly and distinctly than to other things.

Demonstration. Things that we understand clearly and distinctly are either the common properties of things or what are deduced from them (see the definition of reason in Prop. 40, Schol. 2, Part 2). Consequently (by the preceding Proposition), they are excited in us more often, and so it can happen more easily that we regard things together with them rather than with others, and consequently (by Prop. 18, Part 2) that they are joined more easily with them than with others.[9] QED.

Proposition 13

The more an image is joined to several others, the more often it flourishes.

Demonstration. For the more an image is joined to several others, the more causes there are (by Prop. 18, Part 2) by which it can be excited. QED.

Proposition 14

The mind can bring it about that all the affections of the body, i.e. the images of things, are related to the idea of God.

Demonstration. There is no affection of the body of which the mind cannot form a clear and distinct conception (by Prop. 4, Part 5), and so it can bring it about (by Prop. 15, Part 1) that all are related to the idea of God. QED.

Proposition 15

The person who understands himself and his emotions clearly and distinctly loves God, and the more so, the more he understands himself and his emotions.

Demonstration. The person who understands himself and his emotions clearly and distinctly feels pleasure (by Prop. 53, Part 3), and this is accompanied by the idea of God (by the preceding Proposition). So (by Def. 6 of the Emotions) he loves God, and (for the same reason) the more so, the more he understands himself and his emotions. QED.

Proposition 16

This love for God must occupy the mind most of all.

Demonstration. For this love is joined to all the affections of the body (by Prop. 14, Part 5), by all of which it is fostered (by Prop. 15, Part 5), and so (by Prop. 11, Part 5) it must occupy the mind most of all. QED.

Proposition 17

God is without passions, and is not affected by any emotion of pleasure or of pain.

Demonstration. All ideas, in so far they are related to God, are true (by Prop. 32, Part 2), that is (by Def. 4, Part 2), they are adequate, and so (by the General Definition of the Emotions) God is without passions. Next, God cannot pass to a greater or to a less perfection (by Prop. 20, Coroll. 2, Part 1), and so (by Defs. 2 and 3 of the Emotions) he is affected by no emotion of pleasure or of pain. QED.

Corollary

Strictly speaking, God loves no one and hates no one. For God (by the preceding Proposition) is affected by no emotion of pleasure or pain, and consequently (by Defs. 6 and 7 of the Emotions) he loves no one and hates no one.

Proposition 18

No one can hate God.

Demonstration. The idea of God which exists in us is adequate and perfect (by Props 46 and 47, Part 2), and in so far as we contemplate God, we act (by Prop. 3, Part 3). Consequently (by Prop. 59, Part 3), there can exist no pain that is accompanied by the idea of God; that is (by Def. 7 of the Emotions), no one can hate God. QED.

Corollary

Love for God cannot be turned into hatred.

Scholium

But it can be objected that whilst we understand God to be the cause of all things, by that very fact we consider God to be the cause of pain. To this I reply that in so far as we understand the causes of pain, to that extent (by Prop. 3, Part 5) it ceases to be a passion, that is (by Prop. 59, Part 3), it ceases to be pain. So, in so far as we understand God to be the cause of pain, to that extent we feel pleasure.

Proposition 19

The person who loves God cannot endeavour that God, conversely, should love him.

Demonstration. If a man were to endeavour this, he would desire (by Prop. 17, Coroll., Part 5) that God, whom he loves, would not be God. Consequently (by Prop. 19, Part 3), he would desire to feel pain, which (by Prop. 28, Part 3) is absurd. Therefore the person who loves God, etc.

Proposition 20

This love for God cannot be sullied by the emotion of envy or of jealousy, but it is the more fostered, the more men we imagine to be joined with God by the same bond of love.

Demonstration. This love for God is the highest good that we can seek in accordance with the dictate of reason (by Prop. 28, Part 4), and it is common to all men (by Prop. 36, Part 4) and we desire that all should rejoice in it (by Prop. 37, Part 4). So (by Def. 23 of the Emotions) it cannot be stained by the emotion of envy, nor again by the emotion of jealousy (by Prop. 18, Part 5, and by the definition of jealousy in Prop. 35, Schol., Part 3). On the contrary, it must (by Prop. 31, Part 3) be fostered the more, the more men we imagine to enjoy it. QED.

Scholium

We can show in the same way that there is no emotion which is directly contrary to this love, and by which the love could be destroyed. So we can infer that this love for God is the most constant of emotions, and, in so far as it is related to the body, cannot be destroyed except with the body. We shall see later[10] of what nature it is in so far as it is related to the mind alone. With this I have covered all the remedies for the emotions, or, everything that the mind, considered in itself alone, can do against the emotions. From this it is apparent that the power of the mind over the emotions consists: first, in the very knowledge of the emotions (see Prop. 4, Schol., Part 5). Secondly, in the fact that the mind separates the emotions from the thought of an external cause that we imagine confusedly (see Prop. 2, together with the above-mentioned Scholium of Prop. 4, Part 5). Thirdly, in the time in which the affections which are related to things that we understand surpass those that are related to the things that we imagine confusedly, i.e. in a mutilated way (see Prop. 7, Part 5).[11] Fourthly, in the multitude of the causes by which the affections which are related to the common properties of things, or to God, are fostered (see Props. 9 and 11, Part 5). Fifthly and lastly, in the order in which the mind can arrange and interconnect its emotions (see Prop. 10, Schol., and also Props. 12, 13, and 14, Part 5). But in order that this power of the mind over the emotions may be understood better, it must also be noted above all that emotions are called 'great' by us when we compare the emotion of one man with the emotion of another, and see that the one man is harassed more than the other by the same emotion, or when we compare with one another the emotions of one and the same man, and find that he is affected, i.e. moved by one emotion rather than by another. For (by Prop. 5, Part 4) the force of each emotion is defined by the power of an external cause in comparison with our own. But the power of the mind is defined by knowledge alone, whereas lack of power, i.e. passion, is reckoned solely by the privation of knowledge, that is, by that through which ideas are said to be inadequate. From this it follows that that mind is said to be most passive whose greatest part is constituted by inadequate ideas, so that it is distinguished more by its passivity than by its activity. Conversely, that mind is said to act most whose greatest part is constituted by adequate ideas, in such a way that, although there are as many inadequate ideas in it as in the former, yet it is distinguished more by those that are ascribed to human virtue than by those that manifest human lack of power. Then it is to be noted that the sicknesses and misfortunes of the mind derive their origin chiefly from an excessive love for a thing that is subject to many changes, and which we can never possess. For no one is concerned or anxious about any thing except one that he loves, nor do injuries, suspicions, enmities, etc. arise except from love for things which no one can truly possess. From this we easily conceive what clear and distinct knowledge, and especially the third kind of knowledge (on which, see Prop. 47, Schol., Part 2), whose basis is the very knowledge of God, can do against the emotions. For even if it does not destroy these absolutely, in so far as they are passions (see Prop. 3, together with the Scholium of Prop. 4 of Part 5), yet it brings it about that they constitute the least part of the mind (see Prop. 14, Part 5). Further, this knowledge generates love towards an immutable and eternal thing (see Prop. 15, Part 5), of which we are truly the possessors (by Prop. 45, Part 2), and which therefore can be sullied by none of the defects that exist in ordinary love, but which can always be greater and greater (by Prop. 15, Part 5), and occupy the greatest part of the mind (by Prop. 16, Part 5) and affect it extensively. With this I have concluded everything that concerns this present life. For what I said at the beginning of this Scholium—namely, that in these few words I have covered all the remedies for the emotions—can easily be seen by anyone who attends to what we have said in this Scholium, and at the same time to the definitions of the mind and of its emotions, and finally to Props. 1 and 3 of Part 3. It is now time, therefore, for me to pass to those things that have reference to the duration of the mind without relation to the body.

Proposition 21

The mind can imagine nothing, nor can it recollect past things, except whilst the body endures.

Demonstration. The mind does not express the actual existence of its body, nor again does it conceive as actual the affections of the body, except whilst the body endures (by Prop. 8, Coroll., Part 2). Consequently (by Prop. 26, Part 2), it conceives no body as actually existing except whilst its body endures, and therefore it can imagine nothing (see the definition of imagination in Prop. 17, Schol., Part 2), nor can it recollect past things, except whilst the body endures (see the definition of memory in Prop. 18, Schol., Part 2). QED.

Proposition 22

In God, however, there necessarily exists an idea which expresses the essence of this or that human body under a species of eternity.

Demonstration. God is the cause, not only of the existence of this or that human body, but also of its essence (by Prop. 25, Part 1), which therefore must necessarily be conceived through the very essence of God (by Axiom 4, Part 1), and with a certain eternal necessity (by Prop. 16, Part 1), which conception must necessarily exist in God (by Prop. 3, Part 2). QED.

Proposition 23

The human mind cannot be absolutely destroyed with the human body, but there remains of it something that is eternal.[12]

Demonstration. In God there necessarily exists a conception, i.e. an idea, which expresses the essence of the human body (by the preceding Proposition), which is therefore necessarily something that belongs to the essence of the human mind (by Prop. 13, Part 2). But we ascribe to the human mind no duration that can be defined by time,[13] except in so far as it expresses the actual existence of the human body, which is explained through duration and can be defined by time. That is (by Prop. 8, Coroll., Part 2), we do not ascribe duration to it except whilst the body endures. But since there is nevertheless something that is conceived with a certain eternal necessity through the very essence of God (by the preceding Proposition), this something that belongs to the essence of the mind will necessarily be eternal. QED.

Scholium

This idea which expresses the essence of the body under a species of eternity is, as we have said, a certain mode of thinking which belongs to the essence of the mind, and which is necessarily eternal. But it cannot happen that we remember that we existed before the body, since there can exist no traces of it in the body, nor can eternity be defined by time or have any relation to time. Nevertheless, we sense and experience that we are eternal. For the mind senses those things that it conceives in understanding no less than those that it has in the memory. For the eyes of the mind, by which it sees and observes things, are demonstrations. Although, therefore, we do not remember that we existed before the body, yet we sense that our mind, in so far as it involves the essence of the body under a species of eternity, is eternal, and that this existence that it has cannot be defined by time, i.e. be explained through duration. Our mind, therefore, can be said to endure, and its existence can be defined by a certain time, only in so far as it involves the actual existence of the body, and to that extent alone it has the power of determining the existence of things by time and of conceiving them under duration.

Proposition 24

The more we understand particular things, the more we understand God.

Demonstration. This is evident from Prop. 25, Coroll., Part 1.

Proposition 25

The highest endeavour of the mind, and its highest virtue, is to understand things by the third kind of knowledge.[14]

Demonstration. The third kind of knowledge proceeds from an adequate idea of some of the attributes of God to an adequate knowledge of the essence of things (see its definition in Prop. 40, Schol. 2, Part 2). The more we understand things in this way, the more (by the preceding Proposition) we understand God, and so (by Prop. 28, Part 4) the highest virtue of the mind, that is (by Def. 8, Part 4), its power, i.e. its nature, i.e. (by Prop. 7, Part 3) its highest endeavour, is to understand things by the third kind of knowledge. QED.

Proposition 26

The more the mind is capable of understanding things by the third kind of knowledge, the more it desires to understand things by this kind of knowledge.

Demonstration. This is evident. For in so far as we conceive the mind to be capable of understanding things by this kind of knowledge, to that extent we conceive it to be determined to understanding things by the same kind of knowledge, and consequently (by Def. 1 of the Emotions) the more the mind is capable of this, the more it desires it. QED.

Proposition 27

From this third kind of knowledge there arises the highest contentment of mind that can exist.

Demonstration. The highest virtue of the mind is to know God (by Prop. 28, Part 4), or, it is to understand things by the third kind of knowledge (by Prop. 25, Part 5). This virtue is the greater, the more the mind knows things by this kind of knowledge (by Prop. 24, Part 5), and so the person who knows things by this kind of knowledge passes to the highest human perfection and consequently (by Def. 2 of the Emotions) is affected with the highest pleasure. This (by Prop. 43, Part 2) is accompanied by the idea of himself and of his virtue, and therefore (by Def. 25 of the Emotions) there arises from this kind of knowledge the highest contentment of mind that can exist. QED.

Proposition 28

The endeavour, i.e. the desire, of knowing things by the third kind of knowledge cannot arise from the first kind of knowledge but can arise from the second.

Demonstration. This proposition is self-evident. For whatever we understand clearly and distinctly, we understand either through itself or through something else that is conceived through itself. That is, the ideas which are clear and distinct in us, i.e. which are related to the third kind of knowledge (see Prop. 40, Schol. 2, Part 2), cannot follow from mutilated and confused ideas, which (by the same Scholium) are related to the first kind of knowledge. However, they can follow from adequate ideas, i.e. (by the same Scholium) from the second and third kinds of knowledge. Therefore (by Def. 1 of the Emotions), the desire of knowing things by the third kind of knowledge cannot arise from the first kind of knowledge, but can arise from the second. QED.

Proposition 29

Whatever the mind understands under a species of eternity, it understands not from the fact that it conceives the present actual existence of the body, but from the fact that it conceives the essence of the body under a species of eternity.

Demonstration. In so far as the mind conceives the present existence of its body, to that extent it conceives duration, which can be determined by time, and to that extent alone it has the power of conceiving things with relation to time (by Proposition 21, Part 5, and Proposition 26, Part 2). But eternity cannot be explained through duration (by Def. 8, Part 1, and its Explanation). Therefore, to that extent the mind does not have the power of conceiving things under a species of eternity. However, it is of the nature of reason to conceive things under a species of eternity (by Prop. 44, Coroll. 2, Part 2), and it also belongs to the nature of the mind to conceive the essence of the body under a species of eternity (by Prop. 23, Part 5), and besides these two[15] nothing else belongs to the essence of the mind (by Prop. 13, Part 2). Therefore, this power of conceiving things under a species of eternity belongs to the mind only in so far as it conceives the essence of the body under a species of eternity. QED.

Scholium

Things are conceived by us as actual in two ways: either in so far as we conceive them to exist in relation to a certain time and place, or in so far as we conceive them to be contained in God and to follow from the necessity of the divine nature. But those things which are conceived in this second way as true, i.e. as real, we conceive under a species of eternity, and their ideas involve the eternal and infinite essence of God, as we have shown in Proposition 45, Part 2; see also its Scholium.

Proposition 30

Our mind, in so far as it knows itself and the body under a species of eternity, necessarily has knowledge of God, and knows itself to exist in God and to be conceived through God.

Demonstration. Eternity is the very essence of God, in so far as this involves necessary existence (by Def. 8, Part 1). Therefore, to conceive things under a species of eternity is to conceive things in so far as they are conceived as real entities through the essence of God, or, in so far as they involve existence through the essence of God. So our mind, in so far as it conceives itself and the body under a species of eternity, necessarily has knowledge of God, and knows etc. QED.

Proposition 31

The third kind of knowledge depends on the mind, as its formal cause,[16] in so far as the mind itself is eternal.

Demonstration. The mind conceives nothing under a species of eternity except in so far as it conceives the essence of its body under a species of eternity (by Prop. 29, Part 5), that is (by Props. 21 and 23, Part 5), in so far as it is eternal. So (by the preceding Proposition), in so far as it is eternal, it has a knowledge of God, which knowledge is necessarily adequate (by Prop. 46, Part 2). Therefore, the mind, in so far as it is eternal, is capable of knowing all those things which can follow from this given knowledge of God (by Prop. 40, Part 2), that is, of knowing things by the third kind of knowledge (see its definition in Prop. 40, Schol. 2, Part 2). Therefore, the mind (by Def. 1, Part 3), in so far as it is eternal, is the adequate, i.e. the formal, cause of this kind of knowledge. QED.

Scholium

Therefore, the more each person is rich in this kind of knowledge, the better is his consciousness of himself and of God; that is, the more perfect and the more blessed he is. This will appear even more clearly from what follows[17]. But it must be noted here that although we are now certain that the mind is eternal in so far as it conceives things under a species of eternity, yet, in order that what we want to show may be explained more easily and understood better, we shall consider it as if it had just begun to exist and to understand things under a species of eternity, as we have done so far[18]. We may do this without any danger of error, provided that we are careful to infer from this nothing except from premises that are evident.

Proposition 32

Whatever we understand by the third kind of knowledge we are pleased with, and this is accompanied by the idea of God as its cause.

Demonstration. From this kind of knowledge there arises the highest contentment of the mind (by Prop. 27, Part 5), that is (by Def. 25 of the Emotions), pleasure, that can exist. This is accompanied by the idea of itself, and consequently (by Prop. 30, Part 5) by the idea of God, as its cause. QED.

Corollary

From the third kind of knowledge there necessarily arises the intellectual love of God. For there arises from this kind of knowledge (by the preceding Proposition) pleasure, accompanied by the idea of God as its cause, that is (by Def. 6 of the Emotions), the love of God: not in so far as we imagine him as present (by Prop. 29, Part 5), but in so far as we understand God to be eternal. And this is what I call the intellectual love of God.

Proposition 33

The intellectual love of God that arises from the third kind of knowledge is eternal.

Demonstration. For the third kind of knowledge (by Prop. 31, Part 5, and Ax. 3, Part 1) is eternal; so (again by Ax. 3, Part 1) the love which arises from it is also necessarily eternal. QED.

Scholium

Although this love of God does not have a beginning (by the preceding Proposition), yet it has all the perfections of love, just as if it had come into being, as we assumed in the Corollary of the preceding Proposition. Nor is there any difference here, except that the mind will have had eternally these same perfections that we have just supposed to be added to it, with the accompaniment of the idea of God as an eternal cause. So if pleasure consists in a transition to a greater perfection, blessedness must assuredly consist in the fact that the mind is endowed with perfection itself.

Proposition 34

The mind is liable to emotions which are related to the passions only as long as the body endures.

Demonstration. An imagination is an idea by which the mind regards some thing as present (see its definition in Prop. 17, Schol., Part 2), but which indicates the present constitution of the human body rather than the nature of the external thing (by Prop. 16, Coroll. 2, Part 2). Therefore (by the General Definition of the Emotions), an emotion is an imagination, in so far as it indicates the present constitution of the body; and so (by Prop. 21, Part 5) the mind is liable to emotions which are related to the passions only as long as the body endures. QED.

Corollary

From this it follows that no love is eternal except intellectual love.

Scholium

If we pay attention to the common belief of men, we shall see that they are indeed conscious of the eternity of their mind, but that they confuse it with duration and ascribe it to imagination, i.e. to the memory, which they believe to remain after death.

Proposition 35

God loves himself with infinite intellectual love.

Demonstration. God is absolutely infinite (by Def. 6, Part 1); that is (by Def. 6, Part 2), the nature of God enjoys infinite perfection, and it does so with (by Prop. 3, Part 2) the accompaniment of the idea of himself, that is (by Prop. 11 and Def. 1, Part 1), the idea of his cause.[19] And this is what we stated in Prop. 32, Coroll., Part 5, to be the intellectual love of God.

Proposition 36

The intellectual love of the mind for God is the love by which God loves himself; not in so far as he is infinite, but in so far as he can be explained through the essence of the human mind, considered under a species of eternity; that is, the love of the mind for God is a part of the infinite intellectual love with which God loves himself.

Demonstration. This love of the mind must be related to the actions of the mind (by Prop. 32, Coroll., Part 5, and by Prop. 3, Part 3). It is therefore an action by which the mind contemplates itself, with the accompaniment of the idea of God as its cause (by Prop. 32, Part 5, and its Coroll.). That is (by Prop., 25, Coroll., Part 1, and Prop. 11, Coroll., Part 2) it is an action by which God, in so far as he can be explained through the human mind, contemplates himself with the accompaniment of the idea of himself. So (by the preceding Proposition) this love of the mind is a part of the intellectual love with which God loves himself. QED.

Corollary

From this it follows that God, in so far as he loves himself, loves human beings, and consequently that the love of God for men, and the intellectual love of the mind for God, is one and the same.

Scholium

From this we understand clearly in what our salvation, i.e. our blessedness, i.e. our freedom, consists: namely, in a constant and eternal love for God, or, in the love of God for human beings. This love, i.e. blessedness, is called 'glory' in the Scriptures, and rightly so.[20] For whether this love is related to God or to the mind, it can rightly be called contentment of mind, which is not in fact distinguished from glory (by Defs. 25 and 30 of the Emotions). For in so far as it is related to God, it is (by Prop. 35, Part 5) pleasure (if one may still use this term)[21] with the accompaniment of the idea of himself, just as it also is in so far as it is related to the mind (by Prop. 27, Part 5). Next, since the essence of our mind consists in thinking alone, of which the principle and the basis is God (by Prop. 15, Part 1, and Prop. 47, Schol., Part 2), it becomes evident to us how, and in what way, our mind follows from the divine nature, and continually depends on

God in respect of essence and existence. I thought it worth while to note this point here so that I could show by this example how much the knowledge of particular things, which I have called intuitive, or, of the third kind (see Prop. 40, Schol. 2, Part 2), can do, and how it is more powerful than the universal knowledge that I have said to be of the second kind. For although I have shown generally in Part One[22] that all things (and consequently the human mind as well) depend on God in respect of essence and existence, yet that demonstration—although legitimate and beyond doubt—does not so affect our mind as when it is inferred from the very essence of any particular thing which we declare to depend on God.

Proposition 37

There exists in Nature nothing that is contrary to this intellectual love, or, that can destroy it.

Demonstration. This intellectual love follows necessarily from the nature of the mind, in so far as it is considered through the nature of God as an eternal truth (by Props. 33 and 29, Part 5). If, therefore, there existed something that is contrary to this love, it would be contrary to what is true, and consequently that which could destroy this love would bring it about that that which is true is false, which (as is self-evident) is absurd.[23] Therefore, there exists in Nature nothing, etc. QED.

Scholium

The axiom of the Fourth Part concerns particular things in so far as they are considered with relation to a certain time and place; which, I believe, no one will doubt.

Proposition 38

The more things the mind understands by the second[24] and third kinds of knowledge, the less it suffers from emotions which are bad, and the less it fears death.

Demonstration. The essence of the mind consists in knowledge (by Prop. 11, Part 2); therefore, the more things the mind knows by the second and third kinds of knowledge, the greater is the part of it that remains (by

Props. 23 and 29, Part 5). Consequently (by the preceding Proposition), the greater is the part that is not touched by emotions that are contrary to our nature, that is (by Prop. 30, Part 4), which are bad. So the more things the mind understands by the second and third kinds of knowledge, the greater is the part of it that remains undamaged, and consequently it suffers less from emotions, etc. QED.

Scholium

From this we understand that which I touched on in Prop. 39, Schol., Part 4, and which I promised to explain in this Part: namely, that death is the less hurtful, the greater the mind's knowledge is clear and distinct, and consequently, the more the mind loves God. Next, since (by Prop. 27, Part 5) there arises from the third kind of knowledge the highest contentment that can exist, it follows that the human mind can be of such a nature that that which we have shown to perish with its body (see Prop. 21, Part 5) is of no importance in relation to that which remains of it. But I will speak more fully of this soon.

Proposition 39

The person who has a body which is capable of very many things has a mind the greatest part of which is eternal.

Demonstration. The person who has a body which is capable of doing very many things is least harassed by emotions which are bad (by Prop. 38, Part 4): that is (by Prop. 30, Part 4), by emotions which are contrary to our nature. So (by Prop. 10, Part 5) he has the power of arranging and interconnecting the affections of the body in accordance with the order of the intellect, and consequently of bringing it about (by Prop. 14, Part 5) that all the affections of the body are related to the idea of God. From this it will come about (by Prop. 15, Part 5) that he is affected with love for God, which (by Prop. 16, Part 5) must occupy, i.e. constitute, the greatest part of the mind, and therefore (by Prop. 33, Part 5) he has a mind of which the greatest part is eternal. QED.

Scholium

Since human bodies are capable of very many things, there is no doubt that they can be of such a nature that they are related to minds that have a great knowledge of themselves and of God, and of which the greatest, i.e. the chief, part is eternal, so that they scarcely fear death. But so that this can be understood more clearly, it must be noted here that we live in a state of continuous variation, and in accordance with the way in which we are changed into the better or the worse, we are called happy or unhappy. For the person who passes from being an infant or a child into being a corpse is called unhappy, and on the other hand we are said to be happy if we can run through the whole course of our life with a sound mind in a sound body.[25] And indeed the person who—just like an infant or a child—has a body which is capable of very little, and which depends very much on external causes, has a mind which, considered in itself alone, is scarcely conscious of itself, of God, and of things. On the other hand, the person who has a body which is capable of very many things has a mind which, considered in itself alone, is very conscious of itself, of God, and of things. In this life, therefore, we endeavour above all that the body of infancy—as far as its nature allows and is conducive to this— shall be changed into another body which is capable of very many things, and which is related to a mind which is very much aware of itself, of God, and of things. So we endeavour that everything that is related to the mind's memory or imagination is of scarcely any importance in relation to the intellect, as I have already said in the Scholium of the preceding Proposition.

Proposition 40

The more perfection each thing has, the more it acts, and the less it is acted on; conversely, the more it acts, the more perfect it is.

Demonstration. The more perfect each thing is, the more reality it has (by Def. 6, Part 2), and consequently (by Prop. 3, Part 3, together with its Scholium), the more it acts and the less it is acted on. This demonstration proceeds in the same way in the inverse order, from which it follows that a thing is the more perfect, the more it acts. QED.

Corollary

From this it follows that the part of the mind that remains, of whatever size it may be, is more perfect than the rest. For the eternal part of the mind (by Props. 23 and 29, Part 5) is the intellect, through which alone we are said to act (by Prop. 3, Part 3). But the part which we have shown to perish is the imagination (by Prop. 21, Part 5), through which alone we are said to be acted on (by Prop. 3, Part 3, and the General Definition of the Emotions). So (by the preceding Proposition) the former, of whatever size it may be, is more perfect than the latter. QED.

Scholium

This is what I resolved to show about the mind, in so far as it is considered without relation to the existence of the body. From this, and also from Prop. 21, Part 1, and other Propositions, it is evident that our mind, in so far as it understands, is an eternal mode of thinking, which is determined by another eternal mode of thinking, and that again by another, and so on to infinity, in such a way that all constitute simultaneously the eternal and infinite intellect of God.[26]

Proposition 41

Even if we did not know that our mind is eternal, we would count as primary piety and religion, and in absolute terms everything that we have shown in the Fourth Part to be related to courage and nobility.[27]

Demonstration. The primary and unique basis of virtue, i.e. of the way of living rightly, is (by Prop. 22, Coroll., and Prop. 24, Part 4) to seek what is useful to oneself. But in order to determine those things that reason states to be useful, we took no account of the eternity of the mind, which we have come to know only in this, the Fifth Part. Although, therefore, we did not at that point of time know that the mind is eternal, we counted as primary that which we showed to be related to courage and nobility. So, even if we were ignorant of this fact now, we would count as primary the same prescripts of reason. QED.

Scholium

The common view of the multitude seems to be different. For many seem to believe that they are free to the extent that they are permitted to obey their lust, and that, to the extent that they are bound to live in accordance with the prescript of the divine law, they give up their right. So they believe that piety and religion, and in absolute terms all the things that are related to fortitude of mind, are burdens that they hope to lay down after death, receiving the reward of their servitude, that is, of piety and religion. Nor are they led by this hope alone; they are also, and indeed principally, led by fear—namely, the fear of being punished by dreadful torments after death—to live, as far as their feebleness and their weakness of mind allows, in accordance with the precept of the divine law. Indeed, if this hope and this fear were not present in men, but if on the contrary they believed that minds perished with the body, and that there did not remain a further life for wretches worn out with the burden of their piety, they would return to their own way of thinking[28] and would want to govern everything in accordance with their lust and to obey fortune rather than themselves. This seems to me to be no less absurd than if someone, because he does not believe that he can sustain his body eternally by good food, should prefer to fill himself with poisons and deadly food; or, because he sees that the mind is not eternal, i.e. immortal, should prefer to be insane and to live without reason. These are so absurd that they hardly merit consideration.

Proposition 42

Blessedness is not the reward of virtue, but is virtue itself. Nor do we enjoy blessedness because we restrain our lusts; on the contrary, it is because we enjoy it that we can restrain our lusts.

Demonstration. Blessedness consists in the love for God (by Prop. 36, Part 5, and its Scholium). This love arises from the third kind of knowledge (by Prop. 32, Coroll., Part 5), and so this love (by Props. 59 and 3, Part 3) must be related to the mind in so far as it acts. Therefore (by Def. 8, Part 4), it is virtue itself; which was the first thing to be proved. Next, the more the mind enjoys this divine love, i.e. blessedness, the more it understands (by Prop. 32, Part 5); that is (by Prop. 3, Coroll., Part 5), the greater the power it has over the emotions, and (by Prop. 38, Part 5) the less it is acted on by emotions which are bad. So, from the fact that the mind enjoys this divine love, i.e. blessedness, it has the power of restraining its lusts. And since human power in restraining the emotions consists in the intellect alone, no one enjoys blessedness because he has restrained the emotions, but on the contrary the power of restraining lusts arises from blessedness itself. QED.

Scholium

With this I have brought to a close everything that I wanted to show about the power of the mind over the emotions, and about the freedom of the mind. From this it is evident how much power the wise man has, and how he is more powerful than the ignorant man, who is led by lust alone. For the ignorant man, besides the fact that he is agitated in many ways by external causes and never possesses true contentment of mind, also lives as if in ignorance of himself, of God, and of things, and as soon as he ceases to be acted on, he ceases to exist. On the other hand, the wise man, in so far as he is considered as such, is hardly moved in mind; rather, conscious by a certain eternal necessity of himself, of God, and of things, he never ceases to exist, but always possesses true contentment of mind. If the way that I have shown to lead to this seems to be very arduous, yet it can be discovered. And indeed it must be arduous, since it is found so rarely. For how could it happen that, if salvation were ready at hand and could be found without great labour, it is neglected by almost all? But all excellent things are as difficult as they are rare.

The End

PART 3

Supplementary Material

Glossary

Spinoza's technical terms are discussed in various places in the Introduction and notes. I collect here, for the reader's convenience, some brief explanations of his key terms. Words printed in bold are explained elsewhere in the list.

action: in Spinoza's sense of the term, an action is not simply what someone or something does. To 'act' is to do something that follows from one's own nature, and is not determined by something that is outside one. Actions are contrasted with **passions**.

adequate idea: see **idea**.

affection: a term not formally defined by Spinoza, but used by him as equivalent to **mode**.

appetite: *conatus* in so far as it relates simultaneously to mind and body. It constitutes the **essence** of the human being.

aspect of the whole universe: collections of basic particles (see 'body, most simple' and 'individual') are able to preserve their identity through change. The 'aspect of the whole universe' is a complete collection of such collections, i.e. the entire physical universe, which remains constantly the same. It is also a 'mediate infinite **mode**' of **extension**.

attribute: a **substance** consists of an infinity of attributes. These do not have an existence which is separate from that of substance; rather, an attribute is grasped by the intellect as constituting the **essence** of substance. Of the attributes, only two, **extension** and **thought**, are known to us. Each attribute is **conceived through itself.**

axiom: a proposition that is self-evidently true, and from which consequences are logically derived.

bad: see **good**.

blessedness: see **happiness**.

body: a **mode** of **extension**.

body, compound: see **individual**.

body, most simple: a body which is not composed of other bodies. 'Most simple bodies' are the building bricks of Spinoza's physical theory.

cause: *A* is the cause of *B* if *B* follows logically from *A*. *See also* **reason**.

cause, efficient: to say that *A* is the efficient cause of *B* is to say that *B* is generated by, or follows from, *A*. Spinoza regards all genuine causes as efficient causes.

cause, final: that for the sake of which something is done. Spinoza rejects the idea that there are final causes, arguing that purposive behaviour has to be explained in terms of efficient causality, in the form of the **appetite** or **desire** for something.

cause of itself: that whose existence is self-explanatory. **God** alone is cause of himself.

certainty: to be certain about X is not just to be confident about X; it is to be confident and to be able to justify one's confidence. Certainty, therefore, involves knowledge of the truth.

common notions: in Spinoza's epoch a term commonly used to refer to **axioms**.

common order of Nature: to perceive something 'through the common order of Nature' is for one's ideas to be determined externally. In such a condition one does not have ideas that are clear and distinct. (For these, see **idea; idea, clear and distinct**.)

common to all: things which are common to all bodies, or common to all minds, can only be conceived adequately. (Cf. **idea, adequate**.) An example is the fact that all bodies can now move and now be at rest.

conatus: each thing, in so far as it is **in itself**, endeavours to persist in its own being. This endeavour is commonly referred to by Spinoza's term *conatus*.

conceived through itself: **substance** and **attributes** are 'conceived through themselves' in the sense that, for example, we understand the attribute of **extension** through physical concepts only. This means that Spinoza's physics has no use for concepts such as those of perception and will, which belong to the attribute of thought..

contingent: that thing is contingent which is not logically necessary or logically impossible. For Spinoza, nothing that exists or happens is contingent; everything exists and acts as it does by logical necessity.

denomination, extrinsic and intrinsic: an 'intrinsic denomination' is a characteristic that belongs to a thing considered in itself, without relation to others; an 'extrinsic denomination' is a relational characteristic of a thing. For example, being male is an intrinsic denomination of Socrates; being married to Xantippe is one of his extrinsic denominations.

desire: **appetite** of which we are conscious.

distinction, modal and real: two things, A and B, are 'really distinct' if one can be conceived without the other; they are 'modally distinct' if A can be conceived without B, but B cannot be conceived without A. According to Descartes, substances—e.g. this person's mind and that person's mind—are really distinct; on the other hand, shape is only modally distinct from the corporeal substance in which it exists. For Spinoza, there is no real distinction between substances, since there is only one substance; however, Spinoza has a use for the concept of modal distinction. See also **mode**.

duration: for Spinoza, the indefinite continuation of existing. Duration must be distinguished from **time**.

emotion: a word used to translate Spinoza's term *affectus*. An emotion is an increase or decrease in the power of action of either the body or the mind. There are three basic emotions: **pleasure, pain**, and **desire**. Emotions may be either active or passive; see **action** and **passion** respectively.

essence: something, E, belongs to the essence of X if it belongs necessarily to X, and if E is such that, in knowing that it belongs necessarily to X, we also know something that is of fundamental importance to an understanding of X. So, for example, it belongs to the essence of man that he is a mode of God; but the fact that he is, for example, a rational animal does not belong to his essence.

eternity: briefly, eternity is existence that is logically necessary. As such, it is timeless, and is not to be regarded as that which is everlasting.

eternity, species of: to know things under a species of eternity is to grasp them as following with timeless necessity from God, whose existence is necessary and timeless.

extension: that which has spatial dimensions. Extension, for Spinoza, is not an abstraction; it is *that which* is extended. As such, it is one of the **attributes** of God.

false: see **true**.

formal: this means what would now be called 'real', and is contrasted with 'objective'. To talk of the formal essence of X is to talk of X itself; to talk of the objective essence of X is to talk of the idea of X.

free: to call something 'free' is not to say that it is undetermined, i.e. that it has no cause; it is to say that it is self-determined. In this sense, God is free; human beings, though often determined from outside, are at any rate capable of freedom. Spinoza's chief concern in the *Ethics* is to explain what human freedom is, and how we can attain it.

God: a **substance** which consists of infinite **attributes**. God is the sole **cause of itself.** God is also the cause of everything, in that everything that exists is in God .

good: that which we know to be useful to us in our endeavour to persist in our being. Conversely, that is 'bad' which hinders us in this endeavour .

happiness: the condition that one is in when one is successful in one's endeavour to persist in one's being. Cf. *conatus*.

idea: not a mental entity, but an action; namely an act of judgement, or of thinking of something as being of a certain nature.

idea, adequate: an idea which has all the characteristics of a **true** idea, with the exception of its agreement with its object.

idea, clear and distinct: a term, borrowed from Descartes , employed by Spinoza when he wants to contrast the way in which **true** or **adequate ideas** are distinguished from those that are confused. (See **idea, confused**.)

idea, confused: an idea considered in isolation from that on which it depends. Described by Spinoza as being like a consequence without its premisses.

idea, inadequate: the opposite of an **adequate idea**. Inadequate ideas are the preserve of the **imagination**.

image: not a mental picture, but a physical trace left on the brain by something that we perceive by our senses.

imagination: the first of the three kinds of knowledge recognized in the *Ethics*. It includes (among other things) sense-perception, **memory**, and induction. These have in common the fact that, although they provide us with knowledge of a sort, the ideas involved are confused. (See **idea, confused**.) Imagination may also be described as knowledge of a kind that does not involve an understanding of the necessary relations between things.

individual: a group of things which display and maintain a unity of structure. A physical individual may be termed a 'compound body'. Individuals may form parts of a more complex individual, e.g. the human body.

infinite: to be finite, in Spinoza's view, is to be a partial negation; e.g. to say that a man's knowledge is finite is to say that there are things that he does not know. To call something 'infinite' is to affirm the existence of something without any qualification or negation. **God** is said to be absolutely infinite, i.e. to have no limits of any kind, whereas an **attribute** is infinite 'in its own kind'. That is, although (for example) there is nothing extended that is outside the attribute of extension, there are kinds of being, i.e. other attributes, that are different from it.

in itself: **substance** is 'in itself', in the sense that it is absolutely independent.

intellect: that which provides us with genuine understanding. Distinguished from **imagination**.

intuitive knowledge: also called 'the third kind of knowledge' (cf. **knowledge, kinds of**). Unlike the **imagination**, intuitive knowledge provides us with **adequate ideas**. Like **reason**, it understands things under a certain species of **eternity**, but unlike reason it is not abstract or universal, but provides us with knowledge of what is concrete and particular.

joy: pleasure as experienced by the entire **individual**. Contrasted with **titillation**.

knowledge, kinds of: three kinds of knowledge are recognized in the *Ethics*: **imagination**, **reason**, and **intuitive knowledge**. The second and third kinds are superior to the first *as knowledge*; the third is superior to the rest in respect of *power*.

love: **pleasure**, together with the **idea** of the external cause of the pleasure. So, for example, to love money is to feel pleasure, together with the judgement that money is the cause of the pleasure.

memory: not so much the calling to mind of what one has experienced in the past, as the being reminded of something else .

mind, human: not a substance, but a complex idea. Cf. **individual**.

mode: the opposite of **substance**. To be a mode is to be in something else, and to be conceived through that something else.

mode, finite: what would normally be called 'particular things' are called by Spinoza 'finite modes'. So, for example, Socrates is not a substance, but is a finite mode of both thought and extension.

mode, infinite and eternal: such modes are said to be either 'immediate' or 'mediate'. The former are said to follow from the absolute nature of some attribute of God; the latter follow from the former. Examples of the former are **motion and rest**, and the infinite intellect of God; the **aspect of the whole universe** is an example of the latter.

motion and rest: all bodies either move or are at rest; further, bodies are distinguished from one another by motion and rest. See also **mode, infinite and eternal**.

nature: this term has two senses in the *Ethics*. (*a*) It can mean the same as **essence**. (*b*) It can mean the totality of things, and in this second sense the term can be substituted for 'God'. In this translation, this second sense is distinguished by the use of a capital 'N'.

Nature, active and passive: these words translate the Latin terms *natura naturans* and *natura naturata*. The former is Nature considered as a **free** cause, i.e. it is God regarded as active. The latter is Nature conceived as the totality of **modes**, regarded, not as so many separate entities, but as being in God.

objective: see **formal**.

pain: in so far as our *conatus* is diminished or hindered, we experience the **emotion** of pain.

passion: to be passive is to be acted upon. For example, we are passive in so far as we perceive things through the senses, for in such cases we are acted upon by what is outside us. Many, but not all, **emotions** are passions.

perception: Spinoza sometimes distinguishes perception from conception, saying that the former indicates that the mind is passive, whereas the latter indicates that it is active. But he also says, when defining an attribute, that the intellect 'perceives' certain things of substance; in this sense, 'perceive' seems to indicate any activity of the mind by which it 'sees' something.

perfection: for Spinoza, perfection is the same as reality. So the more perfect a thing is, the more real it is.

pleasure: the opposite of **pain**. That is, in so far as our *conatus* is increased or fostered, we experience the **emotion** of pleasure.

power: the power of X is what follows from the **essence** of X. It may also be defined as what X will do, if not impeded.

property: something that belongs necessarily to a thing, but does not constitute the **essence** of that thing. For example, the will of the lover to unite himself with the loved object is, for Spinoza, a property of love.

reason: Spinoza speaks of 'a cause, i.e. a reason'. In this sense, X is the reason for Y if X explains Y, i.e. if Y follows logically from X. The term 'reason' is also used of the second kind of knowledge. In this sense, to exercise reason is to grasp **common notions** and to infer necessary consequences from these. It is a feature of this kind of knowledge that, like **intuitive knowledge**, it understands things under 'a certain species of eternity'. (See **eternity, species of**.)

self-contentment: pleasure which arises from the fact that one contemplates one's own power of **action**.

substance: substance is that which is **in itself** and is **conceived through itself**. There is only one substance, and that substance is **God**.

thought: one of the two attributes known to us, the other being **extension**.

time: though this is not defined in the *Ethics*, Spinoza understands by it a measure of **duration**.

titillation: localized **pleasure**, distinguished from **joy**.

true: a true **idea** is said to 'agree with' that of which it is the idea. It emerges that, for the idea that S is P to be true, not only must it be the case that S is P, but the person who has the idea must *know* that S is P .

understanding: to understand is to have clear and distinct ideas, i.e. it is to be able to say why things are as they are. (See **idea, clear and distinct**.)

virtue: virtue is the same as power. As such, it may be ascribed to any type of thing whatsoever; however, Spinoza's chief concern in the *Ethics* is with human virtue or power.

will: in one sense of the term, will is the same as judgement (on this, see **idea**). In the other sense, will is *conatus* as it is related to the mind alone.

Notes to the *Ethics*

PART ONE

1. On Spinoza's views about definition in general, see Introd., Sect. 3.
2. Cf. Introd., Sect. 7.
3. Cf. Introd., Sect. 4.
4. Cf. Introd., Sect. 4.
5. Cf. Introd., Sects. 5–6.
6. Cf. Introd., Sects. 4, 5, and 7.
7. Cf. Introd., Sects. 7 and 11.
8. Cf. Introd., Sect. 8, on the nature of reason.
9. Cf. Introd., Sect. 3.
10. The Latin word is *ideatum*. On this axiom, see esp. *E*2 P43 S.
11. At this stage Spinoza is prepared to concede that there might be several substances. This possibility is ruled out in *E*1 P14; strictly, therefore, *E*1 P2 and any comparable propositions should have stated, 'If there are two substances . . .'.
12. Spinoza often uses 'nature' and 'essence' as equivalent terms (e.g. *E*3 P56; *E*4 P19, P61). Here, in *E*1 P5, he regards 'nature' and 'attribute' as equivalent, though strictly speaking an attribute *expresses* the essence of God (*E*1 D6). Spinoza also gives the word *natura* another meaning, using it to stand for the totality of existence (e.g. *E*1 P29 S, P33 S2). When the word is used in this sense, I employ a capital 'N'. Spinoza also refers to the totality of existence by the phrase *rerum natura* (e.g. *E*1 P5, P6 and C), which I render as 'the universe'.
13. Sc. of the same nature or attribute. Note also that in the previous sentence the original text had 'by Defs. 3 and 6'; but 'by Def. 3 and Ax. 6' gives better sense.
14. The notion of a substance with one attribute must, like that of a plurality of substances, be only provisional; Spinoza will assert later that God, the one substance, consists of an infinity of attributes (*E*1 P11, P14). Perhaps he is here commenting tacitly on Descartes, who believed that there is a plurality of substances, each of which has a 'principal attribute' (cf. Principles of Philosophy, 1. 53: *PWD* i. 210).
15. *Affectus*. For the translation of this term, see Introd., Sect. 10, first three paragraphs.
16. Another term for axioms. Cf. Introd., Sect. 8, on the nature of reason.
17. This may seem puzzling, for it seems obvious that (say) the proposition that X is white-haired may be false of X when young, but true of X when old. Spinoza's point, however, is that propositions about the nature of substances are either necessary truths or necessary falsehoods (as when, for example, one says that a substance is created). But it makes no sense to say that a necessary falsehood can ever become true, for such a proposition is false under all conditions.
18. *Causa, seu ratio*; more exactly, 'a cause, or in other words a reason'. Cf. Introd., Sect. 7, on the term 'cause of itself'.

19. Spinoza is here using the terms a priori and a posteriori in their standard senses. Roughly, an a posteriori proof is one that involves experience (in this case, the awareness of our own existence). An a priori proof does not need to have any recourse to experience, but rests on definitions and axioms alone. In the present case, the argument rests on the definition of 'power'.

20. Spinoza later says in a formal definition (*E2* D6) that by perfection and reality he means the same.

21. It seems to be implied here that existence is a perfection.

22. *E1* P12 states that whatever the fundamental nature of substance may be (this explains the reference to attributes), no substance can be divided. *E1* P13 says that absolutely infinite substance is indivisible, and *E1* P14 says that no substance besides God can exist or be conceived, from which it follows (*E1* P14 C1) that substance is unique. In sum, Spinoza has now shown that the belief that there is a plurality of substances, which he has so far neither affirmed nor denied, is false (though there is glancing reference to substances in *E1* P15).

23. The original text has 'Proposition 6', but most scholars agree that this is a mistake for 'Proposition 7'.

24. Here, and in several other cases, Spinoza does not complete the proof by the usual 'QED'. In this, and in comparable cases (e.g. *E1* P13, P21, P26), I translate the text as it stands.

25. The reference is to the last sentence of *E1* P12.

26. One may wonder why Spinoza should introduce a reference to corporeal substance at this point. The answer probably is that he is preparing the ground for the long discussion of corporeal substance in *E1* P15 S.

27. This may be a veiled reference to a primitive concept of God to be found in the Bible, where God is represented as walking in a garden (Genesis 3: 8) and as having a face and a back (Exodus 33: 23). As to God's passions, it is notorious that the God of the Old Testament is prone to anger.

28. In other words, although God is not extended in the way that (say) a slab of stone is extended, yet infinite extension is an attribute of God, and is not created by God in the way that theists believe that God created the physical universe.

29. *E1* P14 C2.

30. These arguments are discussed by Descartes, *Principles of Philosophy*, 1, 26: *PWD* i. 201–2, and letter to Mersenne, 15 Apr. 1630: *PWD* iii. 23; cf. Spinoza's geometrical version of Descartes's *Principles*, *PPC2* P5 S. Spinoza seems to have derived the next argument, based on diverging lines, from the medieval Jewish philosopher Chasdai Crescas, with whose work he was acquainted (Ep. 12, G iv: 61–2: *SL* 106–7).

31. This corresponds closely to an argument for the incorporeal nature of God put forward by Descartes, *Principles of Philosophy*, 1. 23: *PWD* i. 200–1.

32. Namely, that corporeal substance is composed of finite parts.

33. Spinoza is probably referring to the Greek philosopher Zeno of Elea (5th century BC). See Spinoza's geometrical version of Descartes's *Principles*, *PPC2* P6 S; also Ep. 12, G iv. 58: *SL* 104, in which Spinoza criticizes a similar argument that is designed to prove that time cannot elapse.

34. On 'real distinction', cf. Introd., Sect. 4, final paragraph.

35. *De quo alias* (literally, 'of which elsewhere'). Spinoza could be referring to what he had already said in his exposition of Descartes's *Principles*, *PPC2* P3; but if so, one

would have expected him to refer to the work by name, as in *E1 P19 S*. It seems more likely, then, that he is referring to a work on physics which he is known to have intended to write. (Cf. Ep. 60, G iv. 271: *SL* 291.) For Spinoza's views on the vacuum, see also Ep. 13, G iv. 65: SL 112, and Jonathan Bennett, 'Spinoza's Vacuum Argument', *Midwest Studies in Philosophy*, 5 (1980), 391–9.

36. This distinction is discussed more fully in *E2 P40 S2*.

37. Hitherto, Spinoza may have given the impression that corporeal substance (i.e. the attribute of extension) can in no sense be said to have parts. But this is not his position; corporeal substance is not a blank unity, but has internal complexity. But this complexity does not imply the existence of many corporeal substances, but rather the existence of modes of the one corporeal substance, i.e. of the attribute of extension.

38. This is the argument based on the supreme perfection of God.

39. This marks a transition to a discussion of the concept of God as cause, which begins in *E1 P16*.

40. For the term 'efficient cause', see Introd., n. 42.

41. *Per se, per accidens*. These were standard Scholastic terms, which Heereboord illustrates as follows: 'When an animal gives birth to something like itself, it is called the cause through itself of the animal that is born; but when it gives birth to a monster, it is called a cause by accident' (*Hermeneia* (1650); cf. Gueroult, *Spinoza: Dieu*, 253).

42. Cf. *E1 A3*.

43. Perhaps a reference to the Scholastic doctrine that the perfections of creatures are to be found 'more eminently' (*eminenter*) in God.

44. Spinoza seems to have in mind here the Aristotelian (and Scholastic) distinction between actuality and potentiality. To speak of God as actually intelligent is to speak of him as exercising his intelligence, as opposed to just having the capacity to think. (Cf. *E1 P31 S*).

45. It must be stressed that the argument which follows is not designed to show that it is only in a stretched sense of the terms that God may be said to have intellect and will; in fact, Spinoza will show later (*E1 P32 C2*) that there is a precise sense in which they do belong to God. His aim here, in *E1 P17 S*, is to establish that intellect and will are not attributes of God, which belong to his essence. The point that he is making is an important one: namely, that God is not to be regarded as in essence a being who forms plans by his intellect, and carries them out by his will. In short, God is not to be regarded as theists regard him.

46. This is a Scholastic distinction, which is also used by Descartes, e.g. *Meditations*, III: *PWD* ii. 28–9. By the 'formal essence' of something Spinoza means something as it is in itself, or, as we should now say, something as it is objectively. But for Spinoza, to say that something exists 'objectively' in the intellect of God is to say (*a*) that its existence is mental, and (*b*) that it is representative of something. For Spinoza's use of these terms in the *Ethics*, see *E2 P5, P7 C, P8 C*; see also *DIE*, sect. 33.

47. See e.g. Descartes, *Principles*, I, 23: *PWD* i. 201, and Spinoza's geometrical version of the work, *PPC1 P17 C*.

48. On these terms, cf. Introd., n. 43.

49. The proof given in this passage (omitting references to other parts of the work) is as follows: 'God is a supremely perfect being, from which it follows that he

necessarily exists. But if we attribute a limited existence to him, the limits of that existence must necessarily be understood, if not by us, at any rate by God, since he is supremely intelligent. So God will understand himself—that is, a supremely perfect being—as not existing beyond those limits, which is absurd. Therefore God has, not limited, but infinite existence, which we call eternity. Therefore God is eternal.'

50. On this, cf. n. 17. on *E1* P8 S2.

51. This introduces the notion of what scholars call the 'immediate infinite and eternal modes'; cf. Introd., Sects. 5 and 6.

52. Later, in *E2* D5, Spinoza gives a formal definition of duration as 'the indefinite continuation of existing'. For other references to duration in Part One of the *Ethics*, see *E1* D8 and *E1* P24 C.

53. The 'idea of God' that is mentioned here is not an idea that human beings have of God; rather, it is an idea that God has—namely, of his essence and of all the things that follow necessarily from it (*E2* P3 and P4).

54. This refers to the so-called 'mediate' infinite and eternal modes. See Introd., Sects. 5 and 6.

55. *Ad aliquid operandum*. In the context of *E1* P26–9, Spinoza is thinking in particular of those operations which involve the production of effects.

56. Spinoza relates here what he has to say about the infinite and finite modes to current Scholastic terminology—namely, the terms 'proximate cause' and 'remote cause'. He explains in the Scholium what he means by a 'remote cause', but he does not explain the two types of proximate cause, namely 'absolute' and 'in its own kind'. Here he was probably following Heereboord, who explained the terms as follows: 'When a proximate cause is said to produce its effect immediately, this is either understood as follows: that nothing whatsoever comes between it and the effect . . . This is an absolutely proximate cause. Alternatively, the "immediately" is understood in this way: that between the proximate cause and the effect there intervenes no other cause of the same order or species . . . This is an efficient cause which is proximate in its own kind' (*Meletemata* (1654); cf; Gueroult, *Spinoza: Dieu*, 255).

57. This translates *et alia mediantibus his primis*, Gebhardt's correction (made on the basis of the Dutch translation) of a faulty passage in the original Latin version.

58. The original text has '27', but '28' seems more likely.

59. *Natura naturans, Natura naturata*. These terms have a long history, going back to the medieval Scholastics, and were still discussed in Spinoza's time. For example, the German Cartesian philosopher Johannes Clauberg (1622–65) pointed out that the Scholastics divided Nature into *Natura naturans*, or God, and *Natura naturata*, or the universe of things. The distinction, he added, was superfluous— the terms 'God' and 'creatures' were enough. (Clauberg, *Opera* (Amsterdam, 1691), 629.) Spinoza, for his part, gives the terms a pantheistic slant: both God, and what is commonly thought of as God's creation, may be thought of as two kinds of 'Nature'.

60. Cf. *E1* P17 S, and n. 44.

61. Cf. *E1* P17 S, and n. 46.

62. These modes of thought are discussed in Part Three.

63. Spinoza here considers will as finite; in the next sentence he considers will as infinite.

64. Spinoza does not show until much later (*E2 P49 C*) that will and intellect are one and the same.

65. That is, will does not belong to the essence of God; rather, it is an infinite mode. Cf. n. 45 above.

66. Spinoza is saying here that his opponents think that God is free in so far as he has an 'absolute' will, i.e. a will which is totally undetermined. But there is no such will; the will is always determined (*E1 P32*). God's freedom lies in the fact (*E1 D7*) that he is *self*-determined.

67. Spinoza of course does not concede this: see *E1 P17 S*, and n. 45. He is saying in *E1 P33 S2* that even if one accepts the assumptions of the Scholastics (as he does not) it still follows that things could not be other than what they are.

68. Spinoza now considers the argument that God could have decided to create a different universe from all eternity. He replies ('And if it is permissible . . . ') that those who maintain this have to admit that God could change things *now* without his perfection being any the less; and this, he implies, is absurd.

69. This reverts to a thesis defended in *E1 P17 S*.

70. Spinoza is here attacking Descartes; see *Reply to Sixth Objections*: PWD ii. 291–2.

71. This refers to a problem which goes back to Plato (*Euthyphro*, 10–11): namely, whether God wills something because it is good, or whether something is good because God wills it. Descartes (*Reply to Sixth Objections*: PWD ii. 293–4) was one of those who took the latter view. Spinoza's reason for expressing a slight preference for this view emerges in the Appendix to Part One, in which he attacks the thesis that God acts for an end.

72. It is important for Spinoza to explain how people come to reject what he regards as truths that are evident to any rational being. He replies that they do so because of their prejudices—pre-formed opinions—and in this Appendix he tries to locate and to remove some of these. On 'prejudices', see also Descartes, e.g. *Principles of Philosophy*, I, 71–2: PWD i. 218–19, and *Reply to Sixth Objections*: PWD ii. 296–300.

73. Spinoza may have in mind Heereboord, *Meletemata* (1665): 'The end of the world is man, the end of man is God. The reason is that the world exists on account of man, and man himself and the world exist on account of God' (cf. Gueroult, *Spinoza: Dieu*, 394).

74. Spinoza has now listed the three parts into which his Appendix will fall: (*a*) The first concerns the reasons for the belief that God created everything for man. (*b*) The second (starting with the paragraph that begins 'With this, I have given') argues that this belief is false, and that Nature has no end. (*c*) Finally, in the paragraph beginning 'After human beings', Spinoza discusses the origins of popular beliefs about good and bad, order and disorder.

75. This slogan goes back to Aristotle, e.g. *De Generatione Animalium*, 2. 6. 744^{a}36, ^{b}16; *De Caelo*, 1. 4. 271^{a}33, 2. 11. 291^{b}13; *De Anima*, 3. 9. 432^{b}21.

76. Cf. n. 74 above.

77. This distinction comes from Scholastic theology. The point made is that God did not create the universe because he lacked something (*finis indigentiae*), but because he willed to create others like himself and so spread his own goodness (*finis assimilationis*). God, as Aquinas put it, is in the highest degree liberal (*Summa contra*

Gentiles, I. 93. 6). Heereboord explained the distinction as follows: 'God did everything on account of an end, not of lack, but of assimilation. The latter is the end by which someone acts, not so that he may seek some advantage for himself, but so that he may do good to other things which are outside him' (*Meletemata* (1654); cf. Gueroult, *Spinoza: Dieu*, 396).

78. Spinoza must here be referring to himself, and in particular to the sixth chapter of his *Tractatus Theologico-Politicus*, which gives a critical account of miracles.

79. Praise and blame, *E3* P29 S; wrongdoing and merit, *E4* P37 S2.

80. For Spinoza, an 'entity of reason' does not have a real existence; however, it is legitimate for us to speak of such entities, in that we use them to explain what does exist. For example, mathematical figures are not real entities, but are 'entities of reason' in that physicists use them in their explanation of the world (*DIE*, Sect. 95). However, the concepts that Spinoza has been criticizing in the Appendix to Part One have no explanatory power, in that they spring, not from the reason, but from the imagination—that is, they spring from sense-experience and non-deductive reasoning. (On the imagination, cf. Introd., Sect. 8.)

PART TWO

1. Spinoza does not offer a historical account of the way in which the human mind comes into existence. Rather, he proposes to explain the nature of the human mind by showing how it follows logically from the one substance, God.

2. Spinoza has used the word 'essence' repeatedly at the beginning of the first Part of the *Ethics* (*E1* D1, D4, D6, D8) without defining it. It may be assumed that he was there using it in what he regarded as a standard sense, and that the present definition (on which, see *E2* P10 S) introduces a refinement on this.

3. I render *conceptus* as 'conception' rather than as 'concept', to indicate that, for Spinoza, an idea is active.

4. Spinoza may here be distancing himself from Descartes, who said that he took the word 'idea' to mean 'whatever is immediately perceived by the mind' (*Reply to Third Objections: PWD* ii. 127).

5. It later becomes clear (e.g. *E2* P49 and S) that the action in question is that of affirmation or denial. To have an idea of *X* is to think of *X*, in the sense of affirming or denying something of it. See also Introd., Sect. 6, first two paragraphs.

6. The terms 'intrinsic denomination' and 'extrinsic denomination' were Scholastic terms, still in use in the 17th century. Roughly, an intrinsic denomination is a property of a thing that belongs to it even when it is considered without relation to any other things; an extrinsic denomination is a relational characteristic.

7. The term 'emotion' (*affectus*) is explained in *E3* D3; cf. n. 15 to Part One.

8. Perhaps a tacit appeal to *E1* D6.

9. This is a literal translation of *vulgus*; but Spinoza sometimes uses the word to refer to the Scholastics—the 'common run' of philosophers.

10. On 'formal essence', see *E1* P17 S and n. 46 to Part One.

11. The original text does not contain a word for 'only', but this is demanded by the heading of the Proposition.

12. This is an interesting example of Spinoza's use of the 'rationalist theory of causality'; cf. Introd., Sect. 7.

13. Spinoza is here attacking a theistic belief, namely that God created the material universe by first grasping in his mind a plan of such a universe and then creating it by an act of will.

14. Although God is called a 'thinking thing' in *E2 P1*, the 'things' referred to in *E2 P7* are extended things. The argument for this Proposition seems to involve the rationalist theory of causality, and runs as follows: for physical state *A* to cause physical state *B* is for *B* to follow logically from *A*; similarly, when we *know* that *A* causes *B*, the idea of *B* follows logically from the idea of *A*. That is, the same deductive order holds both within the physical universe and in true thought.

15. On 'objectively', see n. 46 to Part One.

16. In this important Scholium Spinoza states his version of what is termed the 'double-aspect theory' of the relations between mind and matter. See Introd., Sect. 6.

17. Probably a reference to *E1 P14 C1* and *E1 P14 C2*.

18. The reference is to the medieval Jewish philosopher Moses Maimonides, *Guide for the Perplexed*, 1. 68. The doctrine goes back to Aristotle, *Metaphysics*, (λ) 9. 1075^a 3–5.

19. By this, Spinoza means a physical thing which is circular in shape. He does not mean the circle as a mathematical figure, which would be an 'entity of reason'. (Cf. n. 80 to Part One).

20. This indicates that Spinoza recognizes more attributes than those of extension and thought. Cf. Introd., Sect. 4, n. 27.

21. Cf. *E1 P21*; *E2 P4*; and n. 53 to Part One.

22. For the connection between ' essence' and 'form', see Preface to Part Four of the *Ethics*, final paragraph.

23. *Secundum fieri, secundum esse.* This is a Scholastic distinction. See e.g. Suárez, *De Anima*, IV, 6: 'God is the first cause, on which all effects depend in being and in becoming (*in esse et fieri*).' Descartes uses the distinction in his *Reply to Fifth Objections: PWD* ii. 254–5.

24. Spinoza is referring here to the Scholastics. He once remarked that the common run of philosophers—i.e. the Scholastics—took created things as their philosophical starting-point, whereas Descartes began with the mind and he began with God. (Leibniz, Notes on a Conversation with Tschirnhaus (1675). See Leibniz, *Sämtliche Schriften und Briefe* (Berlin: Akademie Verlag, 1980), vi. 3, 385.

25. This refers to his definition of essence in *E2 D2*. The definition that he criticizes in the present passage is to be found in Descartes, *Reply to Fourth Objections: PWD* ii. 55 (cf. *PPC2 A2*). See also Suárez, *Disputationes Metaphysicae*, 31. 5. 13–15.

26. Inadequate perception is explained in *E2 P24–29*.

27. That this is so is proved in the next Proposition (*E2 P13*). What Spinoza states in *E2 P12* may seem to be obviously false; one is not always aware (say) of the beating of one's heart, or of the movements of one's eyelids. However, it seems that Spinoza means that each state of the human mind corresponds to the total state of the human body at the same time; which is not to say that one perceives clearly each part of that total state.

28. Grammatically, *corpus* could be translated here as 'a body', and not as 'the body', i.e. the human body. But later references to *E2 P13* (e.g. *E2 P15, P19*) show that

Spinoza is thinking here of the human body.

29. Spinoza does not mean that the senses give us a faithful account of the human body; far from it. He means only that the fact that we have sensations shows that there exists a body that we call *our* body.

30. This implies that Spinoza does not accept the view, attributed to Descartes, that the animals not only lack reason, but also do not have feelings. On the desires and appetites of the animals, see also *E*3 P57 S; for Descartes's views about the animals, see J. G. Cottingham, 'A Brute to the Brutes? Descartes's Treatment of Animals', *Philosophy*, 53. (1978), 551–9.

31. The original Latin text has *idea*; but *ideae* (a reading based on the Dutch translation) is better.

32. Spinoza's 'Lemmata' are in fact theorems of his system; they are termed 'Lemmata' rather than 'Propositions' in that they are subsidiary to the rest, forming a kind of digression.

33. Compare Descartes, *Optics*, Discourse 1: *Descartes: Discourse on Method, Optics, Geometry and Meteorology*, trans. P. Olscamp (Indianapolis: Bobbs-Merrill, 1965), 71–2.

34. i.e. the definition following Axiom 2. after Lemma 3 above.

35. Spinoza is here referring to what is termed a 'mediate' infinite and eternal mode of the attribute of extension. See *E*1 P22 and Introd., Sect. 5.

36. i.e. if it were Spinoza's intention to write a treatise on physics.

37. On Postulates, cf. Introd., Sect. 3.

38. This could in principle be translated as 'The idea of any way in which the human body is affected by external bodies'. But the reference to *E*2 P16 in *E*2 P18 S, where Spinoza speaks of the ideas of the 'affections', i.e. of the modes of the human body, implies that Spinoza is thinking of the modes of the body in *E*2 P16 also.

39. Cf. n. 38.

40. The Latin text has *affectu* here, and also in *E*3 P56 and *E*5 P7, which refer to this Proposition. Normally, Spinoza uses the term *affectus* to mean 'emotion' (see Introd., Sect. 10); here, however, he seems to be thinking of an *affectio*, i.e. an affection or mode. In this connection, it is significant that Spinoza speaks of 'affections' in *E*2 P17 S.

41. Spinoza is of course aware of the fact that it is possible to doubt of the senses in certain circumstances, pointed out by Descartes in *Meditations*, VI: PWD ii. 53. His point is that once we can supplement bare sense-experience by a rational theory of sense-perception of the kind that he has sketched, the reasons for rational doubt disappear.

42. Expressed in terms of Spinoza's theory of the attributes of substance, the difference between the two ideas of Peter is this. The idea that Peter has of himself is an idea which expresses in the attribute of thought that which Peter's body expresses in the attribute of extension. The idea of Peter that Paul has is an idea which expresses in the attribute of thought that which Paul's body—or, more precisely, a mode of Paul's body which Spinoza later calls an 'image'—expresses in the attribute of extension.

43. The 'commonly used' terminology is that of Descartes; see Descartes, *Optics*, Discourse 4: PWD i. 165–6, where Descartes notes (as Spinoza does) that the image need not resemble in all respects that of which it is the image. It is important to note here that Descartes and Spinoza are not referring to what would now be

called mental images; for them, an image is a physical trace which is left on the brain of the percipient.

44. Spinoza here explains the term 'imagination', which is of great importance in his theory of knowledge. For a fuller definition, see *E*2 P40 S2.

45. I translate *memoria* by its dictionary equivalent, 'memory'. But in fact Spinoza's chief concern here is with what it is for something to *remind* a person of something. His reason for discussing the topic is this: when we understand Nature, we do so by means of the intellect, and this involves interconnecting ideas in a certain order. But not every interconnection of ideas is an intellectual operation; some are based on 'memory', i.e. on associations of ideas which are personal, and which may vary from one person to another.

46. The equivalence between the idea of *X* and the knowledge of *X* is noteworthy. See also *E*2 P20.

47. This Proposition is used by Spinoza to prove that the mind, in so far as it perceives things through 'the common order of Nature'—i.e. in so far as it and its body are determined from outside—does not have adequate knowledge (*E*2 P29 C and S).

48. The original text has 'Prop. 11 of this Part', but scholars agree that 'Prop. 11, Coroll., Part 2' is the correct reading.

49. Spinoza is referring to *E*2 P43 and S.

50. As Lemma 4 shows, Spinoza is thinking of the way in which the organs of the human body can to some extent repair damage which is done to them.

51. This Proposition complements *E*2 P25, which stated that the idea of any affection of the human body does not involve an adequate knowledge of an external body. *E*2 P27 states that such an idea also does not involve an adequate knowledge of the human body itself.

52. Spinoza is in effect saying that the rest of the proof proceeds as in the Demonstration of *E*2 P25, from 'is in God (by Prop. 9, Part 2)' to the end, changing 'an external body' (or 'the external body') to 'the human body'.

53. Spinoza has already used the term 'clear and distinct' in *E*1 P8 S2, where he took it to mean 'true'. The term is derived from Descartes, who distinguished between 'clear' and 'distinct' ideas: see *Principles of Philosophy*, i, 45: *PWD* i. 207–8. Spinoza seems not to draw such a distinction; he tends to use the term when he wants to contrast true or adequate ideas with those that are confused.

54. This is a helpful definition of the term 'confused', which is used many times in the *Ethics*.

55. Perhaps this should be 'confused and mutilated'.

56. A reference to propositions about 'common notions', which run from *E*2 P37 to P40 S1.

57. Perhaps a reference to Descartes's views about the pineal gland, which are attacked in detail in the Preface to the Fifth Part of the *Ethics*.

58. Spinoza borrows from Descartes here, who said in the *Optics* (Discourse 6: *PWD* i. 173) that we cannot conceive anything that we see to be more than one or two hundred feet away, and (*Principles of Philosophy*, iii. 5) that the true distance of the sun equals six or seven hundred diameters of the earth.

59. On these 'common notions', see Introd., Sect. 8, on the nature of reason.

60. The original Latin version arranged the clauses in the wrong order; the error can be corrected both from the Dutch version and from the first sentence of the

Demonstration. For Spinoza's use of the term 'property', see Introd., Sect. 3 and n. 20.

61. Spinoza means that this was a term commonly used in his day. It referred to what are now commonly called 'axioms'; cf. Introd., Sect. 8, pp. 33–4.

62. Presumably the use of Propositions and Scholia, as in the *Ethics*.

63. Cf. n. 72 to Part One.

64. 'Second notions' is a term derived from Scholastic logic. Such notions (more commonly called 'second intentions') are contrasted with 'first notions', which are abstracted from particulars—e.g. animal, man. Second notions are abstracted from the first notions; examples of these are the notions of genus and species.

65. Clearly a reference to the *Tractatus de Intellectus Emendatione*. Cf. Introd., Sect. 1, p. 7.

66. A 'transcendental term' is one which is of the highest generality—so high that it transcends even the categories (traditionally: substance, quantity, quality, relation, place, time, posture, state, activity, passivity), which were regarded as the highest genera.

67. For man as erect, see Aristotle, *De partibus animalium*, 656ᵃ10, 669ᵇ4; also Cicero, *De natura deorum*, 2. 56. The definition of man as an animal that laughs is ascribed to Martianus Capella (5th century AD), in his *De nuptiis Mercurii et Philologiae*, an account of the seven liberal arts. The definition of man as a featherless biped is discussed by Spinoza in his *Cogitata Metaphysica*, I. 1 (G i. 235), where he ascribes it to Plato. (The reference is perhaps to Plato, *Statesman*, 266e). In the same passage Spinoza ascribes to Aristotle the definition of man as a rational animal.

68. On the three kinds of knowledge discussed here, see Introd., Sect. 8.

69. *Ab experientia vaga*. Not 'vague experience'; the basic sense of *vagus* is 'wandering' or 'vagrant'. In saying that he 'has been accustomed to use' this term, Spinoza is probably referring to the *Tractatus de Intellectus Emendatione*, Sect. 19. Sects. 19–24 of the work throw much light on the three kinds of knowledge recognized in the *Ethics*.

70. See Introd., Sect. 8, first two paragraphs.

71. On the nature of certainty, see also E2 P49 S, p. 157.

72. Cf. E2 D4 and n. 6 to Part 2.

73. Cf. Introd., Sect. 8, on the nature of reason.

74. Spinoza is here anticipating what he will say about *conatus* in E3 P6 and P7.

75. *Eiusque aeternitatem*. 'His eternity' is grammatically possible; but in E2 P46 and P47 Spinoza has spoken of the essence of God as infinite and eternal.

76. Spinoza means that people either use different words in the same sense, or the same word in different senses.

77. Cf. E2 P40 S1.

78. Later (E3 P9 S) Spinoza takes 'will' in a different sense, in which it is closely related to desire. In the present Scholium, and also in E2 P49, Spinoza is opposing Descartes's theory of judgement; cf. Introd., Sect. 6, first two paragraphs.

79. *Ne cogitatio in picturas incidat*: literally, 'so that thinking does not fall into pictures'.

80. Spinoza is here referring to Descartes, who argued that error involves a misuse of human free will, which affirms or denies something beyond the range of human understanding. See on this Descartes, *Principles of Philosophy*, I. 35: PWD i. 204, and *Meditations*, IV: PWD ii. 38–43.

81. *E2 P35.*
82. Cf. *E2 P43 S.*
83. *Sentiunt.* The word can be translated 'sense' or 'feel', but it can also mean 'think', and this seems to be the meaning here. Spinoza is thinking of genuine affirmation or denial, which is the work of the mind, as opposed to affirmation or denial that is merely verbal.
84. The editors of the original Latin version mark the subdivisions of this long paragraph by the use of italics for 'first', 'second', etc. Gebhardt breaks the paragraph into shorter paragraphs, in accordance with the Dutch translation.
85. This point was made by Descartes. See n. 80 above.
86. This objection is also to be found in Descartes: see *Principles of Philosophy,* I. 33, 39: *PWD* i. 204–5 and *Meditations,* III: *PWD* i. 41.
87. Cf. Spinoza, *DIE*, Sect. 38: 'The relation which exists between two ideas is the same as the relation which exists between the formal essences of these ideas.' See also Descartes, *Meditations,* III: *PWD* ii. 28.
88. This argument is attributed to the Scholastic philosopher Jean Buridan (*c.*1300–1358). An ass is supposed to be placed at an equal distance from two equally attractive bundles of hay; the argument is that the ass will die of hunger (since it has no reason for preferring one bundle to the other) unless it makes an uncaused decision to eat one of the two.
89. Spinoza here anticipates a point that he will take up towards the end of the *Ethics,* in *E5 P41 S* and P42.
90. This is somewhat similar to a famous passage in the *Tractatus Politicus,* ch. I, sect. 4, in which Spinoza says of the work , 'I have taken great care, not to laugh at human actions, not to deplore them and not to denounce them, but to understand them.' Compare also the Preface to Part Three of the *Ethics.*
91. Both Latin text and the Dutch translation have 'third', which is clearly a mistake for 'fourth'. The error may be explained by the fact that the *Ethics* was probably once intended to consist of three parts only (see Ep. 28 (1665), G iv. 164: *SL* 180).

PART THREE

1. On the translation of the term *affectus* as 'emotion', see Introd., Sect. 10, first three paragraphs.
2. The reference is to *The Passions of the Soul,* I. 50: *PWD* i. 348.
3. See *E5*, Preface.
4. Note the implication that an effect of X is something that follows from the nature of X. Compare what is said about the rationalist theory of causality in Introd., Sect. 7.
5. It depends on them, in the sense that it takes for granted the truth of these assertions (which concern the identity of an individual and the complexity of the human body). It is not *derived* from them, and for that reason it is presented as a postulate and not as a theorem.
6. This translates the Latin word *absolute*, meaning 'without restriction to special cases'.
7. Spinoza here repeats what he has said earlier in the Scholium, 'For no one has so far determined . . . '.

8. *E*1 P16.

9. A reference to Ovid, *Metamorphoses*, 7. 20–1; see also *E*4, Preface and P17 S. The emotions are those of Medea, whose feelings for her children are overcome by her desire to be revenged on her husband by killing them.

10. Cf. *E*1 Appendix, p. 107.

11. Cf. *E*1 P28 S, and n. 56 to Part One.

12. This proposition states Spinoza's theory of *conatus* (cf. Introd., Sect. 9), which is central to his philosophy of man, and indeed of Nature in general.

13. Here, Spinoza states what the endeavour or *conatus* spoken of in *E*3 P6 really is: namely, the essence of a thing, viewed as having certain necessary consequences. Cf. Introd., Sect. 9, second paragraph.

14. Spinoza has explained in *E*2 D5 what he understands by 'duration', but he does not give a definition of time in the *Ethics*. However, it emerges from an earlier work (*Cogitata Metaphysica*, 1. 4: G i. 244) that when he says that time determines duration, he means that we compare a duration with 'the duration of other things which have a certain and determinate duration, and this comparison is called "time"'. In short, time is a measure of duration. Cf. Ep. 12, G iv. 56–7: *SL* 103–4, and *E*5 P23 and S.

15. With this sense of 'will', compare *E*2 P48 S and n. 78 to Part 2.

16. This shows that Spinoza is prepared to admit the existence of unconscious states of mind.

17. *Appetere*. There is a link here with *appetitus* ('appetite').

18. Spinoza explains this proposition more fully in *E*3 P11 S.

19. Cf. *E*3 D3.

20. The Latin terms are *laetitia* and *tristitia*. Some translators render these as 'joy' and 'sorrow' respectively; but in Spinoza the terms in question are applicable to all sentient beings (cf. *E*3 P57 S), and it is paradoxical to speak of, for example, the sorrows of an insect. It has to be added that 'pain' is not an entirely apt translation of Spinoza's term *tristitia*, which would cover, for example, the emotion of someone who 'feels low'.

21. It is strange that Spinoza should imply by this definition that pleasure is necessarily a passion (cf. *E*3 P56). Later in the same part of the *Ethics* (*E*3 P58) he says that although some pleasures are passions, some are actions. Perhaps the definition given in *E*3 P11 S is a relic of an earlier stage in Spinoza's thought.

22. It will be noted that Spinoza's *melancholia* covers both mind and body. It is worth noting that in medieval and renaissance physiology melancholy was regarded as a physical illness, springing from an excess of 'black bile'; now, however, it tends to be regarded as a mental state only.

23. On desire, pleasure and pain as the three primary emotions, see also *E*3 P59 S and *E*3 DE4.

24. It is not obvious what Spinoza means by an idea which 'excludes the present existence of our body'. Perhaps it is important here to bear in mind his view that an idea involves a judgement (cf. Introd., Sect. 6, pp. 22–3). This being so, Spinoza may mean that when the mind of X does not exist, the situation is that the judgement 'X's mind exists' cannot form part of a system of true judgements.

25. The Latin text uses italics in this sentence; however, as Spinoza seems here to be

talking about what exists rather than about the use of words, I do not use quotation marks.

26. The point of the reference to $E_3 D_3$ is that this defines an emotion in terms of both body and mind.

27. Spinoza is here using the distinction between a cause 'through itself' (*per se*) and 'by accident' (*per accidens*) (cf. $E_1 P_16 C_2$, and n. 41 to Part I). The point that he is making can perhaps be grasped most easily through an example. Suppose that X smells the sea, and that the smell of salt water does not, of itself, produce in him either pleasure or pain. Yet the smell may give X pleasure, in that it reminds him of holidays by the sea that he enjoyed in the past (i.e. it is a cause of pleasure 'by accident'). Spinoza returns to the topic in $E_3 P_17 S$.

28. Spinoza probably has in mind those alchemists who explained chemical reactions in terms of 'sympathy' and 'antipathy'.

29. Like many 17th century philosophers, Spinoza was scornful of 'occult qualities' (cf. Ep. 56, G iv. 261: *SL* 279). Those who appealed to such qualities claimed to explain the observed behaviour, B, of a thing A by saying that there is in A a hidden B-producing quality.

30. *Animi fluctuatio*: cf. Descartes, *The Passions of the Soul* (Latin version), II. 59, III. 170.

31. Spinoza qualifies this in $E_4 P_9 S$.

32. Similar, presumably, to the things considered as imagined in $E_2 P_44 S$, where the 'wavering of the imagination' with respect to past, present, and future is discussed.

33. The Latin is *conscientiae morsus*, and this raises a problem. The literal translation is 'remorse'; on the other hand, the emotion in question seems closer to what would now be called 'disappointment'. Some scholars give this as a translation; but since Spinoza says later ($E_3 DE_20$; cf. Introd., Sect. 3) that he is not greatly concerned with the normal use of words, it seems better to translate the word literally.

34. It is not obvious how this Proposition is relevant here. However, perhaps Spinoza has in mind $E_3 P_12$ and P_13, both of which refer to $E_2 P_17$.

35. The reference is to $E_3 P_27$.

36. It will be noted that Spinoza has no word for having too low an opinion of oneself. This is explained in $E_3 DE_28$.

37. Cf. $E_3 P_22 S$ and n. 35 above. By 'a thing which is like us' Spinoza means a human being. See $E_3 P_29$, which refers to $E_3 P_27$.

38. What Spinoza calls 'imaginations' are mental events ($E_2 P_17 S$, $E_4 P_1 S$, $E_5 P_21$). Here, then, we have a reference to his 'double-aspect' theory of mind–matter relations (Introd., Sect. 6, final paragraph). An imagination (i.e. a mode of thought) is said to 'express' an affection of the body (i.e. a mode of extension).

39. This last sentence concerns a case in which we do have a prior emotion—namely, hatred—towards a thing. In this case, Spinoza says, what is stated in the rest of $E_3 P_27$ does not apply.

40. *Humanitas*. 'Humanity', 'kindliness', and 'human kindness' have also been offered as translations.

41. According to the original Latin text, the cause involved in 'glory' is external, as is the cause involved in 'self-contentment'. But the logic of Spinoza's argument, and the Dutch translation, indicate that the cause involved in each case is internal.

42. *Gloria*. This is hardly a standard sense of the Latin word, nor is 'glory' a standard

sense of the English word; but cf. n. 33 above. Other translations offered are 'honour', 'love of esteem', and 'self-exaltation'.

43. This renders Spinoza's term *gloriosus*. 'Pride' has been defined in *E*3 P26 S.

44. The reference is to Ovid, *Amores*, 2. 19. 4–5.

45. The idea seems to be (cf. *E*3 P29 S) that praise is pleasure accompanied by the idea of an external cause—sc. the person who endeavours to please us—and therefore is a form of love.

46. Perhaps the reference is to *E*3 P27, in which Spinoza refers to images.

47. Cf. *E*3 P27, and n. 37 above.

48. Spinoza does not define friendship, but seems to mean by it 'reciprocal love' (see *E*4 P71).

49. Equal, that is, in the case of a thing which has already been loved and a thing which has not so far been loved.

50. Compare what is said about 'good' and 'bad' in *E*4, Preface, final paragraph, and *E*4 D1–D2.

51. Some translators render *malus* as 'evil'. But this suggests that *malus* is that which is wicked, or morally bad, whereas Spinoza has in mind something that frustrates *any* desire, and may therefore be morally bad or morally neutral.

52. Spinoza presumably introduces timidity and related emotions at this point because of their connection with harm—for so I usually render the substantive *malum*, which is related to the adjective *malus*.

53. On fear as a kind of pain, see the definition of fear in *E*3 P18 S2.

54. In effect, Spinoza claims that it is evident that: (1) people seldom repay benefits, because they often think that those that they have received are no more than their due (cf. *E*3 P41 S: 'This happens . . . quite often'); (2) People often think that they are hated unjustly, i.e. they seldom feel shame (*E*3 P40 S), and so they often try to take revenge.

55. The text speaks simply of 'the memory of the thing', but Spinoza clearly has in mind a remembered thing that is hated.

56. The Latin text does not indicate which of the two Scholia of *E*3 P18 is relevant, but Spinoza's argument clearly involves a reference to the definitions of hope and fear contained in *E*3 P18 S2.

57. The reference is to *E*3 DE13.

58. Here I follow Van Vloten and Land, with whom Gebhardt (G ii. 374) agrees. The original Latin text, and the Dutch translation, have 'Prop. 17. Schol., Part 2'. A reference to *E*2 P11 C has also been suggested.

59. With these definitions, compare *E*3 P30 S.

60. An indication of Spinoza's view that definitions are not to be given in an arbitrary way, but demand much careful thought. Cf. Introd., Sect. 3.

61. On 'more distinct' imagination, see *E*3 P55 S.

62. Cf. *E*3 P30 S.

63. Here, for the first time in the *Ethics*, Spinoza explicitly equates human 'virtue' (*virtus*) with power. The connection between virtue and power is expressed formally in *E*4 D8.

64. *Gaudere*. The translation relates the verb to *gaudium*, translated earlier as 'delight' (*E*3 P18 S2).

65. Cf. *E*2 P40 S1 and S2.

66. Cf. n. 21 above, on *E*3 P11 S.

67. After discussing pleasure and pain and their derivatives, Spinoza now considers the third of the three primary emotions (cf. *E*3 P11 S), desire.

68. *Affectus, seu passiones.* Once again (cf. n. 21 above) Spinoza equates the terms 'emotion' and 'passion'.

69. This indicates that Spinoza has here been using what he calls 'reason', or 'the second kind of knowledge'; cf. *E*2 P40 S2.

70. This might seem to signal the end of Part Three of the *Ethics*, whose purpose, as stated in its title, was to investigate 'the origin and nature of the emotions'. However, Spinoza adds three further propositions, one of them (*E*3 P58) of great importance.

71. But not always: see *E*3 P58.

72. It follows from this that although desire, pleasure, and pain are called 'primary emotions', yet the first of these is basic, in that the other two can be defined in terms of it. Cf. Introd., Sect. 10, first two paragraphs.

73. This Proposition is a pendant to *E*3 P58, explaining why the account of the active emotions in that Proposition involves no reference to pain.

74. This follows the original Latin text. The Dutch translation took the passage to run, 'By pain we understand that which diminishes or hinders the mind's power of thinking', perhaps trying to reconcile this passage with *E*3 P11. But there seems no good reason to emend the Latin text of *E*3 P59, as Gebhardt does.

75. It is stated later (*E*3 DE43) that modesty is equivalent to politeness. Cf. *E*3 P29 S.

76. *Ordine.* In the definitions which follow, Spinoza discusses separately the emotions which arise from pleasure and pain (DE6–DE31) and those which involve desire (DE32–DE48). The first group is divided further into emotions which are accompanied (*a*) by the idea of an external thing as a cause (DE6–DE24) and (*b*) by the idea of an internal thing as a cause (DE25–DE31).

77. *Cupiditas*: cf. *E*3 P9 S.

78. *Laetitia*: cf. *E*3 P11 S.

79. *Tristitia*: cf. *E*3 P11 S. It is noteworthy that when Spinoza defines pleasure and pain in *E*3 P11 S he says that they belong to the mind; here, in *E*3 DE2 and DE3, he speaks of them in terms of *man* (*homo*).

80. In *E*3 P11 S Spinoza says that all these emotions are related both to the mind and the body. Incidentally, it must not be thought that, because Spinoza does not include the definitions of these emotions, they are therefore unimportant. On the contrary, joy (*hilaritas*) plays an important part in his moral philosophy (cf. *E*4 P42 and P44 S).

81. *Admiratio*: cf. *E*3 P52 S.

82. Perhaps Spinoza means that wonder is not a *primary* emotion; cf. Introd., n. 67.

83. On contempt (*contemptus*), veneration (*veneratio*) and disdain (*dedignatio*), see *E*3 P52 S.

84. *Amor*: cf. *E*3 P13 S.

85. This is close to the definition offered by Descartes, *The Passions of the Soul*, II, 79: *PWD* i. 356. See also Introd., Sect. 3, p. 14.

86. *Odium*: cf. *E*3 P13 S.

87. In *E*3 P15 S Spinoza speaks, not of 'propensity' (*propensio*) and 'aversion' (*aversio*), but of 'sympathy' (*sympathia*) and 'antipathy' (*antipathia*).

88. *Devotio*: cf. *E3* P52 S.

89. *Irrisio*: cf. *E3* P52 S. See also *E4* P45 C2 S, in which Spinoza distinguishes derision from laughter.

90. Spinoza does not explain what he means by the word 'despise' (*contemnere*), but it is clearly related linguistically to 'contempt' (*contemptus*), defined in *E3* DE5. Note also the reference to *E3* P52 S, in which 'contempt' is defined.

91. For hope (*spes*), fear (*metus*), confidence (*securitas*) and despair (*desperatio*), see *E3* P18 S2.

92. *Gaudium*. In this definition I follow Gebhardt in reading 'metum' in place of 'spem'. Cf. *E3* P18 S2 and *E3* P57 S.

93. *Conscientiae morsus*: cf. *E3* P18 S2. Some examples may clarify Spinoza's meaning. 'Delight' is the pleasure felt by someone who feared that he would fail an examination, but who discovers that he has passed. 'Remorse' (or, as we would probably say, 'disappointment') is the pain felt by someone who hoped that he would pass, but who discovers that he has failed.

94. *Commiseratio*: cf. *E3* P22 S.

95. *Misericordia*. On this, see below, DE24.

96. On favour (*favor*) and indignation (*indignatio*), see *E3* P22 S.

97. On the importance of this passage for an understanding of Spinoza's theory of definition, see Introd., Sect. 3, p. 13.

98. On esteem (*existimatio*) and scorn (*despectus*), see *E3* P26 S.

99. *Invidia*: cf. *E3* P24 S.

100. *Misericordia*. Spinoza has not defined this term previously in the *Ethics*, though he has spoken of people or things which we pity (*E3* P27 C2 and C3, and *E3* P32 S).

101. Cf. *E3* P15 and n. 41 to Part One.

102. On self-contentment (*acquiescentia in seipso*) and repentance (*poenitentia*), see *E3* P30 S.

103. *Humilitas*: cf. *E3* P55 S1.

104. *Superbia*: cf. *E3* P26 S.

105. *Abjectio*. This has not been previously defined in the *Ethics*.

106. *Gloria*: cf. *E3* P30 S.

107. *Pudor*: cf. *E3* P30 S. By 'some action' in *E3* DE31 Spinoza is thinking of some action performed by the person who feels shame.

108. *Verecundia*: cf. *E3* P39 S.

109. In fact, Spinoza does not return to the topic of shamelessness (*impudentia*), apart from a brief reference to the shameless person in *E4* P58 S.

110. Cf. *E3* DE20.

111. *Desiderium*: cf. *E3* P36 CS. The definition of regret offered there differs from that in *E3* DE32, in that the former definition regards regret as a kind of pain, whereas *E3* DE32 defines it as a kind of desire.

112. See e.g. *E3* P18 and P47 S, which refer to *E2* P17 C.

113. *Aemulatio*: cf. *E3* P27 S1.

114. *Gratia, gratitudo*: cf. *E3* P41 S.

115. *Benevolentia*: cf. *E3* P27 S2.

116. On anger (*ira*) and revenge (*vindicta*), see *E3* P40 C2S.

117. *Crudelitas, seu saevitia*: cf. *E3* P41 CS. There is a difference between the definitions offered in *E3* P41 CS and in *E3* DE38, in that in *E3* P41 CS hatred is said to prevail over

love, and there is no reference (as there is in *E3* DE38) to a third party's love or pity. Scholars have tried to emend the text, but there seems no need for this. Cf. *E3* DE32, in which Spinoza makes changes to a definition of regret given earlier in the work.

118. *Clementia*: cf. *E3* P59 S, where clemency is related to nobility (*generositas*).

119. *Timor*: cf. *E3* P39 S.

120. On boldness (*audacia*) and cowardliness (*pusillanimitas*), see *E3* P51 S.

121. *Consternatio*: cf. *E3* P39 S.

122. On politeness (*humanitas*) and ambition (*ambitio*), see *E3* P29 S.

123. Cicero, *Pro Archia*, 11.

124. On luxury (*luxuria*), drunkenness (*ebrietas*), avarice (*avaritia*) and lust (*libido*), see *E3* P56 S.

125. The reference is to *E3* P56 S.

126. *Generositas, animositas*: cf. *E3* P59 S.

127. *Zelotypia*: cf. *E3* P35 S.

128. Cf. n. 6 to Part Two.

129. Spinoza here uses the Greek word 'pathema'. It will be noted that this 'General Definition of the Emotions' is not a definition of all emotions, but covers only the passions. This is why Spinoza defines an emotion as a 'confused idea', so excluding the active emotions, which involve adequate ideas. (Cf. *E3* P58).

PART FOUR

1. Cf. *E3* P2 S, and n. 9 to Part Three.

2. Spinoza is here stating what he takes to be the original sense of the word 'perfect', which he relates to the idea of being completed, i.e. carried through to the end (*perfectum*).

3. *Exemplaria*, i.e. ideal models.

4. *Deus, seu Natura*. This famous phrase also occurs in *E4* P4.

5. On final causation, cf. Introd., Sect. 9, last two paragraphs.

6. See esp. *E1*, Appendix, p. 107.

7. The reference is to the 'entities of the imagination' discussed at the end of the Appendix to Part One.

8. This is one of the 'transcendental terms', discussed in *E2* P40 S1. See note 66 to Part Two.

9. This 'exemplar of human nature'—a phrase used only in *E4*, Preface—will turn out to be the concept of a person who not only endeavours to preserve his own being, but also (as far as possible) succeeds in doing so. Spinoza's task in the last two Parts of the *Ethics* will be to show just what this concept involves.

10. Perhaps a reference to Descartes, *Optics*, Discourse 6: *PWD* i. 173. There Descartes refers to a distance of one or two hundred feet as being the limit beyond which all objects appear equidistant to an observer.

11. At first sight, this may seem to be an idiosyncratic definition of the term 'end'. In standard usage, if a man is said to take a walk for the sake of his health, then the end of his activity is health, and not the desire of health. However, Spinoza's definition is linked with the attack on final causation in the Preface to Part Four.

His point is that when we are talking about 'ends', we are really talking about desires or appetites, which are the efficient causes (on which, see Introd., n. 42) of what we do.

12. Cf. *E4*D6.
13. A reminder that, for Spinoza, an emotion is both physical and mental. Cf. *E3*D3.
14. *Qua patimur.* Although Spinoza speaks here (*E4*P7 C) of emotions in general, he seems to be thinking of the passions in particular.
15. Cf. Introd., Sect. 11, on the terms 'good' and 'bad'.
16. In fact the reference seems to be to *E3*P18 S2, in which hope and fear are discussed.
17. *Multum distare.* This reading (which most scholars accept) follows the Dutch translation; the Latin text has *non multum distare* ('not very distant'), which must surely be wrong.
18. Ovid. Cf. *E3*P2 S, and n. 9 to Part 3.
19. *Ecclesiastes* 1: 18.
20. One might expect here a reference to *E3*P6, in which the doctrine of *conatus* is stated; but Spinoza may have in mind the fact that this proposition depends on *E3*P4.
21. On justice, see *E4*P37 S2; on faith, *E4*P72; on honour, *E4*P37 S1.
22. On piety, see *E4*P37 S1.
23. Lucius Annaeus Seneca, the Roman statesman, philosopher, and dramatist, was ordered by Nero in 65 AD to commit suicide: Tacitus, *Annals*, 15. 64.
24. Spinoza has already said briefly (*E2*P49 S) that blessedness consists in 'supreme happiness'; cf. *E4* Appendix, Sect. 4. This topic is discussed in detail in Part Five.
25. The original text had 'by Axiom 3', which must go back to a time when this Part of the *Ethics* had at least three axioms. This was corrected in the *Errata* of the first edition to 'by the Axiom of this Part'. But in fact the Axiom of this Part does not seem relevant here. Perhaps the most likely correction is that suggested by Van Vloten and Land: 'by Def. 1, Part 4'.
26. The reference to *E4*P20 shows that in the present corollary, Spinoza is speaking, not simply of people who seek what is useful to them, but of people who do so successfully.
27. Cf. e.g. Aristotle, *Politics*, 1. 2. 1253^{a}2.
28. Spinoza does not define the term 'impulse' (*impetus*) (cf. *E3*DE1). But a few lines later he contrasts acting from impulse with acting from reason, so it may be inferred that an 'impulse' is a desire which is a passion.
29. The passages in question are indicated in the next Scholium, *E4*P37 S2, in which the topic of the commonwealth (*civitas*) is discussed in greater detail. I render *civitas* as 'commonwealth' rather than as 'state', in order to distinguish it from the word *status*, also used in *E4*P37 S2.
30. It is not clear what Spinoza means by 'the law' (*lex illa*) against slaughtering animals. Perhaps he had some knowledge of Indian religion.
31. It is clear from this that by 'right', or 'right of nature' (*E4*P37 S2), Spinoza does not mean something that people ought to have, or ought to be able to do; in his view, 'right' is closely related to power. In this, his views are like those of Hobbes, e.g. *Leviathan*, ch. 14, par. 1: 'The right of nature . . . is the liberty each man hath, to use his own power, as he will himself, for the preservation of his own nature'.
32. *E1*, Appendix, Cf. n. 79 to Part One.

33. This shows clearly that, for Spinoza, 'right' is closely related to 'power'.
34. This is a reference to one of the three basic principles of Roman law: *Honeste vivere, alterum non laedere, suum cuique tribuere* ('Live honestly, do not harm another, give each one his own').
35. Cf. *E2* D4, and n. 6 to Part Two.
36. i.e. by the definition cited in the second sentence.
37. The reference is probably to the Spanish poet Góngora (1561–1627), a copy of whose works was in Spinoza's library. It seems that Spinoza is prepared to say that the living, but forgetful, Góngora issued from the dead poet, and similarly that a living adult has issued from a dead infant. This caused him some concern, in that he feared (*E4* P39 S, last sentence) that it might provide 'the superstitious' with ammunition. Perhaps he had in mind St Paul's views about the resurrection of the body, which is compared to the way in which the living plant issues from the dead seed (1. Corinthians 15: 35–45). Such views would have been rejected by Spinoza: cf. Ep. 78, G iv. 328: *SL* 348.
38. In saying that something is, for example, 'directly bad', Spinoza means that it is bad through itself (*per se*. On this, cf. n. 27 to Part Three). But what is bad through itself can be good in certain contexts; e.g. anguish (a form of pain) can be good when it restrains excessive titillation (*E4* P43).
39. This is in accordance with the text; but perhaps Spinoza meant to write, not *risu* (laughter), but *irrisione* ('derision'); cf. *E4* P45 C2s.
40. *Bene agere et laetari* (cf. *E4* P73 S). A possible source of this saying is the popular Dutch poet Jacob Cats, who in his *Mirror of the Old and New Age* (1632) said that he knew nothing better than *wel te doen en vrolick wesen* ('to do well and be happy').
41. On piety, see *E4* P37 S1.
42. Spinoza may have in mind *E2* P36—namely, that inadequate ideas follow with the same necessity as adequate ideas.
43. Spinoza here refers to Tacitus, *Annals*, 1. 29. 3.
44. On nobility, see *E3* P59 S.
45. The reference is to *E4* P66.
46. The original Latin text has 'by the Corollary of the preceding Proposition', but this must be an error. The same correction has to be made in the Corollary which follows (*E4* P65 C).
47. The original Latin text of this sentence is seriously faulty; I follow the version accepted by Van Vloten and Land and by Gebhardt.
48. It should be remembered that in *E2* P40 S2 Spinoza uses the word 'opinion' as an alternative name for what he also calls 'knowledge of the first kind' or 'imagination'.
49. With this somewhat idiosyncratic account of the Fall of Man compare what Spinoza says about Adam in chapter 4 of the *Tractatus Theologico-Politicus*, G iii. 63, 66; *Spinoza: The Political Works*, ed. A. G. Wernham (Oxford: Clarendon Press, 1958), 77–9, 83.
50. On 'boldness', cf. *E3* P51 S, and DE40–DE42. On passions as 'blind', see *E4* P58 S, P59S.
51. Perhaps Spinoza is hinting that he does not use the term 'courage' in the standard sense.
52. It is clear from this proposition that to preserve one's own being is not to live a life

of ruthless self-aggrandizement. Cf. Introd., Sect. 11, p. 46.

53. On religion, cf. *E*4 P37 S1.
54. *E*4 P50 S.
55. Spinoza is here anticipating the arguments of Part Five. So far, he has not explained the precise way in which the intuitive knowledge of God is important, though he has said that the greatest virtue of the mind is to know God (*E*4 P28). The theme of the intuitive knowledge of God is taken up in a series of propositions beginning with *E*5 P25, and ending with *E*5 P33.
56. The argument of this section is not wholly clear. The editors of the Latin edition took *discordia* and *concordia* to be in the ablative, which would give 'is fostered by discord rather than by concord'. But, as pointed out by Van Vloten and Land, Spinoza could have intended the words to be in the nominative, and I follow this reading. The argument seems to be as follows. Each person endeavours to bring it about that everyone loves what he loves (*E*3 P31 C); i.e. he aims at a kind of concord or agreement. But if *A* loves *B* madly (on which see *E*4 P44 S), then he will want *B* for himself, and will feel fear if others love *B* (cf. *E*4 P37 S1). So he will not want others to love *B*, and in this way he will want to generate discord or disagreement rather than concord.
57. *Officium.* This word can also be translated as 'duty', but elsewhere in the *Ethics* it is to be rendered as 'function'. (See *E*4 P60; *E*4, Appendix, Sects. 27 and 30; and *E*5, Preface). Spinoza seems to have in mind here our playing our part in the whole world-system, in much the same way as that in which a bodily organ performs its function within the body as a whole.

PART FIVE

1. Probably a reference to the opening Propositions of Part Four, from *E*4 P1 to *E*4 P18 S.
2. On this, see Descartes, *The Passions of the Soul*, 1. 31–50: *PWD* i. 340–8.
3. Literally, each 'will' (*voluntatem*). But Spinoza is clearly thinking here of an act of will, i.e. a volition. The reference to Descartes is to *The Passions of the Soul*, 1. 44: *PWD* i. 344.
4. *PWD* i. 338–9.
5. See *E*3 P15 S and n. 29 to Part Three.
6. On these, cf. *E*3 P17 S.
7. On this Proposition, see n. 40 to Part Two.
8. From later in the same Scholium it emerges that these 'fixed rules' (*dogmata*) are precepts of reason, of the kind that Spinoza has demonstrated in the *Ethics*. The point that Spinoza is making here is that as long as we do not have perfect (i.e. intuitive) knowledge of these precepts, we need to reinforce, by means of the imagination, the knowledge that we do have.
9. The 'others' referred to here are the things that we do not understand clearly and distinctly.
10. This is a hint of the discussion of the eternity of the human mind that is to begin in *E*5 P21.
11. It is noteworthy that although Spinoza has just spoken ('Thirdly . . .') of 'affections'

(*affectiones*), in *E*5 P7 he spoke of 'emotions' (*affectus*). The same can be said of the reference to *E*5 P9 and P11 later in the Scholium ('Fourthly . . .'). On the confusion between *affectus* and *affectio*, see n. 40 to Part Two.

12. See the discussion of reason in Introd., Sect. 8. In *E*5 P23 Spinoza makes his first explicit reference to his obscure and controversial doctrine of the eternity of the human mind, or more exactly of a part of it. Some of the difficulties in this doctrine are due to an apparent inconsistency in Spinoza's language. He has insisted in his definition of eternity (*E*1 D8) that eternity cannot be explained by duration or time, and he returns to this point in Part Five (see *E*5 P23 S and P29). Yet he says in *E*5 P23 that something of the mind remains that is eternal, which suggests that a part of the mind endures after the dissolution of the body. Again, in looking ahead to the topic of the eternity of the mind, he has spoken (*E*5 P20 S) of 'this present life', and of 'those things that have relation to the duration of the mind without relation to the body'. See also n. 18 below.

13. On time, cf. n. 14 to Part Three.

14. Spinoza now takes up a promise made in *E*2 P47 S—namely, to speak of the 'excellence and usefulness' of the third kind of knowledge, 'intuitive knowledge'.

15. i.e. mind and body. This is shown by the reference to *E*2 P13.

16. In Aristotelian terminology, the 'formal cause' of X is the structure of X, regarded as providing an answer to the question why something is X. So, for example, the ratio of 2 : 1 is said to be the formal cause of the octave (Aristotle, *Physics*, 2. 3. 194^{b}26–8). However, it does not seem that Spinoza has this sense of the term in mind here. From the last sentence of the Demonstration of *E*5 P31, it appears that he uses 'formal' as equivalent to 'adequate'.

17. Perhaps a reference to the account of the superiority of the third kind of knowledge contained in *E*5 P36 S.

18. Spinoza seems to be saying here that whenever he seems to treat the eternity of the mind as a kind of duration, this is to be regarded simply as a way of making his meaning more easily understood; it is not to be regarded as the literal truth. Cf. n. 12 above.

19. The point is (as shown by the reference to *E*1 D1) that God is the cause of himself.

20. In one of its standard theological senses, 'glory' means 'heavenly bliss' (e.g. 1 Peter 5: 10), and this seems to be what Spinoza has in mind here.

21. Spinoza appears to be uneasy about the ascription to God of pleasure, since pleasure is a transition from a lesser to a greater perfection, and such a transition is impossible in the case of God, who is infinitely perfect (*E*5 P35). Since love is a form of pleasure, it is also hard to see how God can be said to love himself or human beings (*E*5 P35, P36 C). Perhaps one should think of God's love, not as a form of pleasure, but as blessedness, which is said by Spinoza to be perfection itself (*E*5 P33 S).

22. The reference appears to be to *E*1 P25 S. On the importance of *E*5 P36 S, see Introd., Sect. 8, last paragraph.

23. On this, cf. n. 17 to Part One.

24. In his account of the eternity of the human mind, Spinoza has so far concentrated on the third kind of knowledge. He now indicates that the second kind (which also, *E*2 P44 C2, perceives things under a certain species of eternity) has a part to play as well.

25. *Mens sana in corpore sano.* This famous saying is to be found in Juvenal, *Satires*, 10. 356.
26. This is a reference to an infinite and eternal mode of God. Cf. Introd., Sect. 6 and n. 32.
27. Cf. *E*4 P73 S.
28. That is, they would abandon such good moral precepts as they have. Spinoza seems to suggest that such precepts, even if followed for the wrong reasons (namely, hope and fear), are better than a surrender to the passions.

Index of References to the *Ethics*

347

Index of Names and Subjects

McFarland, T. 49 n.
Maimonides 331
man
  consists of mind and body 125
  essence of 114, 121
  free, is courageous 277
    never acts deceitfully 46, 279
    and thought of death 276
  necessarily a part of Nature 231, 282, 286
  rational, acts well and rejoices 263, 280
    useful to other men 249, 282
  substance does not belong to his essence
    121
  various definitions of 148
  whole, advantage of 271
Mandelbaum, M. 39 n.
marriage 284
Martianus Capella 334
mathematics 15, 108
matter, its parts distinguished modally 89
medicine 287
melancholy 173, 257, 260, 333
memory 134, 169, 200, 336
Mendelssohn, M. 49
Mennonites 6
merit 255
Mersenne, M. 10, 326
Meyer, L. 10, 12 n.
mind
  cannot determine the human body 166
  a composite idea 24, 131
  contentment of 305, 310, 312, 315
  endeavour of 172
    highest 304
  eternity of 47 n., 66–7, 303, 307, 309, 312, 314,
    345
  free decree of 168, 218
  good of, highest 245
  idea of 136–7
  non-existent bodies regarded by 132–3
  part of the infinite intellect of God 122
  as percipient 123
  power over the passions 301–2
  presence of 211
  relation to body 25–6, 58, 118, 124, 136, 166–9,
    173, 174
  superiority of one over others 125
  wavering of 178, 188, 191, 202, 211, 223, 290,
    296
miracles 110
miser 259
misery 185

mode
  an affection of substance 19, 75
  of extension 20–22
  finite 56
  God as cause of 117
  immediate infinite 21, 24, 56, 94–5
  mediate infinite 22, 24, 56, 94–5
  a particular thing 20, 56, 97
  of thought 22–6
modesty 211, 222, 284
money 285
monism 18, 46, 49
Moses 276
motion and rest 20, 21, 21 n., 102, 126–8, 130, 255

Nadler, S. 6 n.
nation, love or hatred for 199
Natura naturans, see Nature, active
Natura naturata, see Nature, passive
naturalism, ethical 43
Nature
  active 100, 328
  common order of 58, 141, 232, 268, 333
    and inadequate ideas 141, 333
  laws of 164, 167, 268
  passive 100, 328
  nothing contingent in 29, 99
  right of 254, 282, 342
  state of 255
  supposed not to act in vain 108
necessary 75, 103
  knowledge that things are 293
nobility 211, 223, 261, 282, 296, 314
non-existent things, idea of 119
notions
  common 33–4, 34 n., 42, 59, 145, 147, 148, 153,
    154
  second 147, 334
  universal 148
Novalis 49

objective, *see* formal
Olscamp, P. 332
omens 201
opinion 32 n., 148, 275
order 110
  and connection of things 117, 166, 290
  geometrical 10–12
Ovid 47, 47 n., 238, 336, 338, 342

pain 40, 44, 61, 173, 208, 213, 336
  directly bad 257

Index of Names and Subjects